RACIAL UNION

RACIAL UNION

Law, Intimacy, and the
White State in Alabama,
1865–1954

Julie Novkov

THE UNIVERSITY OF MICHIGAN PRESS

ANN ARBOR

Copyright © by the University of Michigan 2008
All rights reserved
Published in the United States of America by
The University of Michigan Press
Manufactured in the United States of America
⊗ Printed on acid-free paper

2011 2010 2009 2008   4 3 2 1

No part of this publication may be reproduced, stored
in a retrieval system, or transmitted in any form or by any means,
electronic, mechanical, or otherwise, without the written
permission of the publisher.

A CIP catalog record for this book is available from the British Library.

Library of Congress Cataloging-in-Publication Data

Novkov, Julie, 1966–
    Racial union : law, intimacy, and the white state in Alabama,
  1865–1954 / Julie Novkov.
        p.   cm.
    Includes bibliographical references and index.
    ISBN-13: 978-0-472-09885-9 (cloth : alk. paper)
    ISBN-10: 0-472-09885-3 (cloth : alk. paper)
    ISBN-13: 978-0-472-06885-2 (pbk. : alk. paper)
    ISBN-10: 0-472-06885-7 (pbk. : alk. paper)
    1. Interracial marriage—Law and legislation—Alabama—History.
  2. Miscegenation—Alabama—History.   3. African-American—Alabama—
  Social conditions—History.   4. Alabama—Race relations—History.
  5. White supremacy movements—Alabama—History.   I. Title.

  KFA95.N68   2008
  346.76101'6—dc22   2007031012

For all my friends and comrades from Eugene
—to quote Rich Glauber, "you know who you are."

Contents

Acknowledgments

Many generous friends have participated in and patiently suffered through endless conversations with me for the last several years about interracial intimacy, the meaning of marriage, Alabama politics, white supremacy, and the significance of the states as political and cultural entities. As these folks know (some of them all too well), like the state of Alabama, this book has gone through a long process of development, and the interventions they have provided have been enormously helpful and positive.

I was fortunate to have superb research assistance from four students from the University of Oregon: Michelle Diggles, Brian Lee, Mauricio Marcal, and Jason Tanenbaum, all of whom provided me with access to crucial empirical data to build the argument.

I also thank the University of Oregon, which supported my research on this project with a University of Oregon Junior Professorship Development Award and a Bray Award. I acknowledge with gratitude the American Philosophical Society, which awarded me a Henry M. Phillips Jurisprudence Grant, and the National Endowment for the Humanities, which granted me a Summer Stipend.

Many folks took the time to discuss pieces of the project with me formally and informally, helping me to develop key theoretical points in the analysis. Among them were Lane West-Newman, Michael Paris, Carol Nackenoff, Ken Kersch, Amy Bridges, Kevin Bruyneel, Joel Olson, Neal Allen, Ariela Gross, Alicen McGowan, Wayne Moore, Jennifer Culbert, and Duchess Harris. I particularly acknowledge the thoughtful, engaged, and always kind criticism of Ronald Kahn; working on a spin-off chapter of this project for the volume that he and Ken Kersch edited, *The Supreme Court and American Political Development,* helped me to situate the project as a whole more firmly within the literature on political development. Jim Reische of the University of Michigan Press was supportive and encouraging throughout the entire process of getting the book through reviews and into print. Matthew Holden, Rogers Smith, and Mark Graber provided crucial assistance in getting a better handle on white supremacy toward the end of the project. And the entire book is much better than it otherwise would have been because of my participation in the Race and U.S. Political Development conference held at the University of Oregon in the spring of 2006—the presentations and papers greatly assisted me in refining my theoretical framework, and I thank my co-organizers, Joseph Lowndes and Dorian Warren, for their good cheer and hard work in putting this event together with me. I also thank Mark Graber, Paul Frymer, and the anonymous reviewers who provided critical feedback on the entire manuscript. Mark in particular pressed me to work through the significance of judicial decision making on the ground in a racist regime, enabling me to refine my analysis substantially.

At Oregon, this book has been greatly enriched by my conversations with Amy Ash, Deborah Baumgold, Lennie Feldman, Gerry Berk, Priscilla Yamin, Robin Jacobson, Rob Tsai, Keith Aoki, Leslie Harris, Caroline Forrell, Merle Weiner, and Elizabeth Reis. Joseph Lowndes was a terrific sounding board and critic as I was struggling with the relationship between state actors and the meaning of white supremacy as I was finishing the manuscript.

I am deeply indebted to two fantastic scholars who read an entire and rather ugly draft of the manuscript before I was ready to circulate it more broadly. While I have learned so much about these issues simply from reading their work, both of them provided me with crucial guidance in structuring many pieces of the overall argument and figuring out what I could support with my data. Without Pamela Brandwein's and Peggy Pascoe's generosity and brilliant critical insights, this book never would have made it. Much of what is good about this book can be attributed to all of these folks, but to Pam and Peggy in particular, and I take responsibility for the bad stuff.

The book would also not exist without the support of my family. Joel Bloom, in addition to being an amazing partner and father, was (almost) always willing to listen to me hold forth at length about the arguments and cases, and came through for me whenever I had a panicked random question like, "When *was* the Alabama primary election in 1954 held?" While my children were not so interested in discussing the relationship between interracial intimacy and white supremacy, Asher, Shira, and Zachary Novkov-Bloom have always enriched my life and have kept me focused on why I continue to care about politics.

CHAPTER 1 *The Criminal Ban on Miscegenation as a Contested Site*

In November 2000, as Americans were voting for president in a hotly contested and highly controversial election, Alabamans were also voting on a proposed amendment to their state constitution. State representative Alvin Holmes, a black Democrat from Montgomery, had initiated the legislative process to refer the amendment to the people. The amendment sought to eliminate Alabama's constitutional provision barring the state legislature from ever permitting interracial marriage (Sznajderman 1999a: 4B).

In a certain sense, the amendment was pointless. In the landmark case of *Loving v. Virginia*, the U.S. Supreme Court had invalidated criminal bans on interracial marriage in 1967. Even more to the point, a federal district court judge had specifically instructed the state of Alabama in 1970 that it could not persist in enforcing its rule against cross-racial intimacy. The amendment would thus have a purely symbolic effect, as the mechanism for preventing interracial marriage had been judicially dismantled thirty years earlier. The amendment received little discussion in the press in an election that featured more controversial issues like the presidential campaign and a statewide measure to use oil and gas royalties to fund capital improvements. While Holmes had begun the process, he did little other than to provide interviews to newspapers about the need for the amendment, and no significant public campaign was mounted for it. One vocal opponent, Michael Chappell, campaigned against it on the behalf of his Confederate Heritage political action committee and suggested that the votes in opposition would demonstrate a strong "Confederate bloc vote" in favor of preserving the state's Confederate legacy. A poll conducted shortly before the election, however, indicated little controversy: 64 percent of the respondents supported the amendment, and only 19 percent opposed it (Sheppard 2000: 11A).

Holmes, while optimistic that the measure would pass, was not convinced that the margin of victory would be so large. He noted that, except for the state's attorney general, Bill Pryor, who vocally and actively supported the amendment, most political leaders had remained quiet, opting to issue statements of moderate support through their press secretaries (11A). In the end, the amendment removing the ban on interracial marriage passed, but the opposition to removing the ban significantly exceeded the poll's prediction: 40 percent of those voting rejected the amendment. More than half a million voters cast their ballots in favor of maintaining an unenforceable constitutional commitment to prohibiting the legitimation of interracial marriage (Sengupta 2000: sec. 4, 2).

The ban had a long history. It had been placed in the state constitution in 1901, but a statutory prohibition against interracial marriage had been in Alabama's code since before the Civil War. The conscious and contested choice to remove the ban was grounded in years of struggle over the right to marry across the racial boundary and signaled formal closure to a debate over the legitimacy of interracial families that had opened in the aftermath of the Civil War. During these years, the state of Alabama imposed harsh legal penalties on hundreds, perhaps thousands, of Alabamans when they were convicted of engaging in sexual relationships with partners of a different race.

The story of Alabama's efforts to suppress interracial sexual bonds is not just a tale of a bygone era of prejudice swept away by the civil rights movement. The vote on removing the ban suggests that the wounds of these years remain. More than this, however, the history of the legal regulation of interracial intimacy intertwines with a story of conscious, coherent state development, linked to a process of racial construction and reflection conducted both culturally and through the formal organs of the state. At times, legal struggles over interracial marriage played a central part in shaping the process of racialized state development. At other times, defendants' challenges to their convictions and legal state actors' responses to these challenges reinforced and reflected policymakers' efforts to consolidate and legitimate the politics of white supremacy. Telling this story will show how state actors' engagement in the process of constructing race and gender shaped both race and the state, embedding dynamics of domination and subordination within the fabric of life and law. Forgetting or refusing to remember, blinding ourselves to color, has consequences. The narrative to follow will suggest that grappling with this troubling history and confronting it not as an anomaly or exception but rather as a central element in the creation of the modern subnational state yields a richer understanding of race, gender, law, and state.

Regulating Interracial Intimacy and Building the State: Ninety Years of Bounded Development

The constitutional provision that provoked the fight in 2000 was one moment in a contentious history involving race, gender, constitutional principle, legal regulation, and the central meaning of citizenship.[1] This book will narrate that history, tracing the legal struggles over the regulation of interracial intimacy and how these struggles helped to shape and reflect the meanings of both race and the state over a ninety-year period. Through analysis of the appellate cases that defined the law, we will see how and why concerns over interracial relationships so often presented a jumping-off point for state actors to think through racial politics and policies and their relationship to the state. An observation that race was a central factor in the development of the U.S. states, particularly in the South, is not surprising, but understanding how and why race was central to defining the meaning and operation of the state requires significantly more. Studying the legal system's encounters with the problem of interracial intimacy provides a window into the developmental process, while also attending to the meaning of gender in this process. As close consideration of appellate cases will reveal, at times debates over convictions for miscegenation linked tightly to larger debates over the state. At other times, state attorneys' and judges' responses to defendants' challenges of their convictions reflected specifically how key state actors understood race and the necessity for its control and management.

Looking to the regulation of interracial intimate relationships as the preeminent site for developing racial policies unveils this process in Alabama. Alabama's appellate courts regularly confronted the issue, producing more than forty published opinions in the years from the end of the Civil War through the beginning of the civil rights era. Reading the history through these cases clarifies a two-stage developmental process. This process un-

---

1. Struggles over the legacy of white supremacy continue in Alabama. Alabamans voting in 2004 rejected by a razor-thin margin a similar amendment seeking to remove an Alabama constitutional mandate of racial separation in the schools (Roig-Franzia 2004: A1). The state is still governed by the 1901 constitution, a document with troubling roots that will be discussed in this book.

folded in the context of the development of white supremacy as a governing structure and ideology to guide the establishment of the postbellum
order.

While the term *white supremacy* is used most frequently as an ahistorical
description of an ideology of white superiority to other races, in this book it
will be used more specifically to describe the linkage between racial ideology
in politics and culture and its concrete manifestations in state institutions in
the postbellum U.S. South. While white dominance was the defining feature
of Southern politics in the antebellum era, state and social actors were mostly
able to operationalize racial hierarchy through the institution of slavery,
which linked race and formal subordination through the mechanism of status. Certainly the ideas that whites were a superior race and that they had
particular entitlements to power and cultural authority were continuous
throughout, and in this sense, the major shift wrought by the elimination of
slavery and the Civil War was that the South could no longer challenge federal supremacy as long as federal actors agreed to allow the Southern states
to manage "race relations."[2] But this book will show how this process of
negotiation on the ground took place over time, and how the development
and articulation of white supremacy was crucial to it.

White supremacy in the narrower sense of this book was both an ideological and a structural phenomenon, and one major agenda of the book is to
trace its institutional development as state actors expressed, shaped, and contained its ideological aspects within state institutions over time. One could
use the phrase *Jim Crow* to evoke the same sense, but due to its historical
associations, the use of Jim Crow reifies a white-black binary that in fact was
one contested element of the developmental process. But the most apt
description for this period, keeping in mind the dynamism that the book will
reveal, is one in which the social order and state institutions were committed
to some version of an ideology of white supremacy expressed in a structural
sense.[3]

Immediately after the Civil War, the states began to reconceptualize race
in terms of whiteness and blackness, seeking new boundaries for racial categories and meanings in the wake of slavery's demise. In Alabama, this
process, which continued through the rest of the nineteenth century, ulti-

---

2. Thanks to Matthew Holden for clarification on this point.
3. Thanks to Rogers Smith and Mark Graber for thinking through this issue with me.

mately resulted in the state's placement of the white family as the normative center of citizenship. The path to centering the white family was neither smooth nor consensual; the Alabama Supreme Court developed the core principle in a multiple-staged response to an 1872 case in which the criminal prohibition of interracial marriage was declared unconstitutional. Once the core principle was in place, however, Alabama's courts used it as the ground from which to build an understanding of why and how interracial intimacy posed a threat to the state. In developing this understanding, the courts moved toward the idea that mixed-race relationships were most dangerous when they most closely approximated familial relations. This insight grounded a distinction between casual sex or prostitution between blacks and whites, which was viewed with disapproval and sometimes violently sanctioned through private action but not perceived as a fundamental threat to the state, and the crime of miscegenation, which was understood as a fundamental threat to the state. By the early twentieth century, the regulation of race generally and interracial intimacy specifically had been definitively linked to the state and its struggles to develop and progress as an institution.

Placing the normative white family as the central unit of the state in the late nineteenth century initiated the second stage of development. This stage was the establishment and subsequent rationalization and sanitization of the white supremacist state. The most dramatic moment of this stage was Alabama's constitutional convention of 1901, where delegates gathered with the clear intention to rewrite the state constitution around the organizing principle of white supremacy. Constitutionalization was, however, but an early step in the process. The constitutional principle of white supremacy was infused into statutes and their interpretations over the years, and by the 1930s the courts were actively engaged in explicit efforts to rationalize and legitimate the application of the principle. This pattern continued through the early 1950s, when appellate courts actively ignored clear cultural signals that the system itself was under substantial strain. Throughout this process, white supremacy interacted with gendered and racialized normative conceptions of family in interesting ways. The analysis of the interaction between legal struggles over interracial intimacy and the articulation of white supremacy provides a deeper understanding of the dynamic nature of development on the ground than broader models within political development can achieve.

Desmond King and Rogers Smith explain political development as an expression of racial orders, or opposing coalitions of groups struggling over transformative racial change. This theory provides a way of mapping political change and explaining how it happens over time—as different sides of the struggle gain ascendance, change proceeds, the sides produce a stalemate, or racialized repression occurs (King and Smith 2005).

This model, which operates as a macrolevel explanation for political development in the United States, is particularly helpful in explaining the nature of racialized political struggle from the mid-1950s through the mid-1970s, as a strong transformative coalition was gradually built, achieved some victories, and then began to lose the capacity to effect change as the other side responded. A national-level reliance on racial orders can also provide a broad explanation for the radical implications of the statutes and constitutional changes put in place shortly after the Civil War, and the retrenchment that laid the groundwork for the emergence of white supremacy as a political ideology after Reconstruction's failure (King and Smith 2005). King and Smith's major claim, however, is that understanding development as incorporating racial orders sheds significant light on areas of policy that, on the face of it, seem unrelated to race.

A similar but more nuanced approach can assist in untangling the development and institutionalization of white supremacy on the ground in a state context. The dynamism of the racial orders model is one of its great attractions, but its broad scope necessarily obscures the nature of simultaneously ideological and structural changes in white supremacy itself over time. Second, racial orders is a structural model akin to a mathematical or physics equation—change in either direction depends upon the coalitional strengths and weaknesses on the "good" and "bad" sides. It thus does not attend sufficiently to the possibility that the most robust struggles over racial orders sometimes took place between different types of supremacist orders, rather than between a supremacist and egalitarian order.[4]

Rather than seeing white supremacy as pure racist ideology, this book demonstrates how it emerged as a practice and how the state legitimated it over time as a political system. Drawing on recent historical insights to supplement the empirical research, the book situates supremacy as a political doctrine generated through a conversation between culture and state-based institutions, particularly the law. This supremacy was not merely a continuation and moderate institutional transformation of the racial hegemony

---

4. I am indebted to Joseph Lowndes for this insight. See Lowndes's forthcoming book on the roots of modern conservatism (2008).

prevalent in the antebellum era. It was rather a historically contingent ideological basis for constructing a governing structure that its architects and subsequent participants could call democratic and believe this to be true. The struggles over regulating interracial intimacy reveal a state whose policymakers, through their interventions in and development of a specifically postbellum version of supremacy, imagined themselves to be constructing a limited but fully legitimated vision of African American rights and citizenship.

While individuals often based their justifications for white superiority in biological arguments, the shifting nature of white supremacy shown through suppressing interracial intimate relationships suggests that crucial state actors articulated it as a means of governing both whites and blacks. Struggles over racial boundaries were also fundamentally about the state and its legally constructed interests both in defining itself and in state actors' interests in maintaining a certain configuration of conservative political power. Both pieces of the developmental puzzle—the centering of the white family and the legal rationalization of white supremacy—served these interests and ultimately shaped them as well. As these struggles occurred, state actors and institutions also participated in a flattening and bifurcation of the racial landscape into white and black. The story of how this process unfolded reveals much about the intimate and complex connections between racial formation and state-level political development as both took place within the legal arena. At times a key site for development and at other moments a site where development was reflected and consolidated, the state's efforts to eliminate interracial intimacy provide a helpful window.

Likewise, to read this history as a struggle between racially transformative and repressive coalitions provides some insights into large-scale change but does not generate much purchase on the intricacies of law and politics on the ground, where the project was not simply racial repression but also incorporated struggle over particular visions of a racialized state order. Major struggles in individual states in the South did loosely fit King and Smith's racial orders thesis as the conservative white elites gradually gained control over the structures and institutions of state government from the 1870s through the 1890s. But what then of the supremacist states they produced? To understand the dynamism of white supremacy in the late nineteenth and early twentieth centuries, one must move away from the notion of a unified or only marginally shifting coalition around supremacy that persisted over time until the dawn of the civil rights movement.

The research in this book presents a significantly more complex moral and political universe. Even in the post-Reconstruction era, efforts to create labor and agrarian coalitions in light of tensions within the Republican Party over race generated a multilayered and ultimately tragic struggle among groups with competing interests in agrarian populism, labor organization, class reform, and more racial equality. In one sense this coalition did collapse over its inability to negotiate the place of race successfully. But this failure was not solely internal and organic. It was facilitated by conservatives' strenuous efforts to build a workable politics of exclusion that simultaneously united class and race by defining the poor (regardless of race) and all African Americans as unfit for the full exercise of civic membership while dividing class from race as whiteness increasingly became established as a form of cultural and social power. The victory of the conservatives, as institutionalized in the constitution of 1901, guaranteed that, in the early twentieth century, the story would be less about a battle between reformist and repressive coalitions and much more one of struggle between conservative Democratic elites and populists who sought to seize the mantle of reform through the gaudy and flamboyant use of rhetorical and physical racial violence. In a real sense, Alabama's politics did center around a conflict over racial orders at some points, but the conflict was over competing supremacist orders.

Interracial intimacy was the center of the process of negotiation initiated by the surrender at Appomattox because of the enormity of the threat that conservative elite whites perceived from its possible legitimation in the aftermath of the Civil War. When Alabama's high court invalidated the state's prohibition against interracial marriage in 1872, this threat was realized, galvanizing defenders of racial hierarchy into a simultaneously defensive and creative posture. Focus on interracial relationships facilitated the identification of the white family as the fundamental unit of the state, and this identification rendered the initial stakes for suppressing interracial intimacy quite high. While other areas of law—challenges to peonage, struggles over voting rights, efforts to thwart Klan violence, prosecutions of interracial crimes (rape in particular), and struggles over enforcement of contracts— provided locations for the articulation of white supremacy, fears of interracial romance remained significant and present consistently over the decades as such relationships were increasingly defined as direct and public threats to the racial order. The steady supply of reported cases was attributable in part to the fact that defendants had a strong incentive to appeal their sentences: Alabama punished convicted miscegenators with two- to seven-year terms in the state penitentiary. Nonetheless, appellate judges engaged these cases directly and, in many, produced opinions that did more than simply to resolve the fate of the individual in question. The central importance of these legal battles as a site for the articulation and reflection of racial anxieties was also carried over from the late antebellum era, as a brief history of earlier regulation demonstrates.

Antebellum Regulation of Interracial Intimacy

Legal and social prohibitions against interracial intimacy marked the outer parameters of acceptable relations of gender, race, and class. They did so from the colonial era through the 1960s at least, and only in recent years have social norms completely supplanted legal rules. Nonetheless, the history of regulation has not been constant; the stringency of the norms against interracial romance and the means through which the boundary has been policed have changed over time.

A brief history of the development of regulations against interracial romance in the antebellum period provides a rough sense of the consensus that had developed about race and whiteness in the period directly preceding the Civil War. This consensus is significant because it provided content for many whites' nostalgic visions of race in the postbellum era (although, as David Blight [2001] shows, the nostalgic vision itself was a constructed and racially charged memory). Slavery itself ultimately came to serve as a proxy for subordination and inferiority; as a firmly embedded social, political, and legal system, its existence obviated the need for rigorous attempts at racial differentiation. While not all blacks were slaves, most blacks were, and no whites were chattel slaves (though David Roediger [1991] and others address workers' claims concerning their status as white slaves or wage slaves).

Given the state of contemporary racial politics, we are not surprised to see the first evidence of barring interracial sexual relationships quite early in American history. What may be more surprising is that the banning of these relationships was ever in question, but numerous scholars have shown that the status of black Africans and their consequent rights to form intimate attachments were initially debated among the colonial authorities (Williamson 1980; Mumford 1997; Wallenstein 2002). In the early 1600s, when English colonists began to populate the Virginia shores, most of the menial labor soon to be associated with slavery was performed by white

indentured servants or whites whom British courts had sentenced to be trans-
ported to the colonies (Williamson 1980: 7). Such servants were only barely
above slaves in social status, and most of the early mulattoes were the children of indentured servants and slaves (Williamson 1980: 7). While such relationships were problematic, they were not as threatening to the entire social
order as they would become later.[5]

Nonetheless, limiting sexual relations between Africans and whites
became common relatively rapidly, and early colonial courts and legislatures
began to rule that the children of such relationships were themselves black,
with according status. In 1662, Virginia's assembly rejected the English principle that a child's status followed that of its father, establishing instead that
the offspring of slave mothers were slaves regardless of the race of their
fathers (Williamson 1980: 8). This rule was quickly replicated throughout the
colonies, and by the turn of the century, both the permanence of slavery and
the practice of defining mixed-race children as blacks had taken hold firmly
(Williamson 1980). The high rhetoric of the Revolutionary period did little to
change attitudes toward slavery in the South, and while a small class of free
blacks and mulattoes was emerging, their status even in free states was precarious (Wood 1997; Klinkner and Smith 1999). Alabama, which became a
state in 1819, was not exceptional in the South; the overwhelming majority of
blacks were enslaved, but a few free blacks lived in the state, mostly in the
cities (Rogers et al. 1994).

By the end of the 1700s, slavery existed as a separate and coherent category resting firmly upon a racial basis (Hodes 1997: 38). Once the development of slavery as a unique and racially based institution was complete, the
stakes rose tremendously for sexual liaisons between white women and black
men due to black men's extreme structural subordination, and tension over
this type of interracial intimacy rose accordingly (66–67). Nonetheless, Hodes
asserts that "as long as the mighty institution of slavery remained in place,
so, too, did a mostly satisfactory, if at times unreliable, system of
stratification" (122). Even the occasional appearance of a black child born
from a white womb was not enough to disrupt the system substantially,

---

5. Martha Hodes explains that in the 1680s neither whiteness nor blackness had been conceptually and
categorically developed enough for interracial relationships to pose a major threat. The story of a white
indentured servant who married a slave in the 1680s illustrates the early fuzzy line between servitude and
slavery: while the white acquaintances of Nell Butler disapproved of her choice of a black mate, the wedding led to few serious consequences for either party (Hodes 1997: 28–31).

though the placement of such children in the existing racial categories was highly problematic.

Interracial sexual contact took place during slavery, most visibly when white men engaged in coercive sex with black women.[6] Coercion that the legal system recognized as rape also occurred, though the frequency is difficult to ascertain (Sommerville 2004).[7] On some occasions, white masters would free their children upon their death and make provisions for them, but many mixed-race children remained slaves (Rogers et al. 1994: 104–8).[8] Both cross-racial and intraracial relationships contributed to the growth in black and slave populations in Alabama throughout the era of slavery. By the eve of the Civil War, Alabama's Black Belt, a band of plantation land in the southern third of the state, was home to over 200,000 blacks, almost all of whom were slaves; the total black population of the state in 1860 was almost 438,000 (Kolchin 1972: 14). Slaves accounted for nearly half of Alabama's population in 1861; this large group of people found themselves suddenly freed with practically no warning in the spring of 1865 (Rogers et al. 1994: 227; Kolchin 1972: 3).

The specific history of interracial intimacy highlighted the broader question of differentiation between blacks and whites, while simultaneously bringing gender into the analysis. Slavery and blackness were intertwined with each other, and through this relationship conceptions of whiteness emerged and flowered. By the dawn of the nineteenth century, slaveholders and others had successfully defined blacks as a race, destroying the varying cultural and ethnic roots of the people they had enslaved. The association of blacks with slavery trapped eighteenth- and nineteenth-century observers, rendering them unable to confront the problems of blackness and slavery outside of the categories and their association with each other (Fields 1982:

---

6. Coercion was a complicated issue as the iconic example of Sally Hemings and Thomas Jefferson demonstrates. The evidence suggests that Jefferson conducted an illicit relationship with Hemings that spanned some thirty-eight years, during which Hemings bore several children. Hemings was thirty years younger than Jefferson, and their relationship likely began when she was in her teens (Gordon-Reed 1997).

7. While most prosecutions for interracial rape in the antebellum South involved charges against black men, a few instances of prosecutions of white men can be found (Hodes 1997: 65–68, 114–18).

8. Freeing one's mixed-race children was acceptable, but planters could not be too extravagant in their attempts to provide for individuals who were extremely subordinated by their race and gender in the social system. Edmund Townsend, a planter of Madison County, attempted to will the bulk of his half-million-dollar estate and 195 slaves to his two mulatto daughters, Elizabeth and Virginia. An Alabama court overturned the will, though Edmund's brother Samuel successfully manumitted his nine mulatto children in his will (Rogers et al. 1994: 108). Chapter 6 takes up such questions in the postbellum period.

162). The connection between slavery and race (in particular blackness) rendered race a key analytical factor for those confronting questions of sovereignty and citizenship; these questions were also situated across the dimension of gender. As Fields explains, race "became the ideological medium through which Americans confronted questions of sovereignty and power because the enslavement of Africans and their descendants constituted a massive exception to the rules of sovereignty and power that were increasingly taken for granted" (168–69). In some ways the development of the rigid identification of blackness with slavery was accidental, but once the relationship had been established, it had long-range effects that could not be easily undone, and both blackness and whiteness were conditioned by their relationships to gender.

State-Level Political Development and the Construction of Identity

Many studies in political science, law, and history have addressed the relationship between race and political development on the national level, parsing out the connections between race and citizenship (Smith 1997; King and Smith 2005), voting rights (Bybee 1998), immigration (Haney López 1996; King 2000), and national defense (Dudziak 2000; Kryder 2000), to name only a few issues. Such accounts have helped to untangle the meaning of racial hierarchies in their political context, drawing from the culturally constructed elements of the hierarchies to address liberal efforts to bring minorities into the American state. Some regional studies of development, particularly those that have focused on the South, have also explored complex questions of black political agency and resistance (Klarman 2004; Morris 1986; Payne 1995). In addition, an extensive literature on slavery and its political and constitutional significance exists (Graber 2006; Finkelman 1996).

While such scholarship has enhanced our understandings of both identity and constitutional-political development, it overlooks a significant dimension due to its national or regional location. In analyzing development since the Civil War, most scholars have considered citizenship to be a national rather than state-based phenomenon, but many of the specifics of ascriptive conceptions of citizenship have been worked out on the state rather than national level. Indeed, one implication of the Supreme Court's ruling in the *Slaughter-House Cases* in 1873 was to limit moves toward substantive conceptions of citizenship rights on the national level, rejecting the idea that the long-standing practice of allowing states substantial control over defining citizenship and its meanings had been swept away.[9] When we note that for most of the history of the United States, such significant issues as voting, education, marriage, familial relations, and residence have been primarily within the province of state law, we see that the states are far from irrelevant in establishing the grounding context for citizenship and identity, especially when the focus is on subordinated identities and their legal status.

This matters if we wish to understand race and the legacy of formal racial subordination in the United States. The bargain on race worked out after the end of the Reconstruction era was to allow local (meaning state-based) control over race relations, a phrase popularized in the early twentieth century by an Alabaman arguing for local control (Murphy 1901–2). As the book will show, on the state level in Alabama, elites agreed that race was a central concern in a conscious process of state building. As a full-fledged modern state was struggling to be born on the national level, the individual states were managing the day-to-day business of facilitating the exercise of citizenship, administering justice, controlling and defining families, and structuring the political choices that would have the greatest impacts on their denizens.

Relating and analyzing a thick history in one state provides unique insights. If the actual work of racial differentiation and the implementation of its political manifestations took place on the state level, we cannot grasp the process adequately without looking directly at its operation in the states. We also need not assume that the best measure of a theory is its generalizability. Instead we can look to fit, and to the nature of the insights it provides. While the specifics of a narrative concerning Alabama will be less transportable and will cover less geographic terrain than a narrative concerning the nation, the mode of understanding the process and the moments of contingency and closure can provide jumping-off points for future research in other states or regions. Further, an in-depth study of state building in a context where race was unquestionably a central concern can reveal much about the relationship between cultural values and institutions, and specifically how the law mediates between them.

In addition, state-level development did matter nationally. Even if the

---

9. Mark Graber (2006) has shown how thoroughly the states controlled not only access to citizenship, but also its meaning, in the antebellum years. The idea that states had significant authority over citizenship was not a bizarre invention of Roger Taney in *Dred Scott* that the Fourteenth Amendment could simply clarify as incorrect.

process in Alabama did not always directly affect the nation as a whole, the fact that Alabama and other Southern states so jealously guarded their hegemony with respect to race shaped the course of later twentieth-century interventions in racial politics initiated on the national level. Much of the legacy of federalism is the legacy of race, and federalism's design, redesign, and evolution over the past two centuries has explicitly revolved around tensions over race. The national side of the puzzle of federalism and race has been studied and the institutional aspects analyzed. Now we must look to the other side of this puzzle, at the state partners in this process.

Alabama as a Significant Site

When looking to the states, Alabama is an ideal place to start the process of understanding how racial formation and political development meshed on the state level. Alabama's significance rests upon two factors: the close link between litigation over the criminal ban on miscegenation and state-level political development there, and the centrality of Alabama in the history of racial politics in the United States. These factors in combination render a study of Alabama's regulation of interracial intimacy more than simply the history of a particular state, providing a way to see a developmental process that likely had parallels in other states around other issues.

The number of appellate cases addressing the crime of miscegenation in Alabama, while not enormous, dwarfs the number of opinions in other states, many of which only had a single case concerning the constitutionality of their statutes and an occasional criminal appeal or contest of a will. As noted earlier, the narrative to come will show how in Alabama interracial intimacy, racial meaning, and the state were deeply intertwined, with the crime of miscegenation ultimately becoming a premier location for the reflection and construction of the supremacist state. The presence of active and continuous appellate litigation throughout the ninety years of this process renders it visible for historical and theoretical analysis.

Reviewing history through the lens of appellate litigation provides specific benefits. While the rate and outcome of appeals tell us little about the underlying demographics of the trials on a particular issue, the cases themselves preserve the range and scope of legal disputing over the issue. Repeated appellate litigation signals that an issue was unsettled and contested, and courts' choices to publish opinions demonstrate a willingness to use particular conflicts as signaling devices. Particularly at the higher appellate levels, rulings do more than dispose of the cases before the courts issuing them; they establish broad principles for future cases and sometimes attempt to delimit the scope of future conflicts. By closely studying the appeals, we see what the courts themselves thought were the parameters of conflicts and what issues the courts recognized as needing public address. We also see through the way that appeals were framed where the boundaries of argumentation were and what issues were contestable. Finally, the cases themselves make and transform law through a nuanced method that reflects more concretely how the social backgrounds of particular factual scenarios intertwine with the existing statutory or common law governing the situation. They thus provide a way to see the concrete interface between culture and state institutions, and to understand when and how institutions are porous with respect to culture and vice versa.

But why did Alabama produce so much appellate litigation? Two practical factors likely contributed to a larger number of cases going to trial, therefore providing more fodder for appeal. First, Alabama had a higher proportion of black citizens even than many other states in the South—in the 1880s, blacks constituted nearly half of the population, and even by 1950, after waves of mass exodus, blacks still constituted 32 percent (Robinson 1998: 90). Second, Alabama's criminal prohibition was broader than any other state's, declaring not only interracial marriages or cohabitation to be felonies, but also interracial adultery and fornication (90).

Implicit in the detailed historical narrative to follow is a second reason for Alabama's high rate not only of appeals, but of appeals that resulted in reported opinions. At certain historical moments, appeals of convictions for miscegenation and appeals of other questions about interracial sexual relationships were a major site for the state's working out of the meaning of race and the boundary between the races. These intensive periods of appellate litigation established the scope of significant questions that would shape later legal conflicts. At other moments, these cases enabled the courts to reflect and reinforce state officials' uneasy consensus over race and legal norms. In the course of deciding cases about interracial intimacy, Alabama's courts set forth policies on the role of the family, the danger of interracialism to the fabric of the state, the significance of white male patriarchal authority, the proper limits on white feminine behavior, the articulation and rationalization of white supremacy, the differential disciplining of black male and female partial citizens, and a host of other issues that implicated the state, its meaning, and its functioning directly. Regulation of interracial relationships was, the evidence shall show, a prime legal institutional site in Alabama for the creation, articulation, rationalization, and ultimately reflection of the supremacist state, through its attention to the meaning of racial boundaries. Regulating these relationships at times provided a crucial site for the interpenetration of culture and state, as each interacted dynamically with the other. In other states and at other times in Alabama, other issues had similar functions and potentials, but in the years between 1868 and 1954 in Alabama, interracial intimacy was the crucial issue. This insight will be explored further in the conclusion.

In many ways, Alabama was typical of its region, the Old South, but it was also a central location for events of major national significance in the history of racial politics in the United States. Alabama was typical in its less serious regulation of interracial intimacy in the antebellum period than afterward, and in its political turmoil during and after Reconstruction (Wallenstein 2002; Rogers et al. 1994). As in the rest of the South, Alabama's white elites actively pursued the legal implementation of Jim Crow policies, including aggressive disenfranchisement, in the late nineteenth and early twentieth centuries (Rogers et al. 1994). While the Klan was more powerful in Alabama than in some states in the South, Klan violence was present as a social and political factor in most areas of the South and many Northern and Western states as well (Feldman 1999; Tolnay 1995). Alabama's path of moving from violent to nonviolent, rationalized white supremacy in the twentieth century mirrored developments nationally (Klinkner and Smith 1999). Alabama's large cities, like large cities in other Southern states, became targets for mass protest during the civil rights movement (Morris 1984). Finally, Alabama, like almost the entire South, maintained its criminal prohibition against interracial intimacy until forced to relinquish it through fiat by the federal courts, and it joined a few other holdout Southern states in requiring specific judicial admonishment to abandon its policy even after the ruling in *Loving v. Virginia* (Wallenstein 2002).

Several of Alabama's early postbellum legal battles over race had national significance. Alabama's Supreme Court first ruled in *Burns v. State* in 1872 that the criminal prohibition of interracial marriage was unconstitutional, igniting national fears about the impact of the Fourteenth Amendment. The Alabama high court's ruling reversing *Burns* in *Green v. State* also proved a national bellwether that was cited by appellate courts in other states as they uniformly upheld their own measures against interracial intimacy. The case in which the U.S. Supreme Court ruled that antimiscegenation laws did not violate the Fourteenth Amendment was *Pace v. Alabama,* decided in 1883 after the defendant's appeal from the Alabama Supreme Court. In the early twentieth century, Alabama's legal system also produced the leading case of *Bailey v. State,* allowing the practice of peonage under the Thirteenth Amendment.

Alabama's centrality extended beyond the legal arena. While not completely exceptional in its Klan activity, Alabama saw more political consolidation than most Southern states and provided a stage for a focused public and political conflict between the Klan and conservative white elites. Later, the Klan and Alabama became linked in national and international consciousness when Hugo Black, a former Klan member, was nominated to the U.S. Supreme Court. Alabama's notoriety was further enhanced in the 1930s by the international scandal of the prosecution and conviction of several young black men for rape in the Scottsboro case. The Dixiecrat movement was born in Birmingham, and Alabama was one of only a few states able to deliver votes reliably to the Dixiecrat ticket in 1948. An Alabaman, Charles Collins, was the primary theorist and early architect of a new conservative coalition built through the mobilization of racial animus (Lowndes 2008). During World War II and the postwar era, Alabama also saw nationally significant moments of black activism and empowerment, including the establishment of the Tuskegee training program for black aviators. The southeastern headquarters of the National Association for the Advancement of Colored People (NAACP) were in Birmingham, and major chapters of the civil rights movement played out in Alabama, including the Montgomery bus boycott, the Selma march, and the highly public and volatile conflict between Reverend Fred Shuttlesworth and Bull Connor in Birmingham.

To look specifically at the internal struggle in Alabama over interracial intimacy can thus illuminate broader national concerns and developments. The cases considered in this book consist of all reported opinions concerning the crime of miscegenation in Alabama from the end of the Civil War through the ultimate demise of the criminal statute in 1970. Most of the cases are appeals of criminal convictions, but the book also addresses the three cases that concerned interracial bequests of property. In addition it considers the three reported interracial rape cases that took place in the 1910s, which were significant in the context of litigation specifically addressing the crime of miscegenation, as chapter 3 will explain.[10] The total number of cases is forty-seven, of which forty-five were litigated originally in Alabama's state courts.

Appellate cases are informative in describing legal rules and their applications, but they do not necessarily reflect accurately the larger pool of prosecutions from which they are drawn. Almost by definition, these cases only involve situations in which defendants were convicted, giving little sense of the kinds of arguments that might succeed for the accused at trial. The appeals reveal little about how frequently people were prosecuted or what the results were, nor do they provide an overall sense of what kinds of couples were likely to be prosecuted and convicted of miscegenation. Further, the rulings produced by appellate courts cannot give one a sense of the typical case, because the typical case does not raise questions that will necessitate an appeal to a higher court to resolve a legally unsettled issue. As noted previously, however, appellate cases incorporate other significant information.

Some information on prosecutions is available; since the 1880s, Alabama's attorneys general have been responsible for compiling statistics biennially or later quadrennially on the number of prosecutions and their dispositions in Alabama's courts. Unfortunately, these statistics are somewhat unreliable and were compiled only until 1938.[11] The statistics compiled county-by-county from 1883 through 1938 suggest that Alabama attorneys general filed charges against 343 individuals for violating one or the other of

---

10. Since the entire universe of the cases involving interracial rape has not been addressed, the figures that follow exclude them.

11. The statutory mandate to compile and report these records reads as follows: "[The attorney general] must . . . compile a report, which said report shall compromise . . . a statement of the number of criminal cases disposed of in the entire state for the past four years . . . and, taking each character of cases separately, it shall show the number disposed of in each judicial circuit and in each criminal court . . . the number of convictions, the number of acquittals, the number of nolle prosequis entered, the number of cases which were abated or otherwise disposed of, the number of sentences to death, the number of sentences to the penitentiary, the number of other sentences, including fines imposed, and the totals under each head above mentioned" (Ala. Code 1975, Title 36–15–1 [6]). These reports were apparently not compiled after 1938, however, as no records suggest that they were ever delivered to any of the mandated entities. Further, the records themselves are somewhat questionable; for instance, the biennial report covering 1914 through 1916 lists no cases of miscegenation, though every other biennium from 1894 through 1896 on saw at least two cases, and the median number of cases was 12.5. The records listing the number of cases by circuit at times differed from the statewide figures. In 1906 through 1908, two different biennial reports gave two different sets of statistics. In a few instances (1920–22, 1922–24), the sum of the columns indicating the punishments exceeds the number of convictions, though this could be explained by two defendants' having been tried at once and then having received separate sentences.

the antimiscegenation statutes and secured 177 convictions (a 51.6 percent conviction rate). The statistics from the biennial reports, which exist for the years between 1894 through 1938, report 254 cases and 137 convictions, for an overall conviction rate of 53.9 percent. Of these convicts, the largest proportion were sentenced to the penitentiary as mandated by statute (89.8 percent), but a few were sentenced to hard labor (8 defendants), 6 were fined (perhaps for conducting marriage ceremonies), and 1 was sentenced to a jail term.

Charles Robinson's review of state convict records suggests some moderate differences between black male/white female and black female/white male couples. Looking at convictions of 61 individuals between 1884 and 1900, he shows that 39 were white females or black males (20 and 19 respectively). In addition, 10 black women and 12 white men were convicted. He also suggests that a racial hierarchy can been seen in sentencing: black men's sentences averaged 3.84 years, white women's were 3.27 years, white men were sentenced to an average of 3.11 years, and black women to 2.75 years (2003: 69–72). The problematic nature of the statistics, however, makes drawing any conclusions from the data quite difficult, and it is probably safer to look at the numbers and trends as suggestive rather than definitive. We can nonetheless conclude that Alabama's criminal courts took miscegenation seriously and were willing to sentence those convicted of it to significant terms in the penitentiary, regardless of the racial/gender configuration of the couple involved.

The appeals demonstrate the central legal questions concerning these prosecutions and mark the questions that were contentious enough to prompt higher courts to generate opinions to instruct lower court judges. Clusters of appeals around particular issues suggest that these issues were legally and perhaps socially salient questions. They also show where the boundaries of legal interpretation rested, both in the specific framing of the appellate questions and in the ways that the courts resolved them. Appellate opinions function as an arm of the state in the person of the judges who issue them, but the appeals themselves mediate and translate the tensions of cultural forces into legal frameworks. One should also keep in mind that the judges writing these opinions were, with but a few exceptions, representatives of the conservative Democratic Party elites—the so-called Big Mules and Black Belters with strong connections to the center of power in Montgomery. Nonetheless, these political ties did not appear to dictate outcomes, although they did seem to have a bearing in some periods on which version of supremacy the courts were primarily committed to employing in their decision-making processes.

Alabama's appellate courts heard at least one case in every decade between 1865 and 1954. The numbers are somewhat misleading, as in some instances both members of a convicted couple would appeal their convictions and in a few instances both the Alabama appellate division and the Alabama Supreme Court would issue opinions concerning the same case. These complexities aside, the busiest periods were in the post-Reconstruction era and in the late 1910s through the 1940s, with the appellate courts hearing seven cases between 1875 and 1884 and issuing twenty-two opinions between 1915 and 1944.[12] The civil rights era saw no cases, a phenomenon that will be discussed in the conclusion. The only appellate case decided after 1954 was *U.S. v. Brittain,* a ruling in a federal district court that brought Alabama's policies into line with *Loving v. Virginia.*[13]

More interesting than the rate, however, was the clustering of issues. The courts were not considering the same questions throughout; particular issues dominated certain periods of time. These issues may be considered nodes of conflict, or highly concentrated and salient debates among the players within the legal system that are linked to the outside social and political context (Novkov 2001: 15–22). Such nodes are moments of openness in doctrinal development when legal institutions interact with social forces. Those studying nodes of conflict see the legal system as a complex discursive field that is partially porous within its institutional constraints to conscious and unconscious cultural intervention. American law's adversarial nature promotes multivocality and conflict, at times enabling the emergence of sharply focused struggles over the meaning and scope of legal concepts that have cultural import. At these moments, the lay public, lawyers, and judges find themselves in conversation over the proper translation of cultural or political concepts into legal categories. As lawyers seek to defend their clients zealously, they focus on raising ambiguities in legal doctrine that judges must then address, opening some paths and closing others. This process may be

---

12. Two of these cases were appealed from the appellate division to the Alabama Supreme Court, and two other sets of appeals involved a convicted couple, so these twenty-two opinions addressed the situations of eighteen couples. Further, one defendant—Jesse Williams—was tried and convicted three times and successfully appealed each conviction. His story appears in chapter 5.

13. Unlike almost all of the other appeals, *Brittain* was initiated by a couple who had been denied a marriage license by a probate judge. Except for the wills contests, all of the other appeals arose from actions initiated by the state against alleged miscegenators.

partially controlled by state actors as judges and state lawyers seek to implement their views of the state's policies, but their actions within the discursive field often have unintended and broad consequences.

Each chapter of the book covers a particular temporal stretch but also highlights the themes apparent in clusters of doctrine, explaining the significance and consequences of the system's efforts to settle uncertainties, rationalize the operation of the supremacist state, and insulate conservative white rule from political and cultural challenges. The patterns of appellate litigation over interracial intimacy suggest the existence of particular nodes that were important in the development of case law on miscegenation. A clear period of constitutional litigation emerged initially, beginning in 1868 and ending in 1882; Alabama's courts decided seven cases addressing the legitimacy of laws barring interracial intimacy in these years. Evidentiary appeals then became more prominent as seven more opinions addressed these questions between 1883 and 1917. Between 1918 and 1928, a concentrated debate about racial definition took place in six opinions, and then evidentiary appeals dominated again between 1930 and 1951. Constitutional issues reappeared on the courts' agenda in two cases heard in 1954. The wills cases were less concentrated temporally, occurring in 1914, 1940, and 1944. The substantive chapters will describe and explain the debates behind these clusters of cases.[14]

This preliminary presentation of the cases suggests that only by delving into the cases and opinions themselves can we understand the institutional and political dynamics of the process. The outcomes mattered enormously to individual defendants, but the courts' framings of broader rules reinterpreted prior debates and shaped the course of future debates. While an analysis of the appellate cases cannot claim to represent the day-to-day practice of suppressing interracial relationships, it can represent a state process of implementing white supremacy even as it took supremacist impulses from the surrounding culture. Likewise, while a study focusing on Alabama cannot claim

---

14. Some might be wondering about the gender/race breakdown of the couples appealing their sentences and whether couples consisting of black women and white men had more success on appeal than couples consisting of white women and black men. Of the thirty-seven criminal cases in which the races and genders of the couple could be determined, twenty-one involved white women and black men, of whom eleven saw their convictions upheld. The cases involving black women and white men comprised the other sixteen, and nine were successful on appeal. These outcomes suggest that the courts were interested in doing more than reinforcing a strong norm against black male–white female relationships while allowing white men free access to black women's bodies.

to represent precisely the process across the South, it can suggest pathways to the implementation of a regime of white supremacy that may have been followed elsewhere in different forms, contexts, and forums.

Regulating Interracial Intimacy and the Development of the Supremacist State

White elite anxieties about interracial intimacy have long been a crucial location for fights over race and its meaning (see, e.g., Hodes 1997; Bardaglio 1995; Pascoe 1996; Wallenstein 2002; Romano 2003; Robinson 2003; Kennedy 2003). Alabama provides an ideal site to see the development of these conflicts in historical context, because of the thick record of appellate litigation and because of Alabama's own significance in the history of tensions over race in the United States. In focusing on the legal regulation of interracial relationships, this work will tell a broader story about the central role of race in the rise of the modern subnational state, showing how at some moments struggles over these relationships intersected with development and how at other moments these struggles reflected white supremacy's operation on the ground. While this story would not be replicated even across the southern United States in its details, it suggests that race was vitally linked to development, that key state actors played a significant role in shaping the meaning and definition of race, and that the law was a crucial site for dynamic interactions between culture and the state. It also suggests that, because of the deep historical interpenetration of racialization and the state, proposals to get the state out of the business of racialization are likely either naive or disingenuous.

As the narrative will demonstrate, miscegenation itself as a phenomenon was contested throughout the era beginning with the implementation of a new regime at the end of the Civil War and ending with the rise of the civil rights movement in the 1950s. As the courts' grapplings with prosecutions and civil cases demonstrated, the crime of miscegenation changed over time in its significance, its definition, and the nature of its perceived threat to the state. Likewise, as the state itself changed, the particular problem that interracial intimacy posed was understood differently. Both of these dynamisms led to the temporally contained debates that the patterns of issues in appellate cases described here suggest.

Appellate litigation over interracial intimacy reflected and refracted struggles over white supremacy. At times, the legal debate over the definition and scope of the crime of miscegenation directly influenced the process of state-level development. At other times, the appellate cases served more to reflect the operation of white supremacy and to work through the tensions of legitimating a legal system based in structural discrimination. The initial ideological work of creating a new white state in Alabama was largely performed in the legal arena through discussions of the ban on miscegenation. In later years, appeals of convictions for miscegenation would address the meaning of family, shifting conceptions of race, and the problems of sanitizing white supremacy in the face of national and international inquiry. Other sites were significant in Alabama as well; debates over voting rights for blacks persisted intermittently, as did struggles over criminal justice and race more generally, but struggles over interracial relationships produced a continual and thick legal record over time. As noted earlier, interracial intimacy's linkage to racial boundaries as well as Alabama's deep concern with interracial relationships and their possible progeny tied this phenomenon to the development of the supremacist state.

The state's interest in and focus on the crime of miscegenation shifted over time in response to culture but also in response to strategies of litigation. The pronouncements of judges on the viability and interpretation of regulations against interracial intimacy were actions of the state, but they occurred as individual defendants, usually unhappy at the prospect of spending two to seven years in Alabama's state penitentiaries, appealed their sentences. Most of these defendants were not seeking political or social change; they were responding to threats to their liberty or potential property interests. Likewise, the attorneys who represented them were mostly doing what good attorneys do: trying to find fissures through which their clients could escape in a supposedly totalizing regime of white supremacy. The state's interest was necessarily broader in many cases in which the legitimacy or scope of regulations against interracial intimacy was under attack. The judges, however, were simultaneously neutral arbiters and agents of the state charged with maintaining the established order under an overarching commitment to the state's vision of justice.

In negotiating these interests, Alabama's legal system wove a path of doctrinal development beginning with the centering of the white family as the state's fundamental unit, through the legalization and constitutionalization of supremacy, and leading to its gradual rationalization and legitimation.

While establishing the integrity of black family units and encouraging blacks to form relationships that were separate from but structurally parallel to the private elements of white marriages were minor notes for policymakers, the principal focus in early litigation was to elevate and protect the white family as the cornerstone of the state. First articulated as an ad hoc response to emancipation, white supremacy became an ideological support for state policy and ultimately a state constitutional principle. The constitutional convention of 1901 established white supremacy as a foundational principle, and the process of interpreting it through the site of the crime of miscegenation was one of legal rationalization.

While appellate cases involving the crime of miscegenation only at times refined white supremacy, they always reflected its operation as ideology and policy on the ground. As the twentieth century progressed, Alabama's jurists continually reformed white supremacy, transforming it into a facially neutral and objectively applied policy and seeking to limit its operation as arbitrary disordered violence and individually expressed discrimination applied through the state. By the 1930s, this process of rationalization was complete and the legal hegemony of supremacy was totalized. Cases addressing interracial intimacy reflected and highlighted this process. By the 1940s, the courts would no longer engage in legal debates about the meaning of race, sending a message that the state and its relationship to race were fixed.

This lengthy developmental process often had ironic effects for individual defendants. As state actors sought to subjugate their black quasi citizens, they sometimes freed individual blacks and whites suspected of transgressing the most fundamental of boundaries. How and why this happened reveals the uncertain and contingent nature of a developmental process that, from afar, looks monolithic, stable, and unassailable. Appellate outcomes favoring defendants convicted of miscegenation reflected assumptions about the legitimacy of the regime of white supremacy and enabled legal state actors to sanitize and rationalize it. These cases, in which the occasional defendant escaped a lengthy prison term because of technical problems in the trial, highlight the contradiction of a commitment to procedural fairness in the midst of a broadly unjust system, evoking Hannah Arendt's (1994) analysis of the banality of evil. Nonetheless, even in cases focused on procedure, appellate judges remained clear in the twentieth century about their support for some version of white supremacy. In general, these judges appeared to weigh in on the side of the conservative elites seeking to protect and promote white

Democratic Party hegemony against popular expressions of racial violence on the one hand and, as time went on, federal intervention on the behalf of subordinated blacks on the other.

The book considers the development of supremacy by relating a history of appellate litigation over the crime of miscegenation in Alabama. Each chapter will address a specific historical period in sequence, with the partial exception of chapter 6, which considers cases concerning interracial bequests separately. The chapters all open by setting the political and social context in which the cases were litigated and then explaining how litigation both shaped and responded to this context.

The narrative begins in chapter 2, exploring the state's articulated interests in the family as the fundamental unit of state and society and demonstrating how the cases decided after 1872 laid the groundwork for the constitutional order of white supremacy. This struggle set up the initial central place of miscegenation in the state-based and national postbellum debates over race. In these years, legal debates over interracial intimacy played a crucial role in the development of postbellum constitutional commitments to inequality. The empirical focus is on postbellum litigation over the constitutionality of Alabama's 1865 statute rendering miscegenation a felony. The Alabama Supreme Court invalidated its statute on constitutional grounds in 1872, and the attorney general and courts strategized to reestablish its constitutionality in the 1870s and early 1880s.

Chapter 3 describes the refining of state interests in the wake of constitutional struggle, exploring the courts' connecting of the crime of miscegenation to the family. Alabama's courts emphasized the need to prove that an allegedly miscegenous connection involved an ongoing agreement to continue a relationship, which played on the state's interest in preventing the formation of interracial families. The courts also articulated rules about the content and admissibility of confessions touching the elements of miscegenation, grounding debates to come later. These rules emerged in legal battles over prosecutions for miscegenation and interracial rape between 1883 and 1917, which corresponded with the rise of a social and constitutional order of white supremacy. The chapter also addresses Alabama's constitutional convention of 1901, in which the conventioneers forbade the legislature from ever allowing interracial marriages. The chapter places these state actions in the context of the rise of eugenic theories about race and heredity. In these years, appellate cases concerning the crime of miscegenation did not influence the state's development so directly, but they did reflect the growth of white supremacy and negotiations over the place of family in the new regime.

Chapter 4 focuses on the era when the pact popularized in *Birth of a Nation* was finalized: these years saw the consolidation of the agreement that the South was to have free rein over racial politics, as the Ku Klux Klan (KKK) gained political influence in several regions of the nation. While consolidation was taking place politically, the courts faced a vigorous conflict over the state's capacity to regulate mixed-race relationships as defendants successfully challenged their convictions on the ground that the state had not adequately proven their race. The chapter explains how both the Alabama Supreme Court and the legislature grappled with the problems created by strictly hereditary definitions of race. Drawing from rulings in the previous period, the high court ruled that appearance and associations could constitute an admission of one's race, and the legislature endorsed a "one-drop rule," extending the definition of blackness to encompass any individual with any degree of black ancestry.

Chapter 5 addresses the rationalization of the supremacist state during the Depression and highlights the courts' efforts to use earlier successes to consolidate their position. Reversals of convictions in this era reflected the state's endorsement and expression of a smoothly running system of white supremacy in which state policymakers rationalized racism and controlled its legal manifestations. The chapter also explores the growing sense among Alabama's conservative white elite that its racial politics had to be sanitized for outside consumption. Sanitization took place in part around appeals of convictions for miscegenation. The empirical narrative describes the repeated prosecution of a man, Jesse Williams, whose ambiguous racial heritage tested the rules about racial definition established in the late 1920s. Alabama's courts also overturned several convictions during these years on the grounds that prosecutors had engaged in racially inflammatory rhetoric either in questioning witnesses or in their statements to the jury. These rulings articulated a vision of managed and bounded supremacy within the legal realm while allowing free play for violent private action outside of it.

Chapter 6 considers appellate cases addressing white men's attempts to leave their property to their black lovers or interracial children. On the one hand, case law had supported the principle that the testator's intentions were to be respected in the distribution of property through wills. On the other,

Alabama's criminal law and social practices strongly condemned interracial relationships not only as immoral but also as threats to the state. The courts considered white men's interracial bequests through racialized and gender-based frames, enabling them to uphold these bequests by endorsing a strong vision of white male autonomy. The analysis demonstrates how the courts negotiated the collision between two fundamental norms established in post-bellum law and culture, ruling in favor of white men's property interests by stripping black actors of agency.

The final empirical chapter (chapter 7) addresses the closing round of litigation prior to the full emergence of the civil rights movement. It notes the courts' defensive posture during these years and links this posture to state actors' efforts to maintain local control and racial domination in the face of increasing unrest. The empirical narrative describes how cases of the 1940s and early 1950s addressing evidentiary disputes reflected the full development of the supremacist state ,and portrayed this state as fixed. In the appellate cases, lawyers' efforts to challenge the established racialized frame were flatly rejected, and the law of race appeared in court opinions as unchanging and rigid. The appellate opinions thus reflected hardening attitudes toward supremacy. The chapter also analyzes the reemergence of constitutional litigation over miscegenation in the 1950s, tying the masked instability in the legal system to the broader instability in the structure of racial power in the South in the postwar years.

The concluding chapter summarizes briefly the final invalidation of antimiscegenation laws in *Loving v. Virginia* and the need for a federal district court to impose this policy specifically in Alabama three years later. It also describes the removal of antimiscegenation language from Alabama's constitution in 2000. The chapter explores the relationship between these struggles and the legacy of the fully developed supremacist state described in the previous chapter.

The chapter then reflects back on the role of the courts in constructing and maintaining a supremacist state through appellate litigation concerning Alabama's ban on interracial intimacy. The narrative of the book is retold briefly through lenses of race and gender, and the connections between politics and the law are reexamined. Appellate judges' roles as contingent agents who were nonetheless bound by institutional priorities and conditions also receive attention. The chapter emphasizes the way that prohibitions against interracial relationships marked the outer parameters of acceptable relations of gender and race in Alabama and ties these insights to a historical narrative of conscious state building. By the end of the book, it is clearer why remembering this history is so important in an age when many believe that race and racial divisions have declining significance. There is also a brief critique of efforts by legal scholars on the right and left to get the state out of the business of regulating race and intimacy. On the left, I argue against scholars like Randall Kennedy that this aspiration does not reflect the historical reality of the extent of the state's intimate relationship with race. On the right, the argument from an aspiration to color blindness does not take seriously the depth to which racial hierarchy and racialized subordination are historically and institutionally embedded in state and cultural structures.

The book concludes with an afterword addressing the analogy between the historical challenges to bans on interracial marriage and the contemporary struggle over same-sex marriage. While the analogy between bans on marriage based on race and on sexual orientation is imperfect, analysts and activists can draw important strategic lessons from the state-level history discussed in this book.

CHAPTER 2 *Creating a Constitutional Order:*
1865–82

The first postbellum struggles over criminalizing interracial intimacy were structural and constitutional. In these years, the primary flashpoints of conflict were the public and private significance of marriage, the state's perceived responsibility to and relationship with families, the nature of equality mandated by the new federal and constitutional order, and the meaning of contract. The years between 1865 and 1882 were tumultuous for Alabamans, both black and white, as the postbellum political order emerged. The state and social order had to be reconstituted politically and culturally to assimilate the changes wrought by the loss of the war, the freeing of the slaves, and the imposition of military rule. In the decade after the war, Alabama had six different governors, elected six U.S. senators (three were refused seats in the Northern-dominated Senate), and held three constitutional conventions.

Amid all of this turmoil, the central political and social issue was how to construct a new political structure for embedding and expressing racial hierarchy. Questions about interracial intimacy were already understood to be more than questions of sexual mores, as many whites saw interracial marriage as a symbol of the most radical implications of freedom. Alabama's legal debate over the crime of miscegenation quickly became a constitutional struggle over the responsibilities of the postbellum state and its citizens. One can read the litigation over the constitutionality of antimiscegenation laws in at least two ways. First, it provided a window into the uncertainty over the new relationship between the state and the federal government. The authority of national policy, first in the form of congressional legislation and then through the amended U.S. Constitution, had to be determined.

Second, and more significant, the legal problem of regulating interracial intimacy became a visible, high-stakes site for struggling over the postbellum significance of the state itself. The subnational state's responsibilities toward its citizens, its role in defining and separating the races, its capacity to resist national imperatives, and its core legitimacy were all under negotiation in the immediate postbellum era. These issues came up in most institutional settings, but particularly in the courts, as the judiciary engaged the conflict over the meaning of race and equality through the appeals of defendants convicted of miscegenation.

The first cases underlined the uncertainty inherent in the emerging racial repression of the early postbellum era and constituted the foundations of the legal basis for Jim Crow. Between 1865 and 1882, the Alabama courts worked through the question of whether the laws criminalizing interracial intimacy were constitutional. The appellate courts produced written opinions in seven cases, and an appeal of one of these rulings was heard in the U.S. Supreme Court. A full-fledged node of conflict developed around how to understand the state's role with respect to families, race and racial difference, and the proper focus for the guarantee of equality. This chapter details these doctrinal and institutional struggles. In the course of this discussion, we see why the courts heard so many cases that raised fundamentally the same question: were Alabama's criminal prohibitions against interracial intimacy permissible under congressional civil rights laws and the Fourteenth Amendment? Ultimately, the courts settled on the centrality of the white family as the fundamental unit of the state by endorsing a rhetorical conception of race as a type of status, but these understandings emerged only through the developmental process sparked by legal conflict.

Political and Social Upheaval

Richmond, the second capital of the Confederacy (Montgomery had been the first), fell to Union forces on April 3, 1865, and Lee's surrender at the Appomattox Courthouse was solemnized on April 9. The final surrender of the rest of the Confederate forces took place on April 26. Federal authorities arrested Alabama's Confederate governor on May 1, and Alabama had no formal government other than Union troops until the appointment of a provisional governor on June 21 (Griffith 1968: 444–46).

While Alabama's soil was physically relatively untouched by the war—no major land battles occurred there—the lasting effects of war were deep.

Between 75,000 and 100,000 white Alabamans served in the Confederate Army, and estimates of casualties ranged from 25,000 to 70,000. (The white population prior to the war had been just over 500,000.) While the casualty rate for black men was not nearly so great as for white men, more than 50,000 black soldiers served formally in the Union army by the end of 1863, and thousands of others performed vital informal service as scouts, spies, and guides (Klinkner and Smith 1999: 58–63). Death on such a vast scale resulted in an abnormally high female-to-male ratio among whites (Wallenstein 2002: 62). Furthermore, the political infrastructure was substantially damaged, as many prominent and politically active Alabamans were implicated in the Confederacy (Griffith 1968: 398–446).[1] The first task in the postbellum era was to re-create a workable state government, and questions about the role of race in this re-creation were present from the start.

The immediate antebellum period had been one of increasing repression for blacks, and in particular policymakers had worked hard to stymie black literacy. Still, while Alabama had criminalized interracial intimacy, it was not a felony. Prior to 1852, Alabama law allowed marriages "between any free persons" not barred from marriage by degree of kinship or youthfulness. The classification of interracial intimacy as a minor crime did not take place until 1852 (Wallenstein 1994: 373). The 1856 version of the Alabama code allowed marriages between free blacks but specifically barred weddings between members of different races. The statutory language addressed only those who officiated at such marriages, providing, "Any person solemnizing the rites of matrimony . . . when one of the parties is a Negro and the other a white person, is guilty of a misdemeanor, and, on conviction, must be fined not less than one thousand dollars" (Ala. Stat. 1856: Art. I, sec. 1956). No specific provisions mandated punishment for the parties attempting to marry each other. The 1856 code did, however, provide that a black male convicted of raping or attempting to rape a white female would be subject to the death penalty, regardless of whether he was a slave or free black (Art. X, sec. 3307). This pattern of less serious regulation of consensual interracial relationships persisted throughout the lower South in the antebellum years. Further, Deep

---

1. Support for the war was by no means universal in Alabama, despite the fact that Alabama was the fourth state to secede. Northern Alabama, which was mostly white, had many Unionists, and a secret Peace Society was organized in 1862. The First Alabama Cavalry, consisting of 2,678 white Alabamans, fought for the Union. Support for the Confederacy was strongest in the southern and central agricultural regions of the state (Wiggins 1977: 5–7).

Southern states reserved punitive legal measures for whites only, rather than the black participants in interracial relationships (Robinson 2003: 9–10). As one might predict, relationships between white men and black women received far less scrutiny and condemnation than relationships between black men and white women, although in the early part of the nineteenth century, even the latter relationship occasionally existed without exciting violence (Hodes 1997).

As the sectional crisis intensified, free blacks found it increasingly difficult to stay in the Deep South. A network of legal regulations in Alabama made it harder for free blacks to work and live without harassment. By the time of the Civil War, most free blacks (with the exception of a community of more than eight hundred in Mobile), who had formerly composed a fairly significant body of Alabama's population, had left for more hospitable regions (Kolchin 1972; Griffith 1968: 457). Some thinkers have speculated that the legal pressures on free blacks made it easier for Deep Southern states to maintain a low level of regulation directed at slaves. Once almost all of the blacks in a state were slaves, there was no longer a need for explicitly race-based regulation to maintain the subordinate status of blacks (Robinson 2003: 11).

The implications of emancipation were unclear, and the role of blacks in the formation of the new state structure was up for negotiation. Prominent white Alabamans who had not supported the Confederacy assumed that they would manage the transition to a new political structure and began to organize; their assumptions were bolstered when Andrew Johnson appointed Unionist Lewis Parsons as the provisional governor. Governor Parsons called a constitutional convention in keeping with the federal requirement that the Southern states abolish slavery, repudiate their war debts, and repeal their legislation authorizing secession. The convention struggled over the reapportionment of the state legislature, but ultimately the Unionists won, leaving northern Alabama with significantly more political power and the so-called Black Belt with less.[2] Under the new system, white Alabamans elected a new government in November. While the government was composed of many Unionists and was perceived in Alabama and elsewhere as moderate, it was not to be rushed headlong into extending rights to blacks (Wiggins 1977:

---

2. The Black Belt was the region in central Alabama where cotton production was concentrated in the antebellum era. The term *Black Belt* was a double entendre, referring both to the darkness of the soil and to the concentration of large-scale slave-owning planters in the region.

6–15). Alabama's experience of selecting a fairly conservative government after the war's end paralleled that of several other Southern states (Wallenstein 2002: 70).

The reconstituted Alabama legislature met in December and passed several laws restricting blacks, among which was a new antimiscegenation measure (Rogers et al. 1994: 236–41). This measure differed substantially from its predecessor. The law, which persisted in the same basic form until 1970,[3] rendered participation in an interracial relationship a felony while maintaining the crime of officiating at an interracial marriage. The law regarding sexual relations between members of different races was framed neutrally with respect to gender and provided for a lengthy prison term upon conviction.

> If any white person and any Negro, or the descendant of any Negro, to the third generation inclusive, though one ancestor of each generation was a white person, intermarry or live in adultery or fornication with each other, each of them must on conviction be imprisoned in the penitentiary, or sentenced to hard labor for the county for not less than two nor more than seven years. (Ala. Stat. 1866: Art. 1, sec. 61)

The subsequent section provided that anyone attempting to officiate at such a marriage could be fined between one hundred and one thousand dollars and could be imprisoned or sentenced to hard labor for up to six months.

After passing this law and other restrictive measures in late 1865, the legislature turned to other matters, and the formal legal question of managing race relations dropped from the agenda. National events were looming larger, however, as the conflict between President Johnson and Congress became increasingly bitter. Prominent white Alabamans from the range of the political spectrum tried to organize a conservative National Union group and sent delegates to a National Union convention in Philadelphia, but this nascent movement was unable to stop the Republican juggernaut. The November congressional elections of 1866 produced an overwhelming victory for those Republicans who supported major enhancements to federal

---

3. As noted earlier, *McLaughlin v. Florida* struck down Florida's statute barring cohabitation in 1964, and *Loving v. Virginia* invalidated Virginia's antimiscegenation law in 1967. Several Southern states retained antimiscegenation laws in the wake of *McLaughlin*. After 1967, some states, including Alabama, maintained that *Loving* only applied in Virginia. An irritated federal district court judge struck down Alabama's statute in 1970 in *U.S. v. Brittain*. An initiative passed in November 2000 finally reversed Alabama's constitutional prohibition against miscegenation established in 1901. See chapter 8 for details.

power and punitive measures against the South. As soon as the new Congress took office, it began to implement a vigorous Reconstruction that would remake the Southern states' political structure. Race was a key factor, as the first Reconstruction Acts and the Fourteenth Amendment disenfranchised white former Confederates and enfranchised blacks (Wiggins 1977: 18–20).

By mid-1867, it was clear that blacks were going to constitute a significant political force in Alabaman politics; by the end of the summer, more than 90,000 were registered voters and outnumbered the white electorate. In October, the new electorate voted to hold another constitutional convention and selected delegates. At the constitutional convention, black delegates were in the minority and formed a coalition with white delegates seeking to strengthen the hand of the Republican Party. Prominent blacks issued a public statement calling for the abolition of legal distinctions between the races and condemned conservative repression of black voting (Griffith 1968: 459–60). At the convention, a white delegate proposed a constitutional prohibition of miscegenation. Black delegates opposed the clause because they believed that such laws would be used to control the black population. Ovide Gregory of Mobile County argued for the elimination of all laws recognizing racial distinctions, which would have permitted racial intermarriage. John Carraway, another black Mobile delegate, claimed that he would support the prohibition of interracial intimacy only if the clause supported life sentences for white men convicted of having sexual relationships with black women (Robinson 2003: 28–29). Despite the presence of these delegates, little progress occurred in improving blacks' legal standing other than the formal extension of suffrage. Another reapportionment rebalanced the center of power in the Black Belt, but this had new implications in light of the addition of black voters. The constitution also further disenfranchised whites with ties to the Confederacy (Wiggins 1991: 18–32).

The release of the proposed constitution ignited a firestorm of white rage, uniting Democrats and conservatives in opposition, which they expressed in racialized terms. The February election concerning ratification was marked by intimidation and a conservative boycott. While the overwhelming majority of votes cast were in favor of adoption (approximately 70,000 to 1,000), almost 100,000 voters did not turn out. Because majority turnout was required for ratification, the constitution failed. Governor Patton attributed its defeat to its disenfranchisement of whites beyond the disqualifications prescribed in the Congressional Reconstruction Acts and to the constitution's implicit adoption of radical racial equalization. Patton specifically cited two inflammatory examples: the adoption of universal schooling without a specific provision for racial segregation, and the convention's refusal to prohibit intermarriage between whites and blacks (Griffith 1968: 466–67).

Nonetheless, the constitution was not finished. Congress readmitted Alabama to the Union, placing its imprimatur of legitimacy on the constitution through the Fourth Reconstruction Act, which provided that adoption by a majority of those voting was sufficient. The new government was constituted over the summer, and former Democrat and Unionist William Hugh Smith was sworn in as governor. He supported broad suffrage for blacks and the reinstatement of the franchise for whites, but he argued that the extension of the franchise to blacks fulfilled Alabama's duties under the Civil Rights Acts and the Reconstruction Amendments. The Republicans in Alabama were able to install a government, including a judiciary. While some officials hailed from the North, many were Alabamans. The Alabama Supreme Court was composed of Alabaman Republican sympathizers (hostile whites referred to them as scalawags) from 1868 through 1874, and the Alabama circuit courts were controlled primarily by Republicans from Alabama (Wiggins 1991: 36–39, 136–38).

In 1868, however, a new political player arose with a direct interest in racial politics: the Ku Klux Klan. The late-nineteenth-century Klan was not a monolithic organization with unified goals, but the reports of intimidation and violence from different regions of Alabama (and the rest of the South) were similar in their descriptions of tactics and targets. Blacks perceived as "uppity" were threatened, injured, and killed, and these acts were publicized widely. The Klan also acted against whites perceived as supporting the extension of social equality to blacks. The Alabama legislature banned the Klan in late 1868, but the statute had little effect (Griffith 1968: 475–85).

The Klan's power, along with associated formal and informal intimidation from an array of sources, resulted in a dramatic political reversal in the elections of 1870. Democrat Robert Lindsay was elected governor, and Democrats swept back into control of the state legislature. The congressional Radical Republicans responded by legislating against the Klan and sending federal observers to Alabama for the 1872 elections, but this resulted only in confusion as two legislatures—one Democratic and one Republican— claimed to have won the elections. President Grant's attorney general worked out a compromise through which the Republicans held the legislature for the remainder of the term, but by 1874 the North had lost the will to impose its vision of the postbellum order on the South (Rogers et al. 1994: 254–60).

In 1874, the Democrats again took control of the state government under the label of Redeemers (claiming the redemption of the state from evil Northern interests) or Bourbons (referring to the restoration of the House of Bourbon in France after the end of the Napoleonic era) (Rogers et al. 1994: 263–64). The 1874 election also resulted in the establishment of a solidly Democratic bench, including the replacement of three Republican Supreme Court Justices with three Democrats (Wallenstein 1994: 377). The Democratic Party's campaign framed the election in plainly racialized terms, as candidates pleaded for a union of whites in the northern and southern parts of the state against radicals and blacks. The new governor, Democrat George Houston, called for a referendum on holding another constitutional convention, which took place in the fall of 1875. This convention, dominated by conservatives, revised the constitution of 1868. Among other changes, it provided for racial segregation in public schools and ordered yet another reapportionment. The new constitution was ratified overwhelmingly in the fall in an atmosphere of violent intimidation (Griffith 1968: 493–96). A similar process was taking place throughout the South, as conservative Democrats consolidated their strength and took advantage of the national Republicans' fading will to impose strict control in the former Confederate states and to seek alliances through the political mobilization of racism (Wallenstein 2002: 70, 80).

Alabama's Republicans were demoralized and divided, in part because of successful efforts of the Democrats to exploit racial tensions but also because of internal politics of race and patronage between Alabama's Republican senators in the late 1860s and early 1870s (Fitzgerald 1998). The unification of Democrats on racial grounds had contributed significantly to dividing the Republicans, and by the end of the 1880s, black and white Republicans were holding separate conventions. While some Republicans continued to have local and regional success (for instance, Republican William Lowe was elected to Congress in 1878), the party quickly waned as a threat to Democratic hegemony (Wallenstein 2002: 496–99). Significant party-based political conflicts for the next several decades would take place within the Democratic Party rather than between it and the Republican Party. While the national Republican Party passed further civil rights legislation and held hearings on the Klan in the 1870s, no national impetus could be found for the support of genuine two-party competition in the South after 1876 (Kennedy 2003: 250–54).

The end of Reconstruction and the new alliance of whites facilitated the repression of blacks, but separation between the races was beginning to emerge as the acceptable consensus for whites. The foundation of the Tuskegee Institute in 1881 exemplified many whites' belief that the best way to deal with blacks was to educate them for practical and subordinate roles that would facilitate economic self-sufficiency (Griffith 1968: 570–72). Tolerance of those blacks who "knew their place" should not be confused with an acceptance of freedom, however, even though antiblack violence was less visible in the years between the suppression of the Klan and the rise of lynching in the 1890s. Fears of blackness particularly manifested themselves in new popular discussions of the dangers of interracial relationships.

The Threat of Interracial Relationships

No reliable records detail the extent of interracial partnerings in these years. To read the public discussions of it and review efforts to regulate it, one is left with the impression that it was a quiet and relatively uncommon phenomenon primarily involving poor white women and black men. The cases that reached the appellate courts in these years all concerned white women and black men. Nonetheless, the threat of interracial intimacy was a powerful political and rhetorical device for unifying whites and opposing racial liberalization, a device that would bear more fruit as the nineteenth century moved toward a close.

In the early prosecutions, real mixed-race children or adults were not common features. They were rather the image of fear used to drive both increased legislation and vigorous prosecution in the wake of the Civil War. Members of the legal community picked up on the broader fears running rampant in society that the changes wrought by the end of slavery would be horrifyingly deep and sweeping, resulting in absolute social and political equality between whites and the newly freed slaves. While the South recognized that some degree of political equality would be unavoidable, many individuals struggled to rearticulate a conception of equality that would have well-defined boundaries, keeping the races forever separate. This vision had as a significant subsidiary the quick and thorough transformation of black intraracial relationships into formal monogamous heterosexual marriages and families that structurally paralleled those of middle- and upper-class whites (Franke 1999; Yamin 2005).

In this analysis, mixing of the races was itself something to fear greatly. It was biologically dangerous in the minds of many, but it also threatened grave social disruption. This social disruption, though not carefully delineated, related to the nature of marriage as a fundamentally private institution that nonetheless had enormous social and public implications. I will first discuss several popular pamphlets' portrayals of the risks of interracial marriage and racial mixing and then show how these beliefs linked to legal interpretations of marriage, its purposes, and its public significance.

The 1864 pamphlet *Miscegenation* provides a good, albeit ironic, summary of the deepest racist fears that drove opposition to any pushes for meaningful equality. A political "dirty trick," the pamphlet portrayed the full implications of equality, which would ultimately result in racial mixing between whites and blacks.[4] The authors of the pamphlet, pretending to be enthusiastic Republicans, hailed this result as a biological victory, since "if any fact is well established in history, it is that the miscegenetic or mixed races are much superior, mentally, physically, and morally, to those pure or unmixed" (8–9).

As the reader might predict, the response to this suggestion was immediate and condemnatory. Numerous pamphlets were published to address these outrageous claims, and their authors presented their reasons for fearing interracialism. In addition to creating political problems for the newly freed slaves by encouraging them to reach out to grasp an impossible social equality, the promotion of interracial relationships would lead to the destruction of both races, a theme that ran through discussions of miscegenation constantly. The pamphlet provided a focus for a vigorous public discussion of the risks of interracial intimacy.

The risks identified by authors of such sensationally titled pamphlets as *Subgenation* and *Miscegenation Indorsed* were multiple. Some argued that interracial procreation would produce unthrifty and unhealthy children, since whites and blacks were too different to reproduce together successfully

---

4. The anonymous authors, later identified as reporters for the Democratic *New York World*, hoped that prominent Republicans would endorse, or at least would not vigorously repudiate, the ideas presented in the pamphlet. Their strategy failed, as the Republicans largely ignored the pamphlet and ended up winning key victories in the elections of 1864. The pamphlet is generally identified as the source of the word *miscegenation* (Kaplan 1949).

(see, e.g., *Subgenation* 1864). By subverting the natural process of producing children, the mixing of the races would threaten the entire social order, though pamphleteers did not explain precisely how this would happen. Arguments about the need to separate social from political equality often used the example of sexual relationships between white women and black men as the ultimate answer to any general claims about equality. These arguments were logically circular but politically potent among whites. More scientized explanations of the dangers of interracial intimacy would appear by the turn of the century and would enter Alabama's legal system in the 1920s and 1930s, but the legal community of the postwar era largely relied on these vague fears without a great deal of further analysis.

Debates over constitutionality focused on the relationship between the family and the state, and the cases both reflected and shaped this relationship. Ultimately, this discussion would ground later debates, both specifically over the crime of miscegenation itself and more generally over the meaning of race and whiteness in Alabama. The path that the courts traveled in Alabama between 1865 and 1882 involved working out a way to assert Alabama's submission to the national government while simultaneously articulating a state order that depended upon white solidarity and black subordination. The discussions helped to shape and reflect three agendas that crucial state actors privileged: supporting and centering the white family as the fundamental unit of the state, preventing the formation of interracial family units, and providing a structure for the disciplining of black families to fit the strong norms of closed intraracial intimacy and monogamous marriage. Constitutional debates over the crime of miscegenation were a highly congenial site for the building of a new state infrastructure to support and articulate a system of racial hierarchy.

Legal debates over interracial intimacy implicated the political and social order, both reflecting and shaping the turmoil of the state in crisis. The trajectory of case law on the crime of miscegenation in Alabama in the early postbellum period reveals the contested significance of divisions between black and white in the emerging state. The doctrinal path went from an initial tentative approval of Alabama's criminal prohibition of interracial intimacy to a ruling that it was unconstitutional and then through a series of cases reconstitutionalizing the prohibition. In this process, several concepts were under negotiation and found expression through nodes of conflict. Significant debates erupted over whether equality required substantive rebalancing or superficial symmetry, whether blacks' contractual rights included the right to contract marriage interracially, the extent to which marriage and its regulation had public rather than merely private significance, and the extent of the state's responsibility to and relationship with families. After *Pace and Cox v. State* was decided in 1882, these fundamental issues would become part of the structural and constitutional background against which new debates would emerge. The remainder of the chapter will trace this doctrinal path in detail, parsing out the contours of the battle and tracing the legal system's endorsement of a deeply rooted state interest in white families as the fundamental unit of state structure. Judges would simultaneously endorse a reading of race as a status. These endorsements would ground the finer-grained articulation of whiteness and its central importance for the state that would emerge as the twentieth century arrived. At the same time, they sent a message to blacks about the centrality of the normative white family structure and the need to establish intraracial families along these lines.

Throughout this period, the institutionalization of white supremacy was under negotiation in a contingent process. While racist attitudes were prevalent, these attitudes alone could not build a new state infrastructure for the expression and reinforcement of white privilege and power. Rather, that infrastructure had to be built meticulously on the state level, starting in statutory law but expressed and interpreted through judicial decision-making and enforced through the agency of state actors from the governor's office down to local sheriffs and justices of the peace. Judicial interpretation was a crucial chokepoint in this process, as appellate judges had the authority to work out the meaning and legitimacy of the state's initial efforts to generate racialized boundaries that communicated and enforced subordination.

Ellis v. State and the Initiation of the Struggle

Thornton Ellis was classified as black by the state of Alabama, and Susan Bishop was understood to be white. In the spring of 1868, both were arrested for violating Alabama's prohibition against interracial intimacy. Ellis was charged with adultery or fornication, and Bishop with adultery (*State v. Ellis and Bishop*, trial record 1868: 1). The specific charge of adultery suggests that at least one of the two defendants was married to someone else, but the record does not reveal much about the circumstances of the arrest. Both pleaded not guilty to the charge of adultery or fornication but were convicted. The judge sentenced both to pay fines of $100 for their offense; neither was sentenced to a jail or prison term. Both appealed their convictions, possibly in a case set up to test the viability of Alabama's statutory regime (id. at 3).

Their appeals were based on the legal turmoil of the immediate postbellum years, which had disrupted familial relationships on all levels but particularly for African Americans (see Franke 1999). They claimed that the court had erred by convicting them for violating a statute that "was not in force at the time of the cause" (*State v. Ellis and Bishop*, trial record 1868: 4). The argument, while not spelled out in the record, was apparently that Congress's passage of antidiscrimination legislation superseded Alabama's 1865 prohibition of mixed-race relationships.

The Alabama Supreme Court considered the appeal in the summer of 1868 to address the validity of the statute. The justices who heard the appeal were those who had been placed in office in the immediate postbellum constitutional restructuring. They were Democrats though not former Confederates. Arguing for the state was attorney general John William Augustine Sanford, Jr., who served in that capacity from 1865 through 1868 and again from 1870 through 1878. A staunch advocate of states' rights, Sanford would defend Alabama's criminal prohibition of interracial relationships before the high court five times within eleven years (Wallenstein 1994: n. 44). He was thus the main crafter of Alabama's strategy to maintain the implementation of a policy of racial separation with regard to families.

The court opened its opinion by noting that two Alabama statutes addressed adultery or fornication. The first, section 3598, declared adultery and fornication to be crimes punishable by a one-hundred-dollar fine and/or a term in jail or at hard labor for not more than six months. Upon conviction for a third offense, the penalty increased to a term in the penitentiary or at hard labor for two years (*Ellis v. State*, 42 Ala. 525, 525 [1868]). Race was not a component of this offense. Section 3602 addressed miscegenation and prescribed a two- to seven-year term in the penitentiary or at hard labor. Ellis and Bishop, though accused and convicted of the felony of miscegenation, had been sentenced under the statute addressing only the misdemeanor of adultery or fornication.

The court explained the sentence as the circuit court's effort to account for the congressional Civil Rights Act of 1866, reasoning that Bishop and Ellis had been sentenced only for their violation of section 3598. The problem for the court was that the circuit court had erred in believing that section 3602 did not comport with Congress's mandate (id. at 526). The Civil Rights Act of 1866 demanded equal treatment and prohibited discrimination in "the imposition of punishment" but did not prohibit the state from "making . . . race and color a constituent of an offense, provided it does not lead to a discrimination in punishment" (id.). The court emphasized that all parties were punished equally under section 3602: "The white man who lives in adultery with a black woman is punished in precisely the same manner, and to the same extent with the black woman. So also the white woman is punishable in precisely the same manner with the black man" (id.). This interpretation of equality as simple symmetry in punishment partially addressed the mandate of Congress, but it rested on an underlying interpretation of race as a formal legal status.

The court read race as a status akin to one's status as a minor in other contexts; distinctions in status governed the capacity to form a legal marriage. The model of marriage that the court endorsed was not a simple conception of marriage as a contract between two individuals. Rather, marriage was permissible and possible only through the mediation of the state, which defined legally the classes of individuals who could marry (see Van Tassel 1995; Franke 1999). In this interpretation, the state did not simply award a marriage license to approve a relationship. Instead, a state's denial placed a relationship outside of its selective grant of legitimacy. Policymakers used marriage as a tool to encourage and discourage certain types of relationships, privileging intraracial, monogamous, heterosexual connections between two individuals and strongly disapproving relationships involving interracial intimacy or intraracial ties that did not approximate long-term formal connections between two individuals for the purpose of raising children (Franke 1999; Yamin 2005). The importance of marriage as a means of structuring citizens' relations to the state was underlined through the massive campaign to bring former slaves into a pattern of orderly registered marriage in the immediate postbellum years (Regosin 2002: 11–13). Racial status could, like youth, function as an absolute bar to the formation of a marriage. Unlike youth, race would not change, and the bar was unmovable. In this sense, an attempted interracial marriage was more like an incestuous relationship than anything else.

Ellis and Bishop did win reversals of their fines, but the case was remanded to the circuit court to correct the error by resentencing them in accordance with the harsher prohibition of miscegenation. They thus ended up worse off than they would have been had they not appealed (Wallenstein 1994: 378). The court explicitly avoided considering section 3602's compliance with the new Fourteenth Amendment, explaining that the question was not before them and that their ruling should not be taken as an affirmation of the law's validity (378). The end result was thus ambiguous; while the court mandated strict application of the statute in the case at hand, its ultimate validity remained under a cloud.

The case established the initial framing of the questions at issue. The struggle over the meanings of Congress's actions during Reconstruction and the new amendments was to be fought in part around the difficult issue of interracial intimacy. Of course the core question of the constitutionality of antimiscegenation laws had to be settled. But at least as significant was the question of how this issue was to be considered. Was it about the extent of the equality promised by civil rights laws and the Fourteenth Amendment? Was it about the federal government's power to impose national standards in areas traditionally under state, local, or private paternal control? Was it about the nature of contracts and families and their relationship to the state? Or was it about interracial intimacy itself and the precise nature of the threat whites perceived it as posing to the state? These alternative framings would have different implications for the relationship between the family and the state and the significance of interracial connections in this relationship.

The court focused on the meaning of the equality cited in the Civil Rights Act of 1866, reading this equality as a superficial guarantee. Had they wished to do so, the judges in the case could have relied upon the congressional debates over the laws: at least some of the supporters argued that state regulations against interracial intimacy were acceptable as long as the penalties for whites and blacks were symmetrical (Bank 1995). Instead, the justices simply asserted the principle without tying it specifically to legislative intent.

The other significant development in the case was the court's assertion that race was a status. At this stage, the court did not publicly assert that blackness was an inferior status and whiteness was superior, though regulation of interracial intimacy rested upon this assumption and reinforced it. Rather, the identification of race with status highlighted the problematic nature of interracial marriage. If an individual attempted to contract a marriage rendered illegal by his or her status, the marriage was not merely voidable by state officials' intervention but rather was void at the outset. The conception of race as status enabled the court to focus on the differences between intra- and interracial sexual relationships, whether these relationships were legitimated through marriage or not. This distinction, as well as the status-like nature of race, would be significant in later debates over the issue and ultimately would shape the way the U.S. Supreme Court reached the question of banning interracial relationships in the 1880s. Further, it laid the ground-work for later controversies, since status and its legal implications were wholly constructions of the state.

Burns v. State and the Interpretive Challenge

The next case concerning the crime of miscegenation to reach the Alabama Supreme Court was decided in 1872. As noted earlier, by this time Alabama's judiciary had changed dramatically. In place of the Democratic judges who had ruled in *Ellis* were Republicans elected under the controversial constitu-tion of 1868. This case presented the constitutional question squarely, and the court invalidated Alabama's criminal prohibition of miscegenation, becom-ing the only state high court to overturn a conviction on either federal or state constitutional grounds in the nineteenth century. One constant remained from *Ellis:* again John Sanford argued the state's position to the high court.

Little information is available regarding the background of the case. The Alabama Supreme Court's opinion notes that no briefs reached the court reporter. The case involved an appeal by a justice of the peace James Burns, who was tried and convicted in Mobile's city court of violating sections 3602 and 3603 of Alabama's code (*Burns v. State*, 48 Ala. 195, 196 [1872]). Burns's offense was that he had solemnized the rites of matrimony for an interracial couple. Some speculate that his trial and conviction were planned to enable a statutory and constitutional test of Alabama's policy against interracial rela-tionships (Wallenstein 2002: 73). Certainly, Mobile, with its numerically and politically significant black population, many of whom had been free prior to the Civil War, would have been a likely site for planned litigation to question the boundaries of black citizenship (Fitzgerald 1998: 487–89). Upon convic-tion, Burns appealed his sentence (which most likely was the one hundred to one thousand dollar fine prescribed by the statute) on the grounds that the congressional Civil Rights Act of 1866 invalidated the statute and that it was furthermore rendered unconstitutional by the state and federal constitutions

(*Burns v. State*, 48 Ala. 195, 196 [1872]). While the question of the Civil Rights Act's applicability had been answered with respect to section 3602 in *Ellis*, it was worth asking again, given the change in personnel on the bench and in national politics.

The court initiated its inquiry with a discussion of the Civil Rights Act (id. at 197). It first described marriage as "a civil contract, and in that character alone is dealt with by the municipal law" (id.). This description was not, however, the prelude to a discussion of the traditional scope of state authority over the family. Instead, the court emphasized marriage's contractual nature and the Civil Rights Act's command of equality in contractual relations. Like the right to sue and be sued, denied in *Dred Scott* and explicitly granted in the postbellum era, the right "to make and enforce contracts, amongst which is . . . marriage with any citizen capable of entering into that relation" was specifically granted to blacks by Congress (id. at 198). In the court's reading, contractual freedom was one of the hallmarks of citizenship, and marriage was merely a subspecies of contract. This reading also reinforced the Freedmen's Bureau's agenda of pressing black families into formal contractual relations of marriage as the first legitimate and aspirational exercise of their rights (Franke 1999). The Alabama high court described the Civil Rights Act as an example of the kind of scientific government enabled by increasing knowledge (*Burns v. State*, 48 Ala. 195, 198 [1872]).

After summarily dismissing the objection that some citizens (women and children) were justifiably barred from exercising the types of rights characterized as cornerstones of citizenship, the court turned to an analysis of the Fourteenth Amendment. For the justices, the amendment served two purposes. First, it enabled them to dissipate any clouds over the constitutionality of the Civil Rights Act of 1866, and second, it provided them with an alternative and independent reason for invalidating the statute.

In 1872, Congress was still in the midst of crafting regulations within the framework of Reconstruction. Few if any federal courts had addressed the interplay between the Fourteenth Amendment and the legislation that preceded it. Alabama and other state courts thus had the first opportunity to interpret the amendment and its impact; *Burns* was a significant contrast to the widely noted Indiana case, *State v. Gibson*, in which the state supreme court upheld Indiana's ban on intermarriage on the grounds that federal authority did not extend to regulating marriage as an institution traditionally within the states' purview (36 Ind. 389 [1871]). (*Gibson* and a later Alabama case discussed below, *Green v. State,* provided guidance to the numerous states that upheld bans on interracial marriage in the next several years.) With the ultimate question still unsettled in the states in the early 1870s, the Alabama Supreme Court knew that it was blazing a jurisprudential trail that might guide other courts and shape the way that the federal courts ultimately addressed these issues.

The three justices who ruled on the case were Republicans, but they were Alabamans as well. Benjamin Saffold was a lawyer and Unionist from Selma who was also the son of a former chief justice of the Alabama Supreme Court. While he had been born in New York, E. Woolsey Peck was a Tuscaloosa lawyer who had lived in Alabama since 1824 and had been a chancery court judge. He was also elected president of the 1868 constitutional convention in the face of a challenge from the more radical chair of the Alabama Republican Executive Committee.[5] Thomas Peters was a prominent Unionist from Lawrence County and, after his stint on the Alabama Supreme Court, was the Republican nominee for governor in 1876 (Wiggins 1991: 20, 26, 112). They thus could not be said to be unaware of the context and history of race relations in Alabama, nor were they predominantly identified with the Republicans in Congress who were seeking to implement a sweeping vision of equality.

In addressing the relationship between the Civil Rights Act and the Fourteenth Amendment, the court framed its analysis as simply answering the potential objection that the act itself had exceeded Congress's power under the Constitution. The court rejected this claim on the ground that "the cardinal principle [of the Act] is now declared by the 14th amendment to the Federal constitution" (id. at 198). Arguments concerning the permissible scope of federal influence over questions of marriage were percolating in the early 1870s, but they were not yet pervasive or definitive enough for the Alabama court to have to grapple seriously with this concern (Siegel 1997: 1123–24). Further, the constitutional cloud on the act's legitimacy, explained the court, arose from the U.S. Supreme Court's discredited ruling in *Dred Scott.*

The court then explained its vision of the core meaning of the Fourteenth Amendment and the changes it rendered in citizenship.

---

5. Peck had wide powers of appointment as president of the convention, which he used to install white delegates in politically significant positions, while placing blacks as doorkeepers, messengers, and pages (Wiggins 1977: 26).

> The spirit and express declaration of this section are, that no person shall be disfranchised, in any respect whatever, without fault on his part . . . and that persons who acquire citizenship under it shall not be distinguished from the former citizens for any of the causes, or on any of the grounds, which previously characterized their want of citizenship. (Id.)

This sweeping interpretation did not rest on a particular emphasis on any part of section one; rather it read the section as an organic whole designed to change the nature of citizenship for African Americans. The central problem with the statute was that it interfered with blacks' rights to contract freely with other individuals, a right that was the cornerstone of full citizenship and had been enthusiastically extended to marriages encouraged by the Freedmen's Bureau and state policymakers to legitimate black families (Franke 1999; Yamin 2005).

The court implicitly endorsed an abstracted individual model of citizenship, not noting the question of status at all. Drawing on well-rooted ideals of individual freedom, the court conceived of citizenship as a relationship directly between the individual and the state, in which state actors were responsible for governing individuals fairly and equally. This model sought to place blacks and whites on equal footing in the legal sphere through a mandate that the state could not restrict individuals' freedoms differentially. Classical liberal citizenship had contractual freedom as its core, and the court's focus on freedom of contract drew on a rapidly growing body of law invalidating state regulations on this basis.[6]

With individualized freedom of contract at the center, the court was clear that blacks and whites could not be prevented from marrying each other on the basis of race and that to do so violated the principle of equality. The outcome invalidating the criminal prohibition against miscegenation did not reflect white public opinion in Alabama or even in Northern Republican strongholds, but it did reflect arguments that were on the table. Recent legal scholarship, while disagreeing about the implications, points out that Congress seriously debated establishing comprehensive color blindness in U.S. law during their discussions of the postwar civil rights acts and the Fourteenth Amendment (see, e.g., Marcosson 1998; Bank 1995; Berger 1990; McConnell 1995). As Kennedy notes, policies against interracial relationships

---

6. State courts were beginning to consider and invalidate limits on workers' hours under the principle of freedom of contract. See Novkov 2001.

were largely understood to be unassailable by 1875, but significant questions about interracial intimacy arose in congressional debates over both the Civil Rights Acts and the Fourteenth Amendment (Kennedy 2003: 252). The ruling in *Burns,* while perhaps surprising, drew broadly upon legal and social principles under debate at the time and reflected a place on the political and legal spectrum. While the justices in the case were Republicans, they were popularly elected rather than imposed from above and were chosen by a more broadly democratic electorate than any that would select judges in Alabama for years to come.

Burns v. State did not directly challenge the analysis set forth in *Ellis.* Because of the focus on individuals' contractual rights, any connection between citizenship and status remained obscure in the court's reading. The justices did not consider and reject the earlier ruling's reliance on status, probably because the whole question of status was significantly more controversial than the growing consensus around broad contractual rights. While this strategic choice made for a more rhetorically convincing opinion, the antimiscegenation forces would seek to exploit it in later cases.

Ultimately, *Burns* did three important things: first, it invalidated Alabama's antimiscegenation statute, thereby demonstrating that such an outcome was possible and sparking a concerted effort to reestablish the law. Second, it established a framework for interpretation based on the meaning of citizenship as an organic whole and specifically upon contractual rights. Finally, the outcome and reasoning gave attorneys for others convicted of violating the antimiscegenation statute hope that they might be able to extend the ruling to apply to their clients' circumstances. These accomplishments did little to dissuade those who believed strongly that the state had an interest in suppressing interracial sexual relationships, and political reversals would hearten those who supported criminalizing interracial intimacy. Both sides thus had strong incentives to continue litigating the issue as a question of constitutional law, engaging the conflict over the meaning of race and equality fully in the next several cases.

Ford, Green, and *Hoover:* Chipping Away at *Burns*

The next cases concerning interracial intimacy to reach Alabama's high court took place in the mid- to late 1870s. By this time, Alabama's politics had transformed significantly, and the Democrats were once again in control of the supreme court. These cases, all heard by the same court personnel and all of which upheld convictions under Alabama's antimiscegenation laws, demonstrated both the growing acceptance of a distinction between social and civil equality for African Americans and the seriousness with which the Alabama court took the challenge of the broad vision of racial equality articulated in *Burns*.

For a contemporary observer, it is not surprising that Alabama's high court ultimately supported antimiscegenation legislation. What is surprising is that the court did not simply overrule *Burns* at the first opportunity. Instead, the court struggled to harmonize its rulings of the later 1870s with *Burns*, first narrowing it and, even when overruling it, encouraging pardons for all of the defendants. The process through which the court went to revalidate these laws was not simply a process of reversal, but more one of shifting the legal framework through which the cases were being considered. The primary factors in this shift were a move from a focus on liberal individualism and freedom of contract to a focus on the relationship between the state and the family as the fundamental unit of citizenship and the legal and strategic identification of race as a status. This shift was also closely connected with the state-level efforts to generate justifications for the establishment of white supremacy in light of racialized constructions of state interests.[7]

The first case to reach the high court after *Burns* was the case of *Ford et al. v. State* in 1875. Both Ford, a white man, and his unnamed lover, a black woman, were convicted of violating section 3602, which rendered interracial adultery or fornication felonious and its perpetrators subject to a two- to seven-year term in the state penitentiary. The existing record is sketchy in its details, but their attorney John Foster argued on their behalf that *Burns v. State* governed the outcome of their appeal by invalidating section 3602 (*Ford v. State*, 53 Ala. 150, 151). They claimed that the problem with section 3602 was that it made "an act which when committed by persons of the same race . . . only a misdemeanor, a felony when committed by persons of different races" (id.). Their argument did not refer to the Civil Rights Act of 1866, resting instead on the federal and Alabama constitutions.

In response, attorney general John Sanford cited the recently decided *Slaughter-House Cases* for the proposition that "every State has the right to regulate its domestic affairs, and to adopt a domestic policy most conducive to the interests and welfare of its people" (id.). He argued directly that *Burns*

---

7. The circular nature of this claim reflects the logical structure of the arguments.

should be overturned, citing *Ellis* and *State v. Gibson,* which had upheld Indiana's antimiscegenation statute the year before the ruling in *Burns.*

Alabama's high court issued a short per curiam ruling that did not engage these arguments substantially. Rather, the justices explained that *Ellis* had covered the issue adequately and that the specific issue in this case differed from the issue in *Burns. Burns,* they claimed, dealt with the question of prohibiting marriage between blacks and whites. This case addressed adultery. They reasoned, "Marriage may be a natural and civil right, pertaining to all persons. Living in adultery is offensive to all laws human and divine, and human laws must impose punishments adequate to the enormity of the offence and its insult to public decency" (id.). This reasoning differentiated sharply between the legitimate act of marriage, presumed to be the subject of *Burns,* and the illegitimate acts of adultery and fornication. The scope of *Burns* was thus cut back to address only marriage or attempted marriage, defined as (possibly) a natural right governed by the Fourteenth Amendment. The ruling likewise began the process of compromising the category of contract by emphasizing that agreements to engage in sexual intercourse were not within the legitimate scope of contract.

The court did not directly defend the statutory differentiation between intraracial and interracial adultery or fornication against the charge that it violated the Fourteenth Amendment. The court's reasoning seemed to be that since both were illegitimate in a moral sense, the state was justified in punishing each to the extent that it insulted the (or most of the white) community's mores. No further analysis addressed the legitimacy of maintaining a racial classification in the statute, in part probably because the attorneys in the case framed their debate around the question of the applicability of *Burns.* Nonetheless, the specifics of the ruling may have been surprising to both sides—*Burns* did not govern the result, but it still remained as a viable precedent.

The next case the high court considered was *Green v. State,* and it reached the high court twice. While *Hoover* was decided in between the two *Green* cases, the two appeals of Julia and Aaron Green are best considered together. The first *Green* case, decided in early 1878, was the most extensive statement that the Alabama Supreme Court would ever make on the question of the constitutionality of antimiscegenation laws. In it, the court established a dual frame for analysis that rested upon the nature of marriage and the scope of the Fourteenth Amendment's guarantee of equality. This case became a national bellwether, cited broadly by state supreme courts seeking justifications for validating their own criminal prohibitions of interracial marriage.

Julia Green, a white woman, and Aaron Green, a black man, had lived together for several years. At their trial, the state solicitor produced a marriage license dated July 11, 1876; a probate judge in Butler County had issued it (*Green et al. v. State*, 59 Ala. 69 [1878]). Under the probate judge's signature on the marriage license was a notation that Elder Robert Pounds had married the couple on July 13. They had lived together and held themselves out as husband and wife, working as laborers together for one Mr. McCrary prior to their arrest (id.). While Julia apparently went by the surname of Green, she was also charged under the name Julia Adkinson (*Green v. State*, trial record 1878: 6). Both were arrested and charged with violating section 4189 (section 3602 had been renumbered when the Alabama code was reorganized and amended in 1876) in 1877. At the trial level, the case had to be continued briefly because Aaron Green escaped and fled the court's jurisdiction; upon his recapture, the court tried both and found both guilty (id. at 3, 6). They had offered no defense at trial but did ask the judge to instruct the jury that "If the jury believe, from the evidence, that the defendants came to Mr. McCrary's, and represented themselves as man and wife, and openly and notoriously lived together and cohabited as man and wife, this would be evidence of marriage between the defendants" (*Green et al. v. State*, 59 Ala. 68, 69 [1878]). (This instruction recited the legal elements for finding a common-law marriage.) The court refused to give the charge, and the record indicates that they were sentenced to three years at hard labor (*Green v. State*, trial record 1878: 6), though Julia Green's sentence was apparently later changed to a two-year term in the state penitentiary (*Green v. State*, 58 Ala. 190 [1878]).

Julia Green's attorney appealed her conviction on the ground that it fell squarely within *Burns*'s ambit. Because there was direct evidence of a marriage in this case, the question of *Burns*'s validity could not be avoided. The intrepid John Sanford (who had been reelected in 1876) again argued that *Burns* was ripe for reconsideration, repeating his appeal to the court to consider Indiana's exhaustive consideration of antimiscegenation legislation's constitutionality in *Gibson v. State*. This time, the court accepted his challenge to explore the issue comprehensively.

The court's opinion began by explaining previous Alabama precedents, setting up *Ellis* and *Ford* against *Burns*. The justices then began systematically to pick apart *Burns*. They characterized its approach as "narrow and . . . illogical" for several reasons (id. at 192). The first objection to the reasoning in *Burns* was that the antimiscegenation statute did not criminalize marriage itself (still understood to be a civil right) but rather marriage "*between* a white person and a Negro" (id., emphasis in original). They then introduced the principle of symmetry—the claim that no violation of equality or discrimination on the basis of race had ensued because both blacks and whites convicted under the statute faced the same legal penalty (id.; see also Bank 1995).

The court also challenged *Burns*'s interpretation of the history of the Civil Rights Act of 1866 and the Fourteenth Amendment. The *Green* court pointed out that many Northern states prohibited interracial marriage at the time of the passage of both the Civil Rights Act and the Fourteenth Amendment, and that neither the act nor the Fourteenth Amendment referred to miscegenation specifically. Thus, reasoned the court, the extent of black rights should be limited to their furthest expanse in the North during Reconstruction, since the political authorities in Congress presumably reflected these sentiments and thus intended black rights to go no further (id. at 192–93). This discussion dovetailed neatly with the constitutional and legislative changes in Alabama. Alabama's legislature extended the franchise to whites with only those limits provided by the federal government, in contrast to the 1868 constitution's significant restrictions on former Confederates, restrictions that had gone beyond those required even by congressional Radical Republicans. The *Green* court's reasoning did not address the *Burns* court's broad reading of the Fourteenth Amendment as a new understanding of the scope of citizenship, perhaps because the court believed that *Slaughter-House* and *Bradwell v. Illinois* had definitively disposed of this vision.[8]

The heart of the court's analysis, however, was its reconceptualization of marriage and the centering of the white family as the fundamental unit of the state. *Burns* had read marriage as a contract covered by the language in the Civil Rights Act guaranteeing freedom of contract. The *Green* court challenged this reading directly by analyzing the nature of marriage and its rela-

---

8. In *Bradwell v. Illinois*, decided the day after *Slaughter-House*, the U.S. Supreme Court denied Myra Bradwell's challenge to Illinois' refusal to grant her a license to practice law. The Court's majority simply relied upon *Slaughter-House* to determine that the Fourteenth Amendment's scope was insufficiently broad to justify interpreting a license to practice law as a privilege or immunity protected by the U.S. Constitution (*Bradwell v. Illinois*, 83 U.S. 130 [1873]).

tionship to contract. The first principle the court articulated was that marriage contracts differed substantially from other types of contracts. For instance, they could be formed by individuals (women) "not capable of forming any other lawful contract." Marriages, unlike other civil contracts, could be violated and annulled by law. The rights and obligations of marriage were legally determined rather than being subject to the rational will of the contracting parties (*Green v. State* at 193, citing *Townsend v. Griffin*, a Delaware case). This conceptualization of marriage, which the court underlined by citing Joseph Story's well-respected treatise on conflicts, presented marriage not primarily as a private agreement between individuals but rather as a relationship of public significance and under the state's control. Citing a Kentucky case, the court continued by describing marriage as "the most elementary and useful of . . . [all social relations], . . . regulated and controlled by the sovereign power of the State" (id., citing *Maguire v. Maguire*). This interpretation of the state's intimate involvement with marriage had two purposes: it counteracted any claim that marriage was like any other private contract and thus was subject to the civil equality mandated by the Civil Rights Act and the Fourteenth Amendment, and it placed the primary responsibility for regulating marriage squarely in the hands of the state, not the federal government. It also tied in with the emerging policy of encouraging the formal legitimation of long-term, monogamous, intimate relationships that were perceived to serve state interests (Yamin 2006). This process was taking place with respect to black marriages as well, as informal marriages between slaves were transformed into formal and binding monogamous marriages either through the carrot of allowing pensions and benefits to married women or through sanctioning other kinds of relationships between black sexual partners (Regosin 2002: 78–82). The U.S. Supreme Court would endorse this view explicitly in 1888 in *Maynard v. Hill* by refusing to require states to recognize marriages contracted in other states (Wallenstein 2002: 115–16).

The reframing of marriage, however, was not the most important rhetorical shift. Regardless of its nature, why was marriage so connected to the state? The court did not simply rely upon history here—instead it posited marriage as the fundamental relationship for social functioning and the family as the basic unit of the state. The justices reasoned thus.

> It is through the marriage relation that the *homes* of a people are created—those homes in which, ordinarily, all the members of all the families of the land are . . . assembled together; where the elders of the household seek repose . . . ; and where . . . the young become imbued with the

principles, and animated by the spirit and ideas, which . . . give shape to their characters and determine the manner of their future lives. These homes, in which the virtues are most cultivated and happiness most abounds, are the true *officinae gentium*—the nurseries of States. (Id. at 194)

The quoted passage emphasizes the public significance that the court read into the marital relationship; the family's normative importance to the state served as ample justification for careful regulation of the process through which families were created. The emphasis on marriage and family also undercut the *Burns* court's analysis of the individual and her or his rights as the central consideration.

The state's capacity to control and regulate marriage was nonetheless closely bounded. The purpose of prohibiting interracial intimacy was to prevent "the evil of introducing into their most intimate relations, elements so heterogeneous that they must naturally cause discord, shame, disruption of family circles, and estrangement" (id.). Nonetheless, the court explicitly noted that the state had no authority to meddle with the "interior administration" of the family, reserving its power for "guard[ing] them against disturbances from without" (id.).[9] The court's logic was circular—the state had a duty to protect white families against the introduction of blackness because blackness was by definition incompatible with normative family life, regardless of how an interracial family came into existence. This power had to be exercised at the outset, operating as an absolute bar to the formation of the interracial family by rendering an interracial family a logical and legal contradiction of terms. Under the principle of symmetry, blacks' marriages to other blacks had to be legitimated by the state, but the court's clear implication was that white families, not black ones, were both central to the state's future and deserving of special protection by the state.

The opinion sought to mask the inequality inherent in its reasoning by explaining that the protection was as necessary for blacks as for whites (a sentiment that the U.S. Supreme Court would embrace nearly two decades later in *Plessy v. Ferguson*). Nonetheless, the need for separation rested upon a simultaneous assertion that blacks and whites were too different to form successful nurseries of states and that the "more humble and helpless" fami-

---

9. This reservation of power enabled individual men to retain patriarchal authority in their families without undue fear of state intervention. See Siegel 1997.

lies particularly needed the strong hand of the law to prevent them from ally-ing with each other and finding commonalities (id.). (Such reasoning would also support policymakers' efforts to legitimate black unions as appropriate between like individuals.) This disingenuous reasoning also supported mar-riage's noncontractual nature; while marriage was not a contract for pur-poses of unions between blacks and whites, Justice Manning, author of the ruling in *Green,* had in a bigamy case appealed only a year earlier ruled that a marriage between two whites was a contract (Berry 1991: 840). The rhetor-ical removal of marriage from the realm of contract in this case, however, highlighted the extent to which the court was rejecting the whole concept of blacks as autonomous individual actors subject to the same rules and regula-tions that governed whites. Racial relations were a category of interactions set apart and subject to policymakers' careful management because of the state's direct interest in the units that composed it.

The opinion affirmed the judgment of the circuit court, but the court rec-ognized that the defendants had likely believed that their actions were legal. In light of the overruled precedent of *Burns,* the court encouraged the gover-nor to pardon Julia Green (*Green v. State* at 197). The record is silent on whether Democrat Rufus Cobb took up the court's invitation.

The Greens, however, were not finished. A second case, under the man-agement of a different attorney, reached the Alabama Supreme Court in 1878. The second appeal was based on procedural rather than constitutional grounds and was also rebuffed by the court. The Greens argued that the trial court had refused to give a requested jury instruction that might have con-vinced the jury to view their relationship as a legitimate marriage rather than a long-term sexual liaison based on adultery or fornication.[10] This maneu-ver—and its failure—implicitly referenced the criteria establishing a com-mon-law marriage. The record does not provide much information, but likely the Greens attempted at trial to convince the jury to exercise nullification. The court noted that since cohabitation was the key element of the offense of miscegenation, the defendants' own production of their mar-riage certificate merely bolstered the case against them (*Green et al. v. State,* 59 Ala. 69, 70–71 [1878]).

The first *Green* opinion reveals the extent to which white anxiety about

---

10. This maneuver—and its failure—referenced an emerging struggle over the wisdom of extending common-law marriages to those whom the state wished to discourage from marrying (Yamin 2006).

interracial relationships was intertwined with concerns about the family and the composition of the state. The Alabama Supreme Court's need to back away from *Burns* and to validate antimiscegenation laws pushed it toward an analysis that reserved enormous power for the states to regulate racial relations in the public's interest. Likewise, the location of the struggle around the issue of interracial intimacy shaped the court's framing of the dichotomy between social and civil equality. The battles over interracial intimacy fought at the national level during the ratification of the Civil Rights Acts of 1866 and 1875 and the Fourteenth Amendment raised the specter of an African American having a right to sue a white family for not allowing (usually) him access on an intimate basis (Bank 1995; McConnell 1995). The Alabama high court reframed the threat as coming from the established interracial family itself; in its interpretation, the threat was not to individual whites, but rather to the state itself. This reading of the threat of interracial intimacy posed a stronger justification for state intervention and began to outline the contours of a white state threatened by contamination from blackness. Later decades would see the full articulation of a theory and practice of the white state, but the first manifestations of its modern form emerged in *Green* as a response to the triple threat of federal control of race relations, earlier state sanctioning of black equality, and the establishment of legitimate black-white families.

The *Hoover* case, adjudicated in 1878 between the two *Green* cases, also involved an attempt by a black man and a white woman to live together in matrimony. Robert Hoover and Betsey Litsey were arrested and charged with living together in a state of adultery or fornication in violation of section 4189 (the antimiscegenation statute) (*Hoover v. State,* 59 Ala. 58 [1878]). They had been living together in a one-room house in a suburb of Talladega during 1876 and later had moved together to another locale near Talladega. As in the *Green* cases, a marriage license was introduced at the trial. The license had been signed by a probate judge and had a notation indicating that they were married by John Livingston on March 6, 1875 (id.). Only Robert Hoover was tried for the crime of miscegenation; Betsey Litsey (who went by the surname Hoover), according to the record, was too close to delivering their child to appear in court (*Hoover v. State,* trial record 1878: 6). Hoover sought to call the probate judge to the stand to testify that Hoover "had asked him if it was lawful for him (Hoover) to marry a white woman, and that he was informed that it was" (*Hoover v. State* at 58). The state objected, and the court did not allow the evidence to be introduced. Hoover was found guilty and sentenced to a two-year term in the state penitentiary (Trial record at 6).

Hoover's attorney relied upon *Burns* in challenging his client's conviction, but he also argued that section 4189 had never been properly passed in accordance with Alabama law. He also claimed (somewhat confusingly) that "there never was a statute of Alabama forbidding marriage between whites and Negroes, and declaring it to be void *ab initio;* but only a statute . . . declaring that if any white person and any Negro intermarry each of them must, on conviction, be imprisoned in the penitentiary" (*Hoover v. State* at 59). The thrust of this argument was apparently a simultaneous plea for jury nullification and a claim that interracial marriage could not be taken as a crime of strict liability. Rather, implied Hoover's attorney, the defendant had to intend to violate the law. Further, the pleadings again raised the elements of common-law marriage. In response, John Sanford cited *Green I* and the authorities upon which the ruling in *Green I* had relied.

The court opened with a reference to *Green I*, declining to engage in sustained analysis. It also quickly dismissed the challenge to the procedure for passing the antimiscegenation laws, ruling that the somewhat irregular passage of the original acts had been validated by the later adoption of the entire Alabama Code in 1867 and 1876 (id. at 60). The opinion emphasized that the marriage of Robert and Betsey Hoover was not merely voidable but rather was "absolutely void." In technical terms, this meant that any long-term interracial sexual relationship could only be adultery or fornication, not marriage. Thus Hoover was guilty under the law prohibiting interracial adultery or fornication and his attempt to prove marriage, rather than exonerating him, merely strengthened the case against him (id.).

The court went even further in explaining the nature of the crime of miscegenation as one of strict liability. The justices were unpersuaded by Hoover's efforts to introduce evidence that he believed his actions were permissible under the then-current state of the law, ruling that ignorance of the law could provide no defense, even when this "ignorance" rested upon a prior opinion of the Alabama high court itself. Again, the evidence of the marriage worked in precisely the opposite direction as Hoover had hoped— it demonstrated that their act of cohabitation was intentional, and Hoover's question only revealed that he had known of the existence of the antimiscegenation statute (id.). The court's one concession to Hoover's unhappy plight was a recommendation that the case be considered for executive clemency, "on condition there be given satisfactory assurance of a discontinuance of this very gross offence against morals and decorum. Should this crime be repeated or continued, the law should lay a heavy restraining hand on the offenders" (id.).

Hoover added to Green I's comprehensive analysis the court's insistence that interracial marriage itself was a logical contradiction of terms. This reasoning underlined the Green I court's emphasis on the centrality of marriage to the state's purpose and functioning and the interconnectedness of "pure" families with the state's mission. Hoover likewise undercut Burns even more by effectively eliminating the category of interracial marriage as a possibility, including situations in which the formal conditions for common-law marriage had been met. When read in tandem with Ford, an ongoing interracial sexual liaison could fall into but one of two categories: felonious adultery or felonious fornication. The only remnant of interracial marriage logically left in the Alabama code was an attempt to form a marriage that would be legally void and criminally sanctioned from the outset.

The cases of the 1870s thus saw a rapid retreat from Burns and a systematic and thorough dismantling of the adverse precedent. Ford initially limited Burns to cases involving interracial marriage, and Green I and Hoover demolished Burns's remaining governance over interracial marriage. Read together, these cases declared such marriages to be inherently against the state's values and interests and to be logically impossible, given the nature of marriage and the state's intimate relationship with marriage as an institution. They further shifted the focus from individuals' rights to contract freely to the state's responsibility for the protection of the family. The careful trajectory that the state of Alabama plotted in its attack on Burns, both through the efforts of attorney general John Sanford and through the Democratic high court's rulings, shows the seriousness with which the white institutions of Alabama took Burns's challenge to a reestablishment of a status quo of subordination for African Americans. The cases also demonstrated the swiftness with which a refocusing of judicial inquiry could undermine the logical supports of the ruling in Burns. Burns, rather than facing direct challenge and conflict over its reading of the meaning of contract and equality, succumbed to a nodal reconfiguration of the central issues in the cases.

Pace and Cox v. State and Pace v. Alabama: Constituting the State

Pace and Cox v. State would be the Alabama Supreme Court's last word on the constitutionality of its antimiscegenation legislation until the 1950s, and the U.S. Supreme Court's ruling in *Pace v. Alabama* in 1883 would stand until *McLaughlin* in 1964. For rulings of such monumental longevity, the background of the case was fairly unremarkable in the context of its companions at the state level.

As in *Ellis, Ford, Green,* and *Hoover,* the defendants were a black man and white woman who were charged with engaging in an interracial sexual relationship. Not much is known about Tony (or Toney) Pace and Mary Ann (or perhaps it was really Mary Jane) Cox. They met and in 1881 were arrested for violating section 4184 (*Pace and Cox v. State,* trial record 1881: 3). At the time of their arrest, they were living in Clarke County, in the south-central region of Alabama where many former slaves had remained after emancipation (Jackson 1991). They were both charged with adultery or fornication rather than intermarriage or attempted intermarriage (*Pace and Cox v. Alabama,* 69 Ala. 231 [1882]). Both were convicted and sentenced to two-year terms in the state penitentiary (Trial record at 3).

Both Pace and Cox appealed; each appeal had both a procedural and constitutional component. Cox's appeal was based on some confusion regarding her middle name.[11] Pace argued that the evidence was insufficient to prove adultery or fornication (Trial record at 8). He had asked the trial judge to issue a charge pressing the jury to consider the evidence "as to where the parties each lived, and with whom, and where the adulterous acts took place, if they did in fact take place; as whether they took place in a house controlled or occupied by either party or were mere occasional acts of illicit intercourse in out of the way places" (id.). Had the jury found "mere occasional acts of illicit intercourse," Pace and Cox's actions would not have met the appropriate legal standard for adultery or fornication, which required some evidence of ongoing sexual contact. The trial judge refused to issue the charge, and Pace appealed on this basis. Both also claimed that the statute violated the U.S. Constitution.

The Alabama Supreme Court quickly dismissed the procedural claims; for Pace, the dismissal was based on the bill of exceptions' failure to include enough evidence to find an error (*Pace and Cox v. State,* 69 Ala. 231, 233 [1882]). The court spent more time addressing the constitutional challenge; the opinion could simply have cited *Green I* and moved on, but apparently

---

11. She objected that she had been charged and indicted under the name Mary Ann Cox but that her name was in fact Mary Jane Cox. This objection was not nearly as frivolous as it sounds to modern ears; in the heyday of legal formalism, the improper wording of an indictment could easily prove fatal to a prosecutor's case.

the justices felt that further elucidation would be helpful. The court focused directly on the Fourteenth Amendment's equal protection clause and articulated a rule of formal symmetry. The opinion explained that the difference between the punishment for intraracial and interracial adultery fulfilled the mandate of equal protection because it did not differentiate between the races (id.). The justices noted, "The discrimination is not directed against the person of any particular color or race, but against the offence, the nature of which is determined by the opposite color of the cohabiting parties. The punishment of each offending party, white and black, is precisely the same" (id.). This reasoning justified the targeting of differential punishments by focusing on the offense rather than the individuals who committed it. It was the offense of interracial adultery or fornication that differed from intraracial adultery or fornication, not the races of the individuals arrested for engaging in the prohibited activity. This reasoning further directed attention toward the impact that the relationship had on the state.

Once this logical distinction was on the ground (however tenuously), the court was off and running. "The evil tendency of the crime . . . is greater when . . . committed between persons of the two races . . . . Its result may be the amalgamation of the two races, producing a mongrel population and a degraded civilization, the prevention of which is dictated by a sound public policy affecting the highest interests of society and government" (id.). This reasoning picked up on and extended the reasoning in *Green I* concerning the central place of the family in state structure. *Green I* and *Pace*, when read together, present a picture of sharply dichotomous families: the legitimate, intraracial, white cornerstone of the state, and the illegitimate, threatening, destructive interracial not-family.[12] This reasoning rendered racial separation not merely permissible but actually necessary for the future survival of the state. While the court had started with an analysis of equality, any substantive engagement with equality left the table quickly as the comparison between inter- and intraracial relationships and their place in the state became the crux of the constitutional question. Pace's and Cox's convictions would stand, and this time the court showed no sympathy for the offenders.

Tony Pace's attorney, John Tompkins, appealed the ruling against his client to the U.S. Supreme Court, and the Justices placed the case on their

---

12. The cases do not note black families, although the Freedmen's Bureau had worked hard to legitimate them (Franke 1999).

docket. Tompkins's argument was that Alabama's antimiscegenation statute violated the Fourteenth Amendment's equal protection clause. In his brief to the U.S. Supreme Court, Tompkins attempted to reframe the question of equality around racial discrimination. He cited *Slaughter-House* in support of the proposition that the Fourteenth Amendment's specific purpose was to ameliorate black inequality and provide full citizenship for African Americans (J. Tompkins 1882: 2). Citing recent federal precedents acknowledging the unconstitutionality of racial differentiation, he based his analysis on a comparison between the establishment of intraracial adultery or fornication as a misdemeanor and interracial adultery or fornication as a felony (3–4).

Tompkins chose not to go after Alabama's prohibition of interracial marriage. *Green I,* he claimed instead, had answered the question of interracial marriage's illegitimacy definitively. Marriage, he conceded, was a social institution fully under control of the state and its particulars were not subject to federal intervention. Turning around the reasoning used in *Ford* to distinguish *Burns,* he claimed that because adultery and fornication were social evils rather than social blessings, "legislative power may not say how crimes . . . may be discriminately punished (where all are equal before the law) according to the caste of the individual who invades them" (5). This move sought to take interracial intimacy outside of the questions about social equality and render interracial sex a crime parasitic on the simple prohibition of sexual activity between individuals not married to each other.

Despite the careful bounding of his argument, Tompkins concluded his substantive discussion with a hypothetical story designed to elicit sympathy for the interracial family.

> [Let us suppose a] case of two brothers of the Saxon race equal socially and before the law, the one becomes enamored of an octoroon but by reason of local laws cannot make her his wife, the other openly grovels in lowest licentiousness with the most degraded of Indian squaws.[13] Each break the law of adultery and fornication, the statute which Justice Somerville says does not discriminate sends one a felon to the penitentiary and imposes a nominal fine for a misdemeanor on the other. (6–7)

The hypothetical demonstrated the porousness of the categories of adultery/fornication and intermarriage. The prohibition against intermarriage

---

13. White Alabamans held contradictory views regarding Native Americans. See the discussion of the 1901 constitutional convention in chapter 3.

appeared here to work as fundamental a deprivation of rights as the differential punishment of intra- and interracial fornication, but Tompkins likely thought his chances of achieving victory were much higher if he primarily sought only to invalidate the differential punishment for illicit sex. The U.S. Supreme Court Justices would not be taken in by the explicitly narrow scope, seeing its plain implications for interracial marriage.

Henry Tompkins, attorney general for the state of Alabama, filed a response defending the statute in broad terms. (John Sanford, who had defended against the previous challenges, was now the clerk of the Alabama Supreme Court and had overseen the preparation of the trial record for the U.S. Supreme Court's consideration [*Pace v. Alabama*, trial record at 10].) While the law had two purposes—the prevention of intermarriage and the prevention of illicit sexual intercourse between blacks and whites—the ultimate end of the statute was the same: to prevent "the amalgamation of the two different races" (H. Tompkins 1882: 2–3). The defense of the statute was thus not only a claim that punishing interracial adultery or fornication as a felony was legitimate, but moreover that the criminal suppression of interracial relationships was constitutionally acceptable. This reading centered the state's role in protecting the category of legitimate family both for the integrity of the category itself and for the advance of the state's interest in being formed only of normatively correct intraracial families.

In Henry Tompkins's analysis for the state, Pace's argument that the differential punishment of adultery constituted inequality failed on two grounds. First, Tompkins endorsed the principle of symmetry: since both parties were punished alike, regardless of race or gender, the statute did not create any inequality. Second, the crime of interracial adultery was in fact a greater crime than intraracial adultery and warranted greater punishment (1882: 3). In making this claim, Tompkins's brief first noted that adultery between those whose status barred intermarriage often received greater punishment. This simple point introduced the need to examine the relationship between adultery and intermarriage, ultimately implicating the state's authority to regulate marriage.

Tompkins argued that the state had traditionally had extensive power to regulate marriage. Marriage was, as *Green* had noted, more than a private contractual relationship because of its implications for the state's future (4–5). The antimiscegenation statute was akin in one of its purposes to the rules against consanguinity: "the prevention of the evil results which are supposed to be developed in their progeny" (5–6). Because of this particular threat to the state's interests, the state had additional criminal leverage against the couples who purveyed it. Having established the state's traditional powers over these questions, Henry Tompkins now turned to an analysis of the Fourteenth Amendment.

Looking to both the privileges or immunities clause and the equal protection clause, Tompkins articulated a limited vision of national power over state functions and placed the regulation of marriage and family firmly within the ambit of state authority. The primary question for equal protection was not whether the statute created any substantive inequality in its operation, but rather whether the states had the authority to forbid intermarriage. If this power existed, then the constitutionality of antimiscegenation measures was assured "so long as there is no discrimination in the punishment imposed upon the white and that imposed upon the Negro violator of the particular statute" (13–14). To the response that such a measure stigmatized blacks (and possibly to defend against any latent claims under the Thirteenth Amendment), Tompkins argued that such regulations "do[] not place upon either [race] the badge of inferiority; they are based upon the idea of dissimilarity, which does not necessarily mean legal or civil inequality" (14). This analysis led inevitably to the principle of symmetry, but by framing the question as being primarily about the state's power rather than the scope and meaning of the Fourteenth Amendment, Tompkins pushed the court toward a superficial review of the nature of the equality underlying the Fourteenth Amendment. As with the Alabama Supreme Court's ruling in *Green,* this line of reasoning would find its full expression by the high court in *Plessy* in 1896.

The high court heard *Pace v. Alabama* during its October 1882 term and issued its ruling on January 29, 1883. The ruling in the more famous *Civil Rights Cases,* argued the same term, would not be issued until October. The Court's consideration of Pace's appeal was superficial but picked up on the themes emerging from Alabama and other states, ultimately endorsing a thin conception of symmetry as the appropriate departure point for analysis under equal protection. Initially, the Court claimed that Pace was correct to identify the equal protection clause's purpose as that of "prevent[ing] hostile and discriminating State legislation against any person or class of persons" (*Pace v. Alabama,* 106 U.S. 583, 584 [1883]). Equality required accessibility to the legal process on the same terms for all as well as equality in legal outcomes, particularly punishments. In framing the principle this way, the Court relied upon the Civil Rights Act of 1870, which included a clause concerning contracts and a requirement of equal legal consequences (id. at 584–85).

The Court read the equality in punishment, however, as mandating equal sentences for black and white miscegenators, not equal treatment for intra- and interracial adulterers or fornicators. The code sections, claimed the Court, were entirely consistent: "The one prescribes . . . a punishment for an offence committed between persons of different sexes; the other describes a punishment for an offence which can only be committed where the two sexes are of different races" (id. at 585). The discrimination in question was not between blacks and whites but rather between the two different offenses. The Court did not say that it was within the state's rightful power to judge rationally the nature and appropriate punishments for the offenses (the concept of rational scrutiny was decades into the future), but this was implied in the ruling.

The U.S. Supreme Court thus settled the question of constitutionality without delving deeply into the nature of the state's interest in preventing interracial sexual relationships. It was sufficient for the U.S. Supreme Court that the regulation met the low threshold of superficial symmetry. The message was that state policymakers could articulate and enforce their own interests in governing race relations as long as the requirement of symmetry was met in a formal sense.

The state and federal high courts' opinions read together contain an odd dualism. On the one hand, both courts agreed that the mandate for equality required only equality in punishment. In this sense, the statutes prohibiting interracial relationships were models of equal legislation, since, unlike many antebellum measures, they mandated equal punishments for blacks and whites. On the other hand, the statutes survived review because of a significant difference between interracial and intraracial families and between interracial and intraracial adultery. The Alabama high court's ruling that the two types of adultery were indeed different rested on racial differentiation, but because it did so indirectly, the justices claimed successfully that their reasoning did not contravene the mandate of equality.

The U.S. Supreme Court's reasoning had an additional layer of significance. It suggested to the states that their articulations of the dangers posed by black equality and their need to develop legal means of articulating and entrenching white supremacy would largely be allowed to stand without serious review. In the South particularly, state policymakers were not slow to see and accept this invitation.

The New Constitutional Order and the Cornerstones of White Supremacy

The Alabama appellate courts between 1865 and 1882 considered only constitutional questions in ruling on appeals of convictions for miscegenation. These cases reflected the unsettled nature of postbellum federal and state guarantees of equality as well as swiftly changing attitudes about race. In the cases described in this chapter, the judiciary moved from cautious acceptance, to rejection, to increasingly stronger endorsements of the constitutionality and the propriety of the criminal ban on miscegenation. The simple explanation for these shifts is the dramatic shift in the political orientation of the Alabama Supreme Court, which went from Democratic to Republican in 1868 and back again to Democratic in 1874. Nonetheless, the opinions revealed much about the trajectory of the early postbellum process of racial formation. They also articulated the grounding principles of race relations on which later considerations of the ban on interracial intimacy would be based.

The Alabama high court considered the principle of equality and adopted a conception of equality as simple symmetry. As long as differential punishments were not directly based on the race of the individuals suffering them, this conception could be met. Symmetry allowed the state to recognize race and to legislate by using racial categories. The idea likely was popularized in Congress, as it was discussed in debates over the civil rights acts and the Fourteenth Amendment, but it had ready application for postbellum courts that were struggling to accommodate traditional discriminatory legislation to the new constitutional order. The court's struggles over interracial intimacy enabled it to consider and reject alternative interpretations based on individualist readings of the guarantee of equality, resting its reasoning instead upon the embedding of the white family at the center of the state.

The postbellum legal debate over race and equality has often been mapped as a debate over the extent of equality and whether the constitutional changes went so far as to mandate so-called social equality. Strands of this debate were evident in Alabama's legal discussions of interracial intimacy, but social versus civil equality was not the primary axis of conflict. The debate over interracial intimacy instead turned on analysis of the state and its relationship with and responsibility to the individual and the family, central nodes of conflict in the litigation of this period. At least in part, the strong statements of the high court in the late 1870s and early 1880s identifying the normative (white) family as the cornerstone of state structure came directly from the court's need to respond to the *Burns* court's identification of individual contractual rights as the core of citizenship. Likewise, legal rhetoric identifying race as a status enabled legal differentiation between policies that acknowledged racial status without violating the basic principle of equality, read as treating like things alike.

Gender also played a role, as all of these appeals involved white female–black male dyads. As Alabama sought to rework racial hierarchies, these hierarchies interwove with gendered hierarchies as well, particularly in relation to marriage. Alabama's policymakers actively encouraged, both through incentives and punishments, the formation of state-sanctioned marriages between former slaves and between whites, but struggled with interracial intimacy in the wake of *Burns*. Ultimately interracial intimacy was defined in a way that excluded it from the broad practice of finding marriages between people who were living in a marriage-like relationship, leaving only adultery or fornication as possible categories of lasting, intimate interracial relationships. This agenda was exercised on the appellate level against white women who transgressed the racialized boundaries of proper behavior, and against black men who represented dangerous sexual energies that could potentially disrupt the state.

While *Burns* survived only a few years, its significance should not be underplayed. This ruling established that it was possible for courts to find that the prohibition of interracial relationships was unconstitutional. This was despite the apparently widely held sentiment among whites that, no matter what changes were made in regulating interactions among the races, the white family would remain sacrosanct. Miscegenation was always the ultimate threat, the end of the slippery slope, the grave danger articulated for rhetorical purposes by those who opposed change and as an example of a commonsense limit by those promoting change. That this limit could be transgressed not furtively by poor whites and blacks with few alternatives but openly through the formal machinery of the legal process was likely quite shocking to many Alabamans and to those outside of Alabama who heard the news. That the justices ruling in the case were native Alabamans, albeit deemed scalawags by conservative whites, made the ruling more notable.

This dynamic likely accounts for the care with which the Democratic court dismantled the precedent. But in the process of tearing down *Burns,* the high court was also building. It created the groundwork for white supremacy by centering the relationship between the family and the state in its consideration of race and equality. Once the family, rather than the individual, was the key unit for the full growth and health of the state, policymakers could exercise significant power in regulating the family to promote what they saw as best serving its interests. Interracial relationships that mimicked intraracial families were a key threat to the state, not simply because many Alabamans viewed them with distaste, but rather because they undermined the core unit of the state. The principle of the state's interest in racial separation began in the home and would extend outward from it. Reviewing this process in detail demonstrates the dynamic nature of the ideological construction of white supremacy before it was fully institutionalized in its postbellum face.

The process of establishing the constitutionality of regulations regarding interracial intimacy did not directly address definitions of race, which remained what they had been before the war. Nonetheless, this process did facilitate racial formation, primarily by centering the white family as well as establishing race as a status. It was a short step from race as a status to blackness as a justification for subordination, and this step had been taken socially long ago. Establishing it legally would require more manipulations, which would come during the decades of the late nineteenth and early twentieth centuries. The broad-based conflicts of the first era of litigation would narrow and focus more intensively on the meaning of the principle that the white family was the cornerstone of the state, drawing on racial status as the basis for encouraging differential treatment. The first stirrings of freedom were quickly to be repressed through the adoption and justification of Jim Crow policies, which worked hand in hand with a growing campaign of savage extralegal suppression.

It might seem at first blush that dry, technical debates over evidentiary questions had little to do with the rapid rise in racially motivated violence in Alabama and throughout the South after the end of Reconstruction. These debates, however, reflected the process through which white supremacy became entrenched in the state. The constitutional battle had established the state's legitimate interest in regulating race relations—a term that first appeared in an address delivered by noted Montgomery advocate for child-labor regulation Edgar Murphy in 1900 (1901–2). Between 1883 and 1917, social and legal developments resonated with this interest, building on the initial centering of the white family. In the process, the courts considered questions of how general legal rules would apply to racialized contexts and began to establish specific rules for sanctioning relations between blacks and whites.

The appellate courts ruling on appeals of convictions for miscegenation worked within the evolving structure of white supremacy to explain precisely how and why interracial intimacy was a threat. They did this mostly through grappling with the problem of defining what constituted miscegenation. This question seems odd at first glance. Given policymakers' expressed desire for racial separation and the extreme violence directed at some individuals who violated this principle, interracial sex itself would seem to be the most obvious target for the state's coercive and punitive power. In fact, though, judges struggled over defining the elements of miscegenation and ultimately settled on legal principles that extended the earlier period's identification of the mixed-race family as a particular threat to the state. In the process, they turned to general rules governing sexual misconduct and applied them within a racialized context, building a body of cases to which later litigants would turn for guidance about legal rules. White supremacy was not simply to be a matter of embedding black subordination. The constitutional change and more focused legal conflicts of this era would reveal it as an affirmative agenda of consolidating and centering white elite power both institutionally and socially.

As the process of defining the threat of interracial intimacy was taking place, Alabama underwent a significant institutional event. In 1901, delegates again gathered in Montgomery to rewrite the state constitution. In contrast to the turmoil and controversy that had characterized the earlier conventions, this convention proceeded smoothly and produced the constitution under which the state is still governed. The delegates' central agenda for the constitution was the legal rationalization and implementation of white supremacy, and this purpose would overshadow Alabama's politics and laws for years to come.

This chapter will explore the debates of the early Jim Crow era as they played out in the evidentiary considerations that the courts addressed. The debates took place in a broader context of increasingly violent legal and extralegal suppression of African Americans' rights as citizens. The crucial significance of racial mixing was a trope against which white supremacy was the legal and political antidote in both the narrow and broad contexts. Judges drew boundaries between threatening and nonthreatening interracial encounters based on their implications for undermining a coalescing ideology of whiteness. These boundaries both relied upon and reinforced the extra-legally drawn boundaries around which white-on-black violence took place. The appeals of this era did not produce the full-fledged, constitutionally based nodes of conflict of the previous decades. Instead, they were tightly focused conflicts over the evidence necessary to prove the crime of miscegenation. Nonetheless, these debates drew from the earlier establishment of the central nature of the legitimate white family and emphasized state policymakers' commitment to stamping out the direct threat they perceived to family and state from interracial intimacy. The battles thus turned on the nature of the relationship and the parties to it: was the woman involved romantically attached to the man, or was she a prostitute? And how serious was the relationship between the interracial dyad?

Political Consolidation, the Constitution of 1901, and Supremacist Ideology

When the Democrats regained power in Alabama in the mid-1870s, they promoted little forward-looking change. Instead, they emphasized the values of order, stability, and elite rule, actively promoting the unification of whites (especially poor whites) against the threat of black political power. The question of race masked other divisions within the party, most notably those based on geography and economics. The Democrats' main opponents in the 1880s were Republicans, Greenbackers, and Independents, but the Republican Party itself was divided over race as well and could not marshal a serious challenge (Rogers 1970: 35–48).

Nevertheless, the conservative Democrats faced opposition. Small-scale farmers, politicized by their experiences in the Grange, were becoming increasingly frustrated by the failure of land reform and the Democrats' lack of interest in modernization and industrialization. The Agricultural Wheel, which later merged with the Farmers' Alliance, began to promote major reforms. The organization, which enrolled approximately 75,000 Alabamans by 1889, had to be taken seriously. The Democrats became increasingly concerned as some prominent Wheelers sought alliances with labor interests and blacks, forming a Union Labor Party in 1887. While the Farmers' Alliance was more conservative, it also promoted agrarian reform and had nearly 125,000 members by the end of the 1880s. Blacks who were becoming frustrated with the so-called Lily White elements in the Republican Party supported agrarian reform, forming Negro Alliances to parallel the work of the Farmers' Alliance and the Agricultural Wheel as well as contributing directly to these organizations when they could (Rogers 1970: 121–46).

Faced with an increasingly formidable coalition of opponents, the conservative Democrats responded through the exercise of state power, as they were still in control of most of the official organs of the state. They actively engaged in gerrymandering, replaced election with appointment as a means of selecting local officials, and pushed through reforms to the electoral process that drastically cut down voting rights, principally those of blacks and poorer whites. The coalition responded by promoting more formal political action, uniting behind gubernatorial candidate Reuben F. Kolb. In 1892 and 1894, the Jeffersonian Democrats, the Populists, and the Republicans jointly nominated him (Flynt 2001: 69).

The conservative Democrats were likely only able to preserve their hold on power through outright fraud, certifying questionable ballot counts from Black Belt counties under their control in both elections. Populism gradually lost political force in the 1890s, plagued by divisions within and high levels of hostility from conservatives. The conservative Democrats consolidated their stranglehold on Alabama's political structure by the mid-1890s, and the liberal/radical coalition collapsed. Populists, agrarian reformers, and independents largely returned to the traditional Democratic and Republican Parties along racial lines (whites to the Democrats and blacks to the Republicans), though some Northern white Populists established a white reform element within the Republican Party (Flynt 2001: 69–70).

This turmoil and its aftermath set the stage for the constitutional convention of 1901. The Democrats did not wish to take any chances in the future with the establishment of a racially progressive and integrated resistance to their rule and called for constitutional reform. The 155 delegates were far less representative than those selected for previous conventions; none were black, and 141 were Democrats. Of the 14 remaining, 7 were Populists, 6 were Republicans, and 1 was an independent (72). While the convention was aimed primarily at suppressing black political and social gains, the institutional structure it produced also substantially stripped poor whites of access to political influence and participation.

The conventioneers wanted to establish a Democratic hegemony in the state, but the political tool they used to justify their efforts was the emerging ideology of white supremacy. The establishment of white supremacy was ultimately both cause and effect in the Constitution of 1901, as the delegates used it rhetorically to justify their actions and embedded it as the official public policy of the state. While the Democrats could have framed their efforts as an overhaul to replace the patchwork efforts of conventions in the immediate postbellum years, the explicit and stated goal of the convention was to organize Alabama's governmental structure around the ideology of white supremacy.

In his opening remarks, the convention's president, corporate lawyer John Knox, emphasized this goal, explaining, "If we would have white supremacy, we must establish it by law—not by force or fraud."[1] He justified this agenda of legal rationalization through two related arguments: first, the absolute biological inferiority of blacks and second, the political need for massive withdrawing of the basic rights of citizenship from blacks. Relying on theories of eugenics, he argued first that the necessity of grounding white supremacy in the highest laws of the state arose from the inherent differences

---

1. *Journal of the Proceedings of the Constitutional Convention of the State of Alabama* (Montgomery, AL, May 21, 1901): 12 (Mr. John Knox).

between the races, expressed in hereditary terms. He insisted that the new constitution would not discriminate against blacks because of race but rather "on account of his intellectual and moral condition."[2] Because blacks and whites were fundamentally unequal, withdrawing rights from blacks did not constitute discrimination. Instead, it was a form of protection for the state.

The political argument drew on Knox's claims about black inferiority, but could be read independently. He claimed that whites had "an inherited capacity for government" that blacks wholly lacked (Flynt 2001: 12). Nonetheless, the real problem in Alabama was not the presence of an inferior race; instead it was their holding of political rights for which they were inadequately prepared. The experience of Reconstruction had shown that they were mere political tools of outsiders (Northerners) who did not have Alabama's interests at heart. Further, their exercise of political rights generated racial hostility and violence. Institutionalized white supremacy was, for Knox and the conventioneers, the logical solution to this problem.

These statements help to distinguish white supremacy from racist beliefs about white superiority. Supremacy was a political doctrine, grounded partially on racist beliefs but also reflecting a particular view of political power and the state's obligations. Rather than being a simple reflection of racist attitudes, supremacy was emerging in these years as a system for the organization and articulation of governance, and the 1901 constitution sought to embed these developments in the very structure of the state. Knox pressed for as much state-based autonomy concerning racial issues as possible within the parameters set by the U.S. Constitution, justifying the claim for local rule because Alabama, not the nation, had to deal directly with the political problems engendered by black citizenship. He explained, "What is it that we want to do? . . . It is within the limits imposed by the Federal Constitution, to establish white supremacy in this State. This is our problem, and we should be permitted to deal with it unobstructed by outside influences" (Proceedings at 8, Flynt 2001: 71). Constitutionally mandated and legally enforced white supremacy would rationalize the doctrine and apply it within the political sphere to quell what the conventioneers saw as threats to the state.

Controlling interracial sexuality, like restricting the black vote and underlining the necessity for segregated schools, was important enough for the state as an institution for the conventioneers to discuss directly, rather

---

2. *Journal of the Proceedings of the Constitutional Convention:* 15.

than leaving it up to the legislature to manage under the new constitution (Flynt 2001: 69–72). The framers took up the issue on July 22, 1901, considering proposed section 62 of the new constitution. The new section was to read: "The Legislature shall never pass any law to authorize or legalize any marriage of any white person and Negro, or the descendant of a Negro, to the third generation inclusive, though one ancestor of each generation be a white person."[3] This language, which tracked the language of the various statutes barring interracial intimacy in the postbellum years, might have appeared at first to be uncontroversial.

In fact, however, the proposed section initiated a debate because some delegates believed that it did not go far enough. They suggested removing the phrase defining blacks as including only those who had black great-grandparents, instead barring anyone with any black ancestors, no matter how far back, from contracting a legal marriage with a white person. Other delegates believed this to be unnecessary, claiming that the amendment as proposed was sufficient. Supporters of a "one-drop rule" responded that the more expansive version was the only way to assure that no marriages between whites and "the descendants of Negroes" would ever occur, raising the possibility that without the broader rule, the legislature could legalize marriages between whites and people who were fourth-generation descendants of blacks.

When the delegates voted, they opted for the version that did not define any degree of ancestry, thus rendering any marriage between a white person and an individual with any black ancestors at all void. They also briefly considered adding Chinese and Native Americans to the list of people who should not be permitted to marry whites, upon a delegate's suggestion that "Indians and Chinese are sorrier than Negroes." Another delegate objected, pointing out, "The proudest blood that flows in white veins in Alabama is Indian blood, and if we adopt that amendment we would insult some of the proudest and best people of the State" (Official Proceedings 2001: 2652). Ultimately, the delegates did not extend the provision beyond blacks, though multiple racial prohibitions were common in Western states with larger populations of Native Americans, Asians, and Pacific Islanders.

The delegates created a constitution that centralized power in Mont-

---

3. *Official Proceedings of the Constitutional Convention of the State of Alabama,* May 21, 1901–September 3, 1901 (Wetumpka, AL: Wetumpka Printing, 1940), vol. 2: 2650.

gomery to an extreme degree (Allen and Hinds 2001: 7). They also advocated for the massive withdrawal of political rights, particularly the franchise, from blacks and poor whites. Somewhat surprisingly and in contrast to other Southern states that restricted their political citizenry in this era, the delegates submitted the constitution to the then-enfranchised citizens for a referendum. White Populists and most blacks opposed the constitution, seeing clearly that it would entrench conservatism, Democrats, and white supremacy for the foreseeable future. Nonetheless, the constitution passed handily. The white counties in the northern part of the state voted heavily against the constitution, but the Black Belt returns (where African American voters were in the majority) ran overwhelmingly in favor of ratification. Some of these returns were falsified (in ten counties, the recorded votes exceeded the number of males over twenty-one in the population), and many black voters likely experienced open threats and intimidation (Flynt 2001: 74–75).

The immediate results were dramatic. The number of black male registered voters in Alabama plummeted from 181,000 in 1900 to fewer than 5,000 in 1903. Poor whites, another group that had opposed the conservative Democrats, were also removed from the voting rolls; nearly 40,000 fewer white men were registered to vote in 1903 than in 1900. This pattern of structural disenfranchisement persisted over time; a 1940 study revealed that provisions in the state constitution actively disenfranchised more than 1.1 million potential voters (Flynt 2001: 75). The racially charged program of conservative Democratic control would be firmly entrenched for generations to come, rooted in the constitutional structure.

Racial Mixing, White Supremacy, and Violence

Of course white supremacy had cultural roots as well. Much recent scholarship has addressed the grounding of white supremacy in the cultural and political discourse of the South in the late nineteenth and early twentieth centuries. The era was notable for the production of racist tracts that documented the supposed threats of African Americans to culture, society, and the state. Much of this discourse centered around the particular threat of interracial intimacy, not as the ultimate danger generated by freedom and equality for blacks, but rather as a potential contaminant of white blood. At the same time, Southern writers were actively promulgating an interpretation of the Civil War as a tragic fratricidal struggle redeemed by national post-

Reconstruction political consolidation around the idea of white supremacy (Blight 2001).

Specific fears that interracial relationships would produce a race of unthrifty, unhealthy, damaged future citizens were not new; they had been articulated prior to the end of slavery and in response to the original *Miscegenation* pamphlet (see, e.g., *Subgenation*). The differences in this era were that these fears were expressed in scientific language and that the concrete object of fear was the mixed-race child rather than the equality-seeking black man. Authors of pamphlets expressed the danger symbolically as a concern about contamination of blood, but the motif of blood had more than symbolic significance. This framing of the problem of interracial intimacy would develop into the public and lay use of a discourse of heredity, a point that the next chapter will address in some depth.

In the 1880s, concepts of race began to shift to understanding races as subgroups within the human species and to identifying racial characteristics with genetic inheritance through blood. By the turn of the century, anthropologists, sociologists, and other social scientists were becoming increasingly interested in race. Their beliefs about race and mixed race depended on their background assumptions regarding heredity and the nature of race. They generally believed that races existed in pure or ideal forms and generally identified about five, mostly by color: white, Malay, black, yellow, and red, sometimes with the Inuit (Eskimos or Esquimaux in the then-popular terminology) thrown in for good measure. They also believed that individuals inherited racial characteristics in a relatively unitary fashion (see, e.g., Bryce 1902; Smith [1905] 1993; Norwood 1907).

These experts did not have an underlying coherent conception of what race meant, even in the ideal sense, but they did not appear to realize this. With respect to African Americans, all of these beliefs were amplified and reflected among individuals who consciously or unconsciously sought to advance the project of differentiating white from black by creating an unbridgeable analytical gulf between emerging conceptions of whiteness and blackness (Hale 1998). As these beliefs became increasingly prevalent, both scientific and lay analysts identified mixed-race children, particularly those of one black and one white parent, as explicit threats to the purity of whiteness and therefore to the state and society.

Beliefs about the heritability of racial characteristics deserve another few words of explanation. Rather than thinking of race as a composite of skin color, facial features, and other characteristics that children inherited individually from their parents, these scientists connected race with blood. In this analysis, a person's place in the racial order would be determined by how much "black blood" she or he inherited. Such thinking picked up on much earlier theories about the unitary nature of race as an inherited characteristic, but it cast them in the new frame of genetics (Stanton 1960). The quantum of black blood represented unitary inheritance of black characteristics, a confusion about heredity that replicated beliefs about the unitary nature of intelligence.[4] Blood was thus a sign for heredity and ancestry, having the further significance of falling into the category of pure (white) or impure (mixed) (Saks 1988).

These beliefs had direct implications for the late-nineteenth- and early-twentieth-century state, which relied on them to justify regulating marriage and procreation to protect the state's interests in its future citizens. In a study of nineteenth-century restrictions, Peter Bardaglio identifies prohibitions on interracial sexual relationships as "part of a broader judicial trend in the postwar period to promote more rigorous tests of marital fitness that supposedly protected the well-being and safety of the public" (1995: 184–85). Even more directly, in the early twentieth century the city of Chicago instituted a special court that applied theories of eugenics in dealing with wayward youths (Willrich 1998).

Fear of blackness and of racial mixture certainly contributed to violence in Southern states, but some recent work suggests that white-on-black violence was a means of further separating white from black in a cultural sense (Gilmore 1996; Hale 1998). While most of the cases that contributed to the debate over evidentiary standards had no hint of violence in their factual contexts, the danger of violence loomed in the background primarily for the black defendants but also for white transgressors of increasingly rigid racial boundaries. As beliefs about the contaminating potential of black blood became more prevalent and the rate of mob violence against blacks (both men and women) skyrocketed, Alabama's legal system sought to contain blackness both through the constitution and through the application of statutes. The legal system's efforts, though, must be considered within the background context of extralegal white-on-black violence.

---

4. Stephen Jay Gould has thoroughly debunked early-twentieth-century efforts to discover the mystical "g," supposedly the unitary quality of intelligence that some early IQ tests purported to measure (1981: 146–233).

Little reliable information exists on the rates of extralegal violence perpetrated by whites against blacks prior to the 1880s. Certainly such violence
occurred and took place at high rates in the late 1860s and early 1870s. Organizations styling themselves the Ku Klux Klan, the Invisible Empire, the
Knights of the White Camellia, the White Brotherhood, the Pale Faces, and
the Constitutional Union Guard roamed the South, intimidating and attacking blacks and whites who opposed the re-creation of a conservative white
governing structure (Tolnay and Beck 1995: 6). While Congress's efforts to
suppress this violence were initially somewhat successful, Congress's will to
impose wholesale restructuring on Southern politics and institutions had
evaporated by the mid-1870s. Worse, legal analysts aggressively interpreted
the U.S. Supreme Court's ruling in *U.S. v. Cruikshank* as a signal that it
would disallow federal entanglement with the problem of organized violence.[5] (The case itself invalidated the criminal convictions of three whites
under Reconstruction-era federal statutes for their participation in a vicious
confrontation in New Orleans that resulted in the deaths of more than two
hundred African Americans over two days in 1873 [Tolnay and Beck 1995:
6–13].)

Most analysts, however, locate the primary lynching era later as mob violence became increasingly common in the 1880s and 1890s. The lynchings taking place between the 1880s and the late 1920s were largely not the acts of
secret societies or marginalized and racially radicalized outsiders from the
mainstream. Rather, they were conducted by mobs composed of ordinary citizens, often with participation and active incitement by local elites, including
whites responsible for law enforcement. Lynchings ranged from quick
extralegal executions of accused, convicted, or acquitted defendants snatched
from the (often complicit) hands of law enforcement officers (as in the case of
Meredith Lewis in Louisiana in the mid-1890s) to drawn-out tortures and
deaths conducted publicly in a carnival-like atmosphere (as in the notorious
case of Sam Hose in Georgia in 1899) (Wells-Barnett 1969b: 36; Hale 1998:
209–15).

The lynching era featured peaks and lulls in the rate of murders. As reliable statistics began to be collected, the initial phase featured a rapid spike in
the rate from 1882 through the 1890s, with more than 90 blacks being killed

---

5. Thanks to Pam Brandwein for clarification on what the language of *Cruikshank* itself did and did not
establish.

annually by white mobs in 1892 and 1893. The rate then dropped off gradually, falling to less than 10 victims annually in 1928 and 1929 near the end of lynching's heyday. Lynching rates were higher, however, just prior to the 1910s (with a peak of 67 victims in 1908) and again immediately after World War I, when more than 40 murders were perpetrated in both 1920 and 1921 (Tolnay and Beck 1995: 29–31).

Explanations for the phenomenon of lynching are broad, ranging from Williamson's analysis of psychosexual factors to Hale's reading of the cultural creation and performance of whiteness to Tolnay and Beck's economic and class-based understanding. While older work reads lynching as a collision between backward racist attitudes and the gradual expansion of economic and social modernization, newer analyses from radically different standpoints see it as consistent with the drive to build a postbellum economy, state, and society (see, e.g., Hale 1998; Tolnay and Beck 1995). Most likely, a combination of factors influenced the rise and decline of lynching, but most analysts agree that the agenda in the 1890s and early 1900s was largely the exertion of control over blacks through terror.

In these years, Alabama was no stranger to mob violence perpetrated by whites against blacks, though Alabamans were not the worst offenders. Alabama's 262 black victims represented a rate of 32.4 per 100,000 black residents in the state, placing it below Tennessee, Georgia, and Arkansas but above both South and North Carolina. Several of the most lynch-prone counties experiencing multiple events in multiple decades were located in central Alabama, though none of the five bloodiest incidents occurred there (Tolnay and Beck 1995: 29–39). Alabama's newspapers sometimes publicized lynchings before the fact, and Alabamans likely participated in some of the lynchings occurring along the border with Mississippi, where five counties had between nine and nineteen victims each (Hale 1998: 222–23; Tolnay and Beck 1995: 40–41).

What reasons did white mobs give for lynching blacks? The reasons most people would expect to see are allegations of black-on-white violence, particularly rape and murder, and allegations of interracial sex. While such allegations were common, Tolnay and Beck have identified more than eighty separate allegations ranging from what one would expect (arguing with a white man, courting a white woman) to the less predictable (incest, throwing stones). In the Deep South (Alabama, Georgia, Louisiana, Mississippi, and South Carolina), allegations of violating sexual norms constituted 33 percent of the justifications for whites' lynchings of blacks. Within this category, however, 28.7 percent of the alleged violations involved claims of sexual assault, and 3.5 percent were other miscellaneous claims. Direct statements that blacks were lynched because they had engaged in consensual interracial sex constituted less than 1 percent of the justifications. This meant that twelve or thirteen lynchings perpetrated between 1880 and 1930 in the Deep South involved direct claims of ongoing interracial relationships. The use of alleged interracial intimacy as a pretext for lynching was also only a marginal factor in the South as a whole, accounting for approximately 14 lynchings of the 2,314 that occurred in this period (Tolnay and Beck 1995: 48).

Nonetheless, the background context of lynching was ever present in prosecutions for miscegenation. Ida B. Wells engendered a firestorm of controversy when she suggested that many white women's complaints of rape by black men were attempts to cover the fact that their relations had been consensual (Wells-Barnett 1969c: 7–15). So shocking were her claims to whites that she herself only narrowly escaped lynching, and the presses of *The Free Speech,* the Memphis journal that she edited, were burned in 1892 (Tolnay and Beck 1995: 207–9). Given the social and legal costs of interracial sex for white women, the incentives to claim that a relationship was nonconsensual upon its discovery would have been strong. This was particularly true in Alabama, with its prescribed lengthy term in the state penitentiary for interracial adultery and fornication as well as attempted intermarriage. Given this dynamic, it is interesting that only one defendant—a black woman in the 1940s—attempted to nullify a conviction on the appellate level by claiming that the relationship was not consensual.

During the years between 1883 and 1917, the horizons for blacks narrowed quickly across a range of contexts. These years saw the legal implementation of Jim Crow and the rationalization of white supremacy as a legal and political doctrine. They also saw the rapid spread of popular fears of black blood as a contaminant and the popular adoption of racist scientific discourse concerning the threat of blackness to society and the state. Finally, interracial violence was a major factor, as white mobs stalked black victims and often murdered them on trivial pretexts in order to maintain the growing gulf between whiteness and blackness. As these macropolitical and cultural processes were taking place, the courts were painstakingly working their way through a series of evidentiary problems arising from the earlier constitutional debate and foreshadowing later struggles over racial definitions. The focused struggles featured defense attorneys seeking to use the formal elements of miscegenation to create loopholes for their clients. The courts found themselves confronting questions about the nature of miscegenation and its threat to the state by distinguishing between only mildly dangerous casual sexual encounters on the one hand and highly dangerous serious sexual liaisons on the other. This distinction rested on the earlier centering of the white family as the fundamental unit of the state.

Evidentiary Considerations and the Elements of Miscegenation

Regulating interracial intimacy through criminal sanctions was clearly constitutional. Defendants could no longer hope to avoid conviction by claiming either that the statute was unconstitutional or that they reasonably believed that it was unconstitutional or inapplicable. The attorneys representing them thus had to find different means of attacking their convictions. The core challenges to convictions now moved to a close examination of the elements of miscegenation and the adequacy of the prosecution's allegation and proof of these elements. The apparent open spaces for defense attorneys were around the definition of miscegenation, what constituted an admissible confession of miscegenation, and how formally race and gender had to be established. In the late nineteenth century, judges turned to older precedents addressing broader questions of evidence and identity to establish rules for cases involving interracial connections. The engagement of these broad rules with the problem of establishing and maintaining a racial divide produced more specific rules that would apply in later appeals of convictions for miscegenation.

Two long-standing principles of criminal law are that statutory law governs criminal prohibitions and sanctions and that these statutes must be adhered to precisely when the state exercises its punitive power against its citizens. People cannot be punished for vague, broad violations of a community's norms; rather the precise prohibited acts must be clearly defined by statute, and each element of a crime must be proven beyond a reasonable doubt. These basic principles were largely irrelevant during the era of constitutional challenges, which aimed squarely at the statutes themselves. Once the statutes were rendered invulnerable to constitutional challenge, defense attorneys turned to the relationship between the statutes and the alleged acts of the individuals they represented. While these challenges were thus rooted in the relationship between fact and law, they still turned on legal questions of interpretation, generally questions about the kind and sufficiency of evidence necessary to ground a conviction for miscegenation.

What points could be contended? What opportunities existed to use the legal system to vindicate the rights of those convicted for committing miscegenation? Was there any chance to reverse convictions for defendants who, like the earlier defendants, had engaged in an interracial relationship of some sort? Attorneys seeking little more than to vindicate their individual clients contributed to the development of the next body of law concerning the ban on interracial intimacy as appellate defense attorneys forced the courts to confront the elements and nature of the crime.

The Relationship between Interracial Intimacy and Adultery or Fornication

The statutes barring interracial intimacy criminalized only two primary and legally independent acts: the solemnizing of an interracial marriage and the attempt to contract such a marriage (as noted earlier). The balance of the statute required proof of a different criminal act first: the act of adultery or of fornication. Once adultery or fornication had been proven, these misdemeanor offenses could be prosecuted as felonies if their participants were shown to be a white person and a black person. While the statutes did not specify gender, no appellate cases addressed same-sex couples.[6] Most likely, such offenses would have been dealt with as sodomy rather than as adultery or fornication, and interracial sodomy had no special status under the criminal law.[7]

What this meant in practice was that, once the constitutional battle was over, the bulk of litigation would center around couples accused of committing interracial fornication or adultery.[8] Because an interracial marriage was

---

6. In one case involving an intraracial couple, a defendant convicted of adultery appealed, claiming that the affidavit on which the warrant for arrest was issued did not specify that one of the persons was male and the other female. The appellate court brushed aside this complaint, ruling, "The term 'adultery' as used in our statutes means illicit intercourse between two persons of different sex, one of whom is married to another person" (*Rich v. State,* 55 So. 1022, 1023 [Ala. App. 1911]). The genesis of this principle can be found in an interracial case, *White v. State,* discussed later.
7. This was no consolation to defendants charged with sodomy, which was a felony bearing a similar sentence to miscegenation (although attempting sodomy was a misdemeanor). See, e.g., *Brown v. State,* 35 So. 2d 516 (Ala. App. 1947); *Woods v. State,* 64 So. 508 (Ala. App. 1914).
8. Like most states, Alabama defined fornication as sexual relations between unmarried individuals and adultery as sexual relations between individuals of whom at least one was married to a third party.

a logical contradiction of terms in light of the developments of the previous period, and the door to fulfilling the elements for common-law recognition was firmly closed, most prosecutions for interracial relationships involved couples living together or engaging in sexual relations rather than formal attempts to enter into marriages. Even in situations in which a couple was holding themselves out as being married, prosecutors would generally charge them with fornication as a felony because of the interracial element. In fact, in light of the resolution of the constitutional battle, the only legal category into which living together in an interracial marriage could fit was fornication, since the parties could not legally enter into a marriage.

Prosecutors recognized the structure of the regulatory provisions often by charging defendants not with miscegenation but rather with adultery or fornication. Formal charges sometimes reflected the interracial nature of the offense only in that defendants were charged with felonies rather than misdemeanors. Prosecutors could choose how to charge defendants, and in at least one instance, both partners in an interracial relationship were charged only with adultery or fornication as misdemeanors (*Campbell v. State,* 32 So. 635 [1902]).[9] By 1900, most state solicitors were charging defendants with adultery or fornication rather than just one of the two, regardless of the alleged marital status of the defendants. This may have been because of the outcome in an intraracial case decided by the Alabama Supreme Court in 1892 in which the court reversed a conviction because the prosecution had not adequately proven that the defendant knew that her partner had a living wife (*Banks v. State,* 11 So. 404 [Ala. 1892]).

Fornication and adultery both involved allegations of acts of sexual intercourse between individuals who were not married to each other at the time. The courts had developed a significant body of jurisprudence defining these crimes in the context of intraracial offenses, which provided the grounding for early considerations of interracial fornication and adultery. On its face, this principle of definition seemed simple enough. Under Alabama's doctrine, however, even solid proof that two individuals had engaged in sexual relations would not lead inevitably to a conviction for (intraracial) fornication or adultery. In a principle later expanded to include fornication as well, the

---

9. This case, which arose in Montgomery, involved a white man and a black woman. Both were indicted for adultery or fornication, as Mary Calvin was married to another man who testified against defendant Joe Campbell. The case does not reveal why the state solicitor did not charge them with miscegenation, as there appeared to be no question that Campbell was white and Calvin was black.

supreme court explained the meaning of adultery in 1889 in *Bodifield v. State:* "To constitute a living in adultery within the statute . . . , a single or occasional act, without more, is not sufficient. There must be continuation, or an agreement for continuation, coupled with one or more acts, before it can be affirmed that the relation is established" (5 So. 560, 561 [Ala. 1889]). The justices continued, "a single act, or occasional acts, not indicating a consentive or prearranged continuation of the illicit conduct, would not be a living together within the meaning of the statute" (id.). This principle opened up space for objections to convictions for miscegenation when the convictions were parasitic on claims of adultery or fornication.

Four cases involving appeals of convictions for miscegenation addressed questions about the elements of adultery or fornication. Read together, they provide a strong sense of the background belief that, for the state, the real danger of interracial intimacy was the formation of mixed-race families and the legitimation of mixed-race children. Concerns about the formation of such families indeed overshadowed what most scholars have seen as an overwhelming white elite anxiety about controlling white women's sexuality and preventing black male sexual predation. This larger political and cultural problem was manifested, however, through technical discussion of evidentiary concerns relating to adultery and fornication. In these debates, the courts borrowed from existing doctrine addressing intraracial offenses to establish definitional principles for the interracial felonious varieties of the crimes.

This discussion began in 1883, immediately after the constitutional debate was settled. John White was convicted of living in adultery or fornication with Emma Danby; the record and opinion identified White as a white man and Danby as a black woman. Danby was indicted along with White, but the state solicitor dropped the charges against her (the record does not reveal why). The factual circumstances behind their prosecution have been lost, but White's appeal suggests that he could not present a strong case on the facts. Instead of contesting that he had engaged in intercourse with Danby, he challenged the trial judge's refusal to deliver several of his suggested instructions to the jury in an attempt to avoid two years at hard labor.

White was charged with adultery or fornication, and his appeal revolved around the relationship between the two crimes. According to the trial record, the evidence introduced in the case showed that White was married at the time of his liaison with Danby and that she was unmarried (*White v.*

State, bill of exceptions, 1883: 9–10). He argued that the jury should have been required to determine both his and Danby's marital statuses beyond a reasonable doubt, forcing a choice between adultery and fornication (id. at 10–13). The high court brushed aside these complaints, intimating that such precision was unnecessary as long as the parties were not married to each other (a defense unmountable in a prosecution for miscegenation anyway) (*White v. State,* 74 Ala. 31, 33–34 [1883]).

The next chapter in this debate was also brief. Martha Linton, a white woman, was prosecuted and convicted of miscegenation in the late nineteenth century. She was accused of conducting a relationship with John Blue, a black man. One element of her appeal was the trial judge's refusal to issue one of her suggested charges to the jury. She argued that she could not be found guilty unless the jury found that she and Blue had an agreement or understanding that they were going to continue their relationship. The Alabama Supreme Court disagreed, claiming that such a charge would have misled the jury. While adultery or fornication implied an intention to continue the relationship, it was improper to claim that the participants "could not be convicted unless this intention to so continue was evidenced by an agreement—a compact—to that effect, and not withstanding the circumstances might have clearly indicated such intention" (*Linton v. State,* 7 So. 261, 262 [Ala. 1890]). In establishing this rule, the court relied upon litigation over intraracial adultery and fornication, adopting the general principles established there without comment. While Linton also appealed on other grounds discussed later, her claim about the sufficiency of the charges was dealt with summarily in a fashion that set the stage for challenges with more factual and legal depth.

In 1897, the high court considered the case of Will McAlpine and Lizzie White. While the case primarily addressed the problem of admission (to be discussed further), one element is worth noting here. McAlpine and White apparently tried to convince the jury that they had not committed miscegenation because their relationship was one of prostitution rather than an ongoing intimate connection. They asked the judge to charge the jury that "a woman who keeps . . . a house of prostitution is not guilty of living in adultery, as charged in this case, with a man who at such house merely has occasional acts of criminal sexual intercourse with such woman" (*McAlpine v. State,* 117 Ala. 93, 97 [1897]). The high court found these proposed charges to be misleading, for they ignored the fact that, regardless of White's status, if she and McAlpine "lived together in adultery for a single day, intending to continue the illicit connection, a conviction might have been had" (id. at 103). This ruling in conjunction with *Linton* suggested that the courts were carefully bounding the elements of adultery so that prosecutors would not have to prove too much.

Two years later, these bounds were questioned again in the case of *Love v. State*. Love was a white man convicted of interracial adultery. The evidence in the case demonstrated that Love had been seen several times at night in the home of Alice Pinckard, a black woman, during the spring of 1898. Even more damning was testimony that he later rented a house in Opelika and moved Pinckard into it, where he visited her frequently at night and left in the morning. When the couple was arrested, they were found together in a single bed dressed in their nightclothes. In his own defense Love testified that, while he had engaged in sexual intercourse with Pinckard on several occasions, "each was a separate and distinct transaction, and . . . each time he paid her for the pleasure of the act" (*Love v. State*, bill of exceptions, testimony of John Love 1898: 2–6, 6). This claim was unconvincing to the jury, which voted to convict.

Love appealed his conviction on three grounds, one of which involved an alleged confession, which will be discussed below. He claimed that the state had not proven whether Pinckard was married or unmarried, leaving the choice between adultery and fornication in the charge ambiguous. The high court's response was to reiterate that, under the charge of adultery or fornication, such a choice was inapplicable: "it was immaterial whether the woman was or was not a married woman" (*Love v. State*, 124 Ala. 83, 84 [1899]). He also claimed that the trial court should have charged the jury that some agreement or consent to continue an illicit relationship was necessary to ground a conviction for adultery or fornication. The implication was that if his relationship with Pinckard was purely one of client to prostitute, a conviction for the more family-related offenses of adultery or fornication was inappropriate. The court basically disagreed with Love's framing of the facts of the case, pointing out that the uncontroverted evidence showed that they had engaged repeatedly in intercourse (id.). The implied response was that the situation did not seem to be one of a simple series of transactions exchanging money for sex. This case underlined that the courts were not to be troubled by technical distinctions between adultery and fornication. It also showed that underlying evidence of an ongoing relationship between two individuals would not be ignored, even when a white man claimed that a black woman was merely a prostitute (a factual claim that did not even convince the jury).

In these four cases, the high court used intraracial precedents to outline what had to be alleged and proven in order to ground the underlying charge of adultery or fornication in interracial cases. First, the justices made it clear that state solicitors did not have to choose between adultery and fornication. Merely showing that the parties were not married to each other was sufficient if they were charged with adultery or fornication. A charge based solely on adultery was a bit more difficult, as the prosecution had to establish a marriage between one of the defendants and a third party, but if such evidence was readily available, state solicitors sometimes chose only to pursue a conviction for felonious adultery. Because interracial marriage was a legal impossibility, any ongoing sexual relationship between a black man and a white woman or a white man and a black woman necessarily constituted either adultery or fornication. The court's rule that specification was unnecessary eased the burden on state solicitors and squarely demonstrated that Alabama's law forbade interracial relationships between two persons of opposite sexes, irrespective of their marital status.

But the high court also hewed to the principle that interracial relationships, not individual acts of interracial sexual intercourse, were the true targets of the statute. The court consciously emphasized the rule that adultery or fornication required some commitment on the part of the couple to continue the liaison. The justices bounded this rule by pointing out that an agreement or commitment did not need to be formal and could be inferred from the circumstances of the case. If the liaison looked like an ongoing relationship, the jury could rule that it constituted adultery or fornication and therefore that the defendants were guilty of miscegenation.

But as the high court observed, adultery and fornication—regardless of the races of the perpetrators—were crimes of secrecy. With no obvious victim to lodge a complaint and with the site of the offense being the home, how were these offenses to be proven? The most straightforward proof would be to catch the errant couple in bed, but merely observing them in bed would not distinguish between an individual act of intercourse and the ongoing relationship of adultery or fornication. This was the point where the question of admissions became relevant, and here as well, nonracialized cases provided the crucial background rules that judges would adopt for addressing felonious interracial intimacy.

Confessing Miscegenation

The admissibility of confessions has long been a major issue in criminal law. Thus, it is unsurprising that several defendants attempted to convince the appellate courts to overturn their convictions due to improperly admitted confessions. These cases hewed to standard doctrine regarding the necessary foundations for confessions or admissions of guilt, but the technical questions required the courts to consider what constituted a confession of the particular crime of miscegenation. Inquiries based on confessions thus implicated the meaning of miscegenation and the evidence necessary to prove it.

In 1897, the high court considered the first such appeal. Will McAlpine was a married man and "a Negro, a bright mulatto Negro whose hair was nearly straight" (*McAlpine v. State,* bill of exceptions, testimony of C. Bishop 1897: 12). Lizzie White was a white woman who lived with her mother in Talladega (id.). They were accused and convicted of miscegenation for committing interracial adultery. White's social status was likely rather uncertain; she and her mother rented a two-room house that they shared with black man Joe Gantt (or Gant) and his several children. A key figure in the case was one C. Bishop, described by white witnesses as a "before-the-war Negro," on whose initial complaint the prosecution was initiated (id.). Bishop professed distress at the disorderly living arrangements in the house and apparently believed either that both mother and daughter were engaged in interracial relationships or that they were running a bawdy house. He claimed to have remonstrated with McAlpine in an attempt to convince him to end his liaison with White but said McAlpine had responded that "he didn't reckon there was any danger" (id. at 12–16, 13). White, McAlpine, White's mother, and Gantt were all arrested and prosecuted for miscegenation as a result of Bishop's discussion of the circumstances with justice of the peace W. T. Thornton.

In their appeal, McAlpine and White objected to the statements of several witnesses testifying to both White's and McAlpine's admission of their connection. White had allegedly made statements to several individuals along the lines that she did not have to work because McAlpine was keeping her and that McAlpine was her man (*McAlpine v. State,* bill of exceptions, testimony of Alice Madison 1897: 11; testimony of C. Bishop 1897: 14; testimony of Annie Bishop 1897: 17; testimony of Caroline Turner 1897: 19). Both White and McAlpine objected to this testimony, but the trial judge allowed it in. On appeal, the high court ruled that no proper predicate had been laid for these confessions, citing general rules regarding the admissibility of confessions. The prosecution should have been made to show that these admissions "were voluntarily made, without the appliances of hope or fear, without extraneous inducement or pressure in either of those directions from other persons" (*McAlpine v. State*, 117 Ala. 93, 100 [1897]). The court also found error in the state's impeachment of two of the defendants' witnesses, ruling that evidence introduced to discredit them was too remote. While this case basically just rearticulated the fundamental race-neutral rule for the admissibility of a confession, it signaled that such appeals constituted a worthwhile avenue of pursuit for defense attorneys.

The 1899 case of *Love v. State*, addressed earlier, also involved a challenge to an admission of guilt. Love had attempted to clear his name by alleging that Alice Pinckard was a prostitute and that he had paid the black woman each time for the privilege of having intercourse with her. Part of the reason that the jury found this argument unconvincing was the trial judge's decision to allow the chief of police Mills to testify that Love had admitted the relationship. Mills testified that when he had arrested Love and Pinckard, Pinckard appeared to be intoxicated. Both were charged immediately with disorderly conduct as well as felonious adultery later. As they were being arrested, Mills testified that Love exclaimed to Pinckard: "I've spent a heap of money on you to get you out of your troubles, and now you've gone and raised the devil, and if I had a gun, I would shoot your brains out and kill myself" (*Love v. State*, bill of exceptions, testimony of Mills, 1899: 4–5). The record does not reveal precisely how this statement was used, but presumably the state solicitor used it to argue that Love and Pinckard had an ongoing relationship, and that he had been "keeping" her rather than engaging in individual acts of paid intercourse with her.

The high court saw this statement as falling clearly within the nonracialized rules for admitting declarations. Love was speaking to Pinckard, not any official, and he had not yet been charged with adultery. His language "rebuts any suggestion that he was influenced by the appliance of hope or fear from any source" (*Love v. State*, 124 Ala. 82, 84 [1899]). The court did not speak to the conclusions that the jury drew from the statement. This ruling hinted that exclamations that helped the jury to distinguish between an ongoing relationship and one of individual transactions or acts of intercourse would be allowed in.

In 1908 the high court heard a third appeal regarding a confession. In this case, Jackson Jones, a black man, was prosecuted and convicted separately from Ophelia (or possibly Opia) Smith, a white woman. The state's main witness was a police officer who caught Jackson and Smith in bed together in a one-room shack in Birmingham in January 1908. He and another officer arrested the couple and took them to the city jail. He claimed, over the defendant's objection, that Jones had confessed in the jailhouse that "he had been keeping Opia Smith for about three years" (*Jones v. State,* bill of exceptions, testimony of W. M. Burge 1908: 6–7). He also testified that Smith had admitted to having been with the defendant three times in the house where they were arrested (id. at 8). Two other officers testified that Jones had admitted to keeping Smith for three years and that he had confessed to paying her five dollars per week (*Jones v. State,* bill of exceptions, testimony of Officer Nation; testimony of Officer Parker 1908: 9–10). These confessions were crucial in establishing that Jones and Smith had an ongoing relationship and thus were committing adultery or fornication.

The high court considered Jones's plea that the confessions were inadmissible. The opinion began with a summary of the elements of miscegenation, as the justices pointed out that voluntary sexual intercourse between the mixed-race couple was only an element of the offense and not the offense itself. The statute, like the statutes barring adultery and fornication, was aimed against "a state or condition of cohabitation the parties intend to continue" (*Jones v. State,* 156 Ala. 175, 177 [1908]). The officers found the two in a compromising position, and the key question for the court was whether the situation constituted sufficient evidence of the corpus delicti (essence of the crime) upon which the confessions could be admitted. The justices ruled that, while the evidence did not show directly that the couple had engaged in intercourse, "we cannot doubt that it afforded a reasonable inference that sexual intercourse had been indulged in by them" (id. at 178). The jury could then infer from the evidence that the shack was a site for the kind of cohabitation prohibited by the statute, thus rendering the confessions admissible on that ground. The court also found that the confessions were voluntarily given. The court's analysis was not complete, however. The justices ruled that one of the officers' statements that he believed Jones had been telling the truth in his confession should have been excluded. Further, the court had problems with the state solicitor's claim to the jury in his closing argument that "we frequently convict men and women in this court for living in adultery with one another," because no evidence had apparently been entered to support this statement (id. at 181). The supreme court therefore reversed and remanded the case for a new trial. These principles of evidence were not specific to miscegenation or even to adultery or fornication, but they served to enable Jones to escape his conviction. It is unclear whether he was recharged and tried again; the problems with the conviction were technical enough that, with the question of the admissibility of his and Smith's confessions settled in the state's favor, a new conviction would probably have been relatively easy to secure.

The final defendant in this series of cases, George Smith, was a white man accused of living in adultery with Mattie Leonard, a young black woman, in 1916. He had allegedly visited her at her home frequently, and a witness testified that he had stated his intentions of taking Leonard away to the city of Dothan and establishing her there where she would not have to work. Since Smith was already married, the state charged him with adultery or fornication (*Smith v. State*, bill of exceptions, charge 1917: 6, 2). Convicted and sentenced to two years in the penitentiary, Smith appealed; his claims on appeal largely rested upon the admissibility of evidence tending to show the existence of a relationship and upon the trial judge's refusal to give various charges to the jury (*Smith v. State*, bill of exceptions, judgment entry 1917: 2).

The Court of Appeals of Alabama heard the case in 1917 and upon rehearing ruled in Smith's favor. The court believed that a refused charge addressing the credibility of one of the witnesses should have been given. While his conviction was overturned on this basis, the court also held that "statements made by the defendant tending to show his feeling toward the woman with whom he was charged with having adulterous relations . . . were admissible" (*Smith v. State*, 75 So. 627, 628 [Ala. App. 1917]). In general, these kinds of conversations would be admissible to show both that intercourse had taken place and that the defendants had intended to continue their relationship.

The emerging rules concerning admissibility of confessions would be more important in later appeals. Most of the criminal cases during these years involved situations in which the couples were caught together in the same physical location in questionable circumstances, so the admissions that defendants made were simply additional evidence. Nonetheless, these cases provided the fact patterns in which the rule developed, so future defendants would have to be more creative in finding ways to keep their statements to and about each other from reaching juries. Also in these cases, the ruling judges used general precedents developed in cases that ignored race to develop rules for racially charged appeals of convictions for miscegenation. These generally framed rules, when imported into the racialized universe of litigation over interracial intimacy, would take on the broader agenda of supporting the state's investment in white supremacy, and later courts would cite the cases involving interracial intimacy rather than their unracialized doctrinal precedents. In analogous fashion, the idea that admissions or confessions could be used to prove the elements of the crime would transfer readily from the context of questions about whether the defendants had an ongoing sexual relationship to the context of questions about whether the accused dyad exhibited the prohibited combination of qualities of maleness and femaleness and blackness and whiteness.

Establishing Female and Male; Establishing Black and White

Two other elements of miscegenation were that the couple consisted of a man and a woman, as noted previously, and that they were black and white. Some defendants in this era experimented with appeals based on the prosecution's failure to establish these elements adequately. The high court was generally unsympathetic to such appeals, allowing juries to draw conclusions from observing the couple in court. In these cases, the relevant precedents sometimes were racialized, as previous courts in other states had considered the proper means of establishing race. But the court seemed to view the establishment of race and gender as relatively unproblematic matters for jury resolution.

The first such claim took place in 1883, in the previously discussed case of *White v. State*. White was accused of committing miscegenation with black woman Emma Danby. In addition to his challenge to the prosecution's proof of his and Danby's marital status, he claimed that the witnesses' sworn statements did not adequately demonstrate that he was a man. White asked the judge to instruct the jury only to consider the sworn statements, which apparently did not establish his gender. The judge instead instructed the jury that they could look at the defendant and make a judgment as to whether he was male or female. The high court supported this mode of establishing a key element of the crime, explaining, "The defendant was present in court; and it was clearly competent for the jury to draw the inference from his dress and general appearance that he was of the male sex" (*White v. State*, 74 Ala. 31,

34 [1883]). While the appeal may seem absurd to modern readers, Alabama's high court in 1883 likely took this as a serious question about the formal necessities inherent in charging and proving the elements of a crime.

This issue arose again in 1890, in the case of *Linton v. State*. One of the many grounds on which Martha Linton appealed her conviction was that the state had not proven beyond a reasonable doubt that her alleged partner, John Blue, was a Negro. She further complained that the trial judge had not instructed the jury that "if the evidence shows that he is a mulatto, then the defendant is not guilty" (*Linton v. State*, 7 So. 261, 261 [Ala. 1890]). The state had not entered any formal evidence to demonstrate Blue's race; rather, Blue was shown to the jury "in order that they might determine by inspection whether he was a Negro, as charged in the indictment" (id. at 262). The high court ruled that this practice was acceptable as a means of establishing the demographic characteristics of a defendant or witness, and cited *White* in support of this principle. It also cited a Mississippi case in support specifically of establishing race through exhibition of the witness or defendant to the jury. The ruling saw no necessity for specific proof of race, allowing a person to demonstrate or, in effect, to confess to race through his or her mere presence, physical attributes, and speech.

On the question of whether Blue's status as a mulatto could be used to invalidate the conviction, the court noted the legal definition of *Negro* as inclusive of mulattoes and any individual who had at least one Negro great-grandparent. To ground this analysis, the court cited an antebellum Alabama precedent based on the statutory definition of blackness. Under this definition, reasoned the court, the words *Negro* and *mulatto* were interchangeable, since the common understanding of a mulatto was that she or he was "of the half blood" (id.). Thus, whether Blue was a mulatto was irrelevant, as long as he was identified by society (and more specifically by the jury) as a black man.

While both of these efforts were unsuccessful, prosecutors apparently began to worry about the potential for invalidating convictions. In the 1908 case *Jones v. State,* the state solicitor seeking a conviction of Jackson Jones seemed to adopt a trial strategy to ensure that no questions would be raised about Ophelia Smith's race. Over Jones's objection, the state solicitor elicited testimony from the arresting police officer that "Opia Smith looked like a white woman, was a white woman" (*Jones v. State,* bill of exceptions, testimony of W. M. Burge 1908: 7). (The witness also testified that Jones was a Negro, but Jones did not object to this portion of the testimony.) The next act of the state solicitor was to ask the trial judge to order Smith "to be brought before the jury for identification by the witness and inspection by the jury" (id. at 7–8). The court complied, again over Jones's objection.

The high court considered Jones's argument that both the testimony and the proffer of Smith to the jury for inspection were improper. The justices ruled that, even if the testimony that Smith looked like a white woman was an improper statement of opinion, allowing this evidence was harmless in light of the witness's further statement that she was a white woman, a statement of fact. As for Smith's exhibition to the jury, the court saw the practice as falling squarely within the rule established by the *Linton* case (*Jones v. State*, 156 Ala. 176, 180 [1908]). The court thus refused to reverse the conviction on these grounds (though, as noted earlier, Jones did get a new trial based on other errors).

These three cases were harbingers of the next era. The high court tried to clarify that it would not allow successful appeals based on questions about identity, rejecting challenges to identifications of maleness, blackness, and whiteness. Implicit in the court's stance was the belief that gender and race were immediately visible and identifiable qualities of persons. The court used earlier precedents regarding the transparency of gender and race nearly interchangeably, implying a certain equivalence of identity-based characteristics. Also implicit was the finding that ordinary individuals like witnesses or jurors could be trusted to see and judge these qualities accurately. Finally, the court implied that a person's appearance could be treated almost as a voluntary confession of the identity-based elements of the crime of miscegenation.

Interracial Rape

Three of the cases from this era did not involve allegations of miscegenation. Instead, they were appeals of convictions for interracial attempted rape or rape. While a few other cases of interracial rape reached the appellate level in the years between the Civil War and the dawn of the civil rights era, these cases were significant in their temporal clustering and in the work that they did to draw from nonracialized precedents in forming racialized precedents that would ground later developments. The cases also demonstrate the legal and procedural face of the orderly imposition of white supremacy, as contrasted with the disorderly role of lynching and other forms of extralegal violence in the same years.

All of the defendants involved were black men. As discussed earlier, they were in potentially dangerous circumstances, as the three cases were decided in 1908, 1911, and 1912, at or near the second temporal peak in the rate of lynchings. These cases raised evidentiary concerns that related to the developing rules regarding interracial intimacy and also contributed to the legal system's integration of particular images of licit and illicit sex, and of virtuous and nonvirtuous women. The individual circumstances of the cases and appeals were quite different—one defendant claimed that he had not intended to rape, another pleaded mistaken identity, and the third argued that the woman had consented to intercourse—but all three cases addressed issues of credibility and the admissibility of evidence, and in none did the legal actors creating the records acknowledge the background threat of extralegal violence.

Vit Pumphrey's appeal was heard in 1908 after his conviction in 1907 at a second trial regarding an incident between him and Mrs. Anne Crimm that took place in 1906.[10] Crimm testified that she had been sleeping in her room when an unknown individual assaulted her. She woke up to find this individual in her bed, placing pressure on her; when she sprang out of bed, the assaulter fled through her window. She could not tell whether her attacker was white or black, but she was sure he was male (*Pumphrey v. State,* bill of exceptions, testimony of Anne Crimm 1907: 9–11). Pumphrey was later fingered as the assailant by witnesses who identified tracks found at the scene of the crime and leading away from it as coming from a peculiarly damaged pair of shoes he owned (*Pumphrey v. State,* bill of exceptions, testimony of J. T. Powell; testimony of W. C. Kyle 1907: 13–14, 15–16). He presented evidence undermining the state's claim that he was the assailant, but also sought to convince the trial judge to direct a verdict in his favor.

The question he posed to the supreme court was whether the evidence had been sufficient to send the case to the jury. Drawing on rules generated in cases of white-on-white rape, he argued that, while Crimm's narrative provided sufficient evidence of assault, it did not ground a claim that rape had been attempted. Since Crimm and the assailant were the only witnesses to the incident, the substance of her testimony and the implications that might permissibly be drawn from it were the points that the court had to consider. The court reiterated her testimony and then launched into an analysis of rape. It

10. The first trial had addressed a two-count indictment, and Pumphrey had been acquitted of the second count. The record does not reveal the original charges, but he was likely acquitted of rape in the first trial.

began by endorsing the defendant's claim that in the case of an attempted rape (regardless of the races of the assailant and target), "the evidence, to be sufficient . . . should show such acts and conduct on the part of the accused as would leave no reasonable doubt of his intention to gratify his lustful desire against the consent of the female and notwithstanding resistance on her part" (*Pumphrey v. State,* 156 Ala. 103, 106 [1908]). Crimm's narrative, on its face, established no evidence of any attempt to overcome her resistance. The direct application of this principle would thus lead to an invalidation of the conviction.

For the supreme court, however, the issue was more complex. Each case, they explained, had to be considered in the context of its circumstances, which they specified for this case.

> If the accused, a Negro, under the excitement of lust and with the intention of gratifying it by force, entered the bedroom of Mrs. Crimm, a white woman, about 10 o'clock in the night, and with such intention got upon her person, on the bed in which she was sleeping, though he abandoned his design upon her springing from the bed and opening the door, we apprehend that it could not be said, as a matter of law, that he was not guilty of an assault with intent to ravish. (Id. at 107)

The court went on to emphasize that, in the lack of any evidence of any interchanges between the two, "social customs, founded on race differences, and the fact that Mrs. Crimm was a white person and the defendant a Negro" could be taken into consideration (id. at 108). But what, exactly, did this context establish?

The modern legal analyst would likely first look to the question of intent. Accepting Crimm's testimony on its face and accepting that Pumphrey was correctly identified as the assailant does not lead inevitably to the conclusion that he intended to commit rape. The case, however, must be understood both in the context of race and in the context of the early-twentieth-century meaning of rape. The court seemed to assume that the circumstances themselves were sufficient proof of Pumphrey's intent. Any black man breaking into a room occupied by a white woman at night and touching her in her bed could be presumed without discussion or even notice to have lustful intentions in mind.

The real question on which all parties focused was the question of most rape cases in this era: was there sufficient evidence of force to ground a finding of rape or attempted rape? As feminist analysis of rape laws has shown, in the context of intraracial rape the requirement of a showing of force and resistance centered critical analysis on the assaulted woman (or prosecutrix), who had to demonstrate that she had not consented, rather than placing the burden on the state to demonstrate that the defendant had violated the law. *Pumphrey* in effect gave Crimm a free pass on this question. Because of the circumstances, which included the court's explicit acknowledgment that she was a virtuous woman, she would not be held to the usual standard of having to prove force on Pumphrey's part and resistance on her own. This reading racialized the law of rape by lightening the usual burden on the state as representative of the allegedly outraged woman.

Cleveland Toles was tried and convicted of attempted rape at his trial in 1910. The case was probably quite inflammatory, as the alleged victim was a "young woman" still living with her parents. Toles himself was twenty-two and was sentenced to a twenty-year term in the state penitentiary (*Toles v. State,* bill of exceptions, judgment entry 1910: 4). The uncontroverted evidence supported a tale remarkably like that of the *Pumphrey* case. During the day of the assault, the Fonville family was in the process of moving into the house in which it took place. They were assisted by a group of blacks sent to them by a neighbor, Mr. Sikes; Toles was evidently a driver in charge of one of the teams that was hauling the Fonvilles' possessions (*Toles v. State,* bill of exceptions, testimony of J. C. Fonville 1910: 8). This background was relevant because Toles entered every room of the house during the day and had the opportunity to observe its layout. That night, sometime between approximately eleven o'clock and midnight, Claire Fonville was asleep in bed with her mother. She woke briefly, hearing what sounded like two people talking. She then slept again, only to wake when feeling someone's hand against her face. Realizing that it was not her mother's hand, she screamed and struggled with her unknown assailant. The mosquito net over the bed was torn, indicating that the assailant had been under it. The brief struggle ended when the assailant fled through the window (*Toles v. State,* bill of exceptions, testimony of Claire Fonville; testimony of Mrs. J. C. Fonville 1910: 6–7).

No member of the family was able to identify the person who had attacked Claire Fonville, though her mother was sure that "there was only one Negro that created all this trouble" (*Toles v. State,* bill of exceptions, testimony of Mrs. J. C. Fonville 1910: 7). Two men fell under suspicion immediately: Cleveland Toles and another black man, John Colvin. The neighbor,

Mr. Sikes, upon hearing of the assault, went directly from the Fonvilles' home to Toles's home, arriving at about one in the morning with another white man to question him. Toles's account of his activities that evening was contradictory. At first he claimed that he had just gotten in, but then claimed that he had been in since eight or ten o'clock (*Toles v. State*, bill of exceptions, testimony of J. B. Sikes 1910: 9). From there, Sikes went to Colvin's residence, and both Toles and Colvin were jailed. Toles tried to introduce evidence to explain his reaction to Sikes, asking another witness, "Do you know whether Mr. Sikes, who was with you, had whipped or not a Negro with a buggy whip in that house not long before this?" but the state's objection to the question was sustained (*Toles v. State*, bill of exceptions, testimony of W. L. Tatum 1910: 11). A pair of shoes that could not be definitively connected to either Colvin or Toles but apparently belonged to one of them was identified as having made the tracks that appeared outside of Claire Fonville's window, near a large block that had apparently been used for access (*Toles v. State*, bill of exceptions, testimony of J. C. McLendon 1910: 12).

Toles and Colvin were jointly charged, but Toles moved for a severance of the trials. Colvin was convicted of assault with intent to ravish, and Toles and his attorney likely breathed a sigh of relief. The state solicitor, however, pressed forward with Toles's trial. Relying on the conviction of Colvin and the lack of definitive proof, Toles introduced no evidence on his own behalf, trusting to his cross-examinations to convince the judge and jury of the weakness of the state's case. Despite the introduction of evidence suggesting that Colvin had been the real perpetrator and the testimony of Claire Fonville's mother that she believed Colvin to be the assailant, Toles too was convicted. He appealed, claiming that the judge should have directed a verdict in his favor (*Toles v. State*, 54 So. 511 [1911]).

The high court concluded that Toles was trapped. The justices refused to reconsider the evidence in the case, explaining that "there was *some* evidence from which inferences might have been drawn by the jury unfavorable to the innocence of the accused." While the justices saw the evidence as "weak, inconclusive, and unsatisfactory," and "marvel[ed]" that the jury has convicted on such "flimsy proof," they believed that enough was there to justify the judge's submission of the case to the jury in the first place (id. at 511). Given that there was no evidence of conspiracy, if it had been possible to enter evidence of Colvin's guilt and therefore by inference of Toles's innocence, the court indicated that it would have looked even more critically upon Toles's conviction. Unfortunately for Toles, the rules of evidence barred the introduction of Colvin's conviction, and Colvin's guilt had not been proven at Toles's trial. Mrs. Fonville's accusation of Colvin was utterly discounted: "Such a statement, in view of the . . . surprise and terror of the witness while observing the intruder in the darkness of the night, cannot be regarded as either persuasive or convincing" (id. at 512). The innate unreliability of a white woman experiencing an invasion of her home by a black man doomed Toles, though in other contexts, white women's identifications of black men in similar circumstances would also have led to dire consequences.

Cleveland Toles, like Vit Pumphrey, was a victim of the entanglement of race, gender, and sexuality in the early twentieth century in Alabama. The proof of his guilt, which even the Alabama Supreme Court recognized as flimsy, was rooted more in context and the stock story of black-on-white rape than in the concrete facts of the case. As in *Pumphrey,* the white female victim was innocent, blameless, and without agency, though in *Toles* her resistance was not remotely at issue. As in *Pumphrey,* the intent of sexual assault on the part of the assailant was not in question. Toles's trustworthiness as evinced by his management of a team and his intimate association with the inside of the Fonvilles' home simply made him that much more threatening to the jury, which voted to punish his presumption severely. While the court did not express a specifically racialized rule to address these circumstances, it applied a qualitatively different standard by softening the usual requirement of resistance on the part of the woman.

Finally in 1912, the supreme court heard the case of Clarence Story, who had been convicted of rape rather than an attempt. In this case, the circumstances were quite different than in *Pumphrey* or *Toles.* At the heart of the trial were contradictory accounts of the incident between Story and his alleged victim, Beatrice McClure. At Story's trial, both McClure and Story testified about the events leading to Story's indictment. Both narratives, however, made it clear that McClure was not the same type of victim as either Anne Crimm or Claire Fonville.

McClure was the state's principal witness, and she testified that she had just arrived in Tuscaloosa when the incident occurred. She hired Story, who drove a hack, on Friday to take her from the train station to her lodging, which was with Lillie Masters, described by other witnesses as the proprietor of a house of prostitution. She stayed with Masters only a few days, leaving after a long drinking session and a dispute with Masters. As she was searching for another place to stay on Sunday, she encountered Story again, who offered to drive her around. She testified that he took her to a Negro man's house where she procured another bottle of whiskey. She then explained that, after driving around with Story for about three hours and drinking the whiskey with him, he took her to a secluded area and had intercourse with her against her will. She claimed that she was unable to resist effectively due to her drunken state and that, when she resisted him, he told her that "I was not the first white girl he had ever fooled with" (*Story v. State,* bill of exceptions, testimony of Beatrice McClure 1911: 14–15).

On cross examination, McClure admitted that she allowed men to have intercourse with her for money, that she had been doing so for six to eight months, and that her principal means of support was prostitution. She also admitted to having intercourse with as many as two different men the night of her arrival in Tuscaloosa and to having little recollection of the events between the night of her arrival and her reencounter with Story on Sunday. She testified that she had complained against Story only after her own arrest for vagrancy two days after the incident, and that she had engaged in intercourse with additional men Sunday night and Monday. She also allowed that she had been drunk when arrested (id. at 16–17).

Story's testimony was that he had indeed met McClure at the train and had taken her to Masters's establishment on Friday. He also admitted that he had encountered her again on Sunday morning after her stormy departure from Masters's residence. He testified that she hired him to help her find another place to stay. He took her to another white woman's house, where she was refused lodging. At that point, he claimed, she wanted to wash her face and brush her hair and suggested stopping at the house of a black man, Fred Taggett. He warned her that Taggett was black and advised her to go to "some white person's house," but she refused. No whiskey passed hands in Story's narrative. He then testified that he continued to drive her around Tuscaloosa, stopping at several places, all of which refused to lodge McClure. Finally, a white man offered to help her get a room at a hotel, and after Story had picked up lunch for her, McClure departed the hack in the early afternoon. He further testified that she had never appeared to be drunk in the entire three or four hours of their odyssey (*Story v. State,* bill of exceptions, testimony of Clarence Story 1911: 20–22). From other witnesses, Story adduced additional testimony that he had been seen driving McClure around town publicly and that neither was in a state of intoxication.

Story also tried to introduce evidence that McClure had engaged in consensual sexual intercourse with black men on several previous occasions. Such evidence would have hinted that, even if the jury believed that Story had had sex with McClure, the sex was consensual, perhaps a form of prostitution. The prosecution objected, and the trial judge refused to admit this evidence (*Story v. State,* bill of exceptions, testimony of J. H. Hyde; testimony of W. V. Burns; testimony of W. M. Wallace; testimony of J. D. Jones 1911: 26, 27, 28–29). Several of Story's proposed instructions to the jury were refused, and the jury returned a verdict against him. Story appealed, citing twenty-seven separate instances of error for the supreme court's consideration (*Story v. State,* bill of exceptions, assignments of error 1911).

The high court focused principally on the elements of rape, McClure's credibility, and the particular situation of a prosecutrix who was herself a prostitute accusing a black man of rape. As in the previous two cases, the court emphasized the importance of the racial and gender-based context and the reputation of the woman involved. The court began with a race-neutral reminder that any allegation of lack of consent on the part of the woman could be countered by evidence of "a general reputation for unchastity—a condition that argues the consent of the woman to meretricious intercourse with the defendant" (*Story v. State,* 59 So. 480, 481 [1912]). The problem in this case was not the evidence of lack of chastity—such evidence was plentiful and uncontroverted. The problem was whether such evidence as was permitted in was sufficient, given that the accused rapist was black and the alleged victim was white. This focused the court's attention on the trial judge's refusal to admit evidence concerning McClure's relations with black men.

The court reasoned that evidence of prostitution alone was insufficient, because of the vast moral gulf between white women who engaged in paid sexual intercourse with other whites and those who practiced prostitution interracially. Whites engaging in intraracial prostitution might be redeemed; those who accepted black clients, never. Thus, "though a white woman be a prostitute, the presumption is strong, nearly conclusive, . . . that she will not yield . . . even in her confirmed depravity, to commerce with a Negro charged with an offense against her person" (id. at 482). A reputation for lacking chastity was thus qualitatively different from a reputation for engaging in interracial sex, and the defendant should have been permitted to introduce evidence of McClure's liaisons with black men. Only in the presence of such evidence, implied the court, would the jury be able to believe that a white woman had consented to intercourse with a black man, even if she herself had admitted to being a prostitute. Story's conviction and his thirty-five-year sentence were overturned, by virtue of a silently racialized modification in the rule of rape (id. at 483).

Story's case demonstrated the importance of the victim's compliance with traditional norms of sexual behavior for women. More than that, however, it revealed assumptions about interracial intercourse and shaped the way that evidence could be used to subvert these assumptions. No one witnessed the alleged rape, so Story's case hinged on whether the jury would believe his narrative or McClure's. Story's attorney likely saw the evidence of her previous interracial sexual encounters as a means of implying the possibility of consent, thereby negating a key element of rape as framed through the general rules. He could also use this evidence to undermine her credibility in a general sense, to drag her down to a level at which a jury could permit itself to believe the word of a black man over the word of a white woman accusing him of rape. Without the introduction of this evidence of tainting, however, the jury would not take that step, instead accepting McClure's account of the events.

The attempted rape and rape cases show graphically the importance of the relationship between cultural context and the rules of evidence. While the rules of evidence appeared to be race neutral, their application in these cases as a matter of law demonstrated how race made a difference. The high court, even in its review of legal questions, linked its rulings closely to the factual circumstances of the cases, particularly the identities of the defendants and their alleged victims. In *Pumphrey* and *Toles,* the court outlined a stock story of a black invader in a white home at night, terrorizing the chaste victim and escaping through the window, only to leave telltale footprints to testify to his presence at the scene. The account in *Story* was more unconventional, with a problematic, drinking, unchaste heroine accusing the black man only after being arrested herself. But the differences between Anne Crimm and Claire Fonville on the one hand and Beatrice McClure on the other could not in isolation explain the results in these cases.

The juries in all three cases agreed that the black men were guilty. Even in *Story,* the jury was not ignorant of the fact that Story intended to show that McClure had engaged in voluntary sex with black men. The question for the high court in all the cases, however, was what kind of evidence was sufficient to convict and what kind of evidence had to be admitted to exonerate the defendants. In *Pumphrey* and *Toles,* the defendants sought to convince the high court that the evidence at their trials did not prove all of the elements of attempted rape. Pumphrey wanted the court to hew to traditional principles of rape law and demand evidence of lack of consent, while Toles wanted the court to acknowledge that he had not been adequately identified as Fonville's assailant. Story sought to fill out the portrait of Beatrice McClure as an unreliable and degraded woman. While the specific response to these three pleas was different, the court's background reasoning was the same. In cases of interracial rape, the interracial element generated a specific framework for analysis separate from the ordinary operation of laws barring rape and assault. In *Pumphrey* and *Toles,* this framework operated against the defendants, loosening the state's requirement to prove resistance and lack of consent and allowing the state to proceed on weak facts and problematic identifications. In *Toles,* the one definitive identification testified to at the trial was discounted on appeal as an understandable but unreliable product of an overstimulated feminine mind. In *Story,* the framework operated for the defendant, in effect extending the rule that a white prostitute could not be raped across the racial boundary as long as evidence could be adduced showing that she had previously consented to intercourse with black men.

The Constitutionalization and Formalization of White Supremacy

The period of formalizing white supremacy began with the struggles between the Alabaman political establishment and Populist insurgents and ended as the conservative Democratic hegemony centered in Montgomery consolidated its power. The years between 1883 and 1917 saw the rise of a transformed ideology of white supremacy that would be legalized and implemented through legislative and constitutional means. The important cultural developments of the 1910s are discussed at the beginning of the next chapter, as they spoke directly to the initiation of a legal debate over racial definition. The developmental process that took place all over the South from the end of the nineteenth century to the end of the first decade of the twentieth century began with the statutory implementation of Jim Crow and ended with the expression of white supremacy in a wave of state constitution writing near the turn of the century. It was a period of state building, and the builders identified whiteness as the center of their new state (Wallenstein 1994; Hale 1998). The legal process was thus instrumental in the development and articulation of these new modes of thought and their institutional operation.

As this formal process took place, the level of violence against African Americans ratcheted up rapidly, peaking in the 1890s and again becoming high in the early twentieth century. The terror served multiple purposes: it intimidated blacks and warned them against exercising the kinds of freedoms they had enjoyed immediately after the war, it helped to support and entrench a new economic system of peonage to replace the old system of slavery, and it provided a location for the development and expression of new forms of whiteness and white power (Wells-Barnett 1969b, 1969c; Tolnay and Beck 1995; Hale 1998).

In the midst of this developmental process in politics and culture, the courts considered technical questions about the elements of adultery and fornication, the admissibility of confessions, the proper establishment of gender and race, and the framework for considering evidence in cases of interracial rape. These cases reflected the emerging discourse of white supremacy by fleshing out what was meant by miscegenation, how it could be proven, and what kind of threat interracial sex posed to the state. While the cases themselves did not hint at the background context of increasing legal repression and a wave of private, unhampered, white-on-black violence, the courts' reasoning assumed and normalized deference from blacks to whites. They also divided vaguely illicit from deeply threatening sexual partnerings based upon the closeness of the relationship and its potential to undermine the growing state-supported and privately enforced gulf between black and white.

Adultery and fornication were, as the courts described them, crimes of secrecy and concealment, but they were also violations of the legitimate family. The courts did not look at the concrete violations to family—the betrayal of the nonadulterous spouse or the damage to the reputation of a woman engaging in fornication—but rather the violation against the concept of family. A conviction for miscegenation required a showing that the couple had engaged in a relationship that looked more like a familial bond than like individual acts of license or lust. Again, while the normative family that the courts likely had in mind was the white family, various state actors also noted the importance of maintaining the integrity and impermeability of the black family in its humble efforts to mimic white family organization and order. While the courts made it clear that no formal agreement was necessary to ground a conviction, some sort of agreement or arrangement for an ongoing relationship was required. This reasoning tied in with an analysis of what was required to prove such an ongoing relationship. Because of the difficulty in distinguishing between individual acts of illicit intercourse and the formation of a dangerous interracial bond, the best way to determine the nature of the relationship was through looking at the parties themselves and how they described the relationship to each other and to third parties.

In developing these rules, the courts drew heavily from principles articulated in cases decided without reference to race. Rules about the nature of relationships established to deal with intraracial adultery and fornication became the standard for adjudicating appeals of convictions for felonious interracial connections. In the process, these rules took on racial meanings and became linked with the earlier normative centering of the white, intraracial family as the fundamental unit of the state.

Prosecutors operating after the high court's ruling in *McAlpine* would painstakingly lay the foundations for the admissibility of confessions, so interracial couples had to be careful what they said to and about each other; under the right circumstances, such statements could become confessions. These cases built on the analytical framework of white fears regarding interracial sex. A single fleeting encounter that was not repeated did not form the basis for criminal liability, but an ongoing sexual relationship did, even if it was a relationship between a prostitute and her client. Interracial intimacy was primarily a threat to the extent that it subverted or made a mockery of the marriage bond. In the constitutional battles of the 1870s and 1880s, the courts had established that marriage constituted a special kind of contract in which the state had a deep and abiding interest. Now the legal community established a context in which contracts for sex outside of marriage—agreements with prostitutes—could be understood as violating the institution of marriage if such contracts were formed between individuals of different races.

The emerging specific rules concerning the nature of miscegenation and the admissibility of confessions would be more important in later appeals. Most of the criminal cases during these years involved situations in which the couples were caught together in the same physical location in questionable circumstances, so the admissions that defendants made were simply additional evidence. Nonetheless, these cases provided the fact patterns in which the rule developed, so future defendants would have to be more creative in finding ways to keep their statements to and about each other from reaching juries. Later courts would cite these cases, drawing upon the racial boundaries they established and delimited.

The idea that admissions or confessions could be used to prove the elements of the crime would transfer readily from the context of questions about whether the defendants had an ongoing sexual relationship to the context of questions about whether one of the defendants was black. In this period, such questions were framed as formal challenges to the adequacy of the state solicitor's presentation of the case. Had he demonstrated that the individuals charged were indeed black and white and that they were of different genders? The courts vigorously rejected each attempt by defense attorneys to rely on formalistic proof of these identity-based elements, endorsing instead the practice of allowing the jury to ascertain race and gender for themselves. These challenges, however, were formal rather than substantive claims that the state solicitor had not established race. In the next era, the challenges would become substantive.

Attitudes about race, as suggested earlier, were in transition. The late-nineteenth-century cases dealt with race in a straightforward, matter-of-fact manner. In Barbara Welke's analysis of discrimination by common carriers like trains and street cars, she notes specifically that many of the plaintiffs were light-skinned mulattoes who had all of the markers of class status, but the courts did not question their race.[11] The paradigmatic example of this dynamic was *Plessy v. Ferguson;* Homer Plessy apparently had only one black great-grandparent. The same lack of concern prevailed in the appeals of convictions for miscegenation. In *Linton,* for instance, the high court simply approved the practice of exhibiting Linton's partner to the jury in order to prove the element of a racial difference between the couple. This case relied upon an earlier case approving exhibition as a means of establishing gender, implying that both were transparent to jurors and that jurors were competent to make their own judgments without particular argumentation or proof on the point.

In addressing the problem of interracial rape, the *Story* Court, writing

---

11. Welke points out that many of the plaintiffs were indeed trying to differentiate themselves from the lower-class whites and Negroes who traveled in the smoker cars on trains (1995: 284–89).

twenty-two years later, began to articulate a theory of domination and sub-ordination that translated the norms of interaction established during slavery to the modern age. The Justices explained that the white race had taken on a posture of guardianship and generosity toward the black race, endorsing the popular construction of "full-blooded Negroes" as childlike, humble, and dependent. Blending an analysis of old beliefs with new practices, the Justices claimed that Alabama's choice to establish separate social spheres for whites and blacks appropriately protected the white race and "its preservation from the degeneration social equality, between the races, would inevitably bring" (*Story v. State,* 59 So. 480, 482 [1912]). The Court identified in order these key elements necessary to prevent such degradation: the prohibition of intermar-riage, the separation of children of different races in the public schools, and the segregation of passengers on the state's common carriers. It may seem ironic that a full expression of the logic of white supremacy came in a case that overturned a rape conviction for a black man. In fact, though, the case spoke to the domestication and legalization of white supremacy as well as to the growing perception of a normative and descriptive divide between the races so rigid as to require special evidence of its breach even by a white woman identified as a prostitute.

Through these four areas of conflict, the courts began to articulate specific rules about the context of interracial sexual encounters by applying rules established earlier in nonracialized contexts. The standard, race-neu-tral, legal rules of evidence, admissibility, sufficiency, and charges to the jury fit into a context in which judges had to determine the level of threat posed by the relationship they were considering. In the prosecutions for miscegena-tion, this analysis took place against a backdrop of needing to distinguish between a man's paying a woman for individual acts of sex and a man's keeping the same woman, which implied a lasting relationship that could mimic marriage and legitimate family. In the prosecutions for rape or attempted rape, the questions were about the context of the situation in which the alleged incident occurred as well as the nature of the woman involved. Both types of cases demonstrated how broad legal rules articulated in other contexts could be imported into racialized cases and transformed. Further, in both types of cases, the opinions reflected the emerging consensus on the need for separation between the races, the political importance of embedding white supremacy, and the state's crucial role as an enforcer.

Thus in some ways, the women in these cases served as the key points for questions about facts. White or black, was she a kept woman or a prostitute? If the former, both she and her partner were in danger of lengthy prison terms. Was she a virtuous woman, and even if a prostitute, was she the kind of prostitute who would accept black clients? These questions focused the courts' inquiries but tended to mask the underlying assumptions about race and interracial relationships.

While the appellate courts by 1912 had articulated the need for separation and endorsed the idea that the races were fundamentally different and socially incompatible, they did not spend any time articulating a definition or explanation of race as a concept. In 1912, the players in Alabama's legal system still knew what a "Negro" was and felt no need to waste any energy litigating this question with respect to accusations of miscegenation. Only six years later, this certainty began to evaporate in the concrete context of litigation. This litigation would be fueled by the loopholes inadvertently opened by the courts in their efforts to ease state solicitors' burdens in the years between 1883 and 1917.

CHAPTER 4 *Litigating Race: 1918–28*

In the Alabama state courts, more than in any era except the years of constitutional struggle immediately following the Civil War, the decade between 1918 and 1928 featured litigation focused on a single discrete question: What must be proven in order to establish that the defendants in a prosecution are of different races? Since racial difference was a fundamental element of the crime, the lack of attention to this key issue for roughly the first five decades of the statute's operation may seem strange. The sharp and short appellate conflict over this question, however, arose in the context of the prior period of evidentiary challenges in combination with the mass popularization of theories of eugenics. Eugenics, in tandem with the growing popularity of a national narrative of the white state disseminated culturally and socially, simultaneously increased the state's investment in whiteness and purity while biologizing race (see Blight 2001; Guterl 2001; Jacobson 1998). This reliance on biology ironically opened up legal space for challenges to prosecutions on the ground that the state had not adequately proven blackness within the statutory definition. The courts struggled to balance popular and culturally rooted understandings of race with the words of the statute, but ultimately the legislature found it necessary to step in to settle the problem even as the high court manufactured an evidentiary answer.

The struggle over racial definition did not end in 1928, but the legal uncertainty of these years set the parameters for such challenges. Cases involving five different couples provided concrete contexts in which the courts worked to square the evidentiary principles established in the previous period with problems of racial definition.[1] This process would limit the

---

1. One case decided during these years, *Lewis v. State,* did not involve a challenge based on racial definition. *Lewis* was decided in 1921 and addressed an evidentiary challenge similar to those discussed in chapter 3.

scope of possible challenges based on racial definition while providing space for the courts and the legislature to work out the meaning of the white state.

Many political analysts have seen these years as a time of stasis in Southern politics; Jim Crow was firmly in place, and the threats of Reconstruction and Populism had been beaten back (see Brandwein 1999). Nonetheless, while the foundational ideology of whiteness was well rooted by the 1910s, ignoring significant events like the premiere of *Birth of a Nation* and the rebirth of the Ku Klux Klan privileges thin accounts of politics as separate from culture and misses the significant debates over racial meaning that occupied this era. Both whiteness and blackness were still in motion as the process of racial formation continued through both culture and institutions; the legal and social transformations gradually filtered out the ambiguous category of mulatto and pushed Southerners to identify themselves and others as black or white (Bynum 1998). As Matthew Guterl has shown, this process was different in the North, driven more by the tensions over the place of immigrants with respect to whiteness (2001). Nonetheless, racial definitions, their production, and articulation were in play throughout the United States, and significant developments were driving the simplification of the finer-grained racial divisions that had predominated in the nineteenth century and before (Jacobson 1998).

In Alabama and the rest of the South, blacks provided the central contrast to whiteness, and the debate over race moved quickly toward the embrace of a bifurcated racial universe, despite the problematic place of Native Americans both in Alabama's social history and in the cases themselves. Looking at the sharply focused legal debate over how to prove race helps to unveil this process and key state actors' institutional efforts to accommodate conflicting cultural meanings. Through this process, both the judiciary and the legislature ultimately endorsed rigid categories of blackness and whiteness dependent on the kinds of evidentiary principles developed in the earlier legal debates. The appellate courts and ultimately the Alabama legislature worked to remove racial ambiguity at the margins, gradually eliminating the theoretical and legal possibilities for multiple categories of nonwhiteness. The one-drop rule—the idea that any degree of black ancestry rendered an individual black—while reflective of long-term predominant white cultural understandings of race, would finally become the ruling legal definition as a result of the focused conflict over racial categorization in Alabama in these years.

Democratic Hegemony in Alabama's Politics

After the brief struggle over Populism near the turn of the century detailed in chapter 3, the Democratic Party held sway in Alabama, facing no serious challenges. Electoral politics were about choices among Democrats, not between Democrats and alternatives. While Republicans existed in Alabama in the 1920s, they were curiosities; no Republican presidential candidate would carry the state until 1960, and no Republican governor would be elected until 1986. Alabama's political contests thus remained sectional and economic rather than partisan (Rogers et al. 1994: 411–12).

Even sectional and economic conflict remained somewhat muted, however, due to the alliance between Alabama's Big Mules (industrialists) and Black Belt elites (mostly large-scale planters). These conservative interests took active advantage of Alabama's highly centralized government and strong governorship to keep poor whites under tight rein. Occasionally, reformers would gain some leverage through populist appeals, and Alabama endorsed some Progressive causes (Key 1949: 36–57). For instance, Governor Kilby, who took office in 1919, advanced a significant agenda of child protection and increased funding for public health, but policymakers did not engage in the kind of systematic governmental reform common in the West in the 1910s and 1920s. World War I damaged the industrial side of Alabama's economy, and about fifteen thousand Birmingham iron- and steelworkers went on strike in 1919. The strike was swiftly suppressed through Kilby's use of the National Guard and through federal injunction, though periodic multiracial strikes in the steel and coal industries continued in the early 1920s. Union families, faced with blacklisting and repression, left Alabama, and union membership had dropped from 25 percent of miners in 1917 to but 1 percent in 1929 (Rogers et al. 1994: 417–21).

Alabama likewise maintained a brutal system of convict leasing, which was lucrative for the state and advanced the agenda of repressing blacks (though by the 1920s, whites were beginning to rise as a proportion of the prisoners). While Governor Kilby had implemented modest reforms to the system, the next governor, Bill Brandon, elected in 1922, rolled back these reforms and reinstituted the practice of whipping prisoners in response to a rebellion by 500 convicts in 1923. After national publicity about the death of a petty forger in the nation's last convict-leasing program, the system became a significant issue in the gubernatorial race of 1926. Advocate for abolition

Bibb Graves won the election, and convicts were taken out of the mines by the legislature in 1928 (Rogers et al. 1994: 420–23).

Those convicted of crimes continued to work for the state, but in less dangerous conditions. Nonetheless, the implementation of Prohibition led to swift growth in the prison industry; while Alabama had no equivalent institution to Mississippi's notorious Parchman Farm, its five state prisons housed thousands of inmates by the beginning of the 1930s (Rogers et al. 1994: 423; Oshinsky 1996). To be sentenced to a term in the state penitentiary remained a serious, potentially deadly, sanction in Alabama in the 1920s.

Overall, little changed in the formal political system in Alabama between 1918 and 1928. A few modest Progressive reforms were put in place, but the wider call for broader participation by citizens remained unheard, and Progressives' interest in class issues generated no substantive reform. Change did take place in Alabama's political culture nonetheless, but it was change not driven by partisan politics. These years saw the rise of a new political player—the Ku Klux Klan.

The Birth of a Nation and the Rebirth of the Ku Klux Klan

In 1905, Thomas Dixon, a North Carolina novelist and clergyman, published his novel *The Clansman*. An overwhelming success, the novel made Dixon internationally known and established Doubleday, Page, and Co. almost instantly as a major publishing firm. The themes of his novel, which purported to be a romantic history of the Civil War and Reconstruction, were parallel with those in his earlier and later works: "(1) blacks are subhuman, animal; (2) the two races cannot coexist in the same country without miscegenation, which means the destruction of Anglo-Saxon 'purity' and of its driving mission in leading (conquering) the world; (3) blacks must be totally segregated to prevent this disaster, first by denying them political equality (which leads to social equality) and ultimately by physically removing all blacks from the United States" (Kinney 1985: 171, 165). *The Clansman* articulated a new meaning for the Civil War and its aftermath by casting the war as a tragic and fratricidal mistake and white Klan members as heroes seeking to restore order and justice to the topsy-turvy world initiated through Reconstruction.

Popular though *The Clansman* was, however, the story was destined to have a far greater impact. It was first transformed into a play, which toured extensively throughout the South, often drawing mobs who fought over seats (Cook 1974: 102). Ultimately filmmaker D. W. Griffith saw the story as the perfect opportunity to produce an epic drama, breaking from several conventions of film at once and stirring up controversy. Censors threatened to ban it for its inflammatory character prior to its release, but one of its early fans was President Woodrow Wilson, who allegedly exclaimed after a private screening in the White House, "It's like writing history with lightning. And my only regret is that it is all terribly true" (114–15).

The film tracked Dixon's novel relatively faithfully. It opens with the retelling of the story of the Civil War, centering the Camerons of the South and the Stonemans of the North. The families are friendly at the beginning of the story, but the Civil War tragically separates the Cameron and Stoneman sons. Sons from both families confront each other in the war and recognize too late their brotherhood; hero Ben Cameron is injured gravely but is nursed back to health by Senator Stoneman's daughter Elsie. After the war and Lincoln's assassination, Senator Stoneman falls under the evil influence of his mulatto housekeeper and advances equal rights for blacks, including his mulatto protégé, Silas Lynch.

In the second part of the 165-minute film, the action moves to South Carolina, where Senator Stoneman is an active proponent of Reconstruction (Stoneman's character in some respects resembled the outspoken U.S. senator from Massachusetts, Charles Sumner). Silas Lynch travels with him and becomes the state's lieutenant governor. Unruly blacks take over and promote disorder, but Ben Cameron secretly founds the Ku Klux Klan to curb their excesses. Elsie Stoneman, caught between father and lover, breaks with Ben. Soon afterward, however, young Flora Cameron is pursued by rapacious former slave Gus. In a frenzy to escape him, she runs over a cliff and falls to her death (in the novel, she is raped and throws herself over the cliff intentionally after returning home and consulting with her mother, who also commits suicide). The Klan finds Gus, hangs him, and leaves his body on Silas Lynch's doorstep. Vengefully, Lynch swears to pursue the Klan members and forcibly woos Elsie Stoneman. The Camerons initially escape Lynch's disorganized mob but are trapped in an isolated house in the countryside as the black mob advances. The Klan sweeps in on horseback with Ben Cameron at its head, rescuing Elsie and the Cameron family. They rout the blacks and depose Lynch. On the next election day, in contrast to the chaos of Reconstruction elections, the Klan keeps order and prevents blacks from voting. The movie ends with the double wedding of Phil Stoneman to Margaret Cameron and Elsie Stoneman to Ben Cameron; the final frame asks if we dare dream of a day when war shall rule no more.

The Birth of a Nation premiered in the spring of 1915, first in Los Angeles and then in New York. It came to Atlanta at Thanksgiving and helped to spark a revival of the Ku Klux Klan. Alabama native William Joseph Simmons and about twenty other men gathered on top of Stone Mountain outside of Atlanta and burned a cross; three members of the original Klan were present to give the organization the appearance of continuity (Feldman 1999: 12–13). Simmons envisioned the Klan as a continuation of the old organization, but with a broader civic and social agenda. It would be nativist and committed to white separatism, but it would also be a fraternal band that championed the middle class against economic elites (Feldman 1999: 15; MacLean 1994: 79). While most definitely not a liberal organization, the revived Klan endorsed Progressive and Populist ideals of political reform, democratization for whites, and the lessening of the concentration of wealth among elites.

Simmons took advantage of screenings of *The Birth of a Nation,* running newspaper advertisements for the Klan alongside advertisements for the film. Later, the Klan used the film as a recruiting device, showing it to potential Klansmen as a sort of statement of purpose for the organization (MacLean 1994: 13).[2] Initially, the Klan grew slowly, picking up only handfuls of members, but after the heightened xenophobia ignited by World War I and the economic turmoil attendant to the war, the Klan's message became more popular. By the end of 1924, the Klan had established 148 klaverns in Alabama alone, where Montgomery, Birmingham, and Mobile were major centers. The Klan boasted 115,000 members in Alabama and 4 to 6 million members across the nation (Feldman 1999: 16).

The Klan began to permeate Alabama's political structure as aspiring politicians (including future U.S. Supreme Court Justice Hugo Black) became members. While Governor Kilby was not a Klansman and did not support the organization, the Klan had become so influential that he refused to denounce it. The Klan sought recognition as a civic service organization, but its association with violence and secrecy remained prominent. The early 1910s had witnessed a lull in interracial violence against blacks, but by the

---

2. Ironically, Dixon, author of *The Clansman,* deplored the brutality of the new Klan and spoke against the use of his story for this purpose, though to no avail (Cook 1974: 64).

1920s, violence became more common. Ironically, the Klan's reliance on overt intimidation and violence as blunt tools of power probably prevented it from having even more influence than it did. Nonetheless, most outrage over Klan excesses was reserved for their actions against whites, not blacks (Feldman 1999: 70–75).

By the mid-1920s, however, the Klan was politically strong enough to challenge the entrenched conservative order in Alabama. Klan members Bibb Graves, Hugo Black, and Charlie McCall were elected governor, U.S. senator, and attorney general respectively in 1926, shocking conservative Democrats. Black had defeated former governor Thomas Kilby and former state supreme court justice J. J. Mayfield, among others. While all three were more than simple racists and probably used the Klan opportunistically, they openly embraced the Klan upon their elections and relied on its extensive grassroots network for support (Feldman 1999: 81–87).

The Klan's political power had a profound effect on Alabama's legal system. While prominent individuals were identified as Klan members, extra-legal activities were performed in Klan garb, making identification superficially difficult. Under a Klan hood, even a man who was known by all could appear as an anonymous enforcer of the Klan's ideals. When perpetrators of violent acts were identified, law enforcers would first have to arrest them and prosecutors bring charges against them. Even when Klan members were prosecuted, juries often contained Klan members or were frightened of what could happen if they voted to convict. The Klan's permeation of the organs of legitimate government mattered as well: Grand Dragon James Esdale sought to work with Klan governor Bibb Graves to ensure that Klan members would serve on every jury commission in Alabama. The Klan also aggressively campaigned for local offices; by the mid-1920s, nearly every county sheriff in Alabama was a Klan member (Feldman 1999: 86–89).

The Klan did not carry on its work without opposition, though its opponents never united. The NAACP, formed in 1908 in response to a race riot in Springfield, Illinois, that left two dead and forced two thousand other African Americans to flee, worked to collect statistics on Klan activity and confronted its violence. The NAACP was an immediate enemy of the Klan even before its reinception, as it spearheaded efforts to censor *The Birth of a Nation* and took positive measures to counteract its racist message. The group was able to operate more freely in the North than in Alabama, however, as open and vocal membership in the NAACP could provoke a visit from Klan members (Zangrando 1980: 22–50).

In the South, African American resistance was carefully calibrated but exercised nonetheless. NAACP branches, often organized principally by black women, operated quietly and collected information on violence for the compilation of national statistics. Black women in Mobile and Birmingham attempted to exercise the franchise in the election of 1920 despite the application of harsh literacy tests and requirements that they own property. In Birmingham, more than two hundred black women of the forty-five hundred who attempted to register were able to do so successfully (Gilmore 1996: 137–50, 220).

Despite black resistance and despite opposition from conservative interests, it was not until the Klan overreached, flush with its massive victories in the 1926 elections, that it could be reined in politically. Klansmen engaged in an orgy of violence in Alabama in 1927, conducting more than seventy floggings of whites and blacks during the summer alone. Such floggings were vicious physical attacks that occasionally left their victims dead. Ironically, it was an attack on a black farmer[3] that sparked a concerted campaign by the conservative press to topple the Klan. The *Birmingham News* led the attack, calling on the governor to take action before the Klan's lawlessness stretched to encompass whites. The Klan also gained significant negative publicity from beatings administered to white women whom they perceived as violating rigid norms of proper behavior. Soon, national attention began to turn to the situation in Alabama, giving conservatives the leverage they needed to press for change (Feldman 1999: 92–100).

To the Klan's surprise, attorney general and former prominent Klansman Charlie McCall turned on the organization and conducted a public investigation of a particularly notorious incident, securing convictions of the Klansmen responsible. Elites mobilized the media against both the Klan and Governor Graves's modest Progressive reforms, relying heavily on the influential *Montgomery Advertiser* to disseminate their message. The Big Mules and Black Belt elites united to drive the Klan out of its position of political prominence, though they were not able to (or did not have the will to) root out the Klan's embedded power (Feldman 1999: 103–36).

The Klan was successful for most of this period in part because its message resonated so well with popular sentiments about progress and about

---

3. Arthur Hitt was a respected older man, described by locals as a "white man's nigger," who had refused to sell his land to whites for about 15 percent of its value. He was beaten so badly that he was rendered unconscious and was barely able to walk a month after the attack. Three days after the beating, he sold the land to whites for 10 percent of its value (Feldman 1999: 94).

race. The organization self-consciously positioned itself as engaging in a project of creating an ideal society. Integral to the Klan's belief system was an embrace of scientific racism and theories of eugenics; these theories warned stridently about the dangers of racial mixing through interracial procreation.

The Triumph of Eugenics and the Threat of Racial Mixing

The years of the evidentiary battles reflected widely accepted beliefs about race, but a new set of beliefs began to influence the legal community during the late 1910s. While scientific racism was not a new concept in the twentieth century (see, e.g., Stanton 1960: 166–68), the scientific racism that dominated the early twentieth century differed from its predecessors in the scope and breadth of its influence as well as in its basis in the now-dominant genetic theory of heredity. Multidisciplinary investigations of fitness and descent along with their normative implications became known as the science of eugenics. Eugenics and its cousin ethnology emerged at the turn of the century and rose in popular consciousness after that, as writers like Madison Grant and Earnest Sevier Cox wrote books and pamphlets explaining these insights in laypersons' terms (Guterl 2001).

While framed as a science, eugenics was often not based on neutral scientific inquiry. While some practitioners undoubtedly believed themselves to be engaging in disinterested and neutral research that simply led them to racist conclusions, many prominent promoters of eugenics had backgrounds suggesting a commitment to white supremacy independent of their research findings (Gould 1981).[4] While scientific language was prominent in these analyses, discussions of blacks' inferiority in the late nineteenth and early twentieth centuries differed from earlier analyses more in their framing than in any other way. Earlier authors had spoken of mongrelization; the scientific authors of the turn of the century explained difference in the language of genetics. These men were not marginal figures. Rather, they were well-respected professionals in their various disciplines (Baker 1998).

Such individuals first insisted that the social and political difficulties between the races were merely proxies for the fundamental biological differences, which truly grounded the conflicts (Barringer 1900: 3). In the view pre-

---

4. Lee Baker has shown that leading anthropologists at the turn of the century influenced the public realm and popular discourse through their commitment to theories of racial hierarchy expressed in world's fair exhibitions and widely circulated magazines (1998: 51–55).

dominant in the South, the lowest and meanest white remained white and therefore biologically and culturally superior, while the most educated and intelligent black was irremediably linked to inferiority.[5] In such analyses, this inherent inferiority and superiority that would descend inexorably from generation to generation had to be contained within rigid boundaries of black and white. Interracial sexual activity threatened these boundaries and thus attracted attention from the scientists, who predicted unmitigated disaster from any breach. For instance, one author cautioned that the superiority of the white race in absolute physiological terms could only be preserved if the state prevented miscegenation (Smith 1993: 16, 33).

These ideas could have been expressed earlier and in some cases were. But by the turn of the century, scientific authors had the growing prestige of their disciplinary backgrounds and the increasing faith in scientific discovery to bolster their arguments. The 1910s marked a shift from the earlier views about race to popular discussions couched in normative scientific and social-scientific language. Dovetailing with the Progressives' interest in science, a legal system suffused with realism would incorporate these new "break-throughs" in the social sciences, believing that the scientific method would lead to rationalized legal results (White 1997: 10–16). Simultaneously, anthropologists, sociologists, and other social scientists were becoming increasingly interested in race. A debate broke out in the 1910s as Franz Boas presented anthropological research showing that culture rather than nature accounted for differences among groups of people and challenging the very idea of race itself (Baker 1998: 104–7). Eugenicist responses rested upon beliefs about race and mixed race grounded in background assumptions regarding heredity and the nature of race. The tide peaked around 1924, as eugenic theories established a dominant and unified conception of a consanguineous white race (Jacobson 1998: 96–98). Increasingly, scientific voices and their cultural reflections pushed toward a simpler racial ordering configured primarily around whiteness and blackness, with a smaller group of subsidiary non-white groups at the margins (96–98).

As in earlier versions of scientific racism, the key element in blackness

---

5. The racial framework popularized in the North by Grant and others was more complex, naming "Nordic" whites as the dominant race and identifying southern Europeans and Jews as separate and inferior races, albeit superior to the "Negroid" race (Guterl 2001). These distinctions among whites, particularly the separation of Jews from other ethnic groups, persisted into at least the 1950s (Brodkin 1998; Jacobson 1998).

was not appearance, but blood (Saks 1988). The authors spoke frequently in terms of black blood and what was to be done with it, and literary portrayals of interracial romance and tragedy became increasingly popular.[6] Blood was the bearer of blackness, the means through which its dangerous and backward characteristics were conveyed from generation to generation. Ultimately, many of these authors (both scientific and popular) saw only two options regarding blood: either complete amalgamation would take place, producing one race in the United States combining white and black, or a complete separation would have to be enforced, with the current mixed-race people being permanently and irrevocably defined as black (Cox 1926: 93).[7] The problem was thus not simply preventing whites and blacks from marrying. As another author explained, it was also in figuring out a way to deal with the legacy of past intermarriages (Russell 1920: 5). A third motivation was dealing with those "hidden Negroes" who, pamphlet authors feared, had already succeeded in crossing the color line.

For eugenicists and their followers, the proper solution to racial problems was to maintain the purity of the blood of both whites and blacks through complete separation. This solution tied in well with beliefs in a natural antipathy of the races, and white authors encouraged the development of racial pride among blacks as well as whites (Reuter 1969: 355).[8] Racial pride alone was insufficient, however. Only strict prohibitions could reliably protect the integrity of blood. Interracial contact had to be rooted out at every turn through severe legal and social sanctioning (Cox 1926: 92–93).

Ultimately the prospect of complete amalgamation terrified both scientists and popular authors because of the tainting nature of black blood. As Cheryl Harris has shown, whites had a great deal at stake in maintaining the integrity of whiteness and its link to identity (1993: 1725). Much of the ten-

---

6. The most notable example was the leitmotif of interracial romance in Edna Ferber's popular novel *Show Boat*, which, like *Birth of a Nation*, moved quickly and successfully to the stage in the 1920s.

7. While Cox's work was self-published, it was not unread or uninfluential. He was trained in sociology at the University of Chicago and based his findings on his work in Africa. He consciously directed his writing toward the scientific community (Bair 1999: 401).

8. Racial pride was not merely a rhetorical strategy among racist whites. The New Negro Movement was emerging in the North as enterprising blacks fled the stifling cultural and political atmosphere in the South. One of the stranger alliances of the 1920s was between virulent racists seeking absolute segregation and promoting black racial pride as a means of achieving it on the one hand and protoblack nationalist Marcus Garvey and his followers on the other. Garvey attended a conference with Edward Young Clark, Imperial Kleagle of the Klan, in Atlanta in 1922 to discuss their common interest in relocating blacks to Africa (Zangrando 1980: 91).

sion over interracial intimacy rested in the contradictions inherent in thinking about blood. If black blood could be successfully concealed, why was it problematic? On the one hand, both scientists and popular writers agreed that the white race was superior in most ways to the black race and that the natures of both races were determined by genetics. Mulattoes' success in becoming the leaders of the black race was solely due to their superior intelligence and refinement, which was a direct result of the white blood flowing through their veins (Reuter 1969: 355). They aspired to membership in the social class of whites because they were misplaced with the lower fully black race. As white fears of mulattoes grew, the very concept came under attack; in the 1920s, the U.S. Census eliminated the category of mulatto and defined former mulattoes as black.

If this were the whole story, there would be no reason to worry about racial mixture. White blood would simply overwhelm black blood and mask its damaging qualities; the mixture of blacks with whites would ultimately bring the black race closer to the level of the white race. The story was, however, more complex. Along with these beliefs, many people simultaneously believed that black blood had an almost magical quality to it that enabled it to overcome white blood, even when it was only present in the smallest quantities. At bottom was a deep need to render white completely separate and completely pure as its own independent entity (Hale 1998: 284–88). Racists presented the specter of the white person contemplating a grandchild who was both truly a direct descendant and truly and evidently black. The legal and social placement of mulattoes with blacks underlined white fears of the tainting quality of blackness as well as concerns about mulattoes' capacity to conceal their racial heritage and gain full access to white society.

Eva Saks has speculated that these fears and recommendations related to a sense among whites that they had a property interest in their blood (1988: 52). This reading suggests that the fear of taint arose from an interest that people had in their blood and its dispensation in future generations. Both individuals and the state could be understood to possess this interest. State actors enforced the state's interest in preventing the tainting of white blood through continuing and strengthening their legal pursuit of couples who engaged in interracial sex.

These emerging beliefs provided the legal community with a framework within which to justify increasingly rigid separation between blacks and whites and increasingly stringent definitions of blackness. One clear early example may be found in Georgia judge Thomas M. Norwood's remarks delivered in 1907, entitled "Address on the Negro," in which he reflected upon his experiences dealing with black defendants over the years. After detailing the inferiority of the black race, Norwood explained to his audience that interracial intimacy was a horrible threat to the white nation. Even though the law forbade interracial sex, having legal prohibitions on the books was not sufficient to curb the evil: "illicit miscegenation thrives and the proof stalks abroad in breeches and petticoats along our streets and highways" (1907: 26). This proof was the attractive and dangerous mixed-race issue of such unions.

Norwood's beliefs about black inferiority did not permit him to blame "pure" blacks for the increases in racial mixing. He placed the blame squarely on white men, who made and enforced the laws against interracial sexual contact and prevented black men from crossing the color line, while simultaneously "wallow[ing] with dusky Diana with impunity" (1907: 26). This practice by white men, in Norwood's view, was particularly damaging to white women. Women married to men who engaged in interracial sex would bear the shame of knowing that their children had black half siblings. Their white daughters would flinch at having to acknowledge a black child's salute of them as sisters (27).

While Norwood saw "full-blooded Negroes" as childlike, easily led, humble, and nonthreatening, mulattoes were a different story altogether. He believed that mulattoes, due to the admixture of whiteness, were a genuine threat both in their prominence and in their attitudes, arguing that every prominent black person in the United States had white or Native American ancestry to thank for his abilities and that all were hostile to whites. His solution to this problem, which would have been unconstitutional even under *Pace v. Alabama,* was to "Draw a dead line between the races. Tell the Negro, when he crosses it the penalty is death. Tell the white man, when he crosses it the penitentiary is there" (1907: 23, 5). The state had the duty and right to defend itself against the dangerous mulatto through severe punishment of anyone, male or female, black or white, who threatened to bring one into existence. Thus, even as mulattoes were being eliminated as a theoretical and census-based category, they were to be concretely eliminated as well.

The new prominence of eugenics was not the only engine driving the legal debate over racial definition, though it was a helpful catalyst. The new definitions highlighted for the public the disconnect between commonly held understandings of blackness as including any individual with any black ancestry and the formal statutory definitions' reliance on a particular blood quantum as a threshold. At the same time, the spread of segregation and the legal formalization of white supremacy in the previous period raised the salience of racial definition as a legal and social problem, providing policymakers with ample motive for institutionalizing supremacist cultural understandings within state structures. As Jacobson has observed, one important but infrequently noted effect of struggles over the development of segregation in the early twentieth century was the consolidation around a unified conception of whiteness among those of European descent, in contrast to the multivalent classifications present earlier. While this process of consolidation was different, court decisions also played an important role in determining where and how to find whiteness among immigrants (Jacobson 1998: 223–45).

Association and appearance, traditional markers of race that did not rely on heredity, took on new significance in light of the growing bifurcation between black and white.[9] Nonetheless, as eugenics gained prominence, old conceptions of race based largely in the belief that blacks were fundamentally different from whites in their natures and souls began to give way. The implications of genetically based inferiority were significant for policymakers and judges, but an embrace of the belief that blackness was genetic had unforeseen risks for those who wanted to maintain absolute separation between white and black.

Eugenics as an Opportunity for Black Defendants

The problem that racist theories of eugenics presented for prosecutions of alleged miscegenators was in the definition of race and the identification of individuals as black or white. Before the rise of the eugenics movement, Alabamans generally seemed to know what was meant by the word *Negro*. An 1851 ruling had defined a Negro as "a *black* man descended from the black race of Southern Africa" (*Felix v. State,* 18 Ala. 720, 726 [1851]). The statute, as described previously, expanded this definition to include mulattoes down to the third generation, which meant that a person would be considered black for purposes of the antimiscegenation statute as long as one of

---

9. Thanks to Peggy Pascoe for clarification on this point.

his or her great-grandparents was a Negro (Ala. Stat. 1923: sec. 5001). While this formulation was quite specific, it raised few questions—anyone who looked like a black person simply was a black person. Whiteness was even vaguer, not even having a statutory definition.

No one in Alabama had raised a recorded appeal based on not having sufficient black or white ancestry to count as black or white under the statute, because ancestry was simply not as important as appearance. All a prosecutor had to do was to exhibit the defendants to the jury, as in the *Linton* and *Jones* cases, and that would suffice to show race as long as he was careful to claim in the indictment as well that the defendants were of different races. A few scattered cases had raised these kinds of questions much earlier in other jurisdictions. In Virginia in 1885, Isaac Jones successfully challenged his conviction for intermarriage with a white woman on the ground that the prosecution had not adequately proven that he had the required one-fourth quantum of "negro blood in his veins" (Hickman 1997: 1227). Likewise, the Arkansas courts prior to the Civil War had struggled to identify the race of Abby Guy, who sued for her freedom on the ground that she was not black and therefore could not be a slave; ultimately the high court affirmed a jury's verdict that Guy and her children were free (see Gross 1998).

It is impossible to determine for sure why these instances were scattered and did not produce focused attention on this question, since those of questionable race could clearly manipulate this fact to their legal advantage. Nonetheless, it is telling that the debate emerged in Alabama in concentrated form only after eugenics became significant both scientifically and socially, having an impact on understandings of whiteness as well as blackness (Guterl 2001; Jacobson 1998). The clustering of cases in a single decade and the shape of the debate as it developed suggest that these kinds of questions ripened for sustained judicial inquiry in response to the dominance of the discourse of eugenics and the pointed difficulties that hereditary theories of race posed for the everyday process of litigation. The problem of defining race became legally salient just after white supremacy had successfully become legal and constitutional policy, and in the wake of a growing tendency in the South to bifurcate race into blackness and whiteness. The prominence of eugenics likely did not cause the debate over racial conflict to emerge when it did, but the conjunction of the rise of eugenics with the legal and constitutional implementation of white supremacy were likely significant interrelated factors.

The racist eugenicists based their theories in heredity. With this shift, ancestry became much more important. If blackness and whiteness were not simply physical characteristics or natural qualities that existed within individuals but rather were inheritable, defendants had an opportunity to avoid conviction by demonstrating that they or their companions did not in fact have the wrong kind of ancestors. Given that these cases were criminal, a "black" defendant did not even have to prove that he or she had no black ancestors; because of the prosecutor's duty to prove his case beyond a reasonable doubt, the prosecutor now had the burden of showing definitively that the defendant or his or her partners did indeed have at least one black great-grandparent. Even making this showing was difficult, since blood was more significant now than it had been previously. By the 1920s and 1930s, prosecutors were often finding it necessary to go back to the antebellum era to show the requisite black ancestry. The only solution to this pressing problem was to develop a standard that did not require proof of heredity, but this was difficult in light of the statute's language and the cultural beliefs about heredity prevalent at the time. The prominence of eugenic theories also highlighted the contrast between widely held beliefs about blackness as encompassing all those with black ancestry and the blood quantum definitions that prevailed throughout the South. As the cases brought these tensions to the forefront, something had to give way.

Eugenics gave defense attorneys a plausible argument. The fascination with heredity and genetic factors linked to blood generated a scientific definition of race that supplanted other means of defining race (appearance, associations, etc.). The link between the statutory language and the modern eugenic understandings provided the ground for insisting that the state demonstrate ancestry positively before a prosecution could proceed. In some instances, Alabama's courts were caught in a quandary about how to square scientific knowledge and statutory language with what everyone knew to be true about individual identity.[10] The resulting conflict ignited a concentrated node of conflict over racial classification and how to establish it in court. Ultimately, through close analysis in cases involving five different couples, the high court developed standards to bring these contradictory elements into

---

10. Ian Haney López highlights the same tension in federal court decisions concerning immigration and race, but in those cases, newer anthropological understandings of race cut in the opposite direction. The courts largely ignored the science in these cases in favor of endorsing commonly accepted racist standards (Haney López 1996).

agreement, relying on the previously developed groundwork concerning evidence. This debate incorporated gender indirectly, as experts and ordinary witnesses argued over how gendered bodies displayed or manifested race in their physicality.

Metcalf and *Rollins:* Establishing Whiteness

An Alabama attorney first realized that raising questions about the state's ability to prove the races of the defendants could result in appellate reversals of convictions in 1918. Ironically, the claim involved a challenge of white ancestry, not black ancestry. Between the summer of 1916 and the summer of 1917, Ophelia Metcalf and Jim Simmons were indicted, tried, and convicted of living in adultery or fornication with each other in violation of the antimiscegenation statute. The indictment charged that Metcalf was a "Negro" and Simmons was a white person (*Metcalf v. State,* bill of exceptions, indictment 1916). Metcalf was sentenced to seven years in the state penitentiary for her crime (bill of exceptions, Judgment of Conviction). No one had actually caught the defendants together in bed, and much of the evidence in the case centered around witnesses who had seen Metcalf and Simmons together in a buggy or at Metcalf's house (bill of exceptions, testimony of Henry Tice 1916: 1). Metcalf testified that, while she lived near Simmons and had dealings with him frequently, her relationship with him was strictly limited to her use of his livery service. She also asserted that she had never committed adultery with Simmons, nor had she ever had sexual intercourse with him (bill of exceptions, testimony of Ophelia Metcalf: 3). Simmons apparently did not testify at Metcalf's trial.

Metcalf and Simmons both appealed their convictions. The attorney for both, Charles Erastus Mitchell, was a prominent Democrat who had been practicing law in Hamilton, Alabama, since 1893 (Owen 1978: 1212).[11] Mitchell, handling Metcalf's appeal, raised two issues: first, that the state had not produced enough evidence to prove that she had committed adultery with Simmons, and second, that the state had not introduced evidence show-

---

11. Mitchell's representation of a black defendant appealing her conviction for miscegenation seems not to have had any negative impact on his status, and no contemporary large newspapers seem to have reported on the case. This lack of controversy seems to suggest that, at least in some cases, appeals were perceived as part of the ordinary operation of the legal system and not as pointed challenges to the emerging infrastructure of white supremacy.

ing that Simmons was a white man. The appellate court considered her claims and ruled that, while Metcalf's presence at the trial and her testimony before the jury provided the jury with a sufficient opportunity to determine her race, the state had not done enough to establish that Simmons was white (*Metcalf v. State,* 78 So. 305, 305 [Ala. 1918]). Because a crucial element of the crime had not been proven, Metcalf's conviction could not be sustained. The court overturned Simmons's conviction on the same basis, ironically allowing him to escape a lengthy prison term because the state had not sufficiently identified him as a member of the dominant race (*Simmons v. State,* 78 So. 306 [Ala. 1918]). Both defendants thus avoided prison terms on the basis of questions about the meaning of race, in this first case the meaning of whiteness specifically. Defense attorneys were now on notice that this tactic could succeed for their clients, and they were quick to exploit it. The appellate ruling did not give prosecutors any real guidelines about how to prevent this problem from arising again, leading to further litigation.

In 1921, Jim Rollins, a "negro or descendant of a negro" was charged with committing miscegenation (including a blanket allegation of intermarriage, adultery, or fornication) with Edith Labue, a white woman (*Rollins v. State,* record, oral charge 1921: 3). Labue had been married to a white man for about eight years, and Rollins, the defendant who appealed, worked for Labue's father-in-law (*Rollins v. State,* bill of exceptions, testimony of Joe Labue 1921: 6–7). Labue's husband left his wife and two children in Birmingham in June 1918 to serve in the army for six months; Labue was apparently pregnant when he returned and she gave birth to a child of suspicious appearance in April 1919 (*Rollins v. State,* bill of exceptions, testimony of Joe Labue 1921: 15–17). The child was described as "dark brown . . . with kinky hair" (bill of exceptions, testimony of J. McGill 1921: 19). The solicitor for the state had the toddler exhibited to the jury twice, once for Officer McGill to identify and once for the father's identification (bill of exceptions, 19, 21). Likely the second exhibition was to titillate the jury and remind them of the child's damning racial features.

The allegation of miscegenation was not based on the child, however. Rather, a city detective and two police officers, suspecting interracial misconduct, came to Edith Labue's residence one night and entered. Upon kicking open the door to the back bedroom, they discovered Labue and Rollins in the same room, arrested Rollins, and immediately removed him to city hall for interrogation (testimony of B. F. Hubbard 1921: 9; testimony of H. H.

Sullivan 1921: 10–11). What happened during the interrogation was unclear; apparently Rollins was left alone with Officer Hubbard, who admitted to drawing a gun on him, but Hubbard insisted that he had not threatened Rollins or in any way induced him to confess (testimony of B. F. Hubbard 1921: 11). At some point, though the testimony was conflicted about when (and particularly whether it was before or after the incident with the gun), Rollins apparently admitted that he had been having occasional intercourse with Edith Labue since July or August 1918. He also allegedly claimed that Labue had told him about her pregnancy, asking him "what he was going to do about it" once the child was born (testimony of H. H. Sullivan 1921: 14–15).

Rollins's attorney attempted to raise suspicions about Edith Labue's race and the possible source of the third child's appearance. He elicited testimony from Joe Labue that he was from Sicily, where he had lived until he was twelve, and that Edith Labue was also from Italy (though he could not confirm that she was Sicilian) (*Rollins v. State,* bill of exceptions, testimony of Joe Labue 1921: 17–18). In the North, such evidence likely would have raised serious objections to her unproblematic definition as white; in Alabama, the implied question about Labue's race did not convince the jury (Guterl 2001). Witness J. McGill, who described the third Labue child as having Negroid physical characteristics, also admitted on cross-examination that he knew little about Edith Labue's racial background.

> I do not know where she is from. She is an Italian I think. She is either an Italian or a Greek. I don't know which. I do not know whether she has any African blood in her veins or not, but she is not dark. She is of foreign decent [*sic*], and is an Italian or a Greek. I don't know whether she is right adjacent to the Mediterranean Sea or whether she is from Liberia or among those colored races down there or not. I am sorry to say I never had an opportunity to study Geography. (Testimony of J. McGill 1921: 21)

This testimony shows the extent to which Italians were not always reliably white even as late as 1921, when they still occupied a middle ground that was at that time being closed (Jacobson 1998: 62).[12] The witness read her ethnic-

---

12. Jacobson discusses this case briefly and notes that both Italians and Jews were unreliably white in this era, setting mentions of the *Rollins* case alongside a more comprehensive analysis of the racialization present in the lynching of Jew Leo Frank in Georgia in 1915 (1998: 62–65).

ity as Italian or Greek, possibly explaining her own questionable appearance, though he insisted that she was not dark. The comment about geography also suggests the common belief, popularized by noted eugenicist Madison Grant, that some Mediterranean people were of mixed race and could not be definitively identified as white without further investigation (see Guterl 2001). The record does not reveal whether Edith Labue was in the courtroom at any point during the trial; she was apparently not charged and did not testify.

Rollins was nonetheless convicted and sentenced stringently, receiving a six- to seven-year term (Judgment entry 1921). He challenged his conviction on several grounds, claiming that the prosecution had not adequately established the elements of miscegenation, that evidence had been admitted improperly, and that his confession had been coerced. The high court agreed that the trial had been problematic and reversed his conviction.

The main problem for the justices was the confession; without the confession, they explained, "the evidence adduced upon the trial of this case is too vague and uncertain, and therefore insufficient to overcome the presumption of innocence" (*Rollins v. State*, 92 So. 35, 36 [1922]). The confession was problematic because of the possibility of coercion arising from the uncontradicted testimony that a police officer had drawn a pistol on Rollins, but also because the state solicitor had not adequately established the corpus delicti of the crime. Here, as in the earlier application of general rules regarding intraracial adultery or fornication and confessions, the court actively employed race-neutral principles in a case implicating racial boundaries. In general, confessions were only admissible if uncoerced and if a state solicitor could independently establish the basic elements of the crime (corpus delicti). Rollins's confession should have been excluded, they ruled, on both of these grounds.

What basic elements of wrongdoing were missing? In part "there was no evidence whatever to sustain the material allegation that Edith Labue, the codefendant, was a white woman, or that the defendant was a negro or the descendant of a negro." The court made special note that no competent evidence had established Labue's race or that she had no "negro blood in her veins." Nodding implicitly to the rising popularity of theories of racial purity in the North, the court noted that the speculation that she came from Sicily could not be "taken as conclusive that she was therefore a white woman, or that she was not a negro or a descendant of a negro" (id.). Especially since Labue had not appeared in the courtroom, enabling the jury to gauge whether she presented herself as a white woman, the testimony alone was insufficient to establish her race. The court did not mention the child or the use of the child as evidence, finding enough problems with the conviction to overturn it on these grounds alone.

These cases sent a clear message to defense attorneys. Three defendants, two black and one white, had escaped their convictions for miscegenation because the state solicitor had not properly shown that a member of the couple in question was white. This tactic would not work in every case and raised other analytic headaches (think, for instance, of the position of Joe Labue, now married to a possibly racially ambiguous wife), but it could enable some defendants to fight prosecutions if ambiguities could be raised. Defense attorneys could exploit these ambiguities by combining them with the race-neutral rules governing confessions and invoking the ordinary operation of law. The logical next step was to extend this principle to defendants identified as black by the state and see if they, too, could be read as sufficiently racially ambiguous to undermine prosecutions.

Reed and *Wilson:* The Debate Expands

By the early 1920s, the loophole created by eugenically based definitions of race was ripe for exploitation. Defense attorneys could see from the failed prosecutions of Ophelia Metcalf, Jim Simmons, and Jim Rollins that contesting racial identifications was an effective tactic. Given that there was a statutory definition of blackness and that establishing blackness required genealogical information, the shift from challenges to identifications of defendants as white to challenges of identifications of defendants as black was logical. Emergent conceptions of whiteness, while hereditary in a strict sense, were more broadly tied to the absence of taint and people's social embeddedness in white culture. As middling, not-quite-white categories that had encompassed European immigrants were set on the course of extinction in law, whiteness became more monolithic and less subject to question culturally (Jacobson 1998). However, the explicit hereditary definition of blackness in the statute encouraged attorneys who recognized the appellate courts' insistence that the elements of the crime be properly established before convictions could be supported. Two cases in the early 1920s demonstrated dramatically both the shape that these legal maneuvers took and the confusion they engendered both for the courts and for laypersons accustomed to "knowing" race without the need for critical judgments.

Percy Reed and Helen Corkins began living together in around 1915. They had been living alone together in a house for five years when they were arrested for the crime of miscegenation and charged with intermarrying illegally. At their trial, a witness reported that Corkins referred to Reed as her husband, and the pair did not contest the allegation that they considered themselves to be married and lived together as a married couple (*Reed v. State,* bill of exceptions, testimony of Henry Rivers 1920: 12). Instead, they argued that Percy Reed was not black within the limitations of the statute.

The trial did not focus on Percy Reed's race, but rather on the race of his great-grandmother and her daughter, his grandmother. When the trial judge charged the jury, he framed the question in these terms: "Was this woman, the mother of Rose Reed, a Negro; was this child Rose Reed her child; was she the mother of Reuben Reed. Was Reuben Reed the father of this man [Percy Reed]" (*Reed v. State,* oral charge to the jury 1920). If Rose Reed's mother was a full-blooded "Negro," then Rose Reed was black. If she was black, then her son Reuben and grandson Percy could face criminal penalties for marrying or having sexual relations with white women.

Percy Reed claimed that his grandmother Rose had been of mixed race, but not of black descent. Rather, he alleged that her parents had been an Indian woman and Mr. Gaines, a white slaveholder. The court admonished the jury that even if they found that Rose Reed's mother was a "half breed," this would not be sufficient to support a conviction under the statute (id.). They needed to identify a full-blooded "Negro" among Percy Reed's recent ancestors. This would not be easy to do, given that no evidence definitively established the racial makeup of either Rose Reed or of her mother.

The state solicitor relied on witnesses' testimony to establish Rose Reed's parentage. One witness explained in a sworn affidavit that "I knew Rose Reed and heard that she was George S. Gaines' daughter and that one of the Gaines' cooks was her mother" (bill of exceptions, affidavit of John J. Richardson 1920: 1). In his affidavit he could not identify which cook was Rose's mother. At the trial, however, he testified that he knew which cook was Percy Reed's great-grandmother but simply did not remember her name. The unnamed woman was "ginger cake color, and cooked for old man Gaines. She was Percy Reeds' [*sic*] great Grandmother—she was a mighty old woman when I knew her" (id. at 11). While she was a mulatto, her daughter Rose was "brighter" in skin color.

A witness for the defense countered this story, repeating information that had been introduced in an earlier trial regarding the Reeds. This witness claimed that "an Indian woman was the mother of Rose Reed and that George S. Gaines was her father. I always heard and understood that those were the ancestors of the Reeds. I never heard that a Negro cook or a Negro woman in the house-hold of George S. Gaines was the mother of Rose Reed" (bill of exceptions, testimony of George W. Sullivan 1920: 14–15). Another witness corroborated this account, testifying that he had never heard that the Reeds were descended from "Negroes" (bill of exceptions, testimony of Robert Dorman 1920: 15).

This flat contradiction placed Percy Reed's racial identification—an element of the crime—in question. The prosecution could not prove its case through an investigation of Reed's ancestry alone, so it used other tactics as well. Another witness testified that he knew Reed to be a mulatto because he was "moxed [sic] with Negro—have been told that, and I also judge from his looks" (bill of exceptions, testimony of A. G. Richardson 1920: 10). Witnesses' descriptions of the physical appearance of those alleged to be black did not seal the state's case, however. On cross examination, John Richardson admitted, "I don't know about the length of Rose Reed's hair, but remember that she sometimes wore it plaited, and sometimes in a little knot on her head" (bill of exceptions, testimony of John J. Richardson, 1920: 11–12). Another state witness testified that Percy's mother had long straight hair and appeared to be a Native American. Percy Reed's cousin also testified that Rose Reed's hair was one and a half or two feet long and straight, not kinky (bill of exceptions, testimony of Reuben P. Reed 1920: 13–14). These descriptions played into gendered conceptions of racial difference as the defense sought to place Rose Reed as a domesticated Native American rather than a black woman.

Reed's defense attorney also sought to raise reasonable doubt by introducing evidence about Reed's associations. The state's own witness testified that, while he had seen Reed with "Negroes," he did not know that Reed associated with "Negroes" particularly (bill of exceptions, testimony of A. G. Richardson, 1920: 10). A. G. Richardson also testified that the Reed family didn't associate with whites, but the defense attorney was not seeking to prove that the Reeds had white associates. John Richardson testified that Reed's family not only did not associate with "Negroes," but moreover that his maternal relations had owned slaves (bill of exceptions, testimony of John J. Richardson, 1920: 11–12). Reed's cousin, Reuben, testified that Rose Reed did not "talk like a Negro," and both he and Henry Rivers, another defense witness, supported the claim that Reed's family had never associated with "Negroes" (bill of exceptions, testimony of Reuben P. Reed 1920: 12–13; testimony of Henry Rivers 1920: 14).

What was the defense trying to suggest about Reed's racial background? Victoria Bynum has explored the tangled genealogical lines of another such community in southeastern Mississippi (1998: 247–75). In 1948, an appellate court overturned the conviction for miscegenation of a young man named Davis Knight on the ground that the state had not sufficiently proven his blackness. The Knights had descended from a white man who had allowed two of his children to marry mulattoes and possibly had fathered mixed-race children himself. The Knight family largely intermarried with each other and established a separate school for the clan. Without clear physical markers of blackness in the defendant, and with contradictory testimony regarding the physical features and associates of his ancestors, Davis Knight was able to achieve, if not whiteness, at least the ability to continue his married life in peace (id. at 274, 256–58). Likewise, Naomi Zack describes isolated mixed-race communities that existed in the South, East, and Midwest in the 1930s. While members of these communities did not consider themselves to be black, some would acknowledge a small degree of black ancestry. Most emphasized their Native American ancestors to explain their nonwhite physical characteristics, and local whites often understood them socially more as Native Americans than as blacks. They tended to associate neither with whites nor with blacks, choosing rather to keep to themselves. This placed them socially and politically outside of the increasingly bifurcated racial space of the Southeast, but cases like *Reed* signified that they could not remain beside or outside of the law. Their precarious status did not persist in a racially divided society; ultimately they had to deny either their white or nonwhite ancestry (Zack 1993: 86–110). For a time, however, such communities survived and even thrived, as perhaps the Reed clan did.

One of the defense witnesses identified Percy Reed's father as Spanish and Indian, suggesting that Reed's family may have been such a mixed-race community (bill of exceptions, testimony of Henry Rivers 1920: 12). Other witnesses testified that the family associated mostly with each other and that their children did not attend the local school for black children (bill of exceptions, testimony of George W. Sullivan 1920: 12; testimony of John J. Richardson 1920: 14–15). Most damaging for the state's case, however, was the testimony that many members of the family had intermarried with local whites. George Sullivan identified four white families with whom the Reeds and Weavers had intermarried, and Robert Dorman claimed that they had established blood or marital connections with "in fact two thirds of the people in that part of the county" (bill of exceptions, testimony of Robert Dorman 1920: 15). A finding that Percy Reed was a black man would thus have serious implications for the entire community.

The jury, confronted with all of this contradictory evidence, apparently had difficulty in deciding how to decide whether Reed was indeed black. After beginning deliberations, the jury sent their foreman to ask the judge whether they could consider the appearance both of Percy Reed and of the other witnesses as evidence in the case (*Reed v. State,* oral charge to the jury 1920). The judge allowed them to do so, and they found Reed guilty, incidentally determining that he was indeed a black man. Reed was sentenced to three to four and a half years in the state penitentiary. The grounds of his appeal, centering on the process through which the jury identified him as black, highlighted the specific conflict over racial meaning that the earlier cases had unveiled and in part produced.

Reed's appeal claimed that the state had not submitted sufficient evidence of his race to sustain his conviction. The central question was whether Reed's appearance or his associations could constitute an adequate admission that he was a "Negro" or mulatto. The appellate court that reviewed his case took a dim view of the state's evidence, pointing out, "The best that can be said of their [the state's witnesses'] testimony is, from the state's viewpoint, that one of them did state that the defendant was a mulatto or of Negro blood, and that he drew this conclusion from the defendant's color" (*Reed v. State,* 92 So. 511, 511 [Ala. App. 1922]). (The prosecution's use of hearsay evidence to prove the race of Rose Reed's mother was deemed inappropriate by the appellate court; in the future, state solicitors would almost always have to search for people who had actually known the people whose race they were trying to establish.) This application of the rules on hearsay suggested that only direct evidence from the defendant him- or herself or from or about others alleged to be black could be used to prove race. The trial court's error was not in the use of common understandings or classifications of race, but rather in the proximity of the witnesses making these judgments. This ruling, however, left open the question of what would constitute appropriate direct evidence. Thus, the conflict over racial meaning, rather than being resolved, was heightened.

The most significant blunder, however, was not by the state solicitor but rather by the trial court judge. Before sentencing a convicted defendant, the judge was required to assess the convict's occupation, health, and race. After Reed was convicted, Judge Ben Turner found that Reed was a farmer by occupation, that his health was not good, and that he was of Indian and Spanish origin (*Reed v. State*, jury charges and verdict 1920)! The judge on appeal wrote sarcastically, "one cannot help asking how the trial judge made this ascertainment, when the verdict of the jury must of necessity have been arrived at upon an ascertainment that the defendant was of African origin" (*Reed v. State*, 92 So. 511, 512 [Ala. App. 1922]). Reed's conviction was over-turned on the ground that the state solicitor had not sufficiently proved a key element of its case.

As in *Metcalf* and *Rollins*, the appellate court did not issue a definitive ruling in the case. The state had not done enough to prove race, but the court did not explain fully what would be enough. Clearly, concluding that a person was black based solely on that person's skin color was insufficient. Having dark skin was neither proper proof of black ancestry nor an adequate admission that the individual was black. In earlier cases, exhibition had been sufficient to constitute definitive proof of whiteness and blackness, so sufficient that it was almost never even raised as an issue. The inroads that hereditary definitions of race had made allowed Reed's defense attorney to exploit his questionable racial heritage. Further, the trial judge's statements in sentencing the defendant had constituted an admission by the state that Reed was not black, thus negating the racial element of the crime of misce-genation. This finding likewise exacerbated rather than resolved the conflict within the legal system over how to establish race appropriately.

One year after the announcement of the decision in the *Reed* case, the same issue arose at the trial of Sarah Wilson, also known as Shreveport Sarah. The record hints that Shreveport Sarah was a notorious figure in Mobile, perhaps running a speakeasy. The state alleged that Wilson had developed an adulterous connection with Charles Medicus, a white married man. The trial was based heavily on the testimony of Medicus's wife, Ivy, who had gone to Wilson's house looking for her husband; she claimed that, while peering through the window, she had seen Wilson and Medicus having intercourse (*Wilson v. State*, bill of exceptions, testimony of Ivy Medicus 1923: 7). Ivy Medicus was an enthusiastic participant at Wilson's trial, describing her husband's infidelities and her interactions with Wilson in great detail. Her willingness to participate in the trial and her hostility toward Wilson likely stemmed from her allegation that Wilson had openly taunted her about her relationship with Ivy Medicus's husband (id. at 10–12).

On cross examination, Wilson's defense attorney, Edward Grove, sought to raise as many doubts about Medicus's testimony as possible and then turned to the question of race, asking Medicus if she knew how much "Negro" blood Wilson had. Medicus replied, "I cannot prove that, but she lives in a Negro house with Negro people. You can tell by her looks she is Negro." The defense attorney repeated the question and asked Medicus if Wilson's mother, grandmother, or great-grandparents were "Negroes." Medicus, apparently a bit flustered, responded "I do not know which one, but one of them certainly must have been, or two or three." Grove persistently elicited an admission from Medicus that she did not know anything about Wilson's ancestors, and the trial judge interjected to clarify that Medicus had no personal knowledge beyond information about Wilson's appearance. When the trial judge asked Medicus if she knew who Wilson's ancestors were, Medicus answered "No,—but don't she live with Negroes,— she could not surely be white." On redirect, the state solicitor attempted to repair the damage, suggesting that Medicus knew that Wilson was a "Negro" because of her physical appearance, the color of her skin, and her associates (id. at 10–13).

Like the state solicitor in the *Reed* case, the state solicitor in the *Wilson* case introduced evidence about Wilson's associates. One witness testified that he had seen Wilson coming into the courthouse with other "Negroes" and that he had seen her kiss a "Negro" woman goodbye after they left the courtroom (bill of exceptions, testimony of William Earnest 1923: 14–15). Another witness, Cliff Adams, testified that a male associate of Wilson's was a full-blooded "Negro" (bill of exceptions, testimony of Cliff Adams 1923: 17).

Wilson's defense attorney used the same strategy with Adams that had rattled Ivy Medicus, asking him how he knew that either Wilson or her associate was a "Negro." After getting the witness to define a full-blooded "Negro" as a full-blooded African, he asked him whether Wilson's parents were Africans or Americans. Adams answered that he did not know and also admitted that he did not know how much "Negro" blood Wilson had, but he truculently continued to maintain that Wilson was a "Negro," claiming that a great part of her blood was "Negro" blood. When Grove asked Adams how he knew that a high proportion of Wilson's blood was "Negroid," Adams responded that he knew her race by her color and the race of her associates (id.).

Throughout the trial, Wilson's defense attorney's examination of the state's witnesses highlighted the difficulties that arise when concepts such as race are in transition. Repeatedly, state witnesses insisted that Wilson was black while simultaneously admitting that they did not know anything about her ancestry. In the transcripts, their responses to Grove, Wilson's attorney, exhibited both frustration with his repeated questioning and blank incomprehension of the emphasis he was placing on ancestry as a measure of blackness. Their attitude was that they *knew* Wilson was black as a matter of common sense in a society that placed great weight upon categorizing people by race. The trial record preserved no physical description of Wilson, but the witnesses' responses seem to suggest that she was readily identifiable as a black woman. Their attitude appeared to be that a discussion of ancestry was irrelevant when a person was obviously black. The jury also did not see or accept the point at which Grove was driving: Wilson was convicted and sentenced to between three and three and a half years in the state penitentiary.[13]

The main issues that Wilson raised on appeal related to her contention that the state had not proved her race beyond a reasonable doubt according to the legal definition established by the statute. Ironically, the emerging consensus in the racist eugenics movement concerning heredity formed the basis for Wilson's argument. None of the state's witnesses had been able to testify about Wilson's ancestors from personal knowledge, and defense attorney Grove's reading of the statute required the state to prove either that Wilson herself was a "Negro" or mulatto or that one of her parents, grandparents, or great-grandparents was a full-blooded "Negro." The brief explained that the state's witnesses did not establish the legal definition of race in any way: "Well, how did they reach the conclusion that she was a Negro? Can it be said that every dark person, or every brown-skinned person, who happens to be seen with Negroes, is a Negro? Should their association with persons be the sole evidence upon which to base a conviction?" (id. at 25–26, 33).

The appellate court understood Wilson to be arguing that the establishment of race was partly a legal and partly a factual question. In this view, the

---

13. The defense attorney's appellate brief revealed that Charles Medicus was charged but not prosecuted, since his wife refused to testify against him (Bill of Exceptions, Brief of Edward Grove 1923: 38–39).

prosecution would have the duty to introduce evidence about the defendant's ancestry and the jury would then decide if the evidence was credible. The appellate court ruled against this reasoning, finding that these questions were questions of fact. The jury was competent to determine whether a particular defendant was white or black, and the definition of race was not a fully legal issue (*Wilson v. State*, 101 So. 417, 420–21 [Ala. App. 1924]). The court explained its ruling in pragmatic terms. First, it would often be impossible for prosecutors to find conclusive evidence of racial descent. Furthermore, common sense enabled ordinary individuals, including judges and attorneys, to identify a "Negro" when they saw one: "We think that . . . the rule born of necessity . . . permit[s] a witness, if he knows such to be the fact, to testify that a person is a Negro, or is a white person, or that he is a man, or that she is a woman; for courts are not supposed to be ignorant of what everybody else is presumed to know, and in this jurisdiction certainly every person possessed of any degree of intelligence knows a Negro, and also that the term Negro, and colored person, . . . mean the same thing" (id. at 421). The court thus rejected the emerging scientific consensus that race was about heredity, embracing instead the certainty that had predominated in Alabama in the late nineteenth century.[14] Both gender and race were readily transparent to ordinary observers in most cases. Wilson's conviction would stand, though she had the last laugh when the governor commuted her sentence either shortly after she began serving it or perhaps even before she had served any time in the penitentiary.[15]

This solution, however, was not ultimately tenable. It would work with people like Wilson, who apparently had few question marks among her ancestors and easily read as a black woman socially. The court made no attempt, however, to square this ruling with the ruling in *Reed*. By reading

---

14. The court's ruling thus presented an interesting contrast to developments in the North and on the federal level. In the North, whiteness continued to be subject to negotiation as the place of immigrants from southern and eastern Europe remained problematic (Guterl 2001). These developments in Alabama were taking place as a unified legal conception of whiteness was emerging in cases that drew the margins of whiteness at the boundaries of Europe, though not without struggle (Jacobson 1998). Federal courts turned away from scientific evidence and toward folk conceptions of race as well, but instead of eugenics rejected the new ethnological and anthropological evidence that race was a constructed category in favor of rigid and accepted definitions of Asian inferiority (Haney López 1996).

15. The League of Women Voters held a protest meeting in which they vehemently denounced the powerful men who had apparently intervened on Sarah Wilson's behalf. Several members of the organization insisted that it pass a resolution "denouncing the actions of those men 'whose upholding of the most notorious character in the city was an insult to every white woman in Mobile.'" The newspaper report of her release went on to muse, "Poor 'Shreveport Sarah'—human wreck down in Alabama where the perfidy of the sandhiller, degenerate white man, changed the color of a race" ("Mobile Women Protest" 1923).

the two cases together, one could see the emerging contours of a new rule. A defendant could be proven to be black even in the absence of evidence about heredity if a sufficient proxy for that evidence could be found. This appellate court allowed a person's appearance and associations to count as evidence that the person was black, permitting such evidence to substitute for a proper showing that the appropriate degree of heredity was present. It further underlined a tendency to define race on dualist black/white grounds. Such a finding, however, would not be effective if genuine questions existed as to a person's race. Wilson was not able to produce witnesses to counter the state's witnesses, and the court implicitly found that simply attempting to raise doubts about the state's proof was not sufficient without additional evidence on the defendant's behalf.

Weaver v. State and the Effort to Achieve Judicial Resolution

The appellate courts that struggled in the early 1920s with questions of racial definition clearly wished to maintain Alabama's policy against interracial intimacy. They nonetheless recognized the problems inherent in the statutory definition of blackness and in the available means of proving race through readily obtainable evidence. By the late 1920s, the courts were experiencing a crisis, and a resolution had to be reached. Because individuals like Percy Reed who could claim mixed racial ancestry were living throughout the state, the problem was likely to intensify, and legal experts in Alabama were cognizant that this was the case. The prosecution of Jim Weaver and Maggie Milstead provided the context in which an appellate court could craft a comprehensive rule to try to address this problem.

Jim Weaver and Maggie Milstead were convicted of miscegenation in 1927, and the question of Weaver's race was central in the trial. Weaver and Milstead, who went by the name Maggie Weaver, had been living together for about a year before they were arrested for miscegenation. They were tried in the same region of Alabama as Percy Reed, and like Percy Reed, Weaver claimed to be of Native American descent, but the state solicitor used witnesses to argue that he was black through his father.[16] Weaver's father

---

16. It is possible that Weaver and Reed were loosely related and part of the same problematic mixed-race community. Nothing in the transcripts from either trial suggests a relationship, but the Reed trial noted the presence of a mixed-race community composed of individuals with the surnames of Reed and Weaver. No witnesses, however, testified in both trials, and the defendants were represented by different law firms.

testified at his trial that Weaver had no "Negro" ancestry: "There is not any Negro blood in me, my father was Taylor Weaver, he did not have any Negro blood in him, Peggy Parnell was his mother, there is no Negro blood in her. There is no Negro blood in the defendant, who is my son" (*Weaver v. State,* bill of exceptions, testimony of Dudley Weaver 1927: 6). Dudley Weaver also testified that his son did not associate with "Negroes" and that he had not attended a "Negro" school (id. at 7).

The state solicitor attempted to prove his case by using the physical appearance and associations of Weaver's family. Weaver's brother Wade testified at the trial, and the state solicitor exhibited him to the jury, having him stand in front of the jury box and turn around so that the jury could examine the shape of his head (bill of exceptions, testimony of Wade Weaver 1927: 8). This evidence touched on a scientific belief popularized in the mid–nineteenth century that race could readily be distinguished by a careful examination of the cranium (Stanton 1960: 29–37). Another witness testified for the state that Weaver's mother looked "more like a Negro than any other human being I ever saw" (bill of exceptions, testimony of J. W. Henson 1927: 13–14). The same witness also testified that Weaver's grandfather associated mainly with blacks and only occasionally with the "inferior or castoff class" of whites.

The defense attorney countered by raising questions about Maggie Milstead's race. He asked Henson if he knew whether Milstead had "Negro" blood to the third generation, to which the witness answered that he could not swear that Milstead was untainted by "Negro" blood (id. at 11). Weaver himself also swore that he was lawfully married and asserted "I haven't a drop of Negro blood in me. I am White and Indian, neither my parents or grandparents have Negro blood in them. . . . All of my mother's people were clear English people" (bill of exceptions, testimony of Jim Dudd Weaver 1927: 16–17). He also denied associating with "Negroes," claiming to attend a white church. His testimony thus countered the state's efforts to define race as a simple bifurcation between black and white, introducing the question of Native American ancestry as a complicating factor. The jury, however, did not find his testimony to be convincing and convicted both him and Milstead, both of whom were sentenced to two years in the state penitentiary.

In hearing their joint appeal, the appellate court took this opportunity to clarify the standards that were to apply to the determination of race, subtly criticizing the earlier appellate court's somewhat confused ruling in the *Wil-*

son case. The judge claimed that when one was considering a pure racial type, the determination of race could be made simply according to physical characteristics. Ignoring the testimony about Native American ancestry, the court implicitly endorsed racial dualism. This ruling further had the effect of eliminating the category of mulatto. Nonetheless, when a question about a mixed-race individual was raised, witnesses could not be permitted simply to conclude that such a person was black rather than white. In such cases, the state had the duty to prove first that a black defendant had a "Negro" ancestor of the whole blood and second that the defendant was not further removed from that ancestor than the third generation. The problem in the *Weaver* case, according to the appellate court, was that the state solicitor had not shown evidence to prove that Weaver had a "Negro of the full blood" within the requisite degree. If the state could not make such proof, it had to introduce evidence from which the jury could reasonably conclude "that the defendant is not removed more than three full steps from a Negro of the full blood" (*Weaver v. State*, 116 So. 893, 895 [Ala. App. 1928]).

So far, the new rule sounded as if it would be a great advance for black defendants, given the difficulty in finding evidence tending to prove ancestry. The court, however, went on to list additional ways in which race could be proven. If the defendant admitted being a "Negro," such statements could be used as evidence. Likewise, "if he associates with Negroes, in his social intercourse, attending Negro churches, sending his children to Negro schools, and otherwise voluntarily living upon terms of equality socially, such are acts which may be taken as admission" (id.). (Association with whites might provide some evidence that the defendant was not black, but was not as determinative a factor in whiteness as association with blacks was with blackness. Most people likely assumed that no white would associate with blacks voluntarily but that blacks might have valid reasons for wishing to associate with whites.) Physical characteristics, while not definitive with respect to a mixed-race defendant, were not completely ruled out. While the court did not address the proper proof of whiteness to any significant degree, the opinion noted that a witness could "testify that a man is a negro or a white man as the case may be, if he knows the type and is not testifying to a mere conclusion" (id.).

In the case at hand, the court ruled that the state on the trial level had properly presented the defendant's close relatives to the jury so that the jury could "judge for themselves regarding the degree in which defendant stood to a Negro of the full blood" (id.). Furthermore, the state was permitted to prove that the defendant's near relatives had the physical characteristics typical of "Negroes." Under this rule, Weaver's and Milstead's convictions were upheld. Even though the state solicitor was not able effectively to prove his ancestry, the physical appearance of Weaver's relatives and his associations with other blacks, though contested, were sufficient to warrant a finding of guilt for both defendants.

In effect, the court ruled that the state had the alternatives of using the new scientific definition of race to establish that a person was black through proving his or her ancestry or using the older understandings of race within the new framework. The court assumed that if a person did not have "Negro" blood, he or she would not admit to being a "Negro" either directly or indirectly by voluntarily associating on an equal basis with those of the inferior race. In the cultural expression of the scientific terms, only an admixture of "Negro" blood would make such associations acceptable, since even those who had "Negro" blood often tried to escape them. Further, the question of appearance was made somewhat more complex. Rather than simply being a question of whether the defendant looked like a black person and therefore was a black person, the court ruled that a visual inspection of a defendant's relatives could help the jury to make the factual determination that a particular defendant had black ancestors. Because of the belief in the unitary nature of racial heredity, physical features that suggested blackness could legitimately constitute an admission. This determination, furthermore, did not have to rest upon a physical examination of the ancestors in question. Even if a particular defendant had light enough skin to raise questions as to his race, the production of a dark brother or sister could settle the matter for the jury. Racial classifications other than white and black had no place in this analysis. The category of mulatto, which had maintained an important legal and social position in Alabama's law and culture for decades, was being structurally eliminated.

This ruling, which finally clarified the standard, drew on the older rules established with respect to admissions by the defendant, broadening greatly the concept of an admission. In the cases involving prostitution, an admission had been simply a statement by the defendant suggesting that he or she was involved in an ongoing relationship. Such a statement was probative and could be permitted in evidence because it went to one of the elements of the crime, proving an adulterous relationship (as opposed to individual acts of intercourse) between the black and white individuals. The eugenics movement's emphasis on heredity had posed serious problems for state solicitors by linking the definition of blackness strictly to ancestry. The appellate court's solution to this problem was to construct an analytical framework in which the older forms of evidence about race—appearance and associations—could be considered admissions about a person's racial background. This enabled an end run around the problem of heredity and allowed prosecutors to prove race by using evidence that was more readily available than detailed information about a person's great-grandparents. The court was likely satisfied that it had successfully resolved the problem, especially since it had an institutional partner—the Alabama legislature.

The Statutory Redefinition of Race

Even before the ruling in the *Weaver* case, the state legislature had realized that its statutory definition of race was problematic. Scientific interpretations of race mandated that blackness be related closely to heredity, but the ordinary folk concepts of race on which witnesses were likely to rely did not allow interpretive room for distinctions in the degree of ancestry. Race, for these witnesses, was much more a matter of appearance, a person's family connections, and a person's associations, in particular the schools and churches that he or she attended. As other scholars have noted, both whiteness and blackness were strongly related to performance and fit in a particular social context (see, e.g., Gross 1998; Bynum 1998). For the witnesses, this information said something direct about race rather than simply about ancestry. The law, however, had to take ancestry into account in defining blackness. It had to mediate these forms of knowledge to fit them in with statutory definitions of race and therefore read them as admissions. A man who went to a black church was in effect admitting that he had a black great-grandparent. A woman whose sister was dark and who sent her children to a colored school was confessing her racial origins. And as the evidentiary problems mounted, the courts and legislature moved to a binary system of racial identification that eliminated previously meaningful shades of racial difference and hierarchy, including mulattoes and individuals of partial Native American ancestry.

The state legislature could not redefine race to make it based solely on physical appearance and associations, in light of popular acceptance of hereditary definitions of race. What it did was to ease the burden on the state's prosecutors by adopting a so-called one-drop rule in 1927, finally bringing the criminal prohibition of miscegenation in line with the state constitution of 1901. The provision appears to have been uncontroversial; the house and senate journals record no debate over the proposed change. While there is no way to determine easily why the change was made in 1927, legislators were presumably aware of the courts' difficulties with these cases. The member of the legislature who proposed the statutory change at the same time proposed more stringent testing for venereal disease among men prior to the issuing of a marriage license, another issue that interested practitioners of eugenics (*Journal of the Alabama House* 1927: 843). The statute under which the cases of the 1920s had been prosecuted had defined a black person as anyone with at least one "full-blooded Negro" great-grandparent. The new statute simply read, "If any white person and any Negro, or the descendant of any Negro intermarry, or live in adultery or fornication with each other, each of them shall, on conviction, be imprisoned in the penitentiary for not less than two nor more than seven years" (Alabama Statutes 1928: sec. 5001). By not requiring a specific degree of descent, the legislature now defined blackness for purposes of the policy against interracial intimacy as having one black ancestor, no matter how far back. This definition implemented a much harder racial binarism that would no longer recognize mulattoes as a distinct racial group. At the same time, it worked toward reading Native Americans out of the legalized racial landscape as well.

This tendency to adopt more stringent definitions of blackness was national in its scope; the 1930 national census designated individuals with any degree of African ancestry as black (Bynum 1998: 255). Virginia had moved from a one-fourth blood quantum to a one-eighth blood quantum in 1910, but in 1924 it moved legislatively to prohibit intermarriage between whites and people with any nonwhite ancestry (Davis 1991: 9; Finkelman 1993: 2110).[17] Only one state—Tennessee—had such a restrictive definition of race prior to the 1910s; the widespread legislative and judicial embrace of the one-drop rule was an artifact of the 1910s and 1920s (Elliott 1999: 616–17). While little scholarly work has directly addressed the wave of statutory and judicial shifts to more restrictive definitions of race in this era, the wave of

---

17. Finkelman notes that Virginia modified this rule in 1930 to define *colored* as having black blood; the change was likely a result of concern about the delegitimation of prominent families with romantic traditions of descent from Native American nobility (1993: 2110).

problematic cases in Alabama in conjunction with the widespread acceptance of hereditary definitions of race seem like possible triggers. Certainly the widespread assumption that the one-drop rule was uniformly embraced throughout the postbellum era is in need of rethinking.[18]

The Battle over Racial Definition: Resolving Heredity with Common Understandings

This fight over how race was appropriately to be proven spanned only a decade, but it produced much appellate litigation. The appellate courts began by being unsure about how to handle these questions; initially, they simply ruled that the state had not met its duty to establish a key element of the crime of miscegenation. By the end of the period, they had articulated a framework that allowed evidence about associations and appearance to affect trials as admissions rather than as direct evidence of race. Through these years, different courts struggled to square competing conceptions of race and mixed race, accommodating the older folk conceptions to the newer genetic definitions. Individual actors in the legal system had to mesh scientific understandings of race and heredity with beliefs about irrefutable physical markers of race, linking science, popular understandings of race, and the legal principles governing evidence.

Attorneys on both sides were sensitive to these developments and sought to exploit them for their clients if they were defense attorneys or for the state if they were prosecutors. State solicitors were initially at a disadvantage, unsure of what kind of evidence they would have to marshal to secure a conviction that would not be reversible on appeal. They hit on the strategy of proving race through association and appearance in addition to trying to show that the putatively black miscegenator had black ancestors. This strategy ultimately gained the endorsement of the courts and had support from the legislature through the statutory redefinition of blackness.

The litigation addressed the problem of demonstrating whiteness and blackness, and both male and female defendants had success through appeals based on challenges to both racial categories. The structure of the arguments was slightly different, though both produced uncertainty. While blackness

---

18. In making this point, Elliott notes that Alabama's high court itself had ridiculed the one-drop rule as overextending the boundaries of blackness in its 1850 ruling in a prosecution of a mixed-race man for rape (1999: 617).

had a statutory definition linked directly to heredity, whiteness did not. Given that blackness was linked to subordinated status, white defendants might reasonably be expected to eschew any strategy of forgoing their connections to power and privilege; in fact the appeals bear this out, as questions about whiteness were raised by black defendants. The appeals based on shaky identifications of whiteness also reveal the extent to which whiteness itself remained unfixed in the 1920s even in the South, though this tendency was most pronounced in the North and legally contested (Guterl 2001; Jacobson 1998). Were Sicilians fully white? What status should a Mediterranean person have, and how did such an individual differ from the unquestionably white "native" Alabaman? As these answers were worked out, the legal system moved more overtly toward racial binarism.

While whiteness did pose important problems for the courts, this period was a time of adjustment to new standards exogenous to the law relating to blackness. In the early twentieth century, the older scientific and common definitions of race were perfectly adequate to address any problems or questions that arose without giving rise to any appellate litigation. After the emergence of the eugenics movement, however, in Alabama challenges on the basis of genetic understandings of blackness were possible, and state actors had to develop a new analytical frame within which to prove race. The courts enabled this to happen in a way that reflected both the old and new concepts of race, incorporating older beliefs about what constituted blackness with the newer belief in the role of heredity. For about eleven years, these unsettled questions produced repeated appeals, but Alabama's judges finally devised a workable standard, foreclosing this route to overturning convictions as long as the state solicitor did his job competently at the trial. The new scientific beliefs about heredity were successfully sidestepped through a careful application of evidentiary rules regarding admissions developed in the context of challenges relating to adultery and fornication described in chapter 3. The resolution of this instability also contributed to an increasingly racially bifurcated framework, with blackness and whiteness consuming space that had formerly included mulattoes and Native Americans.

Eugenics, however, was not the only scientific theory of race on the table, though it did dominate. The rise to prominence of scientific racism based in genetics took place at nearly the same time as a small group of cultural anthropologists were beginning the project of showing the cultural contingency of race as a concept. Both of these theories were introduced in the U.S.

courts and raised serious questions for judges seeking to interpret and implement the law. As Michael Willrich has shown, the legal system of Chicago relied heavily not only on the policies that a commitment to eugenics prescribed but also to the underlying logic of eugenics itself (1998: 63–65). Ian Haney López argues that the federal courts, when confronted with the new anthropological evidence concerning the problematic nature of race itself, ultimately chose to ignore the evidence and base their rulings on questions of immigration on older naturalistic conceptions of race that enabled increasingly narrow and stringent definitions of whiteness (Haney López 1996).

These examples show that judges and other members of the legal system were often willing to rely on scientific evidence to advance racist agendas, though they ignored it when it cut against the process of establishing white supremacy. In Alabama, genetic definitions of race were subject to litigation and appeal, but the way that scientific framings came into play was different than in either Willrich's or Haney López's analysis. In appeals of conviction for miscegenation, defense attorneys used eugenicist conceptions of blackness not to support eugenicist policies but instead to get their clients off. State solicitors were initially caught off guard, unable to respond to the simple assertion that they had to prove race through heredity. Thus, ironically, one impact that genetic understandings of race had was to make it temporarily possible for couples accused of miscegenation to beat their convictions on appeal.

As noted in chapter 3, prosecutors in the late nineteenth and early twentieth centuries were primarily concerned with maintaining the sanctity of marriage, which was for the state much more than a simple contract. In the immediate postbellum era, interracial intimacy undermined legitimate marriage by making a mockery of the ordered and separate white family; by the turn of the century, the real threat was that it would produce an unthrifty mongrel race that would inevitably fail. In both of these earlier periods, race itself was not in question, since from a white standpoint, blacks' alien nature and appearance made them readily identifiable to the most casual of observers. Neither whiteness nor blackness needed to be defined under these conditions, since the vast gulf between them set them permanently apart. Yet in this earlier era, racial taxonomies were more complex and varied, allowing room for mulattoes and individuals of Native American ancestry to have statuses somewhat different from those of individuals understood as fully and really black.

This way of thinking about race began to shift dramatically in the early twentieth century. During the 1910s, eugenics emerged on the national scene as a political rather than purely scientific or policy-oriented rhetoric, and racist practitioners of eugenics wrote extensively in the 1920s. The discourse of eugenics focused on the concept of blood and mixed blood, portraying racial mixing as a threat to the culture and very nationhood of the United States. Race became increasingly linked with heredity both scientifically and culturally, a fact that caused many pamphleteers to call for stricter rules regarding miscegenation and to attend to white men's partnerings with black women as a danger. Scientific reliance on unitary notions of heredity gave new cachet to old fears about the contamination of white blood by black blood; since racial characteristics were believed to be passed on in a unitary fashion, the stain of blackness could never be erased by genetic chance. The conjunction between the rise of state-based white supremacy and the intensive node of conflict over racial definition exacerbated both the limiting of the racial universe to black and white and the distancing between these two categories. In the process, a more rigid racial binary emerged, and the legal system endorsed it both judicially and legislatively through the adoption of case-centered and statutory one-drop rules.[19]

The discourse of eugenics and its interplay with white supremacy's institutionalization influenced both legislative and legal developments. The legal community was becoming ever more interested in arguments that included scientific as well as legal elements (White 1997). The Alabama legislature, responding both to popular ideas about race and to the courts' emerging dilemma over definitions and evidence, made its interpretation of race stricter. The legal arena, however, was the locus of a deep incompatibility between the newer scientific understandings of race based in heredity and the older folk conceptions of race as something that could simply be discerned. Over a period of a decade, the courts struggled to reconcile these conceptions, finally reaching a solution in the late 1920s. Alabama's legislature, like many others, underlined this solution by adopting a one-drop definition of

19. A commonly reported romantic vignette of the era critical of the one-drop rule features a mixed-race couple on the verge of arrest for miscegenation. The white man resolutely opens his wife's vein, sips her blood, and then challenges the sheriff to arrest the couple, since all of the witnesses are willing to swear that he has a drop of black blood in his body. The sheriff retreats in confusion and defeat. While it is not clear that this event ever really happened, the best example of the stock story appears in Edna Ferber's book *Show Boat*, published in 1926 and adapted as a musical a few years later (1926: 143–48).

blackness. This solution, believed legal elites, would enable prosecutors to use available evidence to convict miscegenators without having these convictions overturned on appeal. It would also further embed the growing social and legal tendency to understand race in binary terms, reading out of the legal categorization scheme the possibilities for mulattoes and Native Americans to situate themselves independently and promoting a more totalizing conception of whiteness. The next decade would show, however, that the craved-for certainty would prove to be elusive.

CHAPTER 5 *Consolidating and Embedding White Supremacy: 1928–40*

The 1930s were a period of retrenchment and consolidation of legal norms. The struggle over race in the 1920s had produced a solid rule on establishing the race of an accused individual, but how this rule was to work in practice was still open. A series of prosecutions of a single individual, Jesse Williams, would provide a testing ground. In Alabama as in the nation as a whole, this experience showed that even the court's acceptance of popular beliefs about race as proxies for the hereditary definition along with the legislature's effort to define blackness more strictly would not make all racial questions easy to answer. At the same time, additional questions relating to evidence arose before the courts, and the appellate courts instructed state solicitors again about what kind of relationship was necessary to demonstrate the crime of miscegenation satisfactorily. The years between 1930 and 1951 saw the continuation and gradual evolution of a discussion regarding evidentiary standards. The courts moved to establish rules about what kinds of relationships constituted the crime of miscegenation, what kinds of people were white and black, and what kinds of evidence could be used to demonstrate these elements of the crime.

Courts adjudicating appeals of convictions for miscegenation in the 1930s worked out the proper application of white supremacy in the legal arena. The turn of the century had seen white supremacy constitutionalized and established in statutory contexts. In the 1910s and 1920s, the legal system's players articulated and hardened the racial boundaries in light of the high stakes inherent in distinguishing whiteness. The Depression years would see a different agenda—key state officials worked to rationalize and embed the principles of white supremacy in and through the legal system. In the process of doing so, appellate courts would distinguish sharply between the legitimate application of supremacist principles through the legal system and the illegitimate expression of prejudice by actors in the system. This distinction highlighted conservative Democratic elite actors' efforts to sanitize white supremacy for national observation and consumption.

In general it is difficult to separate the structural and state-based elements of supremacy from the cultural infrastructure that maintained it throughout. In this period, however, the state—in the person of appellate judges—appeared to be taking an active role to channel culturally supremacist commitments about race through state mechanisms formally committed to the administration of a neutrally situated form of justice within a state structure designed to embed and support racial hierarchy. The legal conflicts emphasized the role of evidence, as they did at the turn of the century, but brought in a debate over what kinds of racialized language would be permitted in the formal setting of the courtroom. This debate tied in with the formal consolidation and application of supremacist norms within a framework that aimed for sufficient legitimacy to forestall any effort to upset Southern state-based control over race and racial questions. As in the previous era, much of this work took place through the transferring of neutral rules about the sufficiency of evidence and appropriate language at trial to a racialized context.

While the discussion in the decades of the 1930s and 1940s was more continual than previous discussions, which tended to fall into sharp categories and periods, considering the 1930s separately from the 1940s is helpful. In the background of the cases of the 1930s was the Depression with its resulting economic and social disruption. The 1940s were marked by World War II and its aftermath. The cultural and political developments of these crucibles forged the groundwork for the mass popular movement for blacks' civil rights, which would be born in Alabama in the 1950s. During the pre–civil rights era, however, much of the work of thinking through the legal boundaries between the races was still taking place in the context of appeals of convictions for miscegenation.

In the 1930s, this thinking took place in the context of debates over the application of the new definition of race and further discussions of what had to be proven to establish an illegal interracial relationship. One individual, Jesse Williams (or Jesse Lundy), a black man from Talladega, was prosecuted and convicted repeatedly for the crime of miscegenation, leading to three appellate cases. Three other cases addressed the sufficiency of evidence required to prove miscegenation, and two cases involving four separate appeals challenged the conviction of one defendant for miscegenation when his partner had been acquitted. Four of the six convicted defendants saw their convictions invalidated by courts of appeal, establishing that state solicitors could not use the stringent standards developed in the late 1920s to become complacent in their efforts. The state's confidence in overturning convictions based on inflammatory racially biased testimony, insufficient evidence of an interracial relationship, or insufficient evidence of the repeated and continued consummation of such a relationship suggested that the racial boundary was well fixed. This confidence prevailed overall even while the individual cases themselves revealed the unstable nature of that boundary and state actors' continuing opposition to the formation of interracial families. As the cases progressed, rules emerged to limit the expression of inflammatory racialized stereotypes in the courtroom, as the appellate courts distinguished such expressions from the legitimated application of white supremacy through statutory law.

Politics and Society in Alabama during the Depression

Times were relatively good in Alabama in the late 1920s, but in the 1930s, the economic and social contexts were quite different. The Depression brought significant suffering and saw the collapse of industrial development as well as more labor unrest. The unrest was not confined to white workers, and it likely heightened conservative whites' anxieties about their capacity to maintain power in the face of national economic and political upheaval. As compared to other states, Alabama's economic straits were particularly dire, as its manufacturing and mining industries were devastated as the agricultural slump that had begun in the 1920s continued. Federal experts identified Birmingham as the large city suffering the worst effects of the Depression nationwide. Both whites and blacks faced severe unemployment; Alabama was one of only three Southern states to experience an absolute drop in white employment in the 1930s (Rogers et al. 1994: 465). In 1929, optimistic city fathers in Birmingham had dissolved its welfare department, and its community chest had served only eight hundred families per year. By 1932, the unemployment rate was more than 25 percent, and the community chest was straining to support nearly ten thousand individuals (Feldman 1999: 239).

This rapid and drastic change destabilized and radicalized elements of the population. Antiunion efforts in the 1920s had been successful, as noted in chapter 4, but the United Mine Workers (UMW) initiated an organizing drive in 1933. Birmingham mine workers sponsored a bitter strike in 1933 and 1934, culminating in a confrontation between strikebreakers and company guards and seven thousand striking miners. Local business leaders and conservative interests branded unionists as Communists and racial radicals, but the federal government had begun to support workers' rights, and by the end of 1934, most mining companies had signed contracts with the UMW (Rogers et al. 1994: 481–82). Disruptive and divisive as this struggle was, it was dwarfed by the textile strike initiated in Huntsville in 1934, in which fifteen thousand workers throughout Alabama walked out of thirty mills. The spark spread nationally, ultimately becoming the largest strike in U.S. history to that point, though the workers failed to gain significant concessions from it. It featured violence, in particular an armed struggle in the streets of Talladega in which two individuals were killed and sixteen wounded (482).

The rapidly growing interest in unionization and confrontation from labor was not solely or even primarily coming from white workers. In sharp contrast to the nadir of the 1920s, union representation increased in the 1930s, and after 1935, unions in Alabama represented fifty thousand workers, of whom more than 67 percent were black. Some of the most prominent black CIO organizers hailed from Birmingham, including Hosea Hudson, Andy Brown, and Henry O. Mayfield (Feldman 1999: 239).

But unionists were not the most radical leftists in Alabama in the 1930s. The Southern Communist Party established its headquarters in Birmingham in 1930, enlisting several hundred members quickly. This development was particularly frightening to white conservatives and remnants of the Ku Klux Klan, as the Communists had their greatest successes with black workers. The Party's membership was about 80 percent black, and several of its most militant and vocal members in Birmingham were black women (Feldman 1999: 238). Black tenant farmers in rural districts were also attracted to communism, and the Communist Party used black fears of Klan violence and repression to recruit rural members. The Party formed a Communist Share Croppers' Union (SCU) that went on strike in the summer of 1931 and was subsequently bloodily suppressed by Klan mobs as the local authorities stood aside. The SCU struck again in 1935, leading to more Klan violence and resulting national embarrassment for Alabama (260–68).

The relief programs of the New Deal likely limited the appeal of radicalism for white Alabamans, even if they did not alleviate completely the dire conditions under which many lived. The establishment of the Tennessee Valley Authority, providing electrical power and the means for more industrialization to northern Alabama, instilled hope, though the promised economic development did not materialize until the 1940s. Major federal initiatives addressed the agricultural crisis, most notably the Federal Emergency Relief Administration's Rural Rehabilitation Division (RRD). The RRD supported rural farmers, enrolling more than one hundred fifteen thousand individuals, who rented land and obtained credit, draft animals, and supplies (Rogers et al. 1994: 446–48). Most of the RRD's programs benefited whites rather than blacks. Despite these programs, in Alabama as elsewhere, the economic crisis of the Depression did not lift until the imminent threat of war began to have an impact at the very end of the decade (510–11).

Politics and Race in the Late 1920s and 1930s

The conflict between the Ku Klux Klan and the conservative Big Mule–Black Belt elites simmered in 1927 and early 1928 but came to a head over the presidential election of 1928. Alabama, a solidly Democratic state, in the ordinary course of events would have been counted as a supporter of Democratic nominee Al Smith. The Klan, which had been deeply shaken by the elites' attack in 1927, saw an opportunity for revitalization through opposition to Smith's nomination. While a Democrat, Smith had two significant liabilities for the Klan and its fellow travelers: he was a "wet" (anti-Prohibition) candidate, and he was a Catholic. The Klan attempted to organize resistance within Alabama's Democratic Party to Smith's nomination but failed; it then established a slate of Klan candidates to be delegates at the national Democratic convention. Joining forces with the Anti-Saloon league and Alabama's chapter of the Women's Christian Temperance Union, the Klan secured the election of most of these delegates, but Smith was nominated nonetheless (Feldman 1999: 160–66).

The Klan and others hostile to Smith vowed to bolt from the Democratic Party and vote for Herbert Hoover in the fall election. Alabama's U.S. senator and Klansman Tom Heflin was probably the most prominent bolter; he made many embarrassing anti-Catholic speeches on the Senate floor prior to the election. The Klan spearheaded the effort against Smith, warning Alabamans that he would institute repressive measures against Protestants and that he was a racial radical who would promote social equality between blacks and whites (Feldman 1999: 168–81).

Democratic elites joined the battle enthusiastically. Conservative newspapers attacked the Klan and accused them of being closet Republicans. The Klan had no monopoly on the use of race as a scurrilous political issue in the campaign. The strategy on which conservative elite Democrats settled was to tap into the *Birth of a Nation* narrative, heightening fears of racial radicalism through Republican rule and Northern intervention in Southern politics and culture. The Klan's extremism would, they claimed, invite a severe Northern response akin to that of Reconstruction. Loyal conservative Democrats publicized Hoover's desegregation of the Commerce Department as evidence of his own plans for implementing racially radical policies. The Democratic Party had, they claimed, established and maintained Alabama as a white man's state and should be trusted to continue to do so (Feldman 1999: 184–89).

Smith barely won Alabama's electoral votes in November amid charges of fraud in the Black Belt, but Hoover won an overall national victory, capturing all but eight states. The Democratic elites now targeted the bolters for revenge, ousting Heflin from the Senate and campaigning vigorously against Klan candidates in the 1930 election. The elites rallied their supporters and faced Democrats who had not chosen sides in the 1928 contest with the imperative to abandon the Klan. Among those who opted to turn on the Klan in 1930 was Hugo Black. The election of 1930 was disastrous for the Klan, which saw its major candidates definitively rejected (Feldman 1999: 194–210).

Formal politics in the era of the Depression thus took place without the participation of the Klan's political machine, which was largely dismantled. The major struggles in the formal political arena centered around Roosevelt and the New Deal, as Alabama's conservative Democrats struggled to square their loyalty to the party with their overwhelming racially motivated fear of federal intervention. As mentioned earlier, this struggle took place in the context of a radicalized and broad political spectrum ranging from the hard-core remnants of the Klan to the burgeoning ranks of the Communist Party, though the range of views represented in formal politics by elected officials and parties was fairly narrow. Within the Democratic Party, which occupied the formal political spectrum almost entirely, the debate was largely between business conservatives who opposed significant intervention in the economy to bolster the cause of labor, and an emerging New Deal wing of the party, which provided Roosevelt with staunch support in Congress and promoted New Deal programs on the state and local level. But as in earlier years, this debate was not a debate between racial reformists and supremacists.

In the 1930 gubernatorial election, outgoing governor Bibb Graves (who had mostly stood on the sidelines in the titanic battles of 1928) supported his lieutenant governor W. C. Davis, who also had the Klan's endorsement. (In the general election, the Klan rallied around longtime supporter and member Hugh Locke, whom vengeful Democrats had driven out of the party over the 1928 fiasco.) Benjamin Miller, the candidate favored by the conservative Big Mules and Black Belt elites, handily won election after a campaign in which he denounced Graves as a tool of the Klan. Miller's promises to return the state to fiscal responsibility and to oust the Klan from its remaining positions of influence and power played well with an electorate exhausted from the 1928 presidential election and suffering the first pinches of the Depression. He governed Alabama through the worst years, serving through 1934, but could do little to convince the conservative Democrats controlling the legislature to take steps to maintain the state's solvency. The financial crisis was so serious that Alabama closed two hundred schools in January 1934, maintaining the others only because federal funds were sufficient to keep their doors open (Feldman 1999: 188–201; Rogers et al. 1994: 496–99).

After his four-year hiatus, Bibb Graves was eligible to run again in 1934, and voters, reeling from the financial disaster of the Depression, reelected him. In contrast to Miller, Graves opposed business interests by siding with labor in some significant disputes and signaling to noncommunist labor leaders that they had a place at the table. Graves was supportive of the New Deal and was instrumental in creating an Alabama Department of Public Welfare in 1935. He also appointed white female reformers to positions in public service, including Daisy Donovan as the head of the Child Labor Division, suffragist and Progressive activist Molly Dowd as a labor mediator, and children's welfare advocate Loula Dunn as Commissioner of Public Welfare (Rogers et al. 1994: 500; Swain 1994: 132–35). Graves's liberalism as demonstrated by his engagement with the New Deal and his willingness to vest governmental power in white women did not, however, extend to racial issues.

In 1938, the gubernatorial race pitted Frank Dixon, supported by organized labor, against Chauncey Sparks, the candidate of business. While laborers were jubilant at Dixon's victory, he quickly disillusioned them by abolishing the Department of Labor and rolling it into his new Department of Industrial Relations. Further underlining his opposition to national New Dealers' liberalism, he fought nationally against efforts to abolish states' poll taxes and to establish national antilynching legislation. His antilabor credentials also included the revival of the practice of calling out the National Guard to break strikes, and he drew on his Birmingham business allies for advice and support (Rogers et al. 1994: 501–2).

Within the struggles between labor and business, between the Klan and the Big Mule–Black Belt alliance, and between New Dealers and their opponents, race remained a visible subtext. Viewing the anti-Klan political efforts as straightforwardly antiracist is a mistake. Rather, opponents of the Klan portrayed the Klan's colorful and violent racism as backward in contrast to a colder and more rationalized racial state that would run things in a sufficiently orderly fashion as to rule out any excuse for federal intervention. The evolution from private violence to public repression mirrored what was happening on the national level (Klinkner and Smith 1999). For the business elites, and even for many Alabaman New Dealers, the key to racial harmony was the smooth and neutral administration of a state system in which white supremacy was the fundamental value. Supremacy was not solely a matter of individual attitudes or even a straightforward ideology or cultural practice, but also an institutionalized principle for the operation of the state. Racially discriminatory laws were to be applied in the interest of the state regime but within a purportedly objective and dispassionate framework. Racial invective in formal legal proceedings was frowned on in part because it communicated directly what was unnecessary to express because it was known by all and, in the idealized version of the white supremacist state, accepted by all. This idealized knowledge was that blacks were inherently inferior to whites, and the state's main interest in them was to ensure that they would serve the white regime with as little disruption as possible.

Alabama's National Scandals: Scottsboro and Hugo Black

Conservative Democratic elites in Alabama worked to ensure that Alabama's citizenry was not perceived nationally as a backward collection of virulent and violent racists, as noted earlier. They campaigned against colorful U.S. senator Tom Heflin in 1930 on the ground that he was an embarrassment to the state for his anti-Catholic speeches on the Senate floor and in other forums. Their goal to keep Alabama's racial politics out of the spotlight suffered two serious setbacks in the 1930s, both arising from incidents that made not only national but also international headlines: the trials and convictions of the Scottsboro Boys and the appointment of former Klansman Hugo Black to the U.S. Supreme Court.

In late March 1931, after a disruption in a boxcar on a train involving alleged fighting between several white men and a group of nine young black men, Jackson County deputies stopped the train in northern Alabama and arrested the young men on charges of raping two white women who were in the boxcar with them. The young men were taken to Scottsboro, where they narrowly escaped an immediate mass lynching. The nine men, referred to in Alabama and nationally as the Scottsboro Boys, were immediately indicted and tried, with a jury returning convictions against eight of them in April. The convicted men were sentenced to death, exciting national and international outrage. The Alabama Supreme Court upheld six of the seven sentences in the spring of 1932, overturning one conviction on the ground that the defendant was twelve years old at the time of the crime (Feldman 1999: 221).[1]

The U.S. Supreme Court intervened, overturning the convictions in *Powell v. Alabama* in 1932 on the ground that the defendants had been inadequately represented by counsel (287 U.S. 45). After a brief turf struggle with the NAACP, the communist International Labor Defense fund took over the defendants' cases for their retrials, in part because the cases had become a celebrated cause internationally. New convictions were obtained after a change in venue (a judge presiding over the first retrial set aside the conviction, and the cases were moved to a court more sympathetic to white interests). In 1935, the U.S. Supreme Court again intervened, this time invalidating two convictions on the ground that blacks were systematically excluded from the juries (*Patterson v. Alabama,* 294 U.S. 600 [1935]; *Norris v. Alabama,* 294 U.S. 587 [1935]). In 1936 and 1937, four of the original defendants were convicted again, and this time the high court declined review. One, Clarence Norris, was sentenced to death. Charges against the remaining four were finally dropped in 1937. By this time, the tide had begun to turn among elites, who recognized the damage caused by the extremely negative national publicity over the cases. While the defendants were accused of inter-

---

1. More information and documents about the Scottsboro trials as well as a detailed time line can be found at UMKC School of Law Professor Doug Linder's Web page on famous trials at http://www.law.umkc.edu/faculty/projects/FTrials/scottsboro/scottsb.htm.

racial rape, the focus on Alabama's criminal justice system in conjunction with perceptions of the purported white victims' lack of absolute purity led to a sharp divergence between national and international media's and elites' reading of the case and that of Alabama's juries. Ultimately, Governor Graves commuted Norris's death sentence, though three of the four convicted defendants were not paroled until the mid-1940s, and Haywood Patterson was in prison in Alabama until escaping and fleeing to Michigan in 1948 (Linder 2003).

The Alabamans who pressured Graves most strongly and pushed most vigorously for the release of all the defendants were not racial liberals. Rather, they were conservatives and well-known opponents of the Klan. Leading newspaper men from the *Montgomery Advertiser* and the *Birmingham News,* which had helped to engineer the conservative defeat of the Klan in the late 1920s, spearheaded the campaign. Grover Hall, editor of the *Advertiser,* initially supported the prosecutions but reversed course in 1937 to call for pardons in order to save Alabama's reputation, which he valued far more highly "than the 'honor' of two 50-cent prostitutes" (Feldman 1999: 226). His real aim was to fend off outside influence or federal intervention as well as to prevent communism from gaining any traction in Alabama, especially among African Americans. The strategy of calling for clemency and Graves's acquiescence, along with the dropping of charges against four of the defendants, had the desired effect: the brouhaha over the Scottsboro trials quickly dissipated in the late 1930s (225–29).

Alabama's racial politics were still in the spotlight in 1937, however, due to Roosevelt's appointment of Senator Hugo Black to replace Associate Justice Willis Van Devanter on the U.S. Supreme Court. Roosevelt was delighted at the opportunity to change the direction of the Court in the wake of the ignominious defeat of his Court-packing plan, and he saw Black as a stalwart New Dealer who would vote to uphold the statutes that the conservative Court had rejected. Black, he felt, would pass muster even with conservative Democrats in the Senate, because Black was himself a senator and a Southerner. The Senate moved to confirm him, despite a brief spat over his Klan membership in the Senate Judiciary Committee. Perhaps anticipating trouble, Black and his wife Josephine departed for Europe immediately after his confirmation and resignation of his Senate seat (Feldman 1999: 229–30).

While the Senate did little probing into Black's connections to the Ku Klux Klan, others found it quite interesting. The *Pittsburgh Post-Gazette,* backed by Republican funds, published a six-piece series detailing Black's involvement with the Klan and trumpeting his acceptance of a grand passport in 1926 entitling him to honorary lifetime membership. A major controversy blew up, and the Blacks found themselves constantly pursued by photographers and reporters in Europe. Leading newspapers across the United States called for him to resign immediately, and numerous political cartoons portrayed him in his Klan regalia alongside the other Justices in their black robes. He drew opposition from a variety of quarters; the right-leaning critics of the New Deal saw the Klan issue as a way to block him, and many Northern New Dealers were genuinely horrified by his past (Feldman 1999: 229–32).

Black had some boosters. Most unhelpful to him was the Klan's initial enthusiasm, even though leading Alabama Klansmen sought to conceal or minimize his connections. Alabamans in general supported the appointment, proud that a native son had the opportunity to serve on the Supreme Court. His most important supporter, however, was Roosevelt himself, along with his staunchest allies. Despite the outrage and controversy (and substantial negative public opinion), Roosevelt never wavered in his desire to have Black sit in Van Devanter's seat (Feldman 1999: 232–34).

Ultimately, the pressure was too great to withstand through simple silence. Black delivered a radio address on October 1, 1937, speaking to approximately 85 million listeners. He was allotted half an hour but spoke for only eleven minutes. In his speech, he addressed the issues squarely and plainly, admitting his membership but emphasizing that he had resigned in 1925. To charges of bigotry, he responded that he had Jewish, black, and Catholic friends and encouraged listeners to consult his voting record in the Senate. He neither apologized for nor explained his membership in the Klan, nor did he say why he had remained silent for the month and a half of the controversy. Roosevelt's closest advisers were appalled, but Roosevelt himself reassured them that the speech would turn the tide. Gallup polls confirmed the canniness of Roosevelt's political instincts: in a poll reported on October 3, 59 percent of those polled believed that he should resign if he had been a member of the Klan, but by October 24, 56 percent of those polled did not want to see him step down (American Institute of Public Opinion 1938). The nation was soon caught up in the looming threat of World War II, and the controversy died down (Feldman 1999: 235). Black of course went on to be a leading liberal voice in his early years on the Court, vigorously defending and expanding the rights of African Americans, Communists, and other politically disempowered groups.

In the controversy over Justice Black, Alabama's elites could do little to challenge the perception of their state as backward and riddled with Klansmen and former Klansmen in positions of authority. In truth, few politicians of Black's generation were untainted by the Klan, though not all had been active members. The scandal over Justice Black, however, obscured the extent to which this was true in other states, even states outside of the South. The Klan had dominated politics in the mid-1920s in Indiana and Colorado, and Oregon and Kansas had both had governors sympathetic to the Klan (MacLean 1994: 18). Nonetheless, the politics of race, memory, and forgetting again served to put Southern elites on notice that they had to ensure carefully that white supremacy would not be perceived as *arbitrary* violence and discrimination against blacks.

The cases of this era served this agenda. National embarrassment and the veiled threat of federal intervention were not direct causal factors in the appellate courts' attention to racist discourse in trials during the Depression, but defense attorneys likely recognized that claims of overt bias were more problematic in the charged atmosphere. Taking up the challenge, appellate judges hewed to the conservative elites' desire to sanitize white supremacy by enforcing it dispassionately and neutrally. This principle arose repeatedly in different contexts as the courts grappled with further questions about the meaning and definition of the crime of miscegenation and its threat to the state. In the process of ruling in these cases, the courts implicitly determined that allowing some defendants to go free was less threatening to the underlying structure of supremacy than failing to sanitize the regime. At the same time, the judges articulated a conception of supremacy as a legitimate form of everyday law that interwove organically through the standard rules of evidence preventing the introduction of inflammatory rhetoric in trials.

Jesse Williams and the Continued Struggle over Racial Definition

By the 1930s, most judges in Alabama were allied with conservative elites, and the cases of the 1930s demonstrate clearly their commitment to the strategy of legal rationalization of white supremacy. As in the 1920s, appellate judges did not hesitate to invalidate convictions of interracial couples on technical grounds, even while maintaining their overall support for the state-based system of white supremacy. In the 1930s, some likely saw the invalidation of convictions as strengthening the state's hand by demonstrating that white supremacy was not based simply in irrational or arbitrary racial prejudice. Instead, it was an embedded, objective, and neutrally applied system, the legitimacy of which ironically rested upon rigorous procedural safeguards for defendants' rights.

Nowhere was this clearer than in the repeated prosecutions and appeals of Jesse Williams, also known as Jesse Lundy. A man of ambiguous race, he engaged in romantic relationships with two white women in the late 1920s and early 1930s, leading to three prosecutions for violation of the antimiscegenation laws. The tale of his trials and appeals demonstrates two things: first, that the state was committed to a rational and neutral application of white supremacy, even at the cost of freeing individual defendants, and second, that the efforts to redefine race in the late 1920s had not been successful in completely closing the loopholes previously exploited by defendants like Percy Reed. Even the stricter standards of racial definition could not provide definitive answers in all cases, and the appellate courts began to carve out a distinction between improper racial invective and the appropriate standard for proving race and thus ensuring that white supremacy would be properly administered.

Jesse Williams lived in Covington County, which is in the south-central part of the state, bordering on Florida. He was arrested, tried, and convicted of miscegenation three times with two different women, once in 1929, a second time in 1930, and finally in 1933. In all three cases, his race was a significant issue at his trial. While different state solicitors handled the first two cases, in all three Williams relied upon the same attorney, E. O. Baldwin, and the same judge presided over the trials.

In the first trial, the question was one of intermarriage. In April 1928, Williams had allegedly married one Louise Cassady, a young white woman.[2] In their marriage license, the couple claimed that he was twenty-one and she was nineteen and that both were white. The couple was married (but not living together) for eight to ten days before being arrested for violating the antimiscegenation statute.

The state solicitor apparently anticipated problems in proving Williams's

---

2. Cassady was between the ages of sixteen and eighteen, so the judge transferred her case to the county probate court (*Williams v. State,* bill of exceptions 1930: 6).

race because Williams's mother was recognized as a white woman and she was married to a white man. It sought to do so in three different ways: by entering evidence regarding Williams's physical appearance at birth and afterward, by arguing that his associations were primarily with blacks, and by arguing that his mother had had the opportunity to have intercourse with a black man. The defense's strategy was to undermine the state's evidence regarding race but not to prove affirmatively that the state's evidence was incredible. In presenting its case on Williams's physical appearance, the prosecution sought to establish certain physical characteristics as touchstones for race, but the defense responded by arguing that these characteristics were not exclusive to blacks.

The state's first witness regarding Williams's race was an eighty-two-year-old black midwife, Sarah Bryant, who testified that she had assisted at between six and seven hundred births of both black and white children (*Williams v. State,* bill of exceptions, testimony of Sarah Bryant 1930: 10). The state solicitor qualified her as an expert due to her vast experience. The jury probably gave her testimony a great deal of credit not only because of her experience, but also because they perceived her as a black woman who accepted and was willing to defend the racial order. She claimed that, while black children were not born with heavy skin pigmentation, certain differences between white babies and black babies did exist at birth: "When a white baby is born it is as fair and as tender as a little tender chicken and a colored baby when it is born is between a white and a yellow color and its skin is rough, it isn't tender. I can tell them the minute I lay my eyes on them" (id.). She was not present at Williams's birth but did see him when he was less than an hour old. She described her first encounter with Jesse Williams and her immediate recognition that the child was not white. "I went to the bed and looked at him and he did not have tender skin. I did not tell any one because I liked his mother's father and mother all right but I told my own man about it. He had thick lips" (id. at 11). On cross examination, the defense got Bryant to admit that she had never delivered an Indian baby and did not know if Indian babies had the same characteristics as black babies, but Bryant maintained on redirect examination that Williams was part black (id. at 12–14). The racial binarism endorsed in the previous era required the placement of Williams into the category of either whiteness or blackness, and the prosecution sought to use the witnesses' expertise to rule out whiteness as a plausible categorization.

Another witness was a local doctor who had some experience in distinguishing race in young children and had examined Williams as a young infant, claiming that he knew the definitive and unmistakable marks of blackness. Dr. Broughton asserted that, while pure black children were easy to distinguish at birth, mixed-race children sometimes had very light skin. One could still identify a mixed-race child by its hair, the texture of its skin and the thickness of its lips, but these were not the best means of identifying race. Broughton testified that "with a boy the characteristics never fail for the testacle [sic] sack is always black and that is the way you can determine" (*Williams v. State,* bill of exceptions, testimony of Dr. L. E. Broughton 1930: 15). He then revealed that, when he had examined Williams at the age of one, Williams's testicles were black (id.). The defense again sought to raise questions about whether Williams's physical appearance might have been due to an Indian ancestor, to Dr. Broughton's extreme annoyance (id.). Broughton admitted that he did not know whether Indian babies had black testicles, but like midwife Bryant, he continued to argue stoutly on redirect examination that the child he had examined was part black (id. at 15–16).

A coworker (race unspecified) of Williams's testified to additional evidence regarding Williams's racial heritage. The state solicitor elicited testimony from him that "I am famaliar [sic] with the odor of a Negro when he gets hot and when he gets hot he smells peculiar. I have seen the efendant [sic] get hot when working with him and could detect the odor about him and it was the odor of a Negro. . . . I got pretty close to him when he tussels [sic]" (*Williams v. State,* bill of exceptions, testimony of H. C. Johnson 1930: 22). White men also smelled when they worked hard enough to break a sweat, but Johnson maintained that the smell of a white man's sweat was substantially different from the smell of Williams's sweat. Here too, the witness was unable to testify on cross examination as to whether Williams's sweat smelled like that of an Indian: "I have never smelled a hot indian [sic] and do not know what kind of an odor they give off" (id.).

Associational evidence was much more difficult for the state to muster. Midwife Sarah Bryant claimed that she had never seen Jesse Williams associating with either whites or blacks particularly, but she did remember that he had been sent home when he attempted to attend white schools (testimony of Sarah Bryant 1930: 11). Likewise, witness Jack Stanley testified that he had never seen Williams associating with white people, but admitted that he had never seen him attending a black church or black school (*Williams v. State,* bill of exceptions, testimony of W. Jack Stanley 1930: 20). Upon pressure, Stanley admitted, "The only thing I base my judgment on that he has Negro blood in him is his color" (id.).

The state solicitor's final tactic was to allege that Williams's father had not been the white or Indian man to whom his mother, Fronie, had been married at the time of his birth, but rather a black man named Joe Atkins. Bryant testified that Atkins was present when Williams was born and that she had seen him at the Williams place several times (testimony of Sarah Bryant 1930: 11). Another witness testified that he had seen Atkins and Williams's mother together prior to Williams's birth in questionable circumstances (*Williams v. State,* bill of exceptions, testimony of H. I. Mitchell 1930: 25). The most damaging evidence, however, was that of Amer Williams, the man who was married to Jesse Williams's mother when Jesse was born. He testified that at the time of Jesse Williams's birth, he and Fronie had only been married for two weeks and further that he had only been seeing her for about six months prior to their marriage (*Williams v. State,* bill of exceptions, testimony of A. J. Williams 1930: 30).

At the end of the trial, the court carefully charged the jury that they had to be satisfied beyond a reasonable doubt that Williams was part black in order to convict him (*Williams v. State,* given charges 1930: 1–2). Nonetheless, admonished the judge, "You do not have to find, as argued by the Counsel for the defense, any degree of Negro blood in him, but all that is necessary for you to do is to find that he is either a Negro or the descendant of a Negro" (*Williams v. State,* bill of exceptions 1930: 2). The jury found that Williams did have some degree of black ancestry and found him guilty; the judge sentenced him to six and a half to seven years in the state penitentiary.

Williams's appeal rested on technical grounds regarding the inadequacy of the charge, but he also claimed that the judge should have instructed the jury that if he honestly believed himself not to be black, he should be exonerated (*Williams v. State,* bill of exceptions 1930: 2). The judge did charge the jury that they had to be convinced "that the defendant has Negro blood in his veins" (id.). The appellate court, apparently unwilling to venture into the minefield of defining race, based its reversal of Williams's conviction on the fact that the state had not adequately proven an intermarriage (*Williams v. State,* 125 So. 690, 691 [Ala. App. 1930]). The justice of the peace who had married Williams and Cassady had been operating under an expired commission and did not have the authority to conduct marriages when he officiated at the wedding (id.). Williams was free, but his status with respect to white women was unclear.

The appellate ruling is somewhat curious. The uncontroverted testimony in the case demonstrates that Cassady and Williams fully intended to marry each other and that they believed themselves to be married after the ceremony. They had a valid marriage license recorded in probate court, and the probate judge who was responsible for maintaining the records testified that the license itself was in perfect order (*Williams v. State,* bill of exceptions, testimony of Judge H. J. Brogden 1930: 7). The intention to form a marriage could be inferred both from their procuring a marriage license and from their participation in a marriage ceremony, even if the ceremony was itself invalid.

The problem was that, because of the lack of proof of cohabitation and because they had not been charged with an attempt to violate the law against interracial marriage, their conviction could only rest upon a legally valid intermarriage, which required a formally valid marriage certificate (the license alone was insufficient). The appellate court did not address the viability of a prosecution for attempt but confined itself to an analysis of whether Woodham could have been acting under color of state law. Because the court concluded that he could not have been acting under color of law with his expired commission, the formal conditions necessary for a valid attempt to contract an illegal marriage had not been met, and the conviction could not stand (*Williams v. State,* 125 So. 690, 692 [Ala. App. 1930]). While this severely narrow interpretation of acting under color of law worked in Williams's favor, it likely reflected a legal context that had built an extremely narrow framework to accommodate white quasi-state actors and their accomplices who had participated in racist violence and intimidation against blacks in the earlier decades.

Jesse Williams found himself in legal trouble again only three years after his initial conviction was reversed. This time, he was accused of committing adultery or fornication with a white woman rather than intermarriage, possibly having realized that attempting to formalize a marriage to a white woman was risky due to his ambiguous racial status. The state solicitor maintained that he had engaged in sexual relations with Bessie Batson, a white woman who lived on the property of Joe Lundy, his maternal grandfather. Williams was again convicted of engaging in an interracial relationship of adultery or fornication.

The question of his race was again a key point. The prosecution recalled Sarah Bryant and Dr. Broughton as witnesses in this trial and qualified them as experts; they both testified that "they had made examination of the defendant in his infancy and from certain infallible signs found on his body they found him to be a person of negro blood" (*Williams v. State,* 146 So. 422, 422 [Ala. App. 1933]). This testimony was unproblematic for the appellate court, but several of Williams's witnesses were asked on cross examination whether Williams "look[ed] like a white person" without having been qualified as having knowledge about the characteristics of the white race. The appellate court ruled that these questions were improper. It also claimed that the state's "two very willing witnesses" who testified to Williams's cohabitation with Batson were not credible. The state solicitor had also not definitively proven that Williams's mother had herself had an illicit relation with a black man resulting in Williams's birth (id.).

Most troubling to the appellate court, however, were the state solicitor's comments to the jury. He claimed, "Since the days of the Carpetbagger colored people have thought, and still think that they are as good as a white man." The defendant objected, and his objection was sustained, but the judge refused to remove the case from the jury. The emboldened state solicitor engaged in a lengthy racial diatribe to the jury in his closing statement, albeit interspersed with the defendant's objections.

> Some negro men, brought from the jungles of Africa, took that white woman and ran off with her—took that woman and lived in adultery with her. . . . This man, gentlemen of the jury, a man of maturity, a man that knows that this law exists, a man that can't help but know it, a man . . . that has stumbled up against it before. . . . And he takes this woman in the face of it, under the protest of the white people in that community and he parades her up and down the street, off in the woods, and says: Do what you can about it. And he does it, gentlemen of the jury, for a period of several months, until there could be convened in this temple of justice eighteen good men, a grand jury of this county, who says to you that, we are going to do what we can to stop it. . . . And then, gentlemen of the jury, up here last year, the first time we see Jesse Lundy, and as the testimony discloses before this jury, the very first time he is in company with a white woman. . . . Old Joe Lundy has stood back of him. I imagine the old man is trying to beat the law of the land with a negro grandchild. . . . Gentlemen of the jury, the desire has existed in this man's brain, years and years, to have intercourse with a white woman. (Id. at 423)

The trial judge allowed the rant to continue and refused repeatedly to sustain objections or to remove the case from the jury.

The appellate court saw this as highly improper. The state solicitor's statements were too inflammatory to the jury and required not only the sustaining of objections but the more serious sanction of a mistrial. The court explained that the state solicitor's argument to the jury, "when considered as a whole . . . discloses an argument filled with an appeal to that racial prejudice, so easily aroused and so hard to control, when it relates to sexual intercourse between a negro man and a white woman" (id.). Such an argument would overpower reasoned deliberation and judgment. The law, admonished the court, "guarantees to every defendant, white or negro, a fair and an impartial trial, free from undue appeals to passion or prejudice" (id.). The opinion cited the solicitor's prejudicial argument as the principal reason for reversing Williams's conviction.

But intrepid state solicitor Reid did not give up, immediately charging and trying Williams again. At the third trial, he again sought to prove Williams's race, addressing the mistakes he had made in the previous prosecutions. He again called Sarah Bryant, who was now eighty-nine years old, as a witness. In this case, she testified again that black or mixed-race newborns had rougher skin than their white counterparts, but she introduced additional evidence about the differences between white children and black children: "There is a mark on them. You never seed a white person with such a mark. The colored children has got a mark across the shoulders and it is just as black as a hat, the girls has, and the boys is marked down below, and it is as black as a hat down below" (*Williams v. State*, bill of exceptions, testimony of Sara Bryant 1933: 10).[3] She again described seeing Jesse Williams as a newborn, but this time she incorporated the definitive testimony that Dr. Broughton had provided in the last trial, claiming that Jesse had the "mark of a darky": black testicles (id. at 9–10). As in the earlier trial, she refused to be shaken from her testimony, arguing throughout that Williams was black, not white or Indian: "If he weren't a Negro I ain't one. . . . You have got my experience in it from my heart" (id. at 10). She also seemed contemptuous of the defense's attempts to suggest that Williams got his skin color from Indian ancestry on his mother's side, maintaining firmly that Williams's maternal grandparents were white people (id. at 8).

The state again entered extensive evidence about Williams's mother Fronie and her alleged connection with Joe Adkins (or Lundy). Much of the testimony paralleled that entered in the earlier trials, but the state solicitor

---

3. The court stenographer in the final trial spelled her first name without an *h* at the end.

had a new white witness, Jerry Woodall, who testified specifically about the relationship between the two. He claimed to have seen them together many times in the daytime and once at night (*Williams v. State,* bill of exceptions, testimony of Jerry M. Woodall 1933: 21). This testimony addressed and attempted to reverse the previous finding in *Williams II* that no illicit relation had been shown between Fronie and Joe Lundy (*Williams v. State,* 146 So. 422, 422 [1933]).

Williams himself had not testified in the first two trials. In his third trial, he took the stand to protest his innocence with regard to Bessie Batson, swearing that "I never did sleep with Bessie Batson in my grandfather's house. . . . I never did walk up and down the public road with my arm around Bessie Batson. I never did go with he [*sic*] to the woods to get flowers. I was never with Bessie Batson a single time in my life. I never had relations with her, in any way, a time in my life" (*Williams v. State,* bill of exceptions, testimony of Jesse Williams 1933: 76). He claimed that an enemy of his, who had sworn to bring him down and had chosen this means of doing so, had triggered the series of prosecutions (id. at 60). Despite his denials, Williams was again convicted and sentenced to five and a half to six and a half years in the state penitentiary.

On appeal, Williams argued that, while the closing argument had not been prejudicial (which had doomed the second conviction), the solicitor's conduct during his examination and cross examination of witnesses had been so laden with prejudice as to warrant reversal. He also argued that his race had not been properly established. Finally, he objected to the prosecution's entrance of evidence about his own prior attempted marriage as irrelevant and inflammatory.

On the question of race, the appellate court clarified that the state had the duty to show credibly that Williams was a descendant of a black man; in order for his race to be established as black, the state had to demonstrate that Joe Adkins was Jesse Williams's father. The state's use of Woodall's testimony was a step in this direction, but the state solicitor had failed to show that "the alleged association between [Fronie Williams and Joe Adkins] . . . occurred within the time to make the testimony material to the issue under inquiry" (*Williams v. State,* 152 So. 264, 265 [Ala. App. 1934]). Other evidence had suggested that Woodall worked in the community several years before Jesse Williams's birth, and thus that the required allegation that any relationship between Williams's mother and Joe Adkins had actually resulted in the birth of Jesse Williams had not been made. The court ruled both that Woodall's testimony had not been properly grounded temporally and should have been excluded and that the state had not adequately proven that Jesse Williams was the son of a black man (id.).

As problematic, though, was the tenor of the state solicitor's questions in attempting to prove Williams's race. In the discussion about the relationship between Adkins and Jesse Williams's mother, the state solicitor interrupted Williams's cross examination of a witness to ask abruptly, "You have always understood that he (Joe Adkins) is the daddy of these colored children, haven't you?" The trial court judge sustained Williams's objection to this interjection, but the appellate court held that the question was sufficiently inflammatory and prejudicial as to warrant an immediate mistrial. The opinion, citing prior case law arising from nonracialized controversies, characterized the question as "so poisonous and improper as to be almost immune from eradication" (id. at 266).

The prosecution also purported to address the question of adultery by raising the issue of Williams's marriage to Louise Cassady. At the trial, the state solicitor had not only asked whether Williams had been previously married but also mentioned Cassady by name (*Williams v. State,* bill of exceptions, testimony of Jesse Williams 1933: 77). The state solicitor also appeared to be attempting to elicit testimony that Williams's relationship with Cassady had continued after the trial and appeal (id. at 78). The trial was taking place before the same judge who had presided over the two previous trials, so bringing Cassady in was not simply an attempt to establish the elements of adultery. Rather, this line of questioning was designed to remind the jury that Williams had previously been involved with a white woman and to suggest that he had perhaps been involved with two white women at once. The appellate court ruled that this line of questioning was "wholly immaterial" and that allowing it was prejudicial and inflammatory (*Williams v. State,* 152 So. 264, 266 [1934]). On the basis of these multiple errors, the court invalidated Williams's third conviction for miscegenation.

In all three attempts, the state was unable to secure a conviction that would survive an appeal. The trial judges, closer to community standards and prejudices about race, sought to apply the rules articulated in previous decades. The question of defining race arose in each trial as a major point of contention, but the appellate cases turned on different legal issues. In the first case, the appellate court had evaded the question of racial definition entirely, basing the reversal of Williams's conviction on procedural grounds unrelated to race. The second and third appeals touched on the question of racial definition but did so indirectly, as Williams was able to convince the appellate court that the state's evidence about his mother's alleged liaison with a black man was not properly grounded and that the state solicitor had made inappropriate comments about Williams's alleged father. In none of these cases was the appellate court willing to tread on the ground established both by the *Weaver* case and the statutory redefinition in 1927, though Williams had asked for consideration on this basis. Still, the end result for Williams was that he three times avoided lengthy terms in the state penitentiary for being commonly perceived as a black man who had been involved with a white woman. Most notably, the statutory change did not produce any marked differences in the ways that state solicitors and defendants argued about race. State solicitors still relied on evidence about the defendant's appearance and associations as well as evidence about heredity, and Williams's defense attorney still sought to convince the jury that Williams was not black for purposes of the statute. In part, though, Williams evaded a lasting conviction because his race was ambiguous even by the stricter terms established in the transformative debates of the late 1920s.

The center of appellate debate had shifted, however. The state, through the agency of appellate judges, insisted that racial invective had no place in a formal legal trial. The appellate court's presiding justice Bricken invalidated convictions of Williams twice because the state solicitor engaged in rhetoric that invoked stereotypes of predatory black masculinity. The first ruling was perhaps not surprising; the state solicitor's conduct during the closing statement was blatant and obviously designed to play directly to the local jury's deepest fears of black male–white female interactions. But what should be made of the second invalidation, based primarily on one inflammatory question interjected during the defense's cross examination of a state's witness? In this case, Bricken insisted that even a judicial instruction to ignore the question would have been insufficient. Once the question had been asked, the only proper course of action was for the trial judge to declare a mistrial. The trial judges, ruling from the bench with concrete white and black individuals before them, did not act definitively to guarantee a sanitized trial, and thus Williams's defense attorney saw an opportunity for his client.

While little information can be located on specific judges without significant political ties or positions, Bricken was likely not a radical advocate for equality. His rulings in the *Williams* cases passed without commentary in major Alabaman newspapers and apparently had little effect on his standing. He remained the presiding justice for the court of appeals, issuing rulings in later appeals concerning convictions for miscegenation in that capacity (see, e.g., *Rogers v. State*, 193 So. 871 [1939]). This suggests that the rulings did not arise from oppositional ideology on his part. Like the conservative Democrats who had opposed the Klan, he challenged explicit and overt manifestations of racism, but not necessarily for racially liberative purposes. Instead, these rulings reinforced the continuing efforts to rationalize and contain racial prejudice and maintain white supremacy within the network of formal legal rules. A "fair" formal trial could mean that no blacks were on the jury. It could mean that it took place in a venue where the individuals were known and where the white male members of the jury could be expected to come down hard on those accused of violating social norms. It meant that state actors would continue to enforce vigorously all of the legal policies designed to implement white monopolies on political power and cultural capital and that blacks would continue to be prosecuted, convicted, and punished differentially for crimes against the system of white supremacy. But all of these things had to happen within the formal legal framework as established and maintained by conservative elites. The ad hoc, personal, individual exercise of racial prejudice and white dominance had to be severely limited within the institution of the law in order to maintain the legitimacy of the legal system and, as many judges appeared to believe by the 1930s, the state itself.

This phenomenon extended beyond cases involving convictions for miscegenation. In 1928, the Alabama Supreme Court overturned a black man's conviction for murder because the state's attorney had misquoted the defendant as directing a codefendant to "kill the white son-of-a-bitch" (witness testimony suggested that the closest the defendant had come was "Kill him, God damn him!") (*Lockett v. State*, 218 Ala. 40, 43–44 [1928]). In another case, *Goldsmith v. State*, the high court reversed a black man's conviction for murder even though uncontroverted evidence showed that he had fatally shot a white man. Goldsmith had killed a white intruder in his black female neighbor's home, and the jury's decision to convict him of murder rather than to consider manslaughter was driven, the court ruled, by "passion or race prejudice" and was thus unsustainable (*Goldsmith v. State*, 232 Ala. 436, 437 [1936]). Nonetheless, while the principle of sanitized trials did help individual black defendants, the Alabama high court ensured that it would not result in a reworking of the power structure, as its steadfast rejection of appeals by the defendants in the Scottsboro trials demonstrated.

Legitimately Proving the Sexual Act and the Intention behind It: *Jackson, Fields,* and *Murphy*

In the 1930s, three appeals touched on issues that had appeared earlier. The appellate courts again had to address questions about the sufficiency of evidence and the formal criteria for convictions resting on the underlying definition of adultery or fornication. In these cases, the appellate courts uniformly found that, for various reasons, the state had not adequately shown that the elements of miscegenation had been properly proven. Given the previous rulings on these questions, what new issues did these cases raise and why were state solicitors tripping up? The gradual consensus building around the need for legitimation of white supremacy in the legal system provided new avenues for defense attorneys who charged that state solicitors had improperly used racially inflammatory language. In addition, the appellate courts delved further into questions about what was required to prove a felonious, as opposed to merely inappropriate or even disgusting, relationship.

Sam Jackson was convicted of miscegenation in 1929 (*Jackson v. State,* bill of exceptions, appeal bond 1930: 5.5). A black man, he was charged jointly with Alexander Markos, identified as a white woman, for committing interracial adultery or fornication. They were tried separately, and the prosecution proceeded primarily on adultery, as the evidence tended to show that Jackson was married (*Jackson v. State,* bill of exceptions, oral charge to jury 1930: 6). The state's solicitor, apparently having attended to the debates of the 1920s, took care to establish both Markos's race and Jackson's. When Jackson's defense attorney elicited testimony that she might have appeared to be of mixed racial heritage, the state's solicitor asked her to remove her coat and exhibited her to the jury (*Jackson v. State,* bill of exceptions, testimony of Alexander Markos 1930: 16). He also called two black witnesses to identify Jackson as a black man; one testified that Jackson was black because he associated with other blacks (*Jackson v. State,* bill of exceptions, testimony of Jessie Collins, testimony of Ivy Collins 1930: 16–17). These efforts were apparently successful, as the defense was unable to raise sufficient doubt either to convince the jury not to convict or to present an issue for appeal.

The state's case rested primarily on the testimony of Alexander Markos. Markos was approximately seventeen years old when the incident giving rise to the prosecution occurred. Originally from Ohio, she had been living in Birmingham for a short while and had known Jackson for about six months. She claimed that she had exchanged three or four notes with Jackson when she was in her father's store, which served a primarily black clientele. While she made no real effort to justify her conduct, she did say that she did not know that Jackson was black and in fact believed him to be white. She testified that one day, she had met him in the street and they had gone to a black woman's house. Jackson paid the woman a dollar for the use of a room; they entered the room and engaged in a single act of sexual intercourse. The encounter took place on a Tuesday and she was arrested on a Wednesday (*Jackson v. State,* bill of exceptions, testimony of Alexander Markos 1930: 9–15). The other significant corroborating evidence the state's solicitor sought to introduce was from the owners of the house where the alleged act of intercourse had taken place. The state's solicitor tried repeatedly to get the male owner to admit that Jackson and Markos had left behind a soiled towel, but Ivy Collins insisted that he could not determine whether the towel was dirty or clean (*Jackson v. State,* bill of exceptions, testimony of Ivy Collins 1930: 17–18).

The defense undermined Markos's story by raising questions about her actions and morals and by eliciting contradictory testimony from her. Jackson's attorney made much of the fact that she was young and had spent most of her life in Ohio, where norms about interracial interactions were different. He tried to get her to admit to having "been with negroes a lot in Ohio," but the question was rebuffed by the trial judge (bill of exceptions, testimony of Alexander Markos 1930: 12). He also elicited testimony that Markos's father had seen the correspondence between her and Jackson and had had no significant reaction, though he had told her "it was not right to write to a negro" (id. at 14). This mild reaction was important, claimed Jackson's attorney, because "surely the presumption is that if a white father knows that a negro is writing to his daughter he would say at least 'Don't buy any more cigarettes here'" (id. at 15). Markos was also trapped into contradictions about her age, her knowledge of Jackson's race, whether her father knew that she had written back to Jackson, and whether she had held herself out to Jackson as white or black (id. at 12–16).

Despite the shakiness of the state's star witness, Jackson was convicted, and Markos was apparently never prosecuted. Jackson was sentenced to four to five years in the penitentiary and appealed on several grounds (bill of exceptions, appeal bond 1930: 5.5). He objected that he had been convicted without the state's having obtained a conviction of Markos, that the trial court had failed to exclude improper evidence, that the questioning of one of the witnesses had been improper, and that the evidence did not support the verdict in the case (bill of exceptions, assignment of error 1930: 25). The appellate court reversed primarily because the state had built too much of its case on the unreliable testimony of Alexander Markos.

To Jackson's charge that the state's failure to prosecute Markos constituted reversible error, the appellate court clarified that the state did not have to pursue both purported wrongdoers in the same trial. If the two had been tried together, a split verdict would have been improper, but when the trials were severed, allowing one potential defendant to testify against another was not improper. This situation raised special concerns, however: "no conviction can be had on such testimony unless corroborated by other evidence tending to connect the defendant on trial with the commission of the offense" (*Jackson v. State*, 129 So. 306, 307 [1930]). The rule was simply an application of the general evidentiary principle regarding the testimony of accomplices to a crime. While the record did not reveal anything about the state solicitor's dealings with Markos, she was possibly convinced to testify against Jackson in exchange for not being prosecuted herself, which made her testimony legally less reliable.

With this caveat in mind, the court ruled that miscegenation had not been adequately established. Even with Markos's testimony read in the worst possible light, the prosecution had shown only that the two had engaged in intercourse once and not that they had intended to continue their relationship. An offhand comment of the trial judge was the final nail in the state's coffin. In a dispute over the defense's effort to develop more details about Markos and her history, the state's solicitor had objected to a line of questioning as irrelevant by claiming, "This man is charged with miscegenation, if the court please. The only issue is whether or not he had intercourse with this woman and whether or not she is a white woman and he is a negro." The trial court judge responded, "I think so." This framing of "the only issue" was improper because it did not include the well-established requirement that the couple in question had to intend to continue their illicit relationship, a key element of adultery. By not pointing this out, the court had possibly left the jury with the impression that proof of a single act of intercourse with nothing beyond it was sufficient to ground a conviction (id.).[4]

This case spoke to the relationship between the alleged miscegenators and what constituted credible evidence of miscegenation. In the early twentieth century, the courts had established a firm rule that a relationship of adultery or fornication had to be proven in order to ground a conviction for miscegenation; this case added nuance to the rule by clarifying how legal actors were to understand the testimony of one alleged miscegenator against another. While it was a crime requiring two participants, their guilt was individual, and, in a severed trial, they were to be treated individually under the prevailing rules of evidence regarding accomplices. Likewise, the case incorporated a particular understanding of young white women's interactions with black men—the appellate court noted Markos's lack of credibility not just in light of the contradictions in her own testimony but in her father's failure to react as one would expect of the white father of a white girl being pursued by a black man.

The next case did not at first glance seem to be a promising candidate for reversal, given its resonance with fears of black men's sexual predation against vulnerable white women. At about twelve or twelve fifteen one night in 1929, two police officers went to the home of a black man, Elijah (Lige) Fields and rapped on the door. After several minutes, they pushed the front door open and entered the house. The single bedroom was bolted shut, but one officer pushed it open. There they encountered Lige Fields and Ollie Roden, a white woman. Both were dressed, but Roden was shoeless and the single bed "seemed to be kind of ruffled." Also in the house were two suitcases full of women's clothing; Ollie Roden admitted owning them. The couple had been seen a few nights earlier alone together in an automobile at about two in the morning (*Fields v. State,* bill of exceptions, testimony of Brigs Wright 1929: 7–8).

Fields, however, had a strong argument to make that the circumstances were not so damning as they appeared. At the time of his trial, he was fifty-five years old (*Fields v. State,* bill of exceptions, judgment entry 1929: 4). His acquaintance with Ollie Roden (who was in her mid-twenties) was through

---

4. In fact, the judge had made this rule quite clear in his charge to the jury. He instructed them three times that they had to find that Jackson and Markos had lived together in a state of adultery and that a single act of intercourse would be insufficient to establish such living together (bill of exceptions, charge to jury 1930: 5–7).

her father, whom he had known for thirty or forty years. He had been drawn into a gradual practice of helping the Roden family, particularly Ollie Roden, over the last year. Roden's father had asked Fields in the spring to transport her to the county hospital, where she apparently spent significant time over the next several months (*Fields v. State*, bill of exceptions, testimony of Elijah Fields 1929: 12–13). While the nature of Roden's ailment was unclear, she had sores on her body and legs, significant bladder trouble, and was continually menstruating. She claimed to be unable to wear shoes for more than brief periods. The clothing was in Fields's room because he had been transporting it for her; due to her condition, she was unable to keep her clothing clean for very long and required frequent changes (*Fields v. State*, bill of exceptions, affidavit of Ollie Roden, testimony of Mrs. Roden 1929: 19, 22).

Ollie Roden's father Rufus was also a witness for Fields. He affirmed that he had known Fields for thirty-five years but that Fields had not met his daughter until the year of the incident. He had asked Fields to pick up Ollie Roden at the hospital because Fields had a large car that traveled more smoothly than Rufus Roden's Ford roadster. He explained Fields's willingness to shuttle Ollie Roden back and forth: "I was not paying Lige anything for coming out there, but I have known him a long time and at one time when I was doing well and had some money I loaned him money at different times, having loaned him as much as fifty dollars at a time. We were friendly and I asked him to do this for me . . . . I knew that he took care of things" (*Fields v. State*, bill of exceptions, testimony of Rufus Roden 1929: 20–21). Ollie Roden's mother also confirmed that Roden's health was poor, that she was continually menstruating, and that her relationship with Fields was strictly based on his driving her to and from the hospital and occasionally driving her on outings with other members of the Roden family (*Fields v. State*, bill of exceptions, testimony of Mrs. Roden 1929: 22–23). Both of Ollie Roden's parents testified that they trusted Fields and that no amorous relationship existed between their old acquaintance and their daughter.

The jury thought otherwise, perhaps influenced by the state solicitor's inflammatory closing statement. He said, among other things, "Do you want your daughter or your wife carried by Lige Fields to his house in the wee small hours of the night? . . . If you find the defendant not guilty, you place your stamp of approval on what Lige Fields did . . . Gentlemen of the jury, suppose it had been your daughter who was treated like this white girl was treated by this negro. . . . You should convict the defendant in this cause in order that similar occurrences may not happen to your daughter." The trial judge excluded all of these statements but did not declare a mistrial (*Fields v. State*, bill of exceptions 1929: 24–25). Fields was convicted, and the trial judge sentenced him to two years plus a day to three years in the state penitentiary, two years being the minimum sentence for miscegenation (bill of exceptions, judgment entry 1929: 4). While Roden was initially charged with miscegenation, like Alexander Markos she was apparently never tried.

In Fields's appeal, the appellate court looked at the totality of the circumstances. The state's case, while damning, required two assumptions: that Roden and Fields had engaged in intercourse and that they intended to continue to do so. These elements had to be inferred from the circumstances in which the case took place, which included not only the night on which Fields and Roden were caught but also the background events and circumstances leading up to that night. The court seemed particularly impressed by the testimony of Ollie Roden's father, not only in its content but by the fact that the father of the white woman accused of engaging in interracial intercourse with the defendant was testifying on the defendant's behalf. Because there was no substantive evidence other than the officers' descriptions of the circumstance in which Roden and Fields were found, the evidence was insufficient to find Fields guilty (*Fields v. State*, 132 So. 605, 606 [Ala. App. 1931]). The ruling implicitly endorsed the defense's efforts to remove the story from a frame of black male predatory sexuality and place it in the alternative gendered frame of the faithful and tame black retainer who willingly effaced himself to help the white folks. Adding to the ruling in *Jackson,* the courts could be seen as tracing out a theory of what constituted adequate proof of adultery or fornication around the sex act itself—without reliable witnesses either to the act or to the defendant's agreement to continue the relationship, a conviction could not stand.

Furthermore, as would occur in *Williams II* and *Williams III,* the court expressed dissatisfaction with the state solicitor's conduct. The opinion explained, "Certain remarks in his argument were a direct appeal to race prejudice with a suggestion of an abuse of the white woman by the negro." While the trial court sustained objections to these statements, the proper remedy was to declare a mistrial because the atmosphere "was not conducive to a fair and impartial trial for one of appellant's race accused of such an offense" (id.). The main problem was the imagery of the vulnerable white daughter assailed by the black man at night; by personalizing this imagery to the jury, the solicitor had instilled an indelible and uncorrectable vision of danger that tapped into the deepest fears of miscegenation for white fathers of white daughters. While this case was litigated on the appellate level as the first Scottsboro trials were taking place, in the much lower profile *Fields* litigation, the appellate judge acted carefully to protect the superficial legitimacy and fairness of the legal process in applying a racially discriminatory law.

The next appeal also involved questions of what had really happened between two defendants accused and convicted of miscegenation. Unlike the previous cases in the 1930s, both the white woman and the black man were tried. Alice Murphy, as the state would argue, was not a young white girl beguiled into a relationship with a man of questionable race (like Louise Cassady or Bessie Batson), a naive child unfamiliar with the racial norms and practices of Alabama (like Alexander Markos), or a sickly woman needing protection and assistance (like Ollie Roden). Instead, she was an adult married woman accused of actively engaging in disgusting and shocking conduct with a black man in an unruly and impoverished mixed-race settlement.

Alice Murphy lived with her husband and children (who were apparently from a prior relationship) in a tent near other families living in tents, a not uncommon living arrangement in areas hard hit by the Depression. Coleman Cole lived nearby in an abandoned dynamite house. The precipitating incident, testified two witnesses, was their overhearing the obvious signs that Murphy and Cole were engaged in an interracial relationship. They claimed that they had heard a conversation between Murphy and Cole in which one told the other "Elmer [Murphy's brother-in-law] is watching me," and then that they heard the bedsprings squeaking (*Murphy v. State,* bill of exceptions, testimony of Felix Perry, testimony of E. L. Bailey 1936: 7–8, 11–12). They also claimed to have seen the two talking together at other times. Bailey claimed that he had overheard a conversation between Cole and Murphy's brother-in-law Elmer in which Cole had told Elmer Murphy that he did not want any trouble over Alice Murphy but joked that if she were up at his house, he would "burn her ass up" (bill of exceptions, testimony of E. L. Bailey 1936: 12–13).

The state solicitor also produced testimony that an intoxicated Alice Murphy had left the tent later that day to search for her husband. Accompanied by Elmer Murphy, perhaps staggering down the road, she allegedly shouted out to her neighbors that if her girls returned to the tent, they should stay with them, as "she was going to blow the town with her sweet daddy" and to tell her husband Buster that she was going to blow the town (*Murphy v. State,* bill of exceptions, testimony of Clarence Ingram 1936: 18). Both spouses were arrested, Elmer for public intoxication and Alice for miscegenation, and Coleman Cole, also intoxicated, was picked up by the police shortly afterward (id.). The deputy who saw Coleman in jail testified that his pants were unbuttoned and that his genitals appeared to be covered with semen; he corroborated other testimony that Cole was intoxicated (*Murphy v. State,* bill of exceptions, testimony of Ray Blakely 1936: 21). The court clerk testified that, when Cole was arraigned shortly afterward and asked whether he pled guilty or not guilty, he replied "Boss, I was just so drunk I don't know what happened" (*Murphy v. State,* bill of exceptions, testimony of Ernest McClure 1936: 35). Cole denied that he had been drunk or that he had said that he was drunk during his arraignment (*Murphy v. State,* bill of exceptions, testimony of Coleman Cole 1936: 34–35).

Buster Murphy, Elmer Murphy, and two of Alice Murphy's daughters testified on the behalf of the defendants, as did both defendants. Buster Murphy testified that he had been with his wife during the entire morning in question, having left the settlement later in the afternoon (he also testified that Alice was unable to find him because he himself was also in jail, having been arrested for public intoxication) (*Murphy v. State,* bill of exceptions, testimony of Buster Murphy 1936: 24–25). Elmer denied that he had suspected his sister-in-law of having an interracial affair or that she had threatened to leave town with her "sweet daddy" (*Murphy v. State,* bill of exceptions, testimony of Elmer Murphy 1936: 26–27). Alice Murphy categorically and indignantly denied that she had engaged in any sexual relationship with Cole or that they had ever had intercourse (*Murphy v. State,* bill of exceptions, testimony of Alice Murphy 1936: 32–33).

The defense tried to explain the prosecution as being motivated by spite on the part of the man who called for the arrest of Cole and Murphy. The attorney asked Felix Perry, who had alerted the police, if he had been operating a bootlegging joint with Cole, who had solicited customers for him until the Murphys moved into the tent and disrupted their arrangement (*Cole v. State,* bill of exceptions, testimony of Felix Perry 1936: 10). This argument was unsuccessful with the jury and judge; the jury voted to convict and the judge sentenced both defendants to six- to seven-year terms in the penitentiary (*Murphy v. State,* bill of exceptions, judgment entry for Cole, judgment entry for Murphy 1936: 57, 58).

The appellate court did not hesitate to condemn Cole and Murphy for their lifestyle, tacitly endorsing the New Deal along the way. The disgusted judges wrote that the evidence presented in the case "affords an unexampled illustration of the degree of moral filth that exists in a few isolated localities in our state. It points the way to renewed and redoubled efforts on the part of those agencies of our government having in view the social welfare of our people. It . . . is nauseating to all that is finer in our natures" (*Murphy v. State,* 176 So. 473, 474 [Ala. App. 1937]). So scandalized was the court that it refused to narrate the facts in the case, characterizing the story as "sordid testimony" (id.).

Nonetheless, the question was a straightforward legal inquiry. Was the evidence so weak that reversal was warranted? Specifically, the court questioned whether, even if one presumed that the state's evidence was correct, the "preponderance of the evidence against the verdict is so decided as to clearly convince the court that it is wrong and unjust" (id.). While the evidence supported a finding that Cole and Murphy lived in a stew of vice, drunkenness, and gendered transgression, they were being tried for the specific offense of miscegenation. For that specific offense, the evidence did not support the verdict.

Why was the evidence insufficient? The attorney general must have wondered also, for he petitioned for rehearing, asking that the appellate court give more specific grounds for its reversal. The court again insisted that the "crucial testimony" was "too vile and disgusting to be repeated any place" (id.). The per curiam opinion, however, outlined sufficiently its reasons for reversal—the court looked to the testimony of the state's key witnesses regarding Coleman Cole's extreme state of intoxication and suggested that Cole, if that intoxicated, would have been incapable of engaging in intercourse. As a result, "the sine qua non of the conviction of appellants was thus positively shown by the state's evidence not to have taken place" (id.). The Alabama Supreme Court denied review, and apparently the case was dropped.

The defendants in these three cases were quite different. Sam Jackson allegedly became entangled in a romantic relationship with a young girl who did not understand the racial topography of Alabama. Lige Fields got in trouble because of his willingness to help an old acquaintance with his sick daughter. And Alice Murphy and Coleman Cole were transgressors in multiple ways tied to their poverty, disorderly lives, and alleged abuse of alcohol. Nonetheless, all had their convictions overturned because the state had not produced definitive evidence either that intercourse had taken place or that the required agreement to continue an adulterous connection was present. In an era when the legal system was working out the distinction between legitimate and illegitimate expressions of racial prejudice, drawing evidentiary lines carefully was significant. Three of the four defendants were not individuals with whom one would expect the courts to have any sympathy—the testimony in *Jackson* suggested without rebuttal that he had indeed had intercourse with a white woman, Alice Murphy was a transgressive figure on multiple levels, and Coleman Cole's drunkenness was his only viable defense against the charge of miscegenation. The courts still emphasized that the elements of the crime had to be established properly and without inappropriate racial invective, even though the individual defendants had engaged in some form of wrongdoing.

Bailey and *Rogers* and the Question of Parallel Outcomes

Earlier cases had hinted that the crime of miscegenation raised complex issues of joint and individual guilt or lack thereof. While most crimes involved separate acts of wrongdoing by culpable individuals, miscegenation was by necessity a joint offense, requiring both parties to agree to continue an illegal relationship or to attempt an intermarriage. The only way in which miscegenation could involve a single wrongdoer would be under the provision that barred the solemnization of marital rites for an interracial couple— a justice of the peace or minister who officiated at an interracial marriage could be prosecuted and treated as any other individual accused would be.

By the 1930s, the law had become settled that both parties to an alleged interracial relationship need not be tried. This was the situation in both *Jackson* and *Fields;* the black male partner stood trial while the white female partner did not, although both had initially been charged with miscegenation. Often, though, the cases were like *Murphy,* with both individuals going to trial for miscegenation either jointly or separately, and both being acquitted or convicted. Given that the evidence in these cases was almost identical, it is not surprising that even when trials were severed for the accused couple, the outcomes were the same. The sort of argument that might convince a jury to acquit would have to be something that would nullify the offense, even if it was directed at only one of the defendants.[5]

---

5. For instance, an argument about one defendant's race might be directed only at that defendant, but by invalidating the racial element of miscegenation, it would work to the benefit of both.

In 1939, however, the appellate court believed that it was dealing with a unique situation in the appeals of Granston Rogers and Wiley Bailey.[6] These evidently unrelated cases were addressed together because they raised the same issue: whether a conviction could be sustained if the other codefendant was not convicted. The appellate court relied upon *Reed v. State* to rule that miscegenation was necessarily a joint offense, and if one partner was acquitted, the other must also be acquitted. Both convictions were overturned on this ground (*Bailey v. State,* 193 So. 873, 873 [Ala. 1939]). The state objected to this ruling and appealed both cases to the Alabama Supreme Court, which also considered them together.

The supreme court disagreed with the ruling of the court of appeals, finding that an acquittal in one case did not necessarily require a directed verdict for the other defendant. The court cited the (race-neutral) rule for adultery that, although a joint physical act was required, the intentions of the parties to the act could differ, thus allowing a split verdict of guilt for the committed adulterer and lack of guilt for the one-shot participant (id. at 874). The court also reversed the court of appeal's ruling in favor of Rogers, ruling that the principle articulated in *Bailey* governed that case as well (*Rogers v. State,* 193 So. 872, 872 [Ala. 1939]). Upon reconsideration, the court of appeals reinstated the convictions of both men (*Rogers v. State,* 193 So. 871 [Ala. App. 1940]; *Bailey v. State,* 193 So. 871 [Ala. App. 1940]).

This principle would not be a factor in most cases in which both accused miscegenators were prosecuted. By the 1930s, Alabaman juries had become accustomed to convicting or acquitting both parties, regardless of their racial configuration. Nonetheless, the rule underlined that miscegenation was an individual offense against the state, and even if one half of the couple escaped, the law would not allow a free pass to the other party. This principle allowed for the freeing of a defendant who perceived an act of interracial intercourse as a mere onetime fling while pursuing his or her partner if she or he took the act more seriously as the initiation of a relationship. This principle, taken with the clarifications about proving intercourse and intentions, underlined policymakers' and judges' fear of the formation of interracial relationships as opposed to single acts of illicit intercourse.

---

6. The records in both of these cases were not locatable at the Alabama Department of Archives and History. The appellate rulings from both the court of appeals and Alabama Supreme Court reveal very little about the factual backgrounds of the cases, not even the races of Bailey and Rogers (both were male).

Depression-Era Evidentiary Refinements and the Rationalization of Prejudice

The tough years between 1928 and 1939 were a time of upheaval nationally and in Alabama, as the political structure dealt with the privations and pressures of the Depression. In Alabama, the end of the 1920s also coincided with the decline of the political Klan, but this decline, fostered by elite attacks, did not correspond to an end to racialized violence. Rather, it heralded a continuing process of rationalization and embedding of white supremacy in the structure of the state. This process was evident in the appeals of convictions for miscegenation, which underlined the themes of the remaining difficulty in proving race, the active disfavoring of individual expressions of racial prejudice in a formal legal setting, and the clarification of the type of evidence required to prove miscegenation. In contrast to the cases decided near the turn of the century, when white supremacy was initially articulated and established, these years saw the courts as more active participants in the effort to express a legitimate racial regime for the public consumption of both Alabamans and national observers.

This process reflected state actors' efforts to channel and control racial animosity, not merely to express cultural values through its exercise of its administrative and institutional power. Rather, key conservative state actors refined the administration of white supremacy and pushed back against the uncontrolled expressions of inflammatory rhetoric and violence, both through the specific rules of evidence in the courtroom and in the broader conservative Democratic efforts to rein in the Klan. While it would be a mistake to ignore social debates over race and racism in Alabama at this time, especially with the reemergence of organized radical politics, the state struggles took place within a narrow political range and incorporated a good deal of political opportunism in efforts to prevent any move toward more federal oversight or intervention.

Jesse Williams was prosecuted unsuccessfully three times in the late 1920s and early 1930s. Each time, the state's solicitor achieved a conviction, but each time the conviction failed on appeal. Williams was a man of ambiguous race, and the state's solicitor had to rely on folk wisdom about racial characteristics, making his case that Williams was black on the basis of a doctor's testimony and an elderly black midwife's. The privileging of Sarah Bryant's knowledge about race—Bryant being in the most structurally subordinated categories of identity available along the axes of race and gender—demonstrated that expertise about race was inherent in accumulated folk wisdom as personified by the old wise woman. Her truculent refusal to be shaken from her conclusion that Williams was black appeared to be rooted in more than a desire to curry favor with whites in power. Like most Alabamans, she expressed implicit disapproval of the crossing of racial boundaries that had allegedly produced Williams, and her testimony was part of a concerted effort to classify him solidly, protecting the social structure and its white supremacist base from disruption in years when disruption was the dominant theme of the day.

The trial records do not reveal why Williams, having narrowly escaped his first lengthy prison term, chose to take up with another white woman (or at least to put himself in a position making such a charge possible). Perhaps he genuinely believed himself not to be black and saw the first outcome as vindication. Perhaps his father really was Joe Adkins, who was posthumously congratulating himself on having put one over on the white community both in sustaining an interracial relationship and in producing offspring who violated the racial boundary. Perhaps Williams was simply the victim of an overzealous prosecutor who was determined to avenge his previous failure to uphold what he saw as the state's need to maintain a rigid color bar.

Nonetheless, Williams's route of escape would not work for most defendants in light of the process of redefinition in the 1920s. Even in Williams's case, two of the racialized reversals were based on the state solicitor's racial misconduct rather than on ambiguity in racial definition. The appellate court did address racial definition indirectly by emphasizing that rhetorical excess could not substitute for solid, admissible proof that a purportedly black defendant had descended from a black ancestor. In the few cases where such ancestry was in question, physical and associational evidence and expert testimony could not always definitively solve the hereditary question.

Negative national publicity for Alabama resulted from the scandalous trials of the Scottsboro defendants and the publicity around the Klan's influence in Alabaman politics connected to Hugo Black's nomination to the U.S. Supreme Court. Alabama was perceived nationally by racial liberals as backward and hopelessly ridden with racism. Such liberals might have been surprised to see Alabama's less visible courts operating in less visible cases to invalidate convictions that may have been influenced by individual acts of rhetorical racism in the defendants' trials. In cases like the second *Williams* case and *Fields,* these rulings were perhaps not surprising, as the state solicitors had used their closing statements as opportunities to play on racism and specific fears of black male encroachments against white females. In these cases, however, objections to these statements were sustained at the trial level, and the appellate court was ruling not simply that the statements were unacceptable but that they required the trial judge to grant a mistrial to the defendant. In the third *Williams* case, tried and appealed just as the furor over the Scottsboro case was reaching its peak, the appellate court ruled that a mistrial should have been granted on the basis of a single inflammatory remark, interjected by the state solicitor as the defense was examining a witness.

In these cases, the courts were not embracing a systematic retreat from white supremacist values. The juries in the cases were all white, and the law under which the defendants were being prosecuted was a cornerstone of the white supremacist agenda. Instead, the courts monopolized and rationalized supremacy as a tool of the state. It had to be exercised carefully, politically, and dispassionately to support the state's interests. In sharp contrast to the Klan's colorful violence in the 1920s, the courts in the 1930s insisted that such overt attitudes and reactions had no place within the formal apparatus of the state. In part, this was likely a reaction to the Klan's overreaching in the late 1920s and its defeat by conservative white elites. These same elites were those most concerned with the public relations problems posed by the Scottsboro trials and Black's nomination to the Supreme Court. Eager to present Alabama as a modern, developed state with opportunities for business, elites sought to suppress the individual, populist, uncontrolled expressions of racial prejudice where they could.

The courts were an ideal location for the development of a white supremacist infrastructure to be administered by the state. The 1930s thus saw the fruition of the constitutional and state-building project of the convention of 1901. What the elite conventioneers envisioned in 1901, a regime that would separate the races in an orderly fashion and provide for the smooth administration of a state designed to advance white elite interests, was precisely what the courts sought to enforce in the 1930s. Ironically, this enforcement took place through reversing convictions for one of the most disruptive individual behaviors against the supremacist state. Perhaps by overturning these convictions, the courts were expressing their confidence that the norms had become deeply enough rooted both in the state's structure and in the social fabric to risk these rulings freeing suspected miscegenators in the greater interest of bolstering their vision of the state.

At the same time, the courts continued to refine the rules about what was necessary to prove miscegenation under the adultery/fornication element. (And the first *Williams* trial clarified that a purported intermarriage had to be a valid purported intermarriage.) The emerging rule of the 1930s was that a prosecutor had to show that an act of intercourse had occurred and show some reliable indication that the parties intended to continue their liaison. Because the defendants of the 1930s (with the possible exception of Alice Murphy) had not made statements that could constitute confessions, the evidence was circumstantial, and the courts had to sort out what kind of circumstantial evidence would be sufficient. In *Jackson*, even one party's admission of the act of intercourse was not sufficient, since the state's solicitor made the error of not convincingly alleging any intention to continue the relationship. The state solicitor in *Fields* was more careful, but the court looked to the surrounding circumstances, particularly the illness of the female partner, and saw the relationship between Lige Fields and Ollie Roden as nonromantic. The outcome in *Fields* was probably also related to the fact that the couple was not the kind of transgressive couple about whom the state had to worry: he was elderly by the standards of the day, and she was not capable of reproduction. The appellate court was able to place their relationship in the nonthreatening frame of one between a loyal, nonsexualized, faithful retainer and his white patron's sickly daughter. In *Murphy*, the state's own evidence (despite the appellate court's extreme distaste with the case in general) suggested that the required act of intercourse could not have occurred. In all of these cases, defense attorneys and prosecutors disputed at trial over how the defendants' relationships met or did not meet the criteria for the crime of miscegenation. On appeal, however, the struggle focused more narrowly on the boundaries for racial invective and further refinement of the proof needed to demonstrate a genuine, ongoing sexual relationship.

These refinements hewed to the general rules regarding adultery but also implied that the state's real fear was of the formation of familial relationships or relationships that might produce mixed-race children. The rules contained an implicit exception for prostitution, and this exception carried over to allow continued access to black women for white men as long as the individuals involved did not take these liaisons seriously as relationships. Because the evidence would generally be circumstantial, prosecutors had to present a holistic picture of the defendants' lives to demonstrate the connections between them, but such stories could be challenged by alternative narratives that recast evidence of sexual involvement as prostitution or recast evidence of connections between defendants as nonsexual. When these reframings were successful, defendants could convince the appellate courts to overturn their convictions, because the state had not successfully elicited enough evidence to support the conclusion that the defendants intended to engage in a long-term, familial interracial connection.

The resonance of the framings of miscegenation versus something else depended upon the gendered and racialized stereotypes available to prosecutors and defense attorneys. One might wonder briefly why prosecutors seemed to be making the same mistake repeatedly in evoking the image of black male predatory sexuality without linking it directly to the facts of the case they were trying, since the courts had made it fairly clear that such rhetoric in the courtroom would not lead only to sustainable objections but to a mistrial. Probably, they had become accustomed to using this tactic because it worked with all-white juries. With respect to the white women involved in these cases, state solicitors were probably making careful choices about charging and offering leniency in exchange for testimony. While some trials were conducted jointly, many were severed, which would theoretically enable a prosecutor to portray a white female partner in a relationship with a black man as an innocent and exploited victim in his trial and an active participant in hers. But if the witnesses' testimony supported a story of victimization, prosecutors in the cases discussed here appeared to choose instead to use the alleged female miscegenator as a supporting witness rather than pursue a conviction for her misdeeds. Such a tactic would not work with an alleged miscegenator like Alice Murphy, whose violations of norms of white womanly behavior likely influenced the state solicitor's choice to try her.

In line with the emergence of these prosecutorial strategic choices, the Depression-era courts ended the decade with a clarification that the crime of miscegenation was an individual offense against the state. While the crime required a partner, both partners did not have to be convicted. Even if one partner were to be acquitted in a severed trial, the other partner could legally be convicted. This rule underlined the relational aspect of miscegenation: if one partner took a sexual encounter more seriously than the other, the more serious partner was the one who could be branded a felon.

These rules taken together, established primarily in the context of prosecutions of black men and white women, emphasized that the most dangerous interracial relationships were those based on serious commitments between men and women of different races. The drunken white woman who may have attempted intercourse with a black man was transgressing and was a threat, but not in the way that a mixed-race couple intending to establish a lasting relationship would be. Even in the latter case, however, the forms had to be followed precisely. *Williams I,* read in conjunction with the other cases of the 1930s, underlines again that state actors wanted to prevent interracial families, and that suppressing the act of intercourse and the intention to continue engaging in it were crucial elements of this interest.

These cases also demonstrate the continued, perhaps heightened, charged nature of relationships between black men and white women. While the appellate courts demanded that racial invective remain outside of the courtroom, decisions about whom to prosecute and whom to convict clearly had racialized and gendered overtones. In the appellate cases of the 1930s, the state portrayed black men as predators (though prosecutors occasionally overplayed this theme) and their white partners as either gullible and vulnerable (like Alexander Markos and Ollie Roden) or as themselves beyond the pale of white womanhood (Alice Murphy). The next chapter will look more closely at the connections between white power and masculinity in the context of interracial relationships that evaded the state's punitive hand.

One of the hallmarks of Southern white masculinity and patriarchal power was the capacity to control property and its disposition within the family. Testator L. Ryal Noble had a valuable parcel of land with two houses on it, and he wished to leave it to his children. In 1901, he wrote a will exercising the full privilege of his gender and skin color to provide for his family after his death, expecting that his desires would simply be fulfilled.

Noble's white male nephew, Gross Scruggs, saw an opportunity when his uncle's will was presented for probate. Despite the fact that Noble apparently had six children, Scruggs would have inherited the property if Noble had died without a valid will. While Noble was unquestionably categorized as white, his six children were legally black, having been produced in the course of a relationship between Noble and black woman Kit Allen that had started in the 1870s and persisted until Noble's death in 1912. Furthermore, Noble's children were unable to produce the original will and provided only a copy to the probate court. When the case was tried before a jury, Scruggs predictably won, but Noble's children appealed on several grounds.

The case raised a welter of questions about race, gender, property, and power in the postbellum South. How would the continuing process of legitimation and rationalization of white supremacy deal with the disruptive element of "private" white male interests in their mixed-race families? Could the courts accommodate both white supremacy and white male control over property? To what extent did legal doctrine and established lines of argument build in modes for recognizing, if not legitimating, the mixed-race family? And could the strongest norms of racism, sexism, and upper-class domination be used to secure access to resources for those on the subordinate end of the spectrum? In Alabama's legal universe, whiteness was clearly both a mark of dominance and a fit subject of state regulation and control. How would key state actors' articulations of white supremacy play out in legal challenges to attempted interracial transfers of wealth implicating interracial intimacy?

By the second quarter of the twentieth century, whiteness had become simultaneously cultural and institutional, as noted in previous chapters. In the South particularly it found expression in the cultural exercise of power and in the various types of formal legal structures established and developed to ground regimes of white supremacy (see, e.g., Hale 1998; Gilmore 1996; Hodes 1997; Wallenstein 1994). In Alabama, this process had as its aim the construction and maintenance of a pure state in which whiteness was intertwined with liberal individualism and civic virtue. While the expressions of this relationship had shifted through the long process of racial formation, the core link between whiteness and power remained at the base. White men's efforts to dispose of property across racial lines created an apparent paradox, as their private desires seemed to undermine the supremacist state. But as in the criminal appeals of the 1930s, appellate courts generated a framework that simultaneously reinforced supremacy while benefiting individual black defendants. While white men's dispositions of property to their lovers and children found favor in the courts, this favor was expressed in a way that underlined supremacist ideology and incorporated an explicitly gendered component.

The families who were the subjects of these cases knew that their relationships took place in the shadow of the criminal law. As noted earlier, much scholarship on interracial intimacy has focused on the commonplace observation that white men were freer to form sexual connections with black women than were black men with white women (Romano 2003; Robinson 2003; Gross 1998; Hodes 1997; Pascoe 1996). In fact, however, in Alabama and elsewhere, many white men were prosecuted for and convicted of violating antimiscegenation codes and sentenced to lengthy prison terms. Ordinarily, interracial couples were charged together and often received the same sentence even when their trials were severed, though by 1940, the Alabama Supreme Court had ruled that this did not necessarily have to be the case.[1]

Still, white male privilege was deeply embedded in Southern society and

---

1. Two appellate cases noted the incongruity of convicting one defendant if the evidence had been found insufficient by a jury to convict the partner, making it difficult to justify punishing black women, white women, and black men while letting white men go free (*Reed v. State* 103 So. 97 [Ala. App. 1922]; *Jackson v. State,* 129 So. 306 [Ala. App. 1930]). As chapter 5 explained, the Alabama Supreme Court clarified that both defendants need not be convicted in *Bailey* and *Rogers* in 1939.

law even after the Civil War. Peter Bardaglio's work shows that while the nature of patriarchy changed from being personally supported and enforced to being supported and enforced by the state, white male power persisted as a structuring factor in the postbellum era (Bardaglio 1995). This power tied in closely with emerging state-sponsored supremacist ideology and legal practice, as the courts negotiated the protections for white male agency in light of the larger goal of maintaining the white state.

This situation was most pointed in cases involving wills through which white male property owners attempted to give their land and personal property to those whom they considered their families although those families were classified as black under Alabama law. Attempts to form interracial families were understood not just as breaches of morality but as specific threats to the state, as the early appellate cases had established. In three cases reaching the Alabama appellate courts between 1914 and 1944, a "mixed" family formed and maintained in contradiction of this strong public policy was at the center as a white patriarch attempted to devise his property to his subordinated black family. These three cases, which were the only reported appellate cases in Alabama addressing interracial bequests by white men, hint at how the legal system linked the larger agenda of rationalization of the white state to the related issue of protecting white male interests in controlling property. While the three appeals were temporally separated and do not provide a thick and continuous story about interracial bequests, they provide a window into how the legal system developed rules to address these tensions. And as with the appeals of convictions, the Alabama courts demonstrated through their handling of such cases the contours of white dominance, even when this dominance meant that individual black litigants would benefit.

Earlier Doctrine Regarding Interracial Transfers of Wealth

Rules of inheritance had long been used as a form of economic control over blacks, as Cheryl Harris points out. During the antebellum era, Southern states, like Northern states, barred illegitimate children from inheriting in the absence of a will, but the prohibition was even stronger with respect to black offspring of white fathers. Such children inherited only their mothers' statuses as slaves, rendering them irrevocably separate from legitimate white families. These principles ensured that the category of legal heirs would not be contaminated by blackness (Harris 1996: 330).

In this regime, property was more than simply a legal matter of who owned what. Ownership of property was a dimension of liberty and a marker of full freedom; only white men had complete access to the entire panoply of potential rights inherent in property ownership. Independence incorporated a concept of self-sufficiency, but this self-sufficiency was itself parasitic not just on property rights but on actual ownership of property. This operation of property excluded all blacks and women from full citizenship, but blacks were doubly burdened by the potential or actuality of their being property themselves (Harris 1996: 344–45).

The framework of white male authority could be tested, however, when a testator left a clear record of his intentions to trespass across these boundaries. Adrienne Davis looks at case law from before and after the Civil War to show that, as in Alabama in the second quarter of the twentieth century, nineteenth-century courts were willing to allow white men's wills to prevail over state-based policies that severely restricted blacks' access to property as owners (1999). Her narrative, like this one, however, is not an unambiguous celebration of black resistance to white power, for the courts' opinions upheld white men's control over property without significantly undermining the underlying principles of white dominance and black subordination.

Davis notes two South Carolina cases addressing testamentary dispositions by white men to their black concubines and their mutual children. By the time of the second case (decided in the 1850s), South Carolina, like most states, had passed a statute barring testamentary emancipations of slaves, which complicated the matter. (Alabama's rule for many years had been that only the legislature could free a slave through a special act, but this was unusual, as most states allowed owners to do this without state intervention.) In both cases, white heirs who would have inherited in the absence of a will challenged the dispositions of property to the black heirs named in the wills, claiming lack of capacity and undue influence (Davis 1999: 249–58).

In both cases, the black heirs prevailed on appeal, despite the high court's expressed distaste for the circumstances. Davis reads the cases as coding formal deference to the established rules for wills within the language of disdain (256). While the testators were engaged in reprehensible relationships, they were on some level adhering to traditional principles of white male obligation and authority over the family, and the court saw these dispositions as natural if disgusting (259).

Davis shows that deference to white male privilege continued in the postbellum era, noting a remarkable case in which the Georgia Supreme Court awarded an estate worth half a million dollars to a white man's illegitimate mixed-race daughter and her family. In this case, the trial court admitted the will into probate, and both the appellate court and the Georgia Supreme Court rebuffed claims by white intestate heirs that the daughter had unduly influenced her father, that she and her mother had defrauded him by misrepresenting her parentage, and that the disposition violated public policy (1999: 279–80). Again, while the court deplored the relationship, it rooted the man's right to dispose of his property in a lengthy history of freedom to control and manage property through contract and will.

To what extent would these principles survive over time and across state lines? Further, how would they look in the context of a fully articulated white supremacist state? In fact, the outcomes and language were remarkably similar, though the particular type of white male authority they supported had shifted subtly in the intervening years. In Alabama, these cases underlined and reinforced the pattern of legitimation established in the early decades of the twentieth century. As in other areas of law, general rules developed in race-neutral contexts proved applicable for the Alabama appellate courts considering property transfers across racial lines, but these rules took on new meanings in their racialized contexts. As a few other Southern judges were beginning to invalidate interracial bequests, Alabama upheld the testators' wishes by maintaining a strict code of facial neutrality as to the racial backgrounds of the litigants on the appellate level.[2] Nonetheless, the trials and appellate opinions relied upon racialized and gendered stereotypes to construct the litigants as the facially neutral rules were being applied to them.

Background Legal Principles Governing Challenges to Wills

Before turning to the analysis of the cases involving attempts to transfer wealth and real property interracially, it may be helpful to sketch the context in which these cases occurred by examining the general principles that governed intraracial transfers of wealth and real property in postbellum Alabama. Just as the general rules governing intraracial adultery and fornication provided a guide for courts considering criminal miscegenation, the rules addressing intraracial wills would provide the background against

---

2. Thanks to Peggy Pascoe for clarification on this point.

which cases involving interracial wills would be heard. In order to understand this context, we can look at cases involving claims of undue influence. In these cases, the testator's intentions were clear, but someone or ones objected to the bequest on the ground that the testator had not been expressing his or her real interests. Many of these cases resulted in appellate decisions in the late nineteenth and early twentieth centuries, and these decisions established the parameters within which the Alabama courts would intervene to nullify a clearly expressed dispensation of property, thereby substituting its own judgment for that of the testator.

Far more of these cases reached the appellate level than cases involving interracial transfers. Between 1900 and 1950, Alabama's appellate courts considered approximately 64 cases in which challenges based on claims of undue influence threatened the testamentary dispositions of white women and white men.[3] In these cases, the formal basis for challenging the disposition was always undue influence, but the nature of the objection and the appellate court's focus often differed. The cases were relatively evenly split between white women and white men, with female testators accounting for twenty-eight cases and males for thirty-six. While the female testators' bequests fared significantly better on appeal than the males',[4] these numerical differences reveal little about the ways that the courts understood the cases and the type of evidence appropriate to sustain a claim of undue influence.

The basic rule governing undue influence was articulated repeatedly in these cases. Undue influence sufficient to nullify an otherwise valid bequest had to "amount to coercion or fraud." This influence had to be "tantamount to force or fear, and which destroys the free agency of the party, and con-

---

3. I say "approximately sixty-four" because I have assumed that the testators were white if race was not specifically mentioned in the case. As discussed later, a few claims of undue influence did involve people of color, but their race was marked in the courts' discussions of the facts. One case that did not mention race, *Barnett v. Freeman*, almost certainly did involve a black female's bequest, but the testator's race was readily identifiable because of her surname. The disparity in the number of cases involving black and white litigants—approximately sixty-four white testators versus two cases involving blacks' bequests, two claims of undue influence regarding transfers inter vivos, and two cases involving intestate succession—arises from several factors. First, blacks were significantly less likely to own property and, if they did own property, to own enough of it to give rise to legal disputes concerning its disposition. Second, in general blacks encountered more difficulty than whites in accessing the legal system on all levels, ranging from obtaining formal legal advice when transferring or willing property to encountering structural and cultural difficulties in resorting to the courts to resolve disputes. These differences were likely magnified on the appellate level, where pro se actions appeared to be relatively rare, if not absent, in the civil cases I have encountered.

4. Women's bequests were upheld or the trial court's invalidation of them was reversed in twenty-one cases; men's bequests survived review in only fifteen cases.

strains him to do what is against his will" (*Councill v. Mayhew*, 55 So. 314 [Ala. 1911]). The burden of proof was on the person claiming undue influence, and affirmative evidence had shown that the testator's will had been overborne. Showing that a testator willed property against what his or her heirs expected was insufficient, and even a showing that significant property was willed outside of the family circle did not give rise to any presumption of undue influence.

The only situation in which the courts were willing to presume undue influence was where a confidential relationship existed between the testator and the beneficiary and "it is shown that the person who is a large beneficiary under the will actively participated in its preparation by making suggestions as to the disposition of the property" (*McQueen v. Wilson*, 31 So. 94, 95 [Ala. 1901]). In these situations, the beneficiary would have to show that the testator had received independent and competent advice in preparing the will, bolstering the argument that the testator's bequest resulted from her or his own decision rather than from improper influence.

Within these parameters, juries (usually) had to decide when testators were indeed exercising their own judgment in preparing their wills and when their true intentions were overborne by beneficiaries' influence. The inquiry, based as it was on questions of autonomy, coercion, influence, and "true" intentions, was infused with expectations rooted in gender and race. The role of gender and race remained unstated, however, and legal rules about what constituted improper influence rested upon neutral language. The situation was complicated additionally because of the tension between the ideal image of the autonomous agent disposing of property—a white man in full possession of his mental and physical capacities—and the real circumstances of most testators in these cases, who, regardless of gender, tended to be old, sick, frail, and often under the influence of opiates or other mind-altering drugs.

While many cases produced appellate opinions, most of them involved technical challenges to the charges issued to juries by judges and questions about the admissibility of evidence. These challenges revealed little about the operation of gender-based conceptions of autonomy, being more directly concerned with procedure. Some cases, however, did address the sufficiency of the evidence. This subset allows the sketching of some general beliefs about testators' legal capacity to dispose of their property.

In cases involving male testators, the courts applied the general rule that undue influence claims had to meet strict evidentiary standards. The courts seemed more inclined to rule against the validity of a man's will if contestants were able to introduce some evidence that his true intentions were not expressed in the document submitted for probate or if they could claim credibly that the man suffered from legally defined insane delusions. Both of these legal frameworks avoided creating the impression that the court was clearly substituting its own judgment for that of the testator. For instance, in *Posey v. Donaldson,* the Alabama Supreme Court ruled that the question of undue influence should have been for the jury to decide, overturning a directed verdict. In this case, the testator, a "very old and very infirm" man, had declared repeatedly his intent to give a share of his estate to his granddaughters, the children of his deceased son (66 So. 662, 663 [Ala. 1914]). His will, however, awarded the entire estate to his previously estranged wife and his surviving sons; his wife had returned to live with him shortly before his death and had discouraged contact between him and his daughter-in-law and granddaughters (id.).

In several cases, claims of undue influence merged with claims of lack of capacity, and the lack of capacity appeared to be a stronger basis for invalidating specifically expressed dispositions of property. Successful challenges on these grounds largely arose when a male testator disinherited "the natural objects of his bounty," usually his children. While a will disfavoring direct descendants was not per se questionable, "if the manifested prejudices of the testator against the natural objects of his bounty can be explained on no other theory than that of insane delusion, and the will is the direct offspring and fruit of such insane delusion, this is sufficient to avoid it" (*McLendon v. Stough,* 118 So. 647, 648 [Ala. 1928]). Such insane delusions generally took the form of persistently held negative and incorrect beliefs about potential legatees (see, e.g., *Batson v. Batson,* 117 So. 10 [Ala. 1928]; *Wainwright v. Wainwright,* 137 So. 413 [Ala. 1931]), though in one case the problem was that the testator had given extraordinary powers to a trustee and there was some question as to whether the testator fully understood his own actions (*Zeigler v. Coffin,* 123 So. 22 [Ala. 1929]).

Only in *Tipton v. Tipton,* decided in 1947, did the court unambiguously present the male testator as a weak party whose will had been overborne through outside influence. In this case, the ordinary dominance of parent over child was reversed. In the context of the parent-child relationship between J. J. and Victor Tipton, the court explained that the son Victor was in fact the dominant party: "The father was over 80 years of age, deaf, and feeble both in body and mind. The son . . . was about 50 years of age, apparently in good health. . . . The evidence shows that . . . Victor handled financial matters for the father and exerted considerable influence over him" (*Tipton v. Tipton,* 32 So.2d 32, 34 [Ala. 1947]). As the court read the relationship, the father's age and ill health had "reversed the order of nature and that dominion of the parent finally became subservience to the child" (id.). J. J. Tipton had been ill for several months prior to signing the deed but had recently become obsessed with fear of his imminent death, which he expressed to a doctor. The doctor advised the family that his mental and physical condition was poor, and a few days after J. J.'s contact with the doctor, Victor contacted an attorney and had the deed prepared. The court found that the circumstances under which the deed was signed were suspicious and that Victor had not adequately shown the fairness and equity of the transaction.[5]

In cases involving male testators, the courts upheld bequests by men in various circumstances of enfeeblement or dependency. In two cases in which the sufficiency of evidence was in question, the testators allegedly had used intoxicants excessively (see *Sharpe v. Hughes,* 80 So. 797 [Ala. 1918]; *Watkins v. Yeatman,* 66 So. 707 [Ala. 1914]); in four others, the testators signed wills as they were suffering terribly or under the influence of mind-altering drugs for their fatal illnesses (*Ritchey v. Jones,* 97 So. 736 [Ala. 1923]; *East v. Karter,* 118 So. 547 [Ala. 1928]; *Abrams v. Abrams,* 144 So. 828 [Ala. 1932]; *Towles v. Pettus,* 12 So.2d 357 [Ala. 1943]). Nonetheless, without specific evidence that these men had acted contrary to their own expressed desires, the courts reviewing these cases were unwilling to direct trial courts to invalidate their bequests or to conduct new trials in which further evidence of undue influence could be adduced. The Alabama Supreme Court also ruled explicitly in 1926 that the mere existence of an illicit relationship between a testator and his beneficiary would not ground a finding of undue influence (*Hobson v. Morgan,* 110 So. 406). In this case Frank Morgan's intestate heir, his

---

5. Somewhat lost in the case was the fact that Naomi Tipton, who survived her husband, had also signed the deed. Her testimony, according to the supreme court, suggested that she did not know what she was signing although she recalled hearing Victor ask his father if he could have the property. She was not a party to the case, and the court did not discuss either the relationship between her and her husband or between her and her stepson. The appellate court as well as earlier participants in the suit apparently assumed no agency on her part despite the fact that she was a co-owner of the property in question (*Tipton v. Tipton,* 32 So.2d 32 [Ala. 1947]).

mother, challenged Morgan's bequest of half of his estate to Lula Hobson, a married woman with whom he was allegedly conducting an affair; the court ruled that even if adultery had been proven, that alone would not permit the invalidation of the will.

The appellate courts were also not eager to invalidate women's bequests, but the circumstances the courts described were somewhat different. The white women in the cases involving claims of undue influence often appeared in subordinated positions or at least in positions in which others were contributing substantially to their decisions. While the abstract rules regarding undue influence remained constant, the opinions described a narrowed scope of autonomy for female testators, and the courts required no evidence that they were independently managing their affairs to rule that they had exercised their own judgment in disposing of their estates. For instance, in a case decided in 1911, the testator, Mary Smith, was "a frail and sickly woman, and could not attend to her business." Two of her sons managed her business and "she would take no action without their advice and approval" (*Smith v. Smith,* 56 So. 949, 951 [Ala. 1911]). She disinherited two of her six children; the two left out of the will claimed that their brothers had unduly influenced their mother, but the court disagreed. Likewise in *Scarbrough v. Scarbrough,* the testator's affairs were managed entirely by her brother, who was also a substantial beneficiary under her will. While Mary Scarbrough was of sound mind, "she had the limitations one would expect to find in one of her sex whose life had not been troubled by matters of business," and the court upheld her will despite the fact that she had suffered her final illness in her brother's home and had made her will there with her brother's assistance (*Scarbrough v. Scarbrough,* 64 So. 105 [Ala. 1913]). Certainly in instances in which a female testator appeared to have acted with the control and dominance one might expect to see in a male testator, charges of undue influence had little chance of success (see, e.g., *Hyde v. Norris,* 35 So.2d 181 [Ala. 1948]).

As with white men, the touchstone was whether the female testator's preferences had prevailed. Cases in which courts allowed findings of undue influence to stand or ruled that the jury should have been permitted to consider undue influence largely revealed circumstances in which the bequests themselves raised questions. In *McQueen v. Wilson,* the testator had left significant property to her priest, who was "a constant visitor at the home of testatrix prior to and during her sickness which terminated in her death" (31

So. 94, 95 [Ala. 1901]). *Cox v. Parker* involved a dual claim of undue influence and lack of mental capacity in a challenge to a deed that a passive mother made over to her stepson. In this case, the mother died of malaria after spending her final two weeks in the stepson's home; during this time, he prepared the deed and presented it to her for her signature in the presence of her physician and a notary. The argument accepted by the lower court and upheld on appeal was that the widow Parker was "so reduced by mental and physical weakness as to become the mere passive agent of the dominating will . . . of another" who had confidential relations with her (101 So. 657, 659 [Ala. 1924]). The crisis of her illness, however, operated in conjunction with a high degree of dependence on her son-in-law for the management of her business.

A case over which the court disagreed further reveals the tricky nature of circumstances. In *Mullen v. Johnson,* the majority upheld the expressed desires of a woman who willed her entire estate to her husband as she was dying painfully from cancer and relying on opiates for relief. A wife's will awarding her estate to her husband would not ordinarily have raised any problems, but her brother (who would have been her intestate heir) objected on the ground that the husband had exercised undue influence. The majority disagreed, but the dissent pointed out that the husband was "a young, strong, and healthy man, not shown to be possessed of any estate, with a wife feeble and sick unto death with a painful and mortal disease, and constantly under the influence of narcotics" (*Mullen v. Johnson,* 47 So. 584, 589 [Ala. 1908]). The husband's attorney had prepared mutual wills for Thomas and Annie Johnson, and the wills were executed at nine o'clock at night in the absence of any other family members. The dissent argued that Thomas Johnson had not adequately shown that his wife had exercised her own wishes; some evidence at the trial suggested that she had previously declared her intent to leave much or all of her property to her biological relations (id. at 589–90).

The scope of autonomy and its meaning thus appeared to be subtly different for male and female testators. In the cases, the male testators largely appeared either to have exercised their own independent judgment or to have been incapacitated by illness or insanity. They were portrayed as active agents and had their bequests upheld, or were portrayed as passive vessels for another's will and had their bequests invalidated. For female testators, their situations and those of the individuals around them seemed to matter more to the courts. Those supporting female testators' bequests did not have to show definitively that the women were in control of their financial holdings or that they could exercise significantly independent judgment about the disposition of their wealth. Rather, they had to demonstrate that the circumstances were not too questionable, either by contradicting previously expressed desires (as with male testators) or by presenting a picture of a woman acting completely against her natural feelings for her offspring or biological relations to the benefit of a questionable outsider.

These parameters still allowed substantial room to invalidate bequests. The courts looked dimly upon challenges to male testators who expressed their intentions clearly and unequivocally and who had firm grasps upon their business and finances. Nonetheless, the option of framing a male testator's beliefs as delusional existed, as well as the less viable but still possible path of showing both contradictions in his intentions and the presence of someone whose will could conceivably have overborne that of the testator. The fact that more male testators' bequests lost out on appeal than female testators is interesting, though not definitive; at least it enables us to conclude that avenues for invalidation existed.

Set against this background, one can imagine different ways to try to challenge interracial bequests. Appellate courts could have been convinced that interracial intimacy so violated the public's interest that a cross-racial bequest in the context of such a relationship should simply be void, just as a bequest provided in consideration of the initiation of an illegal sexual relationship would be void under the law. They could have determined that engaging in a long-term interracial relationship constituted per se evidence of mental instability. They could have decided that leaving one's property across the color line evinced such hostility to one's family as to qualify as the type of monomania that grounded the invalidation of the will at issue in *Batson v. Batson*. In fact, the appellate courts took none of these steps. Their considerations of cases involving interracial bequests reflected their negotiation of the process of stabilization of white supremacy through potentially destabilizing private actions on the part of white men. The appellate records also hint that gender played a significant role in shaping racialized notions about autonomy and prevailing legal conceptions of the state's proper scope of influence in enforcing public policy.

As noted earlier, only three appellate cases, which were decided between 1914 and 1944, addressed challenges to legacies of white men involved in interracial relationships. Despite the juries' findings in favor of white challengers, the appellate opinions in these cases incorporated strong conceptions of masculine autonomy and resulted in the granting of the contested property to the black legatees. White challengers to white men's wills that left property to black women and mixed-race children alleged that such wills were invalid because they violated public policy. The courts, relying primarily upon the established nonracialized structure of legal rules governing bequests to reject these challenges, agreed that the relationships posed serious threats to the state's continued existence as a white state, but they recognized a stronger countervailing right to control property within the family unit. This authority was an essential component of the white masculinity well represented in the fact patterns and legal analysis of cases addressing intraracial transfers of wealth. Ultimately, upholding white male authority over property even under adverse circumstances served the state's larger interest in maintaining a consistent commitment to the ordered application of white supremacy and contributed to the institutionalization of supremacy. In this regard, these cases fit in well with the appeals of convictions for miscegenation.

Allen v. Scruggs: Providing for the Children

The first challenge to the validity of a will granting a white man's property to his black partner or children reached the appellate level in the case of *Allen v. Scruggs* in 1914. This case juxtaposed white masculine authority against the subordination of both children and blacks. L. Ryal Noble, the white testator in the case, controlled and provided for his black family all of his life, only to have his intentions and capacity questioned after his death. Nonetheless, the court ruled that the evidence in the case was sufficient to award the property to the black legatees, largely because the grant of property was configured and presented in such a way as to be, in the judgment of the court, beyond the capacity of the black legatees to fabricate (*Allen v. Scruggs*, 67 So. 301, 306–7 [Ala. 1914]). The background context of the relationship between Noble and his children clearly evinced his intention to provide for them and protect them after his death. Nevertheless, when he died, his will could not be located, and the Allens found themselves having to prove Noble's intentions toward them through the testimony of witnesses.

Gross Scruggs, Noble's nephew and intestate heir, contested the will, which named Noble's children, the Allens, as the legatees. The evidence for the Allens suggested that Noble had had six children with Kit Allen: Joe,

Robert, Alma, Lucy, Duff, and Berry. Noble and Kit Allen had become involved after the Civil War; Allen lived on his land and worked with his mother on domestic tasks, primarily cooking and milking cows (*Allen v. Scruggs,* bill of exceptions, testimony of Kit Allen 1913: 134). Noble had quietly acknowledged the children upon their births and had provided for them as they grew up. In July 1900, he became seriously ill and thought himself to be on the point of death. With his black family around him, he called for the local justice of the peace and executed a will leaving all of his property to his children in equal shares (*Allen v. Scruggs,* bill of exceptions, testimony of O.H. Watson 1913: 39–42). He gave the will to his daughter, Lucy Randolph, and told her to keep it safe, for she would need it someday (*Allen v. Scruggs,* bill of exceptions, testimony of Lucy Randolph 1913: 103).

The major problem for the Allen children (who apparently were all adults by the time of Noble's death several years later) was that this will could not be located. The Allens thus had to prove the existence of the will through parole evidence and a copy with no established provenance (id. at 111).[6] In light of Gross Scruggs's claim that Noble had later decided to wash his hands of his troublesome black family as well as public sentiment against the Allens,[7] their burden was significant indeed. The trial resulted in a verdict for the white intestate heirs. The judge in the case was convinced by the testimony and most likely by his own internal frameworks of racial boundaries that the Allens should not inherit over the objection of Noble's white kin.

In order to analyze the image of white masculinity that emerges from the case, one can look to the trial record, which provides information about the relationship between Noble and Kit Allen, the mother of his children, the nature of the patriarchal control that Noble exercised over his children, the children's relationship to him, and white responses to his expressed desire to give his property to the Allen children. All of this information provides the necessary background to the question of the missing will and its contents, demonstrating the ways that the court had to negotiate the tension between white male autonomy and the legal disapproval of interracial relationships.

Kit Allen and Ryal Noble apparently initiated their intimate relationship,

---

6. Parole, or spoken, evidence, would ordinarily be inadmissible in a will contest. The rules of evidence provide a specific exception that the Allens were able to exploit, but ordinarily such testimony is understood to be significantly less reliable than written evidence about a testator's intentions.

7. The Allens sought a change in venue due to hostility against them in the local community, but their motion was denied (*Allen v. Scruggs,* bill of exceptions, motion to change venue 1913: 22).

which was to last for nearly forty years, sometime around 1874, when Allen
was a domestic servant in Noble's mother's household (bill of exceptions,
testimony of Kit Allen 1913: 135). Noble was initially unmarried but married
a white woman at some point during this period.[8] Allen's relationship with
Noble was contradictory. On the one hand, she was the mother of his children, whom she claimed he always recognized as his own (id. at 133). While
he did discipline them, she believed that he was always "crazy about them"
and wouldn't be without his illegitimate family. She cooked for him, cared
for him when he was sick, and worked in his fields throughout their association. Kit Allen felt it unbecoming to her to publicize her children's parentage,
but she claimed that Ryal Noble had wanted their five surviving children to
have his property upon his death rather than his white blood relatives (id.).
She also claimed that he supported her, since "what he wanted me to have he
would give me" (id. at 137). In this sense, their relationship was much like
that of husband and wife.

In other ways, however, their connection was more one of master and
servant. Allen lived in a "place of her own" close to Noble, which she rented
from him. She claimed that he "gave me new ground and I would work" and
that "I always gave Mr. Noble money" (id.). In addition evidently to share-
cropping his land, she also had a business relationship with him, using part
of her money to "go into the mercantile business" and trade her cotton,
which he would sell for her. White witnesses for the intestate heirs framed
their relationship as fundamentally unlike a stable marriage. They claimed
that Allen had two or three other children not fathered by Noble who were
"full-blooded Negroes" (*Allen v. Scruggs,* bill of exceptions, testimony of
J. A. Green, testimony of Thomas H. Callis 1913: 204–5, 209). They also
explained the status of Kit and her children as tenants rather than as family,
pointing out that they were working the land as Noble's other tenants were
(bill of exceptions, testimony of Thomas H. Callis 1913: 209).

Likewise, the relationship between Noble and the Allen children was
ambiguous. In many ways, he exercised patriarchal control over them. Several witnesses, mostly blacks, testified that he openly acknowledged the Allen
children as his own. Lucy Randolph testified extensively about her relationship with the man she called "Uncle Ryal," claiming that he "treated her just

---

8. The trial testimony did not reveal definitively what happened to Noble's legitimate wife; at the trial,
Allen claimed that she had died, but a white witness claimed that she was still alive (id. at 135). In any
event, the legitimate marriage produced no issue.

like any other man would treat his daughter, that he sent her to school and took care of her, that he provided for her support and the support of her brothers and sisters from the time she grew up till she married and moved off" (*Allen v. Scruggs,* bill of exceptions, testimony of Lucy Randolph 1913: 106). While she only knew her parentage from what her mother and Noble told her, she had no reason to doubt that Noble was her father.

Noble apparently invested significantly in his children's upbringing and future. He sent Robert and Alma to "the University at Selma" (most likely the University of Selma, a historically black college), where they went by the last name of Noble (id. at 108). Some of the children occasionally got into legal trouble for fighting, and Noble paid their court fines (id. at 113). Noble also contributed to their medical expenses; when Joe Allen was shot, Noble brought in three doctors to attend him and paid their bills (*Allen v. Scruggs,* bill of exceptions, testimony of Joe Allen 1913: 127). When Alma died, Noble furnished the funeral expenses and the coffin for her (bill of exceptions, testimony of Kit Allen 1913: 132–33). Kit Allen also testified that he had provided unspecified financial support the entire time the children were growing up. Noble also treated them paternally by giving them livestock and responsibility in his business (bill of exceptions, testimony of Joe Allen 1913: 125).

In some of the testimony, however, Noble's attitude toward the Allen children seemed ambiguous. Were they treated as his children or as his retainers? When Noble was apparently trying to protect some supporting documents, he allegedly asked a white man to hold the papers in his safe; when Charley Williams (a store owner in the community) asked Noble what he wanted him to do with them, Noble replied, "I give them to my Negroes up here." Williams asked which Negroes he meant, and Noble replied (apparently with some impatience) "You know my Negroes, give them to Joe" (*Allen v. Scruggs,* bill of exceptions, testimony of Charley Williams 1913: 138). Another witness testified that Noble never publicly referred to the Allens as his children but rather as "Kit and them chaps" (bill of exceptions, testimony of J. A. Green 1913: 203). Noble lived close to but never with the children, and the children were generally known in the community by Kit's last name, not Ryal's. Noble certainly recognized that even if he acknowledged the Allen children, he could not hope to have the boys inherit his status after his death, and thus he arranged with whites to protect their interests rather than leaving them to protect their own interests.

The children testified that they had a loving relationship with "Uncle

Ryal." While accepting his largesse and support, they responded by working for him and tending to him in his illnesses. The black witnesses portrayed the scene of the will's preparation as a family gathering—most of the surviving children surrounded their father (bill of exceptions, testimony of O. H. Watson 1913: 41). When he died, Robert, Joe, and Duff Allen along with Kit Allen buried him, and Lucy came up immediately after the funeral to help in winding up his affairs (*Allen v. Scruggs,* bill of exceptions, testimony of Robert Noble 1913: 168). Apparently none of his white relatives were involved in planning, nor did they attend, his funeral.

The white opponents of the will attacked this picture of a familial bond. First, they argued that the will itself was invalid because it violated legal norms regarding the capacity for a white man to legitimate his black family. Second, they argued that even if a familial relationship had existed when the purported will was created, Noble had later severed that relationship. They also argued that the will had not been validly witnessed (bill of exceptions, testimony of Joseph N. Scruggs 1913).

White witness and justice of the peace O. H. Watson had also questioned the will's legal legitimacy on the ground of the illegality of Noble and Allen's relationship. In discussing the will in the town store, Watson had allegedly pointed out two sections in the civil code mandating that mixed-blood issue did not inherit and that bastards did not inherit (bill of exceptions, testimony of O. H. Watson, testimony of W. S. Melton 1913: 51–52, 206).[9] Watson and other whites interpreted these provisions broadly, assuring each other that they would bar Noble from implementing a specific desire to devise his estate to his mixed-race offspring. Their belief was not totally unreasonable, given that they certainly knew that interracial relationships were crimes under state law. (None of the evidence suggests any explanation for why Noble and Allen were never charged, but Noble appeared to have significant property and some standing in the community.) Implicit in the belief that mixed-race issue could not inherit under any circumstances was a belief that a family composed of white and black members was a logical and legal impossibil-

---

9. The code provisions to which Watson was referring almost certainly addressed the problem of intestate succession. Alabama, like most states, did not allow nonmarital children to inherit their parents' property until much later, and a specific provision barring interracial issue from inheriting was obviously a necessity in a culture in which white men were relatively free to form loose sexual liaisons with black women.

ity.[10] The only legitimate frame available for the relationship between Noble and the Allen clan was that of white symbolic patriarch and faithful retainers, a frame that was a nostalgic throwback to constructed romantic white memories of slavery.

The fallback position of white witnesses opposing the will was that Noble had grown tired of his "family" and had been taking steps to sever his relationship with them, a process that would have been much easier if the "family" itself were not a real family. Justice of the peace Watson claimed that Noble had told him that he was through providing for "these Negroes" and that he "wanted them to get hungry and to know the need for a dollar," testimony seconded by J. A. Green (bill of exceptions, testimony of O. H. Watson, testimony of J. A. Green 1913: 57, 200). Green furthermore claimed that, while Noble had written a will when he was ill, he had destroyed it immediately upon recovering (id. at 202). Another witness asserted that Noble was actively trying to extricate himself from the Allen clan at the time of his death, looking into either leasing or selling his land (bill of exceptions, testimony of Thomas H. Callis 1913: 209).

Overall, the testimony in the case presented a conflicted picture of the relationship between Noble and the Allen children. In many ways, they were like legitimate children, and the relationship was within the range of normal family relationships; the emphasis on Noble's willingness to support the children financially was a significant marker of male parental behavior, just as Kit Allen's and the children's participation in his medical care marked their familial and gendered contribution to his welfare. Still, the analogy with white family was not perfect. The question of a breach between Noble and the Allens was relevant and important only because their races were differ-

---

10. At least one man, O. H. Watson's nephew Frank, had trouble even convincing himself that the will, valid or not, had been drawn up. On the stand, he displayed evident discomfort with the subject, claiming, "I don't like to tell it." He then explained that he had heard that Watson had drawn up the will but didn't believe it. He then went to his uncle and asked him, but Watson refused to discuss it, claiming that he had "promised not to talk" (*Allen v. Scruggs*, bill of exceptions, testimony of Frank Watson 1913: 117). Frank was still skeptical and went so far as to challenge Lucy Randolph directly; she testified that he had told her that he didn't believe in the existence of the will and bet her five dollars that there was no will. The next time she was in town, she brought the will with her and showed it to him (bill of exceptions, testimony of Lucy Randolph 1913: 104–5). Watson related the same incident, acknowledging that she had indeed shown him the will in his uncle's store. When Lucy then asked him for the five dollars, he responded "Hell no" and never paid the wager, but quickly explained that his failure to pay was not the reason that he disliked discussing the matter of the will (bill of exceptions, testimony of Frank Watson 1913: 120).

ent; Noble had been estranged from his white family for years, but very little testimony addressed the relationship between them. The testimony also could not answer the question of whether he treated the Allens as his children or as cherished but not necessarily related subordinates who were destined to remain in subordinate status for the rest of their lives.

The trial court judge was unconvinced by the familial portrait painted by the Allens. He ruled in favor of the white heirs, explaining that he was "not satisfied from the evidence that the copy of the purported will . . . is a substantial copy of the said instrument in writing" (*Allen v. Scruggs,* bill of exceptions, judgment entry 1913: 238). While he did not explain why he found the testimony regarding the will to be unconvincing, his response was most likely connected to the high level of community disapproval for the Allens' rights of inheritance. Notably, he made no reference to either legal or social prohibitions against interracial intimacy, ruling instead on formal legal grounds connected to the rules governing wills. In this sense, the case played out much like future cases in the 1930s would; the racialized justification for ruling against interracial couples remained under the surface.

The appellate court deciding the case opened with a condemnation of Noble's relationship with Allen, describing it as "meretricious" and attributing his estrangement from his white relatives to "his reprehensible manner of life, boldly maintained and sustained." The court further reasoned that he was aware and ashamed of his conduct, surmising that "doubtless he realized his voluntarily established immoral status, and . . . withdrew . . . from that social association and relation normally to be expected and observed between kindred and friends" (*Allen v. Scruggs,* 67 So. 301, 304 [Ala. 1914]). The court placed total responsibility for the illegal and immoral conduct upon Noble's shoulders. Implicit in this condemnation, though, was an acknowledgment that Noble had formed a familial association with Kit Allen and her children. The court read the scene of the will's creation as that of a tender and humble moment growing out of the years of connection, claiming that when Noble became seriously ill, "it was both reasonable and natural that they should gather around him" (id. at 305).

The real question for the Alabama Supreme Court was whether the evidence was sufficient to show that the will had existed and had not been revoked. The court saw the evidence of the black witnesses as reliable, explaining that their testimony was "direct, clear, and without any degree of unnaturalness or improbability. They did not testify as if by rote. Their statements do not describe the abnormal or invoke belief of that which would not reasonably be expected" (id.). Further, the court implied that the story was beyond the capacity of these humble people to concoct: "It cannot, *on the evidence here,* be for a moment conceived that a gigantic, criminal conspiracy was organized" (id. at 306–7, emphasis in original). Despite the direct interest of most of the black witnesses, the court believed that their simple testimony in conjunction with the complexity of the story made their narrative plausible.

Their testimony alone, however, was not dispositive. The court pointed out that several white witnesses corroborated this story. For instance, the justices explained that Frank Watson was "a white man, and his testimony is unimpeachable," implying that his whiteness lent a significant element of veracity to his words (id. at 305). Likewise, the narrative of the will's creation beside Noble's sickbed was supported by O. H. Watson's testimony.

For the court, the two keys to the case were Noble's relationship with the Allens and the Allens' subordinate position as both children and blacks. Their dual subordination and presentation of themselves in a sufficiently humble way made them somewhat less of a threat than they might otherwise have been to the established order. But the main principle for ruling for the Allens was the consistency of Noble's behavior in the court's eyes. Once he had set his course of disrespect and contempt for law and cultural expectations, he maintained it throughout, ironically leading the court to find his ultimate disposition of his property to be more credible and acceptable than if it had conceived of him as an upstanding citizen. The court accepted that he had established an interracial family, though his children were defined as black, and read his agency as an evil and illegitimate choice, but not as a reason to overbear his will.

The court's bottom line was that it had ample, credible evidence of Noble's act in preparing the will that granted his estate to his black family. Contradicting the trial judge's findings, it found no credible evidence showing that Noble had revoked the will. In light of Noble's whiteness and the testimony of white men to his intentions, the legal system at the upper level elected to validate his will. The Allen children would inherit his estate despite the fact that they could not produce the physical document because the legal system adhered to its own internal logic of vesting authority, power, and credibility in white men and subordinate status in blacks of both genders. The granting of property to the Allen children foreshadowed developments in the 1930s, when the state would apply the law in ways that maintained supremacy while allowing individual black defendants to benefit.

Mathews v. Stroud: The Primacy of the Testator's Intentions

The next challenge to a bequest reached Alabama's Supreme Court in 1940. While the substantive issue for the court was the validity of Charlie Stroud's naming Estella Mathews as his beneficiary for a life insurance policy, Stroud's children in fact had challenged not only the naming of Mathews as the beneficiary but also his gift of most of his property to her shortly before his death. The case, which arose from a simpler factual background than the *Allen* case, was set up as a straightforward question of whether the life insurance provider's interest in white supremacy should override Stroud's decision to name a black woman as his primary beneficiary. Underneath this issue was a larger question of the state's capacity to enforce the policy against a black beneficiary without undermining the principle of white male autonomy. The case, reaching the high court immediately after the consolidation of white supremacy reflected in the appellate rulings of the 1930s, proceeded along a formalistic framework.

Charlie Stroud had a life insurance policy with the Woodmen of the World Life Insurance Society, a beneficial secret society with by-laws limiting membership to whites only. When Stroud enrolled initially, he had named his daughter, Pearl Grace Stroud, as the beneficiary for the $3,000 policy. On January 21, 1938, however, he changed the beneficiary to Estella Mathews, "a colored woman with whom the said Charlie C. Stroud was living in a state of miscegenation and unlawful cohabitation" (*Mathews v. Stroud,* bill of exceptions, bill of complaint 1939: 1–2). On June 9, 1939, Stroud deeded his real property to Mathews in exchange for consideration of one dollar; there was no evidence that the dollar was ever paid (id. at 4). Less than two weeks later, Stroud died, leaving Mathews in possession of all of his property of any significance. Stroud's children filed a bill in equity against Mathews, challenging her title to the property and the insurance policy; Mathews responded through her demurrer that she was indeed entitled to the proceeds of the insurance policy. The trial court judge overruled her demurrer, granting the proceeds of the policy and the property to the Stroud children.

The Stroud children challenged Mathews's appointment as the beneficiary for the life insurance policy on two grounds. First, they claimed that the terms of the policy prohibited Stroud from naming Mathews as his beneficiary. Second, they claimed that she had exercised undue influence upon him, which also caused him to deed his real property to her shortly before his death. The first claim was based on both the nature of the fraternal organization in question and the relationship between the insurance policy's terms and state law.

Stroud's children introduced into evidence the by-laws of the society, which specified that the membership of the society was limited to "white persons of sound bodily health, exemplary habits, and good moral character." The by-laws further limited beneficiaries to a long list of family members "and such other beneficiaries as may be permitted by the laws of the state in which the Camp is located" (id. at 2). The white heirs claimed that because Mathews fell into none of the relational categories and was not Charlie Stroud's dependent, her status as a black woman with whom Stroud was living in an illegal relationship rendered her an ineligible beneficiary under both the society's by-laws and Alabama's state law (id.).

The second element of their challenge directly questioned Stroud's capacity to act independently, portraying him as lacking full control of his circumstances. They claimed that he had been an invalid "in a weakened physical and mental condition" for the six years preceding his death and that he had been involved with Mathews for fifteen years (id. at 3). They presented no real evidence to support their assertion that Mathews had unduly influenced him other than the timing of his signing over of his assets to her. Drawing on the established line of doctrine that Stroud's autonomy had to be overcome to ground the claim, the challenge implied that if Stroud had been of sound mind, he would not have disinherited his children in favor of a black woman. While the trial judge addressed none of these claims directly, he was convinced enough to rule in favor of Stroud's white children.

The high court explicitly considered the relationship between Alabama's statutory framework and the policy's limitations. First, it examined the provisions of the policy, which allowed the policy's holder to name as a beneficiary any person permitted by the laws of the state to be named, and saw no specific limit expressed in that language. Any limit, therefore, had to come from Alabama's code (*Mathews v. Stroud*, 196 So. 885, 887 [Ala. 1940]). The predecessor provision in Alabama law had apparently established a narrow range of individuals who could legitimately be named as beneficiaries, but in 1931 it was amended to allow the member "to name any person permitted by the laws of the society to be such" (id.). This move expanded the autonomy of benefactors, but the legislators likely did not anticipate this outcome.

This change in the policy rendered the question simple in the eyes of the court. If a society wished to limit potential beneficiaries, it could do so, and the law of Alabama would support such efforts. If, however, a society did not specifically prevent a white policyholder from naming a black beneficiary, the law would not override the white man's choice about the dispensation of his property. While the Stroud children were permitted to go forward with their complaint of undue influence, they would have to prove that undue influence had taken place—the high court would not impute it from the circumstances (id. at 888). The court portrayed this outcome as the simple and orderly implementation of standard rules, in line with the cases of the 1930s that overturned convictions due to irregularities in prosecutorial behavior. Here as well, the application of a general rule developed in a race-neutral context benefited a black litigant. After the resolution of the appeal, no reported case reveals whether the white intestate heirs pursued and won their claim in a second trial conducted under the more difficult standard.

Like *Allen v. Scruggs,* this case sidestepped the tension between Alabama's prohibition of interracial intimacy and the possibility for white men to give property to black women with whom they had interracial relationships. The Stroud children had based their claim on the assumption that the state's policy against interracial intimacy would provide sufficient reason for the Alabama courts to rule that Mathews could not be a legitimate beneficiary. The paucity of their evidence on the claim of undue influence suggests that they believed that merely showing Stroud's stubborn continuation of a relationship violating the community's mores would demonstrate his mental instability satisfactorily. The high court, however, privileged the white man's capacity to determine the dispensation of his property over his white children's losses. In doing so, it followed the line of intraracial cases suggesting that some significant evidence of mental instability or lack of capacity to form meaningful intentions would be required to overturn the clearly expressed desires of a white male benefactor. In doing so, the *Stroud* court marked Stroud as a conscious transgressor, rather than a mentally unstable person, underlining the criminal nature of interracial intimacy.

Dees v. Metts: Does Public Policy Prohibit Interracial Inheritance?

In 1944, the plaintiffs in *Dees v. Metts* presented the main question in their appeal as a direct conflict between a private testator's nefarious intent to will his property across the racial boundary and the state's public policy against interracial cohabitation. The basic dispute was over Ben Watts's decision to deed a parcel of land to Nazarine Parker, a black woman with whom he had had an interracial relationship for over ten years. When Watts died, his will confirmed the granting of the deed to the property to Nazarine Parker, and one of Watts's intestate heirs, Olga Metts, sued to invalidate the deed. Loxley Dees, Ben Watts's executor, filed a proceeding to probate his will, which was also challenged by Olga Metts. In both proceedings, Metts claimed that allowing Parker to retain possession of the land would violate public policy interests. The trial court sustained the contest and issued a ruling following a jury verdict canceling both the will and the deed, allowing Watts's intestate heirs to inherit rather than Parker. The Alabama Supreme Court, however, ruled for Parker, finding that Watts's authority over his property fell within the regular parameters for intentional distribution. The high court's ruling simultaneously validated the state's support for white male control over property while vigorously condemning interracial relationships, maintaining consistency with the rulings of the 1930s that had legitimated the state's application of supremacist norms.

Nazarine Parker and Ben Watts had become involved somewhat more than ten years before his death. Watts lived with Parker on the property in question, of which Parker had possession at the time of the trial (*Dees v. Metts,* bill of exceptions, testimony of Leonard Wiggins 1943: 29). During much of his life, Watts had a troubled relationship with his white family (id. at 30). In 1938, he contacted Loxley Dees, who worked at the Monroe County Bank, to make provisions for Parker (*Dees v. Metts,* bill of exceptions, testimony of Loxley Dees 1943: 48). After the will was drawn up, he took it to an attorney in Monroe County, A. C. Lee, and asked him if it would accomplish his aim of "giv[ing] everything he had to her" (*Dees v. Metts,* bill of exceptions, testimony of A. C. Lee 1943: 56). Lee assured him that it would, and later assisted him in drawing up the deed that legally conveyed his land to Parker but retained a life estate for himself (id.).

Metts's challenge to will and deed had three elements. First, her witnesses testified about the details of the relationship between Parker and Watts, which must have been shocking to the jury and observers of the trial. Second, she claimed that Watts's treatment of his white family demonstrated his mental incapacitation. Finally, she suggested that Parker had unduly influenced him. The three arguments worked together to suggest that any white man who willed property to a black woman with whom he had a sexual relationship was presumptively either of reduced mental capacity or under undue influence and thus that such testamentary intentions were subject to invalidation by the state. Furthermore, to allow such bequests to proceed would in effect provide a stamp of state approval on behavior that all decent individuals condemned.

Witnesses hostile to Parker's interests testified about the details of the relationship between Parker and Watts. Watts's land had two houses on it, one five-room house as the principal residence and another one-room house by the road. Leonard Wiggins testified that Parker lived in the larger house and "Ben stayed there with her," explaining that Watts had died there, in Parker's bed (bill of exceptions, testimony of Leonard Wiggins 1943: 30). Nevada Nelson, a black woman who lived nearby also had seen Parker and Watts in bed together. She further asserted that he treated her "just like his wife," taking care of her until his death. She testified to witnessing Parker sitting on Watts's lap and to seeing Watts embracing Parker (*Dees v. Metts*, bill of exceptions, testimony of Nevada Nelson 1943: 34).

Most explosive along these lines was the testimony of Dill Brooks, a black man who worked for Watts and Parker. He waited on them in the morning and testified that they indeed slept together in the same bed at night. He described finding them regularly in the morning: "They would be in bed in the mornings when I would get there just as man and wife" (*Dees v. Metts*, bill of exceptions, testimony of Dill Brooks 1943: 36). This shocking state of affairs was apparently well known in the locality, but the local sheriff testified that he had never "tried to break it up" (*Dees v. Metts*, bill of exceptions, testimony of J. L. Bowden 1943: 56). As in previous cases of notorious cohabitation, local authorities provided no explanation for their failure to pursue the wrongdoers, but like Charlie Stroud and Ryal Allen, Ben Watts was a man of property.

While Metts's attorney was obviously trying to provoke and shock the jury, the main agenda was to prove the elements of the crime of miscegenation satisfactorily. Prosecutions for miscegenation in the absence of an attempt to intermarry required proof of all of the elements of adultery or fornication in addition to a demonstration that the defendants were of different races. Metts's attorney had to show that sexual intercourse had taken place regularly with the intention of continuing the relationship. Since interracial intimacy was against the state's public policy and all of the elements of miscegenation had been proven, implied Metts, the inheritance should be void.

The evidence in the case did not explicitly address *Hobson v. Morgan,* the case in which the Alabama Supreme Court had rebuffed a challenge to an intraracial bequest from a white man to his alleged mistress, but Metts's attorney emphasized the scope and enormity of the breach of public mores in the graphic evidence presented.

The second element of Metts's argument was that Watts's capacity was diminished when he deeded his property to Parker. The story was that Watts had suffered from syphilis about eighteen years before his death, and afterward he was a changed man (bill of exceptions, testimony of Leonard Wiggins 1943: 28–29). The implication was that mental deterioration from syphilis bore some relationship both to his choice to become involved in an interracial relationship and to give his property to his black partner. This argument fit less problematically within the scope of established case law governing intraracial bequests.

Watts was, by many accounts, a difficult man. Wiggins testified that if things were all out of order in his house, he would "throw the water bucket off the shelf and kick the stove, and knock the victuals off and break the dishes" (id. at 29). Wiggins described him as having moments when his mind would go and he would become angry and curse everyone vigorously. His temper was apparently both unpredictable and violent, although no one testified to seeing him unleash it against Parker.

His venom, rather, seemed to be reserved for his white family. According to witnesses for Metts, his mother and sisters tried to treat him with love and concern, but he rejected them. When his mother remonstrated with him for his lifestyle, "he would tell her it wasn't none of her damn business what sort of life he lived, that he was grown and would live like he pleased" (bill of exceptions, testimony of Nevada Nelson 1943: 35). Nevada Nelson concluded that "from the way he treated his color and folks in my opinion he was of unsound mind." As a black woman, she was not willing to go so far as to say that he had lost his senses, but she implied as much with her testimony. Another witness claimed that he regularly cursed his mother and sisters and would often "say he wished they were dead and that they ought to have been dead forty years ago" (*Dees v. Metts,* bill of exceptions, testimony of E. M. Salter 1943: 58).[11] Another witness corroborated this information, claiming to have heard Watts call his mother "a crazy old God damn bitch"

---

11. The modern reader should keep in mind that, while such language sounds mildly reprehensible to twenty-first-century ears, it was most likely much more disturbing in the conservative Southern culture of 1940s Alabama, particularly in light of the fact that it was directed toward Watts's sisters and mother.

and curse his sisters (bill of exceptions, testimony of Leonard Wiggins 1943: 29).

Metts's witnesses portrayed Nazarine Parker as a schemer who took advantage of Watts's incapacitated state to exercise undue influence over him. Leonard Wiggins claimed to have had a conversation with Parker in which she boasted to him that she had convinced Watts to will all of his property to her and further that the idea of establishing her ownership through deed prior to Watts's death was hers (id. at 30). Nevada Nelson also testified that Parker had told her that Watts had willed her "every damn thing he had" and that "she was going to get it." She presented the relationship as one in which Parker was clearly in control: Parker would sit on his lap and "tell him what she wanted and he would give her what she asked for" (bill of exceptions, testimony of Nevada Nelson 1943: 35–36). In this testimony, Parker appeared as the wily black seductress intent upon using her native duplicity to bedazzle and swindle Watts, alienating him from his natural connections to his family.

According to Wiggins, Parker was not content to stop there. She also insinuated her family into Watts's good graces. Wiggins testified that he had seen Watts and Parker frequently traveling on Sunday evening to visit Parker's grandchild (bill of exceptions, testimony of Leonard Wiggins 1943: 30–31). As Watts's health began to decline, he increasingly turned over his business to Parker's adult son Chapman rather than obtaining assistance from his white relatives.

Metts's witnesses sketched Watts as an unstable and volatile man under significant influence by a clever and manipulative woman. Incapable of managing things for himself, he increasingly relied on Nazarine Parker's suggestions and judgment. In Metts's theory of the case, it was no wonder, under these circumstances, that she had arranged things so effectively to benefit herself in his declining years. This evidence suggested that Watts's decision to give his property to Parker was not a valid expression of competently formed testamentary intent, and that the more rightful result was to reward his long-suffering family.

Unfortunately for the intestate heirs, other white witnesses supported a countervailing narrative. Loxley Dees, Watts's executor, presented a different image of the man who had willed and deeded his land to Parker. In Dees's testimony, Watts was a confident and assertive businessman seeking the best way to ensure that his wishes would be fulfilled. Dees testified that when

Watts approached him to see if Dees could write a will for him, Watts explained,

> I want to leave what I have for this Negro woman that has been taking care of me all the time. You know how white people are about Negroes and I want to be sure this thing is handled right because I want her to have what I've got. All my own people have ever done for me was to borrow money and never pay it back. I want to see that she gets it and I want to see that some white man sees that she does get it. (Bill of exceptions, testimony of L. L. Dees 1943: 48)

In this testimony, Watts appeared both shrewd and fully aware and in control of his intentions. He consulted not one, but two, white male professionals to ensure that when Parker's inheritance was challenged, she would have credible witnesses on her side as well as perfectly drafted documents. Not only did he know what he wanted Parker to have, he also knew that she needed "some white man" to support her claim.

A. C. Lee, the attorney he consulted regarding the deed, corroborated this image of Watts as planning ahead to protect Parker. Like Dees, Lee testified that Watts was concerned that his white relatives would "try to break the will" and that he had consulted Lee in order to "do everything possible to make sure that his will would be carried out" (bill of exceptions, testimony of A. C. Lee 1943: 56). Lee, like several other witnesses, testified that he saw no signs of lack of judgment on Watts's part.

In addressing the relationship between Watts and his family, Parker's witnesses proposed an alternative explanation for Watts's behavior. One witness claimed that Watts's anger was due to the fact that he had wanted them to come and live on his land so that they could care for him. He had offered them the large house, proposing to take the small house for himself, but they had refused. This, claimed the witness, "hurt him all over," given that he had provided for many of them and had received nothing in return (bill of exceptions, testimony of W. G. Daniels 1943). Parker, on the other hand, cooked for him and nursed him when he was ill; his white nieces and nephews apparently never visited him or nursed him before his death (bill of exceptions, testimony of Leonard Wiggins 1943: 31). The implied argument was that Parker behaved more charitably and in a more familial sense than his own extended family and thus that, given his clear intentions to reward her, she was entitled to have permanent possession of the land.

The jury disagreed with this picture of the relationship, finding in favor of the intestate heirs. Presented with these competing conceptions of the relationship between Watts and Parker, the Alabama Supreme Court questioned whether the fact of the interracial relationship gave rise to a presumption that Watts was either mentally unsound or under undue influence when he willed and deeded his property to Parker. The white heirs posed the question as whether the state's policy against interracial intimacy rendered such a testamentary intent void as conflicting with public policy. This inquiry set the state's protection for white male control over property in direct conflict with the state's desire to prevent mixed-race families and children. The case produced a split, with the Chief Justice writing for himself and three other justices, with the remaining three justices dissenting.

The majority rejected the proposed framing. Given that the ruling came out in favor of Parker, the justices took pains to ensure that no one would read the case as approving mixed-race relationships. The opinion strongly endorsed the principle that state actors should move vigorously to "prevent race amalgamation and to safeguard the racial integrity of white peoples as well as the racial integrity of Negro peoples" (*Dees v. Metts*, 17 So.2d 137, 139 [Ala. 1944]). While it was morally reprehensible to live with any woman outside of the marriage bond, for a white man to engage in such behavior with a black woman was "a much lower grade of depravity" (id.). The court flatly condemned Watts's conduct as felonious as well as destructive of the state's moral nature. This language echoed that used in the antebellum cases from South Carolina, exhibiting disdain for the white male's conduct (Davis 1999: 256).

As in these earlier cases, however, the majority noted that Watts was a man of strong character who could make his own choices. Chief Justice Gardner's opinion accepted Dees's and Lee's testimony about Watts's shrewd planning to protect Parker's interests, highlighting his reasonable fears that his white relatives would try to thwart Parker's inheritance (id. at 138). As to the allegations of mental instability, the court weighed his treatment of his family against evidence regarding his business dealings. His behavior toward his mother and sisters, explained the majority, could be attributed to his "resentment of their criticism of his conduct," but this evidence provided no reason to believe that he was mentally impaired (id. at 141). Further, his public presentation of himself as a credible and reliable businessman in relationships with other white men was more significant than his abuse of his white female relatives. This abuse could be understood if not justified as a reaction to their criticism of a white patriarchal figure.

The majority addressed the question of undue influence relatively summarily. Rejecting Metts's argument that Parker's relationship with Watts enabled her to beguile him, the justices framed the connection as being rooted in power relations with Watts as the instigator and controller. They pointed out that "in the instant case testator was of the 'dominant race'. . . . And the dictates of common sense tell us that this unlawful relationship must have been initiated by Watts himself, and the proof is abundant that he in fact was a man of determined will" (id. at 141). As the white man, Watts was presumed to have power and influence over his black female partner in crime; in sharp contrast to the trial testimony, Parker herself was practically absent as an agent in the majority opinion. The majority emphasized Watts's agency and authority, claiming that he had freely chosen to live "this life of shame, and face the criticism, or perhaps ostracism, that would naturally follow" (id.). Parker, implied the majority, had little or no choice or responsibility in the relationship.

Thus for the majority, Metts's attempted narrative of black female agency could not displace the well-established narrative of white male agency and the regularized application of rules from the intraracial context. While the formal law set heavy penalties for such behavior, in this case the law did not intervene while Watts was alive (possibly because of his standing in the community). Regardless of how wrong his conduct was or how stringently the formal law punished it, a white man's authority to dispose of his property was analytically distinct and not to be disturbed (id. at 139). For the court, the fundamental principle at stake was white male freedom: "so far as one's own conscience is concerned . . . there is a freedom also in the moral world for one to choose his own way of life. Ben Watts chose the evil way" (id. at 142). While the court could (and did) condemn this choice, "however . . . reprehensible it may have been, the courts must not lose sight of the fact that his accumulated estate . . . was his own" (id.). The courts could not concern themselves with the question of to whom property was distributed but had to be deeply concerned with protecting the right to dispose freely of one's property, which inhered in property ownership. The high court cited the intraracial case of *Hobson v. Morgan* as the controlling precedent on this point, further ruling that an "illicit relationship is not sufficient per se to warrant a conclusion of undue influence" and that trial courts could not presume undue influence when a man of sound mind favored his illicit paramour in his will (id. at 139–40). The ruling thus maintained the practice of legitimating Alabama's legal system even though this resulted in the disposal of significant property to a black heir, as well as the practice of adapting race-neutral precedents to address racialized controversies.

The majority possibly could have differentiated between intraracial and interracial illicit relationships but chose not to do so. But while the majority did adopt a race-neutral rule of not finding per se undue influence, race was nonetheless present in the ruling. The case revolved around Ben Watts's "evil" and "reprehensible" *choice*. As in the earlier cases, understanding Watts's actions as a result of conscious choice underlined the criminal wrong he had committed in living his intimate life with a black woman. Watts was not a madman, nor a man enthralled to the point of overcoming his own will. Rather, he was a bad man who had exercised his judgment in favor of transgression. Allowing miscegenation to be framed as a nonagentive act in this context could conceivably have undermined the nature of the prohibition in the criminal context and rendered it a less serious crime than the direct attack on the foundations and morals of the state that the appellate courts expressed it to be.

The case, however, was controversial. Justice Bouldin, writing for the three dissenting justices, rejected the strong conception of white male agency presented in the majority opinion in favor of a reading of the case based on black female manipulative behavior. In his reasoning, he focused on the question of undue influence after explaining his fundamental agreement with the state's policy against racial intermingling. It was necessary, he claimed, to take into account the totality of the circumstances. A white man engaging in an interracial relationship

> faces a loss of respect on the part of friends and neighbors of his own race, the better element of both races; is probably ostracized to a degree by the social laws of his community; sacrifices his own self-respect; humiliates his family, his blood relatives. . . . Keeping up such criminal relations at such a price may be considered by the jury in connection with all the evidence, and found to support a reasonable inference that the man has become so infatuated with his Negro mistress as to render her the dominant party in matters of special interest to her. (Id. at 144, Bouldin, J., dissenting)

In this reading, the mere fact of a relationship between a white man and a black woman raised the question of undue influence, and the balancing of sexual gratification against the loss of status inherent in pure whiteness rendered the black woman the dominant individual in the relationship. In discussing this case briefly, Joan Tarpley describes how Bouldin's dissent presented Parker as a Jezebel figure invested with frightening seductive power (1996: 1374).

Furthermore, Bouldin's reasoning implied that, ironically, the more status and influence a white man had, the more likely it was that he was significantly under the influence of his black partner. White men with more property and status in the community and pride in their families had far more to lose from connections with black women than those without property, status, or honorable families. One therefore would have to assume a higher degree of influence or trickery on the part of the black woman in order to convince such a man to engage in such a damaging relationship. Given Watts's clear standing in the community, claimed Bouldin, the jury could reasonably conclude that only under a condition of undue influence would he become so deeply and publicly involved with a woman of the subordinate and despised race.

While Bouldin acknowledged *Hobson*'s rule that a man could will his property to his partner in an illicit relationship, he argued that evidence of an illicit relationship could be used along with other evidence to ground a finding of undue influence by the jury (id. at 144). The other evidence in this case was the interracial nature of the relationship; Bouldin did not see Watts and Parker's relationship as a garden-variety case of adultery to be governed by *Hobson*. His preferred legal rule would not have been a per se finding of undue influence in cases of bequests by white men to black women or their children, but would have amounted in practice to a presumption of undue influence, reversing the usual burdens of proof in such cases.

In the final analysis, the high court maintained its commitment to the regularized application of legal principles developed in intraracial cases. On one reading, the two competing narratives invoked common beliefs about the attributes of white masculinity and black femininity, but for the majority of the court, the narrative of white masculine power and authority was more convincing and resonant with the facts of the case than the narrative of black feminine manipulation. Furthermore, none of the justices was willing to argue directly that the state should bar the inheritance of white men's property by black women or children; such a rule could only be achieved through a formal means of presuming that the white man's will was overridden through the evidence of his violation of strong social norms. While this rule comported with earlier opinions in other jurisdictions, it took on additional layers of meaning when articulated in the context of a fully developed regime of white supremacy. Just as the appellate courts' rulings overturning convictions based on the inappropriate use of racist invective sanitized and supported the regime of white supremacy, so too did the orderly granting of property to black heirs of white men involved in interracial relationships.

What about Black Property Owners?

An additional relevant comparison is to survey the authority of black property owners in these situations. Would their wishes be treated with the same deference as those of white male property owners, and how would the context of the cases figure in? As one might predict, very few appellate cases address transfers of property by black property owners. By casting a slightly broader net, we can get a sense of how courts viewed agency and autonomy when blacks' wishes were at the center of the inquiry. The abstract legal rules cited were those established and explained in the cases discussed previously, but the courts applied them within racialized and gendered contexts.

In the few cases reported on the appellate level, black women's formally expressed wishes fared poorly. Three cases addressed claims of undue influence and findings of undue influence were upheld in two of them. These two involved interracial transfers; the remaining case addressed an intraracial transfer. Reading these cases as the legal system's racist overriding of black women's autonomy is too simple, however: the circumstances of the cases influenced the outcomes. The two cases in which claims of undue influence succeeded were not challenges to bequests but rather were suits brought by black female plaintiffs to set aside conveyances of land by deed. These cases are not perfect parallels to the wills cases, but the Alabama Supreme Court had ruled repeatedly that many of the same legal principles governing undue influence prevailed in cases involving wills and cases involving transfers inter vivos.

The supreme court presented the facts in the two cases addressing deeds as very similar. *Yarbrough v. Harris*, decided in 1910, involved a conveyance of a piece of land worth between $500 and $1,900. Recent widow Ann Harris, described by the court as "a poor old ignorant woman," conveyed the land in exchange for $25 (*Yarbrough v. Harris,* 52 So. 916, 917–18). The purchaser was a white businessman, and he was assisted by the white male attorney who had handled Harris's legal business after her husband's death (id.). The facts in *Kirby v. Arnold,* decided in 1915, were portrayed even more egregiously. The case questioned a deed conveying a parcel of land from Lucy Arnold to A. Collins Kirby. After the transfer, Arnold, described by the court as "an ignorant Negro woman," challenged the "intelligent man of affairs" to whom she had deeded the property, claiming that the conveyance had taken place under conditions of fraud and duress. Evidence entered at trial for Arnold purported to show that she had not realized she was transferring the entire parcel and that she had been threatened that if she did not sign the deed, her grandfather would be imprisoned at hard labor in the mines (*Kirby v. Arnold,* 68 So. 17, 18 [Ala. 1915]).

In both cases, the Alabama Supreme Court exercised principles of equity to uphold the chancery court's initial invalidations of both deeds. In *Yarbrough,* the court framed the facts as obviously over the boundary, writing, "There is not a single fact to show that it [the transaction] was fair or just; but to the contrary, every circumstance shows it to have been unfair and oppressive—oppressive of the ignorant, weak, and confiding, by the intelligent, strong, and dominating" (52 So. 916, 918 [Ala. 1910]). Likewise, the court summarized in *Kirby:* "To protect the weak and ignorant from imposition by the strong and intelligent is the exercise of a high-minded honesty and 'the crowning glory of courts of equity'" (68 So. 17, 20 [Ala. 1915]). While no other comparable cases could be located, the discussions in the opinions are suggestive. Likely the egregious facts would have constituted valid claims of fraud and/or undue influence if the transactions had occurred intraracially. Nonetheless, one wonders if the distance between the two parties was enhanced for the court by their races and genders. In the court's opinions, the women's ignorance and men's competence appeared to weigh as significantly as the concrete lack of adequate consideration and the allegations of threat.

One case involved an intraracial challenge of a black woman's will.[12] In

---

12. In fact the reported opinion did not mention the races of the participants or the testator, but the surnames of the testator and challenger were both Freeman. It is highly unlikely that a white family in Alabama in the 1910s would have borne that name. The likelihood that the family was black is increased when we note that the court referred to the testator as "Lizzie Freeman" rather than "Elizabeth Freeman." Many thanks to Professor Amilcar Shabazz at the University of Alabama for clarification on this point.

this case, the high court endorsed various complaints by contestant Jack Freeman. At trial, a jury rejected the will, but the supreme court noted that some of the evidence should not have been admitted. Furthermore, the court ruled that the evidence presented did not meet all of the elements of undue influence (*Barnett v. Freeman*, 72 So. 395, 396 [Ala. 1916]). The court's opinion was short, but clearly portrayed the testator as in control of her actions.

Finally, one case involved an intraracial contest of a black man's will.[13] William Nesbitt, the testator, had married twice, and his daughter Willie King from his first marriage contested his will. Nesbitt owned two pieces of real estate, one of which he left to his daughter and the other of which he left to the niece of his second wife and her husband, his housekeeper Adeline Tate, and attorney William McCullough (*King v. Aird*, 38 So.2d 883, 885–86 [Ala. 1949]; Aird was the estate's executor). King claimed that McCullough had exercised undue influence in procuring the bequest on his behalf. McCulloch's race was not identified in the court's discussion of the facts. While Nesbitt was hospitalized for the month prior to his death and executed the will while in the hospital, the court upheld the trial court's admission of the will to probate because the evidence was insufficient to ground a reversal (id.). Among other things, the court ruled that McCullough's attorney's inflammatory reference to King as "the woman in New York who not only gets . . . the most valuable of that William owned, . . . but modifies that problem by contesting this will" was not a ground for reversal (id. at 888). Nonetheless, the court upheld the will, finding that Nesbitt had expressed his own desires when he signed the will. There was no discussion of his business acumen in supporting the finding that he was of sound mind. Instead, the court particularly noted his break with his daughter, the "woman in New York" whom he did not visit in a trip there a few years prior to his death.[14]

These cases followed the general rules but applied them within racialized contexts. Black women's autonomy was recognized to be limited, particu-

---

13. One other case actually involved an interracial relationship, but this case, *Locklayer v. Locklayer*, was a black son's challenge to a white widow's request that the court grant her an elective share in her black husband's estate. The court refused, claiming that the attempted marriage violated public policy and thus was void. The widow tried to evade this principle by claiming that she had not known her husband's race, but substantial evidence demonstrated that she knew or should have known that he was black (*Locklayer v. Locklayer*, 35 So. 1008 [Ala. 1904]).

14. Without the trial transcript, we can only speculate on how Willie King was portrayed to the jury, but given that the case took place in 1949, it seems likely that she was presented as violating norms of subordination based in both race and gender.

larly in encounters with white men, and black women were twice portrayed as hapless victims. This victimization, however, was an individual result of imbalances in the education and experience of the deeders and their beneficiaries. The single case involving a black man portrayed him as having exercised autonomy, but the evidence for his soundness of mind was implicitly located in his wisdom in rejecting an uppity daughter who had moved to New York. While it was possible for a black woman to defeat a white man in a court of equity, the framing of the case rested upon the racial and gender-based order rather than disturbing it. These cases thus echoed the principles established in the 1930s, which allowed for the invalidation of convictions due to the inappropriate use of racial invective by state actors. Taken in isolation from the broader social context, both sets of opinions presented a legal system that operated through norms of neutrality and fairness and without incorporating formal disfavor for black litigants. Nonetheless, they rested upon a legal structure that incorporated culturally held beliefs about the appropriate relationship between black and white, and enabled the operation of these beliefs within society as long as they were expressed through the channels approved by state actors. While formal legal rules provided the justification for the outcomes, the substance of the cases deeply internalized racialized beliefs about will, power, agency, and coercion.

Legitimation and White Male Control over Property

The background established by extensive litigation over white intraracial bequests suggests that framing undesirable bequests by men as the product of either madness or extreme debilitation and control by an outside party was the likeliest route to invalidation. Discussions of the bequests of female legatees, on the contrary, turned more closely on the circumstances and the familial or nonfamilial relationships at stake. When addressing facially outrageous interracial transfers from black women to white men, the courts emphasized the ignorance and implicit feminine weakness of the women as set against the business acumen and intelligence of their bilkers. This analysis attributed the injustices to individual attributes rather than to socially and culturally embedded structures of inequality.

The three cases addressing interracial bequests by white men underlined legal actors' presentation of the state both as legitimate and committed to white supremacy. This balance rested upon the relationship between masculinity and whiteness in law and culture in Alabama before the dawn of the civil rights movement. While, as all of the justices on the *Dees* court agreed, the principle of white supremacy was a paramount value in Alabama's legal structure, under some circumstances black legatees could face white intestate heirs in the Jim Crow court system and win substantial awards of property through the appellate process's commitment to the neutral application of rules. These outcomes were particularly interesting in light of the fact that these black legatees were marked not only by their race but also by their violation of the strong legal and social prohibitions against interracial sexual relationships and the formation of interracial family units. The overall results emphasized both key state actors' commitment to supremacy and their desire to administer supremacy through the ordinary operation of law, even when the ordinary operation of law would benefit black litigants. They also underlined the principle that miscegenation was a crime, and a result of individuals' choices to set themselves against the dominant racial order endorsed by society and embedded in the law.

How were litigants like the Allens, Estella Mathews, and Nazarine Parker able to prevail? In a sense, asking the question in this way obscures the underlying ideology of the cases. In all of the twentieth-century appellate cases, the dead white men who had willed their property to the legatees were far more present and active than the legatees themselves, most of whom were active witnesses at the trials. With the testimony appearing on paper rather than in the flesh, white male agency became the dominant narrative. While the testator's agency was always the focus of legal inquiry even in cases involving only white litigants, the centering of white men's agency and choices in the interracial cases had particular meaning. These cases thus were not triumphal stories of the power of legal norms to overcome rooted prejudice, but rather familiar stories about the capacity for white men to act as agents and to control property. The rulings that granted property to black heirs in no way upset the stabilized supremacist state. Rather, they endorsed and applied the generally framed rules of bequests, which evolved in a context in which almost all property was held by racially and ethnically privileged men. The stories of white male autonomy had their genesis in the antebellum era, as Adrienne Davis shows, and the appellate courts merely cast them in the context of the fully developed supremacist state (1999).

As the courts had determined in the disputes over racial definition in the 1920s and 1930s, whiteness in these cases was far more related to performance and action than to skin color or heredity (see also Bynum 1998; Gross 1998; Hale 1998; Welke 2001). The male testators in these cases were aided in their performances of white privilege and power by the courts. Most pointedly in *Dees v. Metts*, the courts ruled that, despite the men's illicit actions that undermined the boundaries between whiteness and blackness, the paramount principle of validating white masculine dispensations of property was a core right that could not be gainsaid. Ryal Noble, Charlie Scruggs, and Ben Watts exhibited their whiteness by acting freely, exercising their liberty to make "evil choices." While their relationships were threatening to the state, judges were faced with undermining white power no matter how it ruled. Supporting white men's patriarchal (in the specific sense) capacities tied in effectively with racial supremacy, underlining the conception of white male honor, responsibility, and authority first formulated in the antebellum era (Wyatt-Brown 1986). It simultaneously enabled the branding of these white men, dead though they were, as criminal transgressors worthy of condemnation by the state and complete and legitimate exclusion from the circles of their white relations due to their evil choices and contamination.

The wills cases highlighted the contrast between white male agency and the absence of agency on the part of the black litigants. No surprises arise from the portrayal of the white men as dominant figures and the appearance of the black women and children as subordinates, but the high court's opinions presented portraits of active agency only on the behalf of the white men. To the extent that the black parties acted, they did so only out of natural affection, almost instinct, as in the scene presented in *Allen v. Scruggs* with the children gathered around their father. The few other instances of black action (for instance, Lucy Randolph's possession of the will) were directed and controlled by the white testators. The opinions thus contrasted sharply with the testimony set forth in the cases, which present active and careful black litigants taking independent precautions to preserve the legacies that they expected to receive. In the trial testimony, not only did the black litigants tell their stories, but they also described their relationships with the white testators and their active efforts to behave like family toward these men. This image of mutuality was flattened in the court's rulings, replaced by an analysis of the testators' side of the relationships and their attitudes toward their passive and silent subordinates. The one-sidedness of white agency and black passivity in these cases contrasted with the prosecutions for interracial intimacy and their appeals, in which black actors, both female and male, often appeared as agents. While the contrast resulted in large part from the differences between wills contests' legal focus on the testator's intentions and criminal prosecutions' legal centering on the defendants' joint intentions and actions, the trial records in the wills cases presented significant evidence demonstrating and contesting agency on the part of those standing to benefit from bequests.

In all of the opinions concerning interracial wills, the high court was quick to condemn interracial intimacy in general and the particular manifestations of it that gave rise to the cases it had to consider. Nonetheless, as *Dees v. Metts* explained explicitly, the general rules allowing the testator to control property would apply even in the context of an illegal interracial relationship. The apparent contradiction between the principle against interracial intimacy and the principle of private control over property was least partially illusory, for the authority to control and dispose of one's property evolved in the context of whiteness and maleness. A significant component of whiteness was the capacity to control the property that one had. Further, access to property enabled the white man to enhance his patriarchal authority. While the cases do not reveal why the mixed-race couples involved were never prosecuted, all of the white men involved had significant property and felt secure enough to conduct their interracial relationships fairly openly. Property was both insulation from legal sanction and a marker of authority and power. The testators used their property to protect and nurture in a masculine sense their unorthodox families. Upon their deaths, the Alabama high court allowed their control over property to remain continuous and unbroken; the state could have invoked the criminal law to interfere in the relationships in life, but presumably even prosecution and imprisonment could not impair the ultimate authority of the white man to control and distribute what he owned.

Judges in these cases thus applied the abstract rules within the cultural expectations and beliefs about the litigants they faced. The courts likely could have adopted a narrative of madness or presumed influence to address these cases, as Justice Bouldin urged in *Dees v. Metts*. The judges instead supported a strong reading of male autonomy grounded in images of competent white businessmen whose clearly expressed desires were under attack. The courts maintained their commitment to the white state as well by branding these men as criminal transgressors who were fully aware of the import of their choices both for their white relations and for their own lives. The courts' endorsement of these images of white men as bad but nonetheless as real agents ultimately enabled subordinated black litigants to prevail, despite a consistent insistence by state actors that interracial families were a threat. These cases thus fit well in the larger context of appeals of convictions for miscegenation: even when the outcome favored the individual black litigant, the legal framework underneath supported the institutional project of white supremacy. This pattern would prevail in the 1940s and 1950s, serving as a prelude to the civil rights revolution.

CHAPTER 7 *Portraying the Static State: 1941–54*

      In the appellate criminal litigation over miscegenation in the years between 1941 and 1954, little major doctrinal development occurred. The appeals mostly involved questions about the sufficiency and admissibility of evidence. Cases involving four couples modestly refined established understandings of what constituted valid evidence of a miscegenous relationship. One case raised again the question of racial definition, this time focusing on the alleged child of an accused couple. The final two cases, decided in 1954, raised the question of constitutionality again for the first time since the early 1880s, but the appellate court hearing the cases did not see any reason to move away from the established acceptability of these prosecutions based in years of unquestioned practice. In contrast to earlier periods, the appellate courts steered away from nodal conflicts, leaving little room for the opening of new debates on race and steadfastly refusing to engage the types of questions that had sustained concentrated struggles earlier.

      In reading these cases, one might get an image of a static state, despite the fact that these years encompassed World War II, in which many Alabamans, black and white, served; the postwar economic boom; and the initial stirrings of the civil rights movement. The contrast between judges' official pronouncements in legal cases and the tumultuous broader context is not accidental. As Alabama was dragged forward into a new world of conflict and rebuilding, it struggled to maintain the fully articulated and institutionalized structure that it had so painstakingly built throughout the twentieth century. This struggle helps to explain both why the scope of substantive debate over the statute prohibiting miscegenation was so narrow, and why the question of the statute's constitutionality suddenly reemerged in the state courts in the mid-1950s.

The system of domination that civil rights activists confronted in the 1950s looked solid, comprehensive, and impregnable. In his classic study of the civil rights movement, Aldon Morris characterizes it as a near-totalitarian structure of economic, political, and personal domination that was thoroughly embedded in the state and in culture (1984: 2–3). Given that the major jurisprudential questions had been settled and the significant loopholes closed, why did a single law firm in Alabama seek to confront head-on the keystone of the supremacist state, the criminal prohibition against interracial intimacy?

Looking to the broader history of the era as well as the cases and their dispositions suggests that these years, while they did represent the fullest articulation of white supremacy before its challenge and disruption, were not a period of stasis. Rather, groundwork was being laid, both intentionally and unintentionally, for the major changes that would shake the foundations of the Southern state and require a reworking of the legal principles of supremacy nearly as substantial as that which had followed the Civil War. Alabama would be a crucial location for this process. Much of this groundwork was social and occurred outside of the context of legal struggles over interracial intimacy, but these developments help to explain why constitutionality suddenly arose again as a question in 1954. The cases of the 1940s and early 1950s helped to define the parameters of the fully developed supremacist state that the civil rights movement would confront. They did so by looking intensively at evidentiary questions about the types of gendered relationships that could fit into the prohibited miscegenist frame. Considering these cases in depth thus helps us to understand both the fully developed supremacist state prior to the full emergence of a popular civil rights movement and why constitutional questions about miscegenation became salient again in the 1950s after seven decades of silence in Alabama.

Politics and the Hesitant New Progressivism

As the end of the Depression was overshadowed by the widening conflict in Europe, Frank Dixon's term as governor was ending. While he had been disappointing to staunch New Dealers, anti–New Deal forces continued to oppose him vigorously and faced the 1942 election with trepidation. Dixon was ineligible to run, but longtime popular New Dealer Bibb Graves had decided to seek a third term as governor. Conservative Democrats backed

Chauncey Sparks, tagged "the Bourbon from Barbour [County]" as the alternative, but they had little hope of combating the popular Graves. Graves, however, died in March, leaving the liberals in disarray. Sparks was elected after some liberals reluctantly supported him and the CIO backed a relative newcomer, James Folsom. Sparks won handily, but his election coincided with the election of a strong New Deal congressional delegation. During his tenure, he presided over tax revisions that raised corporate rates, and he expanded social services. His modest reformism, however, did not reflect the temper of the state, and in 1946, a more progressive administration took over (Rogers et al. 1994: 525–26).

The most significant constitutional change that took place during Sparks's administration was not progressive—it was the passage of the Boswell Amendment. Conservatives and racists banded together to pass it in the wake of the U.S. Supreme Court's ruling in *Smith v. Allwright* striking down the all-white primary in 1945 (Feldman 1999: 195). The amendment, which required all applicants for voting registration to demonstrate their understanding of the Constitution, was described by the chair of the State Democratic Executive Committee as a means to "prevent from registering those elements in our community which have not yet fitted themselves for self government" (Norrell 2001: 152). In addition to the threat of federal intervention, in the summer of 1945 a black man, William Mitchell, had filed a class action lawsuit against Macon County for denial of his effort to register; he was represented by NAACP lawyers Arthur Shores and Thurgood Marshall. The amendment was ratified in the November election of 1946 and soon after was challenged, again with the NAACP's Legal Defense Fund's help (Clemon and Fair 2001: 1134). The federal district court for Alabama's southern district invalidated the amendment on the basis of the Fourteenth and Fifteenth Amendments, finding that its explicit purpose was to discriminate against potential black voters (*Davis v. Schnell*, 81 F. Supp. 872 [S.D. Ala. 1949]). The U.S. Supreme Court affirmed in a per curiam ruling with no opinion (*Schnell v. Davis*, 336 U.S. 933 [1949]).

In the 1946 election, Jim Folsom was elected, building on the momentum established in his surprisingly strong campaign in 1942. Folsom was liberal by anyone's standards, having bolted from Alabama's delegation in the 1944 Democratic convention to support Henry Wallace for vice president over Alabama senator John Bankhead, Jr. He had strong New Deal credentials, having administered the Work Projects Administration (WPA) for Marshall County in the 1930s, but had run an unsuccessful campaign against New

Deal congressman Henry Steagall in 1936, attacking him from the left by demanding more federal aid. Flamboyant and personable, he mobilized a mixed constituency of liberals, racial progressives, rural whites, and union elites (Rogers et al. 1994: 526–29). Upon his election, however, he ran into the Montgomery establishment, a bastion of conservative Democratic power that maintained significant control in the highly centralized institutions of state governance.

Folsom could not deliver completely on his vision of progressive change. He sought to reform poll taxes but was blocked in the Alabama Senate. He appointed registrars who would allow blacks to register despite the Boswell Amendment, and this maneuver raised the proportion of blacks registered to vote in Alabama from 1 percent in 1947 to 5 percent in 1952, but he could not push through liberalizing state constitutional reform or reapportionment. Still, after the 1946 election, Alabama's senatorial delegation featured two staunch New Deal supporters, Lister Hill and John Sparkman, and Alabama had several strong liberals as congressional representatives (Rogers et al. 1994: 529–32).

Liberals and progressives, however, had little time. Again, racial politics and fears of federal intervention enabled elite mobilization and coalition-building among opponents of the New Deal and strong supporters of white supremacy. In 1943, Governor Dixon had issued a public call for the formation of a Southern Democratic party dedicated to maintaining segregation. When President Harry Truman promoted civil rights legislation repealing poll taxes, enforcing the prohibition of discrimination in employment based on race, and making lynching a federal crime, the match was lit (Rogers et al. 1994: 533–34).

Alabama's Democrats fractured in the early months of 1948. Folsom's faction supported Truman and his program for civil rights. A second group stuck by Truman but expressed strong opposition to his positions on civil rights while praising his containment of Communism. The third faction revolted against Truman. Reminiscent of Alabama's 1928 repudiation of Democratic presidential nominee Al Smith, the 1948 bolters claimed as leaders former KKK members Horace Wilkinson and Hugh Locke. A less radical subgroup led by former governor Frank Dixon advocated attending the national convention to try to block the adoption of any planks supporting civil rights for African Americans. Alabama's electorate selected a split slate of delegates; the delegation to the national convention was evenly divided (Rogers et al. 1994: 354). The states' rights delegates from Alabama and other states walked out of the convention hall when the other delegates passed a platform plank calling for the desegregation of the armed services, an issue that was explosive for reasons addressed later (Higginbotham 2000: 315).

The formal birth of the Dixiecrats took place in Birmingham on July 17, 1948, attended by five Southern governors. The Dixiecrats controlled Alabama's state Democratic Executive Committee and ensured that Truman's name was not on the ballot in Alabama in November 1948. As a result, 80 percent of Alabama's vote went to the Dixiecrat ticket of South Carolina governor Strom Thurmond and Mississippi governor Fielding Wright. The ticket won in Louisiana, Mississippi, and South Carolina as well but failed miserably in its ultimate goal to throw the presidential election to the U.S. House of Representatives (Rogers et al. 1994: 534–35).

The Democratic Party, as it had in 1928, endured conflict and chaos in the resulting contest for control. The gubernatorial election of 1950 was seen by many as a referendum on the Dixiecrats' actions, and the election of loyalist Gordon Persons and the loyalists' winning of several key seats on the Democratic executive committee answered concerns in Alabama and nationally about Southern Democratic solidarity. The Birmingham *World,* a black newspaper, trumpeted the election of Persons as a return to liberalism and reformist policies on race (Rogers et al. 1994: 536).

Persons, like Folsom, was a mild disappointment to progressives. While he did lower poll taxes significantly, he supported a right-to-work law that enraged unionists. Progressives rallied again around Jim Folsom in the 1954 gubernatorial race, and he was the overwhelming winner in Alabama's Democratic primary, which was held on May 4.[1] After the results were announced, the Birmingham *World* editorialized (just before the explosion of the civil rights movement in Alabama) that the politics of race-baiting had become a losing tactic (Rogers et al. 1994: 537–38). As further evidence of the strength of the new progressivism and racial moderation, in the same primary Alabamans also selected reformer John Sparkman over the Big Mule candidate from Birmingham, Laurie Battle, for the Senate. The relative quiet and edging toward reform that preceded the primaries, however, was destroyed when the U.S. Supreme Court announced its ruling in *Brown v. Board of Education* less than two weeks later on May 17, 1954.

---

1. Thanks to Joel Bloom and Ed Packard in the Alabama Secretary of State's Office for clarification on this point.

War and Its Implications

Alabama had a long military tradition, and the state's elites were generally inclined to support U.S. intervention in World War II fairly early. Alabama's congressional representatives supported Lend-Lease as well as a peacetime draft, and the major papers began to press for intervention as the situation in Europe worsened. In addition to mobilizing thousands of Alabamans as servicemen, the war jump-started Alabama's economy, as Birmingham transformed swiftly from being the nation's large city worst affected by the Depression to being a national center for the manufacture of arms. Two air force bases were located in Montgomery; at Maxwell Air Force Base alone, more than 100,000 airmen were trained during the war. During the war years, rural dwellers flocked to the industrial cities, military bases, and ports; the Census Bureau estimated that Mobile County alone gained 89,000 new residents during the war (Rogers et al. 1994: 510–12).

Ultimately, a quarter million Alabamans served during the war, and about 6,000 died in the line of service. Birmingham's residents responded patriotically to rumors that Birmingham was Germany's second industrial target after Pittsburgh. Mobile endured blackouts as German submarines roved the Gulf of Mexico in the summer of 1942. Alabama was also a center for prisoner-of-war camps, housing some 15,000 Germans by the end of the war (517–18).

Blacks contributed to the war effort, both by laboring in jobs that ordinarily would have gone to white men and by serving in the armed forces. Nationally, as white women entered the factories, black women took their places in laundries, cafeterias, and domestic service (Dudziak 1988: 71). Black men in Alabama flocked to the good industrial jobs now available to them, which sparked resistance from resentful whites; in Mobile, race riots occurred in 1943 in response to the federal Fair Employment Practices Commission's ruling that twelve black welders had to be promoted (Rogers et al. 1994: 514).[2] The riot was quelled by a combined force of the army, the U.S. Coast Guard, state and local police, and the Alabama National Guard. Alabama governor Chauncey Sparks responded publicly by excoriating "out-

---

2. The FEPC itself owed its existence to racial agitation. A. Philip Randolph, president of the Brotherhood of Sleeping Car Porters, threatened a massive march on Washington in 1941 to protest President Roosevelt's inaction on promises of racial justice. Roosevelt narrowly averted the march by signing Executive Order 8802 in June 1941, establishing the FEPC to investigate and ameliorate discrimination in the defense industry (Feldman 1999: 286).

side influences" and their attempts to meddle in "matters which are entirely local" (Feldman 1999: 287).

Blacks served in the military but were held back by segregation and other racist policies. Black men were limited by caps on black enlistment, and achieving the status of officers was even more difficult. Black marines were confined to the steward's branch, and nearly 80 percent of black men serving in the navy were cooks, stewards, and stewards' mates. While the army allowed blacks to become officers, the ratios demonstrated widespread discrimination: for whites, there was one officer for every seven enlisted men, but for blacks, there was one for every seventy. The black men not excluded from combat duty faced the enemy in segregated units. Black women also served, making up 10 percent of the Women's Army Corps. Like black men, they experienced significant discrimination, were rarely sent overseas and were routinely assigned to perform menial tasks (Dudziak 1988: 72).

The most well-known contribution of blacks to the war effort was through the Tuskegee Institute's training program for black aviators. The federal government established the Civilian Pilot Training Program at Tuskegee in 1939; inspectors were astonished when they administered the CPT examination to the first class and every black student passed, an accomplishment that no other college in the South had achieved. The Army Air Corps, acting under heavy pressure from the NAACP, grudgingly allowed the creation of a segregated unit of airmen, and the Ninety-ninth and One Hundredth squadrons were ultimately commissioned. The Ninety-ninth became a highly decorated unit that produced two future air force generals (Rogers et al. 1994: 515–16).

Many blacks nationally believed that World War II would change things. After all, the United States rallied around democracy and excoriated the Nazis' racist policies, framing the war as a just struggle against evil regimes. In particular, blacks who were in the armed services believed that their fight for democracy abroad would heighten sensitivity to these principles at home. While some consciously chose to defer their struggle against racism until the war against fascism was won, many viewed dramatic change in racial policies across the United States as their entitlement after the war was over (Dudziak 1988: 72–73).[3]

---

3. These optimistic views were somewhat dampened by the U.S. Supreme Court's ruling in *Korematsu v. United States* during the war. While those seeking racial reform could take comfort in the Supreme Court's pronouncement that racial policies required strict review, they saw that the Court upheld the policy of interning Japanese and Japanese American citizens on the basis of racial suspicions linked to national security (*Korematsu v. United States*, 323 U.S. 214 [1944]).

The war created a class of blacks in Alabama and elsewhere who were less content to wait than their predecessors of a generation or two before, given their experiences. Many had worked in better paying and more skilled jobs than had been available to blacks in the early twentieth century. Others had served their country, some in combat positions. They had experienced the war as the triumph of American justice over fascism and could see the obvious application of these principles to their circumstances. The process of racial formation would acknowledge these voices as they became increasingly hard to ignore in the postwar years, and as state actors reacted to them initially in contradictory ways ranging from accommodation to violent repression.

Early Stirrings of the Civil Rights Movement

On December 1, 1955, Mrs. Rosa Parks violated Montgomery's segregation ordinance by refusing to relinquish her seat on a bus to a white man. This event, which sparked the Montgomery bus boycott, has acquired an almost mythic quality as the first salvo in the civil rights movement. In the popular narrative, Parks was simply tired and decided on that particular day that she "had had enough." In fact, not only was Parks a longtime member of the NAACP, having served as the secretary for the Alabama State Conference of NAACP since 1943, but she had also had several prior confrontations with white Montgomery bus drivers (Morris 1984: 51).

Parks was not alone, even in Alabama. In 1942, Birmingham's buses and streetcars had experienced trouble, with the companies logging 88 incidents of blacks' taking seats reserved for whites in addition to 176 other racial incidents. Twenty-two were fistfights between passengers and white drivers. As early as the 1930s, black women were sporadically confronting the segregation ordinances, sometimes physically, after the long hiatus resulting from the settlement of the constitutionality of segregation in *Plessy v. Ferguson* in 1896 (Feldman 1999: 288).[4] Despite this history of individual activism, the urgency of race on the national agenda increased and the resulting windows of opportunity for blacks in the South opened more broadly in the postwar era.

One sign of the new, confrontational attitudes in Alabama can be seen in

---

4. Barbara Welke describes a somewhat similar earlier period of testing performed primarily by black women challenging segregation on trains in the late nineteenth century (2001).

an appellate case decided in 1946, involving a conviction for assault and battery. The assault and battery, allegedly committed by a black man against a white man, unsurprisingly resulted in a conviction and punishment of a fine of fifty dollars and thirty days' hard labor for the county. The circumstances of the case, however, revealed the potential for unrest wrought by the war. The man assaulted was a seventy-one-year-old custodian for the DeKalb County courthouse. One day when he entered the court's restroom, he encountered "some young colored men using the urinals established for white persons" (*Malone v. State*, 26 So.2d 916, 916 [Ala. App. 1946]). When he brought this fact to their attention (the record does not reveal how), the defendant Samuel Malone, a "twenty-three year old negro soldier weighing 194 pounds," informed him that blacks would use "whichever urinal they took a notion to." The opinion then relates that Malone violently swore at the custodian and followed him out of the bathroom with curses. The custodian seized a stick from a broom closet, and Malone took it away from him and struck him in the forehead, leaving him semiconscious. When Malone's friends urged him to leave, Malone truculently remained. In his defense, Malone had represented himself, claiming that the custodian had cursed him, though he did admit to having said that the bathroom was a public place and he would leave when he "took a notion." He also claimed that the physical altercation had been started by the aged custodian, who had jabbed him in the ribs with the stick first. Unsurprisingly, the appellate court found that the evidence was sufficient to uphold Malone's conviction (id.). While the case testifies to black servicemen's simmering rage over facing segregation upon their return, it also speaks to the depth of the embedded nature of white dominance, a force that could embolden a seventy-one-year-old janitor to confront a large, twenty-three-year-old soldier and expect his immediate compliance.

Other such incidents occurred across the South, most of which likely left little record or impression. A black man, George Smith, just discharged from the army but still in uniform, was convicted of maiming a white man with a whiskey bottle, an act that he had allegedly performed against an uninvolved white bus passenger in revenge for the bus driver's insistence (backed with army support) that he relinquish his seat in the white section (*Smith v. State*, 211 P.2d 538 [Okla. 1949]).[5] A young black soldier in North Carolina in 1952

---

5. The precipitating incident, as well as Smith's original trial and conviction, took place during the war, in 1943 (*Smith v. State*, 165 P.2d 381 [Okla. 1946]).

was convicted of assault with intent to kill for an incident between him and a gasoline station owner.[6] During the war, several black airmen were arrested in England because white officers became offended at their fraternization with white English women in a bar. In the resulting altercation, three black servicemen and three military police were wounded, and thirty-two of the black airmen were convicted in courts martial (Higginbotham 2000: 302–3). Additional violent clashes took place between black and white soldiers at several military bases during the war (303–4).

As in World War I, such assertiveness on the part of black soldiers and former soldiers sparked rage among some whites. In Mobile during the summer of 1942, a white bus driver shot a black private who was on his way back to his barracks. The private died (Feldman 1999: 288). In Missouri, a white man's drunken argument with another black man led to a black soldier's death when the white man, James Eaton, entered another bar looking for the first man and broadcasting racial epithets. William Van Ross, a discharged veteran still in uniform, confronted Eaton and his similarly loud and obnoxious white friend, seizing Eaton's companion and physically restraining him and demanding that they stop. Eaton shot several times, striking Van Ross twice in the back and killing him (*State v. Eaton*, 195 S.W.2d 457, 457–59 [Mo. 1946]). A race riot in Athens, Alabama, in 1946 injured nearly one hundred individuals, most of whom were black (Feldman 1999: 289).

These sporadic incidents ultimately coalesced in mass action against the white power structure in the form of a boycott. The first mass boycott was not in Montgomery, however. It took place in 1953 in Baton Rouge and, like the later Montgomery boycott, involved segregated seating on public buses. The boycott, which lasted less than a month, resulted in a compromise significantly reducing the racialized reservation of seats but not eliminating the practice. While the news of the Baton Rouge community's victory disseminated across the South through black church networks, its impact in the media was overshadowed by the Supreme Court's ruling in *Brown v. Board of Education* (Feldman 1999: 21–24).

The Montgomery bus boycott, while initiated in response to Rosa Parks's arrest, began in the context of longer-term tensions over segregation. In 1954, community groups had met with Montgomery's city commission to request changes to the bus system, to address the condition of parks and playgrounds

---

6. Defendant Elgie Wagstaff allegedly pistol-whipped the owner, then threw him on the ground and kicked him, fracturing his hip. He appealed his conviction and won a reversal on the basis of several procedural errors in the trial (*State v. Wagstaff*, 68 S.E.2d 858 [N.C. 1952]).

in black neighborhoods, and to ask for the hiring of black policemen. The city commission agreed to hire black policemen and placed four on the police force in May, but it did nothing to address the other issues. The community groups prepared for action and, when Parks was arrested, initiated the boycott in early December (Feldman 1999: 53–54).

The community, organized through the black churches, responded nimbly. Community activist E. D. Nixon organized with progressive black ministers to form a single umbrella group, the Montgomery Improvement Association (MIA), directed by an energetic new minister, Dr. Martin Luther King Jr. The boycott continued for a year as the city and the bus company refused to back down and the black community refused to ride the buses, supported by a transportation network organized by the MIA. Ultimately, the U.S. Supreme Court thwarted Alabama's legal efforts to break the boycott, demonstrating that determined, organized resistance could triumph over segregation (Feldman 1999: 55–63).

In response to *Brown* and the rise of mass protest, Alabama's officials and other officials across the South lashed out against the NAACP. Mirroring the NAACP's own affinity for legal maneuvering, attorneys general in Alabama, Louisiana, and Texas obtained injunctions against the organization. Legislatures across the South passed laws limiting the NAACP, investigating its links to communism, and demanding access to its financial and membership records. By mid-1956, Alabama had succeeded in outlawing the NAACP entirely. The NAACP's dedication to the legal forum was such that it could not effectively resist attacks of this nature (Feldman 1999: 30–32).

In Birmingham, the attack on the NAACP had unintended effects. Birmingham had long been a center for biracial organization and was the site of the NAACP's southeastern headquarters. Reverend Fred Shuttlesworth, observing the ongoing bus boycotts in Montgomery and Tallahassee, decided that Birmingham blacks could develop an effective response. Following the Montgomery template, he created an organization, the Alabama Christian Movement for Human Rights (ACMHR), to coordinate protest activities. Despite violent responses and attempts on Shuttlesworth's life, the ACMHR filed lawsuits and sparked mass actions in violation of segregation ordinances. These actions initiated a decade-long epic conflict between Shuttlesworth and Birmingham's notorious Commissioner of Public Safety, Eugene "Bull" Connor (Feldman 1999: 68–72).

This surge of activity dramatically affected racial formation and the state's relationship with white supremacy. After the turn of the century and prior to the emergence of mass movements, racial formation had been an incremental process, played out in various political and cultural forums but nonetheless largely controlled and directed through conflicts between and among whites. The legal arena as such was focused on key state actors' efforts to stem the rising tide of protest, both through the prosecution of defendants who violated norms and boundaries governing race and through the courts' consideration of appeals based on criminal and private questions about race. The civil rights movement shifted the central arena to conflicts primarily between black activists and white supporters of the state's articulated vision of white supremacy, overshadowing prior conflicts among whites over race. The legal forum remained significant but was used more strategically by both sides to advance competing visions of race and the state. And even though the law was significant, it was secondary to action and response; the legal cases that largely shaped the trajectory of the struggle over segregation arose from mass protests and state legal actors' responses to it.

The period between 1941 and 1954 was the final era when appeals of prosecutions for criminal miscegenation were significant in either reflecting white supremacy or shaping its future course. As the civil rights movement picked up steam, negotiations over white supremacy and the state took place in the context of state actors' responses to mass movements. The embedded supremacist state that the civil rights movement confronted was, however, articulated and developed in part in the context of the legal regulation of interracial intimacy. The state structures that elites used to contain black protesters appeared to be rationalized and deeply embedded in large part due to the developmental work that the courts engaged in the 1930s and their subsequent refusal to renew jurisprudential debates over race in the 1940s and early 1950s. The roots of the movement are thus entangled with key state actors' institutional efforts to maintain rigorous separation between the races prior to the upheavals of the mid-1950s.

Framing Relationships and Avoiding Racialized Debate: *Jordan, Brewer,* and *Gilbert*

Five of the seven cases decided in these years addressed evidentiary concerns about convictions for miscegenation. These cases, while evidentiary in their nature, differed from the cases of the late 1920s and the 1930s. In clarifying the rules for proving the crime of miscegenation, the appellate judges in these cases avoided racialized issues or questions, even though the defense attorneys appealing their clients' convictions explicitly raised such issues. Instead, the cases turned on neutrally framed evidentiary issues, some of which were not even related to the statutory prohibition of miscegenation. The appellate courts' refusal to engage in debates on explicitly racial grounds portrayed the state's stance on race as static and stable, building on the process of legitimation that had taken place in the 1930s.

Along with the debates over proving race, the earlier cases had dealt with questions of whether the requisite sexual act and intention to continue the relationship had been proven. A significant theme of preventing uncontrolled individual outbursts of racist rhetoric established in the 1930s continued in the appeals. Although at trial, one case in the later period raised questions of racial definition (*Agnew v. State*) and another raised questions about the proper proof of the sexual act and intention to continue a relationship (*Griffith v. State*), the dominant theme was continued investigation of the nature of the relationship. Appellate courts considering evidentiary appeals confronted the question of whether a relationship that appeared to be miscegenous could be framed in different terms, thereby lessening its threat to the state and the urgent need for its suppression. The implicit understanding of miscegenation as an effort to form a familial relationship across the color line remained in the background and likely influenced the reasoning in three of the appeals. In these appeals (two of which addressed the same couple), the outcomes turned in part on whether an alternative credible gendered and racialized framework to the framework of miscegenation could be articulated. In one, the modern reader can readily construct the alternative framework, but the court simply saw a failure to establish the required relational elements of miscegenation. The racial elements were not in contest in these cases, though the presumed racial difference animated the alternative frameworks.

This theme emerged in the first cases of the era, *Jordan v. State* and *Brewer v. State*. These cases arose from the prosecution of two individuals, Tom Jordan and Mary Brewer, for miscegenation. While they were both indicted, Jordan demanded a severance (*Brewer v. State,* bill of exceptions, court's oral charge to the jury 1940: 26). Brewer was tried first, in late 1940, and Jordan's trial followed in the spring of 1941. Represented by the same Florence law firm, Barnett and Bradshaw, which would figure prominently in two later cases discussed, both were convicted and both appealed.

Tom Jordan, a white man, was a salesman living in Florence, Alabama (*Brewer v. State,* bill of exceptions, testimony of Clara Sinbeck 1940: 6). He was in his early seventies, and his wife had died in August 1940 after a long period of illness and decline (*Brewer v. State,* bill of exceptions, testimony of Mrs. Grover Goodwin 1940: 7). They had apparently occupied their house alone prior to Mrs. Jordan's illness but had hired Onice Graham, a "white girl," through the WPA, to assist with Mrs. Jordan's care when she became seriously ill (id. at 8).

Mary Brewer was a black woman who worked for the Jordans, doing housework, cooking, washing, and ironing. Tom Jordan testified that Brewer "worked day and night—any time I wanted to call her to do work," not an unusual circumstance for black domestic workers (Palmer 1989). He reported having requested that she come to his house in the middle of the night "lots of times." He ultimately moved Brewer into his house and stored her furniture there because he was unable to afford to pay her enough for her to maintain her own residence (*Brewer v. State,* bill of exceptions, testimony of Tom Jordan 1940: 19).

The evidence of interracial misconduct came principally from two witnesses, a Mrs. William Mefford and Onice Graham. Mefford, a neighbor of the Jordans, testified to a conversation she had allegedly had with Mrs. Jordan prior to her death in which Mrs. Jordan accused Mary Brewer of "trying to come in between she and her husband" (*Brewer v. State,* bill of exceptions, testimony of Mrs. William Mefford 1940: 9). She also claimed to have observed Mary Brewer sitting at a table with Mrs. Jordan (a significant breach of racial etiquette) and disputing with her about Brewer's relationship with Jordan (id. at 9–10). More damning by far, however, was Onice Graham's story. Graham testified that Mrs. Jordan had protested against Brewer's moving into the house, admonishing her husband that "you will cause people to talk and I ain't going to put up with it" only to have him respond that she would have to accept it if she wished to stay in the house (*Brewer v. State,* bill of exceptions, testimony of Onice Graham 1940: 11). Graham also claimed to have witnessed Jordan and Brewer go into the bathroom together, where they stayed for forty-five minutes, and to have seen them emerge in a disheveled state. She testified further that she had seen them hugging and kissing each other. Finally, to audible shock from the courtroom's audience, she stated that she had overheard Tom Jordan tell his wife that he had been going with Mary Brewer for sixteen years and that "he loved her better than anything in the world" (id. at 11–12). While other witnesses testified to having seen Tom Jordan and Mary Brewer driving around together, their testimony was not nearly as damaging as Graham's (*Brewer v. State,* bill of exceptions, testimony of James Horrace, testimony of Sam Smith, testimony of Granville Brackeen 1940: 15, 16).

Mary Brewer testified in her own defense and denied the allegations completely. She insisted that she had known Jordan for only two years and that she had never had any kind of familiar relationship with him. She also claimed to have had only a remote relationship with Mrs. Jordan, confined within her role as a domestic worker. She pointed out that she had moved out of the Jordan residence after spending about a week getting things in order after Mrs. Jordan's death (*Brewer v. State,* bill of exceptions, testimony of Mary Brewer 1940: 21–23).

At Jordan's trial the following spring, the same witnesses with a few additions testified to substantially the same facts. Again, Onice Graham provided the main case against the defendant, with only minor variations (*Jordan v. State,* bill of exceptions, testimony of Onice Graham 1941: 8–12). Jordan's defense attorney attempted to impeach her credibility by highlighting some contradictory details between her earlier narrative at Mary Brewer's trial and her testimony in Tom Jordan's trial, and also sought to gain an admission that Graham had been living with a man out of wedlock but was unable to shake her from the crucial portions of her story (id. at 12–15). Jordan introduced several witnesses who testified to his good character and expressed bewilderment at the suggestion that he had conducted an inappropriate relationship with a black woman (see, e.g., *Jordan v. State,* bill of exceptions, testimony of O. R. Fielder, testimony of R. M. Sims, testimony of M. J. Carter, testimony of Arthur South 1941: 20–21). Three witnesses also testified on his behalf that Onice Graham's reputation and character were poor (*Jordan v. State,* bill of exceptions, testimony of J. D. Moseley, testimony of Ed Brewer, testimony of Carl Copeland 1941: 22–23). Jordan's testimony in his own trial was substantially the same, though more detailed, than his testimony in Mary Brewer's trial, and like Brewer, he flatly denied any romantic involvement (*Jordan v. State,* bill of exceptions, testimony of Tom Jordan 1941: 23–27).

When the appellate court decided Jordan's appeal, it framed the main legal issue as the credibility and admissibility of Onice Graham's testimony. It characterized Onice Graham's report of Mrs. Jordan's statements as "the rankest hearsay—and in nowise admissible" (*Jordan v. State*, 5 So.2d 110, 111 [Ala. App. 1941]). The court continued that, even if the testimony had been permissible, information about Mrs. Jordan's perception of the relationship between Mary Brewer and Tom Jordan did not constitute sufficient proof of an illegal interracial relationship. Another intraracial case had established that tension between a purported paramour and a spouse could not ground a charge of adultery. Further, it was prejudicial to Jordan. The spousal relationship between Jordan and his wife posed an additional problem, as Onice Graham's use as a mouthpiece for the deceased Mrs. Jordan had in effect constituted "testimony wrung from her dead lips," violating the principle that spouses could not be coerced into testifying against each other in criminal cases (id. at 112).

The appellate court thus based its ruling on problems with the testimony of Onice Graham regarding Mrs. Jordan's statements and forewent any consideration of the other evidence that supported a finding of criminal behavior. (While the court did not state explicitly that the prejudicial nature of the testimony was sufficient grounds for invalidating the conviction, the failure to consider the sufficiency of the other evidence implied that this was its reasoning.) As in the cases from the 1930s, a neutral evidentiary rule provided assistance in a racialized context. Nonetheless, the circumstances of the case made an impression on the judges. The opinion noted particularly that Jordan was aged and that he had a good character (id. at 111). In marked contrast to Graham herself, he was an upstanding member of the community with some property and status, and these factors likely helped him, as he had greater credibility for the appellate court rooted in his class and gender than Graham did. Jordan's positive qualities possibly influenced the appellate court to consider and write on his appeal in depth, while disposing of Mary Brewer's conviction with a reference to Jordan's appeal, despite the fact that her appeal reached the court first (*Brewer v. State*, 5 So.2d 112 [Ala. App. 1941]).

Another helpful fact for the defendants about the case was that it fit into an alternative racialized frame. Brewer was Jordan's servant, and having a black servant to help out (or to manage a household completely), particularly when the white lady of the house was indisposed, was a familiar situation. White men had a certain degree of latitude in dealing with black female domestics, as long as these relationships did not cross the line into a criminal interracial relationship. This latitude included a wide range of sexual harassment up to and including rape but would not extend to the formation of a familial or romantic attachment on the part of the dominant white man, as the courts had implied in their condemnatory statements in the wills cases. The age gap between Jordan and Brewer and her clearly subservient domestic position made the court less likely to perceive the relationship as a dangerously close or familial one. Graham's credibility as a woman dependent on a WPA program could perhaps have influenced the appellate court, though the judge and jury at trial framed the case as an instance of the violation of racial boundaries, believing Graham over Jordan.

In a second case, released by Alabama's Court of Appeals the day after the bombing of Hiroshima, the court considered an appeal by Myra Gilbert of her conviction for miscegenation. While the record for the case was unavailable, the context suggests that she was likely a black woman. Gilbert was married, with six children, and had represented herself at her trial. She was tried along with a codefendant who remained unnamed in the appellate court's opinion. Her conviction was perhaps unsurprising, as she openly admitted to having had intercourse with the codefendant. Nonetheless, she had a significant point to raise on appeal: she had insisted at her trial that the codefendant had raped her. She had testified, "He overpowered me and held me and told me he would kill me if I told it" (*Gilbert v. State*, 23 So.2d 22, 23 [Ala. App. 1945]). For his part, the codefendant maintained that he had never engaged in sexual intercourse with Gilbert (id.).

The court did not explain how the alleged act of intercourse had come to the attention of the authorities, nor did it cite any other witnesses to the event. The case thus rested on two contradictory stories: Gilbert's story of coerced sex and the codefendant's story that nothing had happened. Of course, if the codefendant were to be believed, there would be no basis for a conviction. Gilbert's explanation also raised problems for the prosecution, however. A rape, even if it involved a completed act of sexual intercourse, would not by its nature imply any agreement to continue the relationship. In fact, coerced sex would imply the opposite. The court reiterated the rule that even when an act of sexual intercourse had been proven, the statute further required proof of "a living together in adultery" (id.). In the appellate court's view, this required element had not been adequately proven. The jury should have been charged that, if they believed the appellant's testimony, she could not be convicted; instead they apparently had the impression that the veracity of Gilbert's testimony would work against her (id.).

Presiding Judge Bricken, in granting the motion for a new trial, noted the irony in the way Gilbert's testimony was used and justified the appellate court's ruling as the restoration of justice. He wrote, "our courts of justice are not to be the medium of injustice or oppression. . . . The guilty, as well as the innocent, have a right to be tried in accordance with the law of the land. The innocent ought not to be punished, and the law does not intend or provide that they shall be punished [quoting *Patterson v. State*]" (id.). While he did not discuss race in the opinion, he was likely reinforcing the principle that even blacks accused of violating the racial boundary deserved fair trials. In this case, justice demanded a new trial, in which Gilbert's story, if credible, would exonerate rather than condemn her.

The appellate court thus found that, whatever the relationship between Gilbert and the codefendant was, it was not miscegenation because of the lack of an agreement to continue the relationship. The modern reader easily sees the alternative framing of rape, but the appellate court did not use the word *rape* in its entire opinion. The appellate court's admonition to the trial court about fairness and justice reads oddly outside of the context of white supremacy. Why did "justice" constitute a simple reversal of Gilbert's conviction for miscegenation and the removal of the threat of a lengthy term in the penitentiary, rather than a call for the investigation of the alleged crime committed against her? While the appellate court does not mention the races of the defendants, their races are likely clear from the context of the case.[7] Quite possibly, the alleged assault on Gilbert was not read as rape because of stereotypes about black women's sexuality. If black women could not withhold consent to sex, any sexual intercourse between black women and white men had to be casual encounters, transactions involving prostitution, or criminal miscegenation (see, e.g., Tarpley 1996). Such a narrative involving a white woman and a black man would probably not have led to an allegation of miscegenation and the conviction of both parties, but rather to a prosecution for rape and the possible imposition of the death penalty, particularly since the woman in question was married and had children.

---

7. Between 1900 and 1955, Alabama's appellate courts published judicial opinions disposing of more than thirty appeals by black men convicted of raping white women and approximately eight appeals by black men convicted of raping black women. While four cases did not specify the race of the rape victim, it seems reasonable to assume that a published opinion involving an appeal by a white man convicted of raping a black woman would have mentioned the unusual racial configuration of the individuals involved.

The model for these prosecutions was laid out clearly in the cases discussed in chapter 3. If a sexual relationship between an individual identified as black and an individual identified as white seemed to be more than a casual encounter, the relationship was criminal and miscegenous. The discourse in those cases, however, tied in with the threat to the state that interracial intimacy posed, particularly when the cases were read in conjunction with the interracial rape case of *Story v. State,* decided in 1912. In *Jordan* (and by extension *Brewer*), although the racialized framing of the relationship was significant in making the case look less like an instance of an illegal interracial connection, the appellate court's ruling turned on the inadmissibility of Mrs. Jordan's statements as hearsay. Likewise, the problem in *Gilbert* was not explicitly linked to the hidden narrative of interracial rape but instead to the inappropriate use of Myra Gilbert's testimony. Notably in *Gilbert,* race was kept so invisible that Gilbert's own racial identification was not mentioned by the appellate court. The appellate court's only formal reference to race was due to Gilbert's appeal of a conviction for miscegenation.

As World War II raged and a new black assertiveness was just beginning to emerge, the appellate courts continued to clarify the proper means of proving the crime of miscegenation but did so without much reference to race. In both the joint *Brewer/Jordan* appeal and in *Gilbert,* the court had to determine whether the defendants' own narratives of the facts revealed either an alternative framework for the alleged interracial relationship or a credible denial that all of the elements could have been fulfilled. For both couples, their efforts were successful. Mary Brewer and Tom Jordan convinced the appellate court that the trial court and jury could, without the improper testimony of Onice Graham, have considered and believed that their relationship was simply that of servant and master. Myra Gilbert was unsuccessful in articulating a credible alternative frame of rape, but her appeal did use the issue of lack of consent to defeat the requirement that an agreement to continue the relationship be proven. In both of these cases, the racial configuration of the defendants as well as their genders were crucial, and one cannot imagine these cases coming to trial as prosecutions for miscegenation (or in the case of Brewer and Jordan, perhaps even occurring) had they involved black men and white women. The initial charges, trials, and convictions as well as the outcomes on appeal depended upon the established—and by now unspoken—structure of gender- and race-based individual relations of power supported by various layers of state actors.

The Necessity of Proving Intercourse: *Griffith*

The prosecution, conviction, and appeal of Lubie Griffith in the early 1950s resembled an earlier case, that of Alice Murphy and Coleman Cole, in which Murphy had appealed her conviction successfully. Like Alice Murphy, Lubie Griffith was a white woman who violated several norms for appropriate white feminine behavior. She was not as destitute as Murphy; her husband, Frank Griffith, ran a store. Nonetheless, they were likely somewhat marginal, as they apparently lived near blacks and the clientele of their store was at least part black (*Griffith v. State*, bill of exceptions, testimony of Miley More 1950: 27–28). She was convicted of miscegenation separately from her alleged partner, Nathan Bell, and the trial and appeal were based on the sufficiency of the circumstantial evidence that an illegitimate interracial relationship had taken place between them.

The initial connection between Griffith and Bell may have been the store. Bell worked at a local sawmill, but he also worked for Lubie Griffith's husband Frank in the store, which sold groceries and other general merchandise (*Griffith v. State*, bill of exceptions, testimony of Mattie Leonard 1950: 74). The state's principal witness was a black woman named Miley More, who claimed that Lubie Griffith had confronted her in a jealous rage about a supposed relationship that More was conducting with Nathan Bell. More testified that Griffith had asked her if she was going with Nathan Bell and had threatened her, "If I catch you and Nathan Bell together again . . . I am going to kill you, both of you" (bill of exceptions, testimony of Miley More 1950: 25). More also testified that she had seen Griffith and Bell riding together in a car, and that Griffith had told her that Bell had been "her man" for four years (id. at 36–37).

Griffith and More had a complex relationship. The women apparently both did their washing at and got their households' water from the same spring and occasionally encountered each other there (id. at 34). They had known each other for five or six years, and Griffith had sometimes employed More to bake and do "different little jobs" (*Griffith v. State*, bill of exceptions, testimony of Lubie Griffith 1950: 102). In contrast to this typical relationship of white use of black labor, however, Lubie Griffith did sewing for "most of the colored people in that community." She also claimed that More sold her husband whiskey, and that More's damaging testimony arose from a conflict between the two women over money that More owed Griffith for some sewing that she had done (id. at 96). More denied that any such conflict had occurred or that she had engaged in any relationship with Nathan Bell (bill of exceptions, testimony of Miley More 1950: 26).

More's story was corroborated by another black woman, Mattie Leonard, who also testified to having seen Bell and Griffith traveling together by car (bill of exceptions, testimony of Mattie Leonard 1950: 73). A white woman, Louise Stallworth, related that Lubie Griffith had been driving in a car with her when they had observed Miley More on her front porch; Griffith, she testified, had exclaimed "I am going to kill Miley and Nathan," though she did not explain her outburst (*Griffith v. State,* bill of exceptions, testimony of Louise Stallworth 1950: 77). Other witnesses also testified to having seen Griffith and Bell together on various occasions and in compromising circumstances.

Griffith categorically denied that anything inappropriate had ever occurred between her and Bell. She explained away some witnesses' testimony as arising from grudges or conflicts over unrelated events. The state attempted to elicit testimony from her about a fight that she had allegedly had with her daughter Inez about her conduct with Bell, claiming that Inez had initiated the fight by accusing her mother of ruining her by maintaining the connection. The fight had become unruly, implied the state's solicitor, with Lubie Griffith chasing her nineteen-year-old daughter down the road with a stick. Griffith admitted that the conflict had taken place but claimed that it was because Inez had refused to hoe the garden (bill of exceptions, testimony of Lubie Griffith 1950: 110). This testimony was challenged by the state's white witness R. B. Williams, who claimed that he and Griffith's brother-in-law had heard Inez's concerns about her mother's conduct after leaving home (*Griffith v. State,* bill of exceptions, testimony of R. B. Williams 1950: 124–25).

As in some of the cases in the 1930s, the prosecutor made questionable arguments to the jury during his closing statement. He opened his remarks by saying, "Society says you can't do certain things. When an individual comes along and defies all these things . . ." and immediately faced an objection from the defense, which the trial judge sustained (*Griffith v. State,* bill of exceptions 1950: 126). In a second closing argument, the prosecution also tried to inflame the jury, belittling Griffith's dismissal of the witnesses arrayed against her: "They [the defense] say there is some sort of conspiracy. It all started in her own flesh and blood. . . . That is where it started, when her daughter remonstrated against her cohabiting" (id. at 127). Again the defense objected on the ground that the daughter's alleged castigation of her mother had never been testified to in the trial. The defense argued that this statement of a white daughter's shame was prejudicial enough to warrant a mistrial, but the judge settled for instructing the jury strictly to discount it (id.).

Griffith's appeal was based on several claims that testimony should not have been admitted and on a claim that the circumstantial evidence had not adequately proven the allegation of criminal miscegenation. The appellate court worked through the claims and dismissed each. In particular, the court noted that the state was not obligated to prove directly that intercourse had taken place. Because the crime involved the secretive act of sex, reasoned the court, circumstantial evidence would often be the only means of proof, especially in situations where the defendant issued a categorical denial (*Griffith v. State,* 50 So.2d 797, 799 [Ala. App. 1951]). The court was evidently impressed by the wide range of witnesses who had testified for the state, even though many of the witnesses could only testify to having seen the defendant in compromising circumstances, generally in inappropriate places like an automobile or a pasture, alone with a black man (id. at 798–99). The court also found that the defendant's denial that she had fought with her daughter over her relationship with Nathan Bell opened the door for the state's solicitor to introduce witnesses who testified that her daughter had known of such a relationship and had disapproved (id. at 799). All in all, evidence about the circumstances suggesting the relationship, rather than direct evidence of the relationship, was sufficient to sustain Griffith's conviction. The trial judge's instruction to the jury—that "the offense of . . . miscegenation [is a] crime of darkness and secrecy, and hence always difficult of direct proof. . . . when acts and complicating circumstances are proved, it becomes largely a question for the jury to determine . . . whether there was in fact such continuation as amounted to miscegenation"—was a proper statement of the law (*Griffith v. State,* bill of exceptions, oral charge to the jury 1950: 130).

These circumstances incorporated an embedded understanding of what was appropriate behavior for white women. Unlike black defendants Mary Brewer and Myra Gilbert, who complied with expectations about behavior for black women, Lubie Griffith violated norms governing the conduct of white women. As the state's solicitor was arguing before being cut off, "society says you can't do certain things." And the reference to societal norms, not cast in racial language, was insufficiently prejudicial to render the trial invalid. Griffith, unlike Alice Murphy, would not go free through the appellate court's application of sanitizing neutral law.

By 1951, rationalized white supremacy operated to dictate that evidence of compromising circumstances, even in the face of flat denials by the defendant and the absence of direct evidence of sexual interaction, were sufficient to warrant a sustained conviction as long as other rules governing trials had not been broken. *Griffith* proved a warning to any defendant lulled into a false sense of security by the outcomes in the cases decided in the 1930s. Violation of gender- and race-based norms of interracial interaction could be as dangerous as being caught in the act of interracial intercourse or confessing to it. The courts in these cases (unlike the *Story* court, for instance) had no need to lay out the norms of behavior for white women; these norms were now part of the background against which trials and appeals would take place, and violation of them could constitute circumstantial evidence of felonious conduct.

Agnew and the Court's Final Word on the Problem of Prejudice and Racial Definition

The case of Hosea Agnew was about a baby. A white woman, Vena Mae Pendley, gave birth to a child in 1950, and immediately afterward, people began to talk (*Agnew v. State,* bill of exceptions, testimony of Sherman Brasher 1950: 28). The local officers of law enforcement discussed the situation and took two trips out to see Pendley and the baby. Upon determining with expert assistance from two doctors that the child was black, they pursued the case as an instance of criminal miscegenation (*Agnew v. State,* bill of exceptions, testimony of Sherman Brasher, testimony of Dr. J. H. Ashcraft, testimony of Dr. B. W. McNease 1950: 28, 30–31, 32–33). To add fuel to the rumors, Pendley's husband had left her at some point during her pregnancy and had visited only occasionally to see his three daughters, refusing to acknowledge the newborn boy as his own child (*Agnew v. State,* bill of exceptions, testimony of Hosea Agnew 1950: 56). While Hosea Agnew had been observed hanging around the Pendley residence in 1949 and part of 1950, no witnesses testified to having seen Agnew and Pendley in compromising circumstances (*Agnew v. State,* bill of exceptions, testimony of Oscar Watkins 1950: 17).

After examining the baby, the police picked up Hosea Agnew and questioned him. The sheriff claimed that he readily admitted to having had intercourse with Pendley at least once. In making this confession, he was apparently told that Pendley had already admitted their relationship, and he allegedly said in response that if she had admitted it, there was no use in his denying it (id. at 25). While the officers who testified saw nothing untoward in his confession, Agnew protested that it had taken place under duress. On his way to the police station, he claimed, the officers had warned him that "a mob was liable to get me any time" (bill of exceptions, testimony of Hosea Agnew 1950: 53). He also insisted that he had told the officers that he was not guilty at the police station, but that they had told him that they knew he was guilty and had continued to imply that they might turn him over to a mob (id. at 53–54). Under these circumstances, he explained, he had told his interrogators that he could not hope to overcome the word of a white woman in court, but he continued to insist that he had never had intercourse with Pendley (id. at 54). While Pendley was also indicted, the trials were conducted separately, and Pendley was also convicted at trial.[8]

Because the main source of suspicion was the baby, the defense sought to raise doubts in the minds of the jury as to the child's parentage. Hosea Agnew's race was not contested at the trial, but Vena Mae Pendley's was. The state's witnesses identified her as white, but the defense contended that she had Native Americans as ancestors. No one could provide definitive proof one way or another, but this question opened a path for the defense to explain away the appearance of the baby. The defense first tried to elicit testimony from a state's witness that Pendley's appearance varied from the white norm: that she had darker skin, thicker lips, and higher cheekbones (bill of exceptions, testimony of Sherman Brasher 1950: 26). The state had attempted to prove that the baby had a black parent through expert testimony; Dr. Ashcraft claimed that the baby appeared to "have negro blood" because "its genital organs were very dark, and it had spots on the hips and in the main it was different from a white baby" (bill of exceptions, testimony

---

8. Pendley also appealed her conviction on the ground that the judge, after denying a motion for separate trials, allowed jury selection to proceed and then granted separate trials. The effect of this procedural irregularity was that Pendley's and Agnew's defenders exercised their peremptory strikes and strikes for cause jointly instead of separately, and Pendley ended up having fewer strikes than she would have had if the motion had been granted initially. Unfortunately, her attorney raised no specific objections to the jury on this basis when it was empaneled, and the appellate court therefore ruled that, while the process incorporated irregularity, this did not constitute reversible error (*Pendley v. State*, 53 So.2d 811 [Ala. App. 1951]).

of Dr. J. H. Ashcraft 1950: 30). Dr. McNease largely concurred; he described the baby's private parts as having "a purplish hue, and its scrotum was dark" (bill of exceptions, testimony of Dr. B. W. McNease 1950: 32).

The defense countered this testimony and the testimony of the other doctor by questioning them about the possibility of throwbacks, getting them to admit that such instances had happened before. Because Native Americans were darker than white people, the baby's physical characteristics could, argued the defense, reflect a genetic throwback to an ancestor of the mother. Dr. Ashcraft admitted that "Indian blood" might "cause some departure from the white characteristics," while Dr. McNease admitted that a child of fourth-generation Native American ancestry could exhibit strong physical characteristics traceable to that strain (bill of exceptions, testimony of Dr. J. H. Ashcraft, testimony of Dr. B. W. McNease 1950: 31, 33). To cover all bases, the defense also introduced witnesses who had known Pendley and her children for a long time who swore that the baby looked like its mother and was definitely white (*Agnew v. State,* bill of exceptions, testimony of Clara Courington, testimony of Edna Franklin 1950: 40, 42). Between them, these women had birthed twenty-three of their own children, and the defense hoped to use their home expertise as experienced mothers to counter the medical professionals' assessments.

Unfortunately for the defense, the prosecution had another piece of evidence regarding the child's race. Some readers might wonder why, given this controversy, the child himself was not exhibited before the jury so that the jurymen could assess for themselves whether he was white or black. The reason was that the child was unavailable, having been relinquished for adoption by Vena Mae Pendley when he was but three weeks old. In Alabama's system of closed adoptions, it would be very difficult, if not impossible, to locate the child, as a representative from the state's child welfare department testified (*Agnew v. State,* bill of exceptions, testimony of Aline Williams 1950: 60). The state's solicitor entered into evidence a petition signed by Pendley requesting that the baby be adjudged a ward of the state. As a reason for the relinquishment of parental rights, the petition stated, "Petitioner [Pendley] further says that the father of said child is a negro and she cannot provide a normal life for him. She thinks it is to the best interest of said child and his three half-sisters that he be adjudged a ward of the State" (*Agnew v. State,* bill of exceptions, Exhibit B 1950: 66). In granting the petition, the juvenile court ruled in passing that the baby was in fact black (*Agnew v. State,* bill of exceptions, Exhibit C 1950: 67). While none of this evidence addressed Hosea Agnew specifically, no testimony at the trial on either side suggested that any other black man could have been the father of the baby.

Agnew's attorney vigorously attacked the conviction, identifying fifty-two grounds on which he believed Agnew should have been granted a new trial. While many of these grounds overlapped, the basic argument was that the evidence did not support Agnew's conviction, as an interracial relationship had not adequately been shown, and that several pieces of prejudicial evidence were erroneously admitted. In considering the appeal, the court first took up the question of whether the solely circumstantial evidence was sufficient to ground the elements of miscegenation, thereby paving the way for the proper admission of Agnew's confession. Following implicitly the ruling in the recently decided *Griffith* case, the court ruled that the facts and circumstances elicited by the state's witnesses were sufficient on their face to show the corpus delicti of the crime. Echoing its sister court in *Griffith*, the court found the reliance on circumstantial evidence appropriate, "particularly in view of the nature of the offense charged, which is rarely actually seen, but must, because of its usual secret and devious character, of necessity be established by circumstantial evidence" (*Agnew v. State,* 54 So.2d 89, 90 [Ala. App. 1951]). The court did not address the circumstances of Agnew's confession, although Agnew's attorney raised concerns about its admissibility under the circumstances that Agnew described (*Agnew v. State,* bill of exceptions, motion for a new trial 1950: 6–7). The court thus declined the invitation to scrutinize the meaning of voluntary confessions in racialized contexts, an invitation that earlier courts might have accepted. Perhaps the subject was simply too risky to engage by 1951.

The court did spend some time addressing the question of racial definition, responding to issues with Pendley's racial categorization and the baby's identification as black. The defense asserted that evidence of Pendley's Native American ancestry undercut the state's claim that she was white. The court disagreed, ruling that the defendant's mistake regarding Pendley was to reason that her mixed ancestry rendered her nonwhite because the statute defined blackness as comprising any person with any degree of black ancestry. The theory, claimed the court, rested on a mistaken attempt to draw a mirrored analogy in defining whiteness as encompassing only those of "pure" racial ancestry. Referring to the rule of stringent statutory construction for criminal statutes, the court refused to accept the analogy (*Agnew v.*

State at 90–91). The question of the baby's race, as based on the testimony of the witnesses, was simply a factual issue for the jury to decide (id. at 91).

The court did, however, find a reason to invalidate the conviction. The trial judge should not have admitted into evidence the documents from juvenile court that identified the baby as black. The opinion explained the straightforward race-neutral rule: "The petition and judgment . . . was in an entirely different proceedings; the appellant was not a party, the rules of procedure, and the burden of proof in the ex parte proceedings in the Juvenile Court were not the same as in this criminal prosecution" (id.). The purported reason for admitting the documents was to demonstrate that the child was a ward of the state, but the defense had not contested the witnesses' testimony on this point. The real use for the documents was thus to support the state's contention that the child was indeed black, and to do it in a way that would persuade a jury of laymen.

The court's real intentions are difficult to ascertain. Perhaps the appellate judges were troubled by Agnew's story of the threat of lynching. If so, why did they not address this question directly, turning instead to a problem of admissibility that at bottom had nothing to do with race? And why the insistence on not considering seriously the question of racial definition?

The answers to these questions turn on the developmental narrative underlying the history of appellate rulings on convictions for miscegenation and the relationship between cultural and political development and these cases. Earlier courts had established clearly that racial invective had no place in the courtroom, but little had been said about the exercise of extralegal racial threats. By 1950, these threats were embedded in the culture and society of Alabama, although elites had publicly decried the Klan. Extralegal modes of oppression worked in conjunction with the law, but overtly racial individual threats and maneuvers, the courts had established in the 1930s and 1940s, had to be purged from the formal setting of the courtroom. The appellate court's choice not to engage the question of coercion implied that it wished to make no further statements clarifying the relationship between the threat of extralegal violence and law enforcement's use of such threats to extract confessions. The outcome for Agnew was positive, as it might have been had the racial questions been engaged, but the reignition or continuation of conflicts over racial meaning and the boundaries between acceptable and unacceptable racialized state action was avoided.

The question of racial definition, too, had been debated extensively in the courts in the 1920s. The statutory redefinition, along with the landmark ruling in *Weaver v. State* in 1928, purported to settle such questions definitively. While the circumstances of *Agnew* and the arguments the defense attorney raised suggested that additional room to maneuver could be found, the appellate court declined the invitation to initiate a new round of debate over these questions. Instead, it fell back on the established rules that appearance could serve as a proxy for definitive proof of heredity and that the jury could adjudicate questions of fact raised by conflicting expert testimony. The court flatly refused to open any discussion regarding definitions of whiteness, perhaps foreseeing a period of uncertainty like the 1920s at a potentially more explosive moment in the broader scope of racial politics in Alabama.

Ironically, reading between the lines of the appellate court's ruling suggests that the conviction was thrown out for both of the reasons that the court refused to address directly. The petition itself was problematic both because its identification of the child as black was unnecessarily inflammatory to the jury and because it inappropriately implied a definitive settlement of the question of racial categorization, a question that should properly have been left to the jury. Nonetheless, the court signaled cloture on these debates, issuing an opinion that would stand as the final word from the state of Alabama about the concrete operation of its prohibition against interracial intimacy. In the cases of the 1940s and 1950s, courts repeatedly worked around conflicts directly implicating racial definition and racialized acts of the state, signaling to defense attorneys that such avenues were not worth pursuing on appeal. After 1951, the door on evidentiary appeals closed completely. No Alabama state court would again produce a published opinion addressing the elements of the criminal prohibition against interracial intimacy.

Constitutional Challenges Arise Again: *Jackson* and *Rogers*

The closure of appellate debate on the crime of miscegenation was not complete, however. In 1954, two remarkable cases reached Alabama's courts of appeal. In fact, they reached the same court of appeal, having both come from Florence, Alabama, in Lauderdale County, near the northwestern border of the state. In one case, *Jackson v. State*, the court's ruling was announced prior to the U.S. Supreme Court's ruling in *Brown v. Board of Education;* the second case, *Rogers v. State,* was announced after *Brown.*[9] The cases were not remarkable because they involved black women's appeals of their convictions for miscegenation; as we have seen, many black women appealed their convictions and got hearings from the higher courts. These cases were remarkable because of the grounds for the appeals: forgoing the long history of fairly effective procedural and evidentiary challenges, they instead directly attacked the constitutional legitimacy of Alabama's criminal prohibition of miscegenation.

Alabama was not the first state to confront this question judicially in this era. The California Supreme Court, in a 4–3 vote, invalidated California's antimiscegenation statute in *Perez v. Sharp* in 1948. While more than half the nation—twenty-nine states—still maintained statutory prohibitions of miscegenation in 1950, legislatures also began to respond by removing the bans. Oregon, Montana, and North Dakota led the way in 1951, 1953, and 1955, respectively. These changes marked a surge of critical state-based consideration not matched since the 1880s, when four states had removed their bans legislatively (Wallenstein 2002: 199, 254).

In Alabama, both defendants were represented by the same firm in Florence, and the same young attorney argued their cases at trial and on appeal. Elbert Haltom, Jr. was a member of Bradshaw, Barnett, and Haltom, described as "one of the leading firms in Florence and Lauderdale County" (Moore 1954: 263). In his early thirties, Haltom had served in the air force as a sergeant from 1943 through 1945, attending law school afterward and receiving his LL.B. from the University of Alabama in 1948. He immediately went into private practice but also had significant political connections. His representation of two defendants in miscegenation cases apparently did not hurt him politically; he served as a representative in the Alabama House from 1954 through 1958 and then in the Alabama Senate from 1958 through 1962 (Federal Judicial Center 2003).

Linnie (or Lennie) Jackson was accused of committing miscegenation with A. C. Burnham, identified as a white man in the appellate documents

---

9. *Brown I* was announced on May 17, 1954. *Jackson* was announced on February 16, and *Rogers*, less than a month after *Brown I*, on June 15. By the time that *Jackson* was announced, however, most elites were likely anticipating the ruling in *Brown*, which had been delayed due to its reargument. The reargument was in December 1953. Richard Kluger's *Simple Justice* (1977) remains an outstanding in-depth history of the legal mobilization behind *Brown* and its genesis.

(*Jackson v. State,* bill of exceptions, demurrer to indictment 1953: 5). As the objection at the appellate level was constitutional, none of the testimony at trial was presented in the bill of exceptions. From the charges given to the jury, it appears that the case, litigated in the summer of 1953, was fairly typical of those taking place during this era. The judge cautioned the jury that the evidence was necessarily circumstantial, and the defendant's and state's requested charges focused on the requirement that an agreement to continue the relationship be present (*Jackson v. State,* bill of exceptions, given charges for defendant, given charges for the state 1953: 12–13). Jackson had apparently testified in her own defense (*Jackson v. State,* bill of exceptions, oral charge 1953: 10). The record does not reveal what happened to the white man with whom Jackson was accused; she was convicted in July 1953.

Gold Lillie Rogers was accused of committing miscegenation with R. L. McCurry, identified as white. McCurry was apparently tried separately, and the record does not reveal his fate (*Rogers v. State,* bill of exceptions, oral charge 1953: 9). Her trial was in December, and as with Jackson, Haltom asked the judge to emphasize to the jury that proof of a single act of intercourse was not sufficient to ground a conviction for miscegenation (*Rogers v. State,* bill of exceptions, defendant's given charges 1953: 13). He also asked for a directed verdict, which the court declined to issue (*Rogers v. State,* bill of exceptions, defendant's refused charges 1953: 15). Although she faced a different judge and jury than Jackson had, Rogers's one-day trial likewise resulted in a conviction.

Sparse records in both cases shed little light on the circumstances leading to these defendants' charging and conviction by the state. An investigative reporter from a Baltimore newspaper, *The Afro-American,* wrote an article about the cases in the fall of 1954. This article, along with a few others, suggested that Jackson had at a minimum a long-term liaison with A. C. Burcham if not an attempted marriage (Jackson 1954; *Black Dispatch* 1954; *Birmingham Herald* 1954). One of Rogers's neighbors told the reporter that Rogers had been "caught," but few people were willing to talk about the circumstances around either case.

Haltom had sought to stop both cases from going to trial in the first place, attacking the initial indictments. His challenges, which were identical, were both filed on the same day. He argued several separate constitutional grounds to the trial judge. He objected on Fifth Amendment grounds, claiming first that the differential punishment prescribed by the statute was sufficiently arbitrary to constitute a denial of due process and second that the due process clause of the Fifth Amendment prohibited discriminatory legislation. Challenges under the Fourteenth Amendment included the claim that the statute constituted "arbitrary and unreasonable discrimination by the State of Alabama against this Negro Defendant, and members of her race similarly situated," that it abridged Jackson's privileges or immunities, and that the prohibition on intermarriage generally violated the entire first section of the amendment (*Jackson v. State,* bill of exceptions, demurrer to indictment 1953: 4; *Rogers v. State,* bill of exceptions, demurrer to indictment 1953: 3). He also cited the violation of a general "constitutional right and privilege of intermarrying with a white person" (id.). These grounds formed the basis for his appeal, as he argued that his motion to quash the indictments before either woman was tried should have been granted.

The court of appeals opened its discussion in *Jackson* by noting that the challenge was constitutional but without specifying the grounds in detail. It then highlighted the Alabama Constitution's prohibition on the legislative recognition of miscegenous marriage and emphasized the statute's persistence in Alabama's criminal code over the years. The court provided a brief history of litigation over the law, focusing on the constitutional era. It noted in particular that, while the Alabama Supreme Court had initially invalidated the statute in *Burns,* its constitutionality had been affirmed in three other roughly contemporaneous cases. The court also noted the U.S. Supreme Court's approval of Alabama's law in *Pace v. Alabama.* To provide additional continuity, the court cited the *Wilson* case as an example of an appellate court that had upheld a conviction for miscegenation in the 1920s, stressing that the Alabama Supreme Court had refused to reconsider the maintenance of Wilson's conviction (*Jackson v. State,* 72 So. 2d 114, 114–15 [Ala. App. 1954]).

In effect ducking the constitutional question, the court disposed of the case by ruling that precedents from the Alabama Supreme Court governed its holdings and decisions. The case was apparently of some general interest and concern; the *Montgomery Advertiser* reported the outcome the day after the ruling without editorial comment (*Montgomery Advertiser* 1954: 14B). Haltom moved for a rehearing, which was denied in early March. In response to his request, however, the appellate court agreed to extend its original opinion by articulating the constitutional grounds on which his challenge was based. To do so, the court simply quoted the language he had used in framing his initial demurrer to Jackson's indictment (id. at 115–16). Haltom continued to press, seeking certiorari from the Alabama Supreme Court to address the constitutional question directly. The Alabama Supreme Court declined the invitation on April 15, 1954 (*Jackson v. State,* 72 So.2d 116 [Ala. 1954]).

The irrepressible Haltom refused to admit defeat, and his firm appealed to the U.S. Supreme Court (Wallenstein 2002: 179–80).[10] The high court, dealing with the political fallout from *Brown I,* denied certiorari in November (*Jackson v. State,* 348 U.S. 888 [1954]). While nationally some legal scholars were beginning to speculate about the constitutionality of Alabama's statute and those like it, they recognized that the issue would be politically difficult for the Court to address. One of Justice Douglas's clerks noted this tension, writing in a memo to Justice Douglas that, while Alabama's statute seemed to be clearly unconstitutional, "review at the present time would probably increase the tensions growing out of the school segregation cases and perhaps impede solution to that problem" (Wallenstein 1994: 416). Not foreseeing the long, winding road ahead for desegregation, he recommended deferring the question briefly "until the school segregation problem is solved," but taking it up immediately afterward because of the serious personal consequences of these criminal statutes (416). Jackson went to the penitentiary to serve her two-year sentence.

Alabama's court of appeals dealt even more summarily with Gold Lillie Rogers's case. This time the court reprinted the constitutional challenges as Haltom had initially framed them without Haltom's having to request it, but the court simply cited its ruling in *Jackson* and stated its intention to "adhere to that view" (*Rogers v. State,* 73 So.2d 389, 390 [Ala. App. 1954]). On June 29, the court announced that it would not rehear the case, finally ending Alabama's appellate courts' conversation on the crime of miscegenation, initiated in *Ellis v. State* eighty-four years earlier.

While Alabama's courts abruptly stopped considering miscegenation in published opinions, one more significant development occurred in Virginia in these years signaling that the issue would not be deferred forever. In 1952, Ham Say Naim, a Chinese sailor, had married a white woman, crossing the state border to do so, as Virginia prohibited marriages between Asians and

---

10. While Haltom had handled the case up through the Alabama Supreme Court, more experienced firm partner H. A. Bradshaw took over for the federal petition for certiorari (*Jackson v. State,* 348 U.S. 888 [1954]).

whites. They separated soon afterward, and in 1953 Ruby Naim sought an annulment of the marriage on the ground that it was never a valid marriage due to Virginia's prohibition on miscegenation. A Virginia judge granted the annulment, and Ham Say Naim appealed, fearing that his application for an immigrant visa would be jeopardized. The case worked its way up through Virginia's courts, leading to a ruling by Virginia's highest court upholding the statute and its application in this case (Wallenstein 1994: 417).

Like Linnie Jackson, Naim appealed to the U.S. Supreme Court. Rather than denying certiorari, the U.S. Supreme Court evaded the case by issuing a statement that the record was insufficiently clear for the Justices even to determine whether to accept it for review (*Naim v. Naim,* 350 U.S. 891 [1955]). The ruling was issued in November, after the Court had released *Brown II* in May, but the Court was considering whether to accept the case in the context of expected continuing tensions over desegregation.[11] In a conversation with Walter Murphy in 1963, Justice Douglas suggested that he, Earl Warren, and Alabaman and former Klansman Hugo Black all wanted to grant certiorari in both *Jackson* and *Naim* in order to invalidate the statutes on constitutional grounds. Most vocal in opposition was Felix Frankfurter, whom Douglas described as having "spoke[n] at great length, with great feeling, pounding the table, shouting. He spoke so vehemently that I was beginning to feel that perhaps he was less sure on the inside than he seemed to be on the outside" (Douglas and Murphy 2000). Douglas believed that Frankfurter's reluctance to consider the cases arose from a pragmatic concern about their volatile potential for the South, though he reported that no one had made this argument openly in conference. Upon remand, the Virginia high court insisted that the record was sufficiently clear and refused to order further proceedings. This maneuver helped both courts to evade an open confrontation over the issue but left the criminal prohibitions against interracial intimacy standing across the South (Wallenstein 2002: 220–23).

The implications of the Supreme Court's evasion as well as Alabama's silence on miscegenation will be explored in the next chapter, but Alabama's legal elites undoubtedly watched the developments in Virginia with great interest and concern. Three constitutional challenges had reached Southern

---

11. The ruling in *Brown II* was delayed by the retirement of Justice Jackson and his replacement by Justice Harlan (*Brown v. Board of Education,* 348 U.S. 886 [1954] [continuing *Brown II* in the absence of a full Court]). As with *Brown I,* the members of the Court were wary about issuing anything less than a unanimous opinion from nine Justices.

states' appellate courts within a year, and two of these cases had been appealed up to the U.S. Supreme Court. In light of the newly ignited legal struggle over white supremacy, white Southern elites likely saw the constitutional attacks on bans on interracial intimacy and the Supreme Court's refusal to hear them as highly salient information in crafting strategies to defend the state that had been so painstakingly established over the previous half century.

The State Courts' Final Words on Miscegenation

The cases of the 1940s and 1950s constituted the final developmental appearance of the criminal statutes barring miscegenation. They emanated a false sense of stability and continuity in light of the massive disruption that would take place in the coming years. This surface tranquillity could not mask the tensions that were emerging in Alabama throughout the era, as the experience of World War II at home and abroad galvanized a generation of blacks there and elsewhere.

Previous eras had featured major and thematically focused debates that broadly shaped the legitimacy and operation of the prohibition against interracial intimacy. Between 1868 and 1882, the courts had considered whether the statute was constitutionally valid and had established the fundamental state interest in protecting white marriage and family. Between 1883 and 1917, the courts had laid out the basic principles of the statute's operation, clarifying the nature of the miscegenous relationship as one that mimicked family and introducing the theme of the integrity of blood as a state interest. In the 1920s, the debate focused on racial definition and the proper modes for proving race in an era when heredity was increasingly salient. The debates began to narrow in the 1930s, but the period nonetheless saw the courts developing principles about the state's monopoly on acknowledging and legislating racial difference, barring individual expressions of racial invective in trials for miscegenation—through this process the white supremacist state was legitimated and rationalized. Even the cases addressing wills, widely spaced though they were, established the major principle that white male authority over property would override the state's policy against miscegenation.

The nonconstitutional challenges of the 1940s and early 1950s were not so coherently focused, nor did they address major issues with the statute.

Instead, they worked further refinements in the long-established rules about miscegenation, albeit with a significant tendency to steer away from the sharp and direct conflicts over race that had characterized several of the earlier periods. *Brewer* and *Jordan* reinforced the principle that the crime of miscegenation was really the attempt to establish a familial relationship, and that the appellate courts could sometimes place an interracial link between a man and a woman within an alternative recognizable but legitimate frame for a relationship of dominance and subordination: that of black servant to white master. *Gilbert* also involved a relationship that fit within an alternative frame, but the frame was one that the court could not see or at least could not acknowledge: the relationship in question was not one involving consensual sex but rather a rape. Even though Myra Gilbert introduced all of the required elements of rape to defend herself from her own prosecution for miscegenation, the court did not acknowledge such a violation against a black woman. Gilbert's consolation was that she was not branded a criminal and imprisoned, because the court did recognize that her narrative of coercion invalidated the requirement that the relationship be ongoing. While a black woman's consent was generally presumed to a solitary act of intercourse (a familiar frame of prostitution, sexual license, and black hypersexuality), this presumption could not be extended to the establishment of a familial relationship without specific evidence addressing this point.

Lubie Griffith's appeal demonstrated the legal system's further refinement of another set of elements: the role of circumstantial evidence in proving intercourse and the role of intercourse itself in a prosecution for miscegenation. Previous cases had implied, and even at times had stated, that the state had to prove that intercourse had taken place, but no case had directly questioned these implications or statements. The evidence in *Griffith* certainly suggested that something untoward was occurring, but unlike the situation in previous appeals, no witnesses could provide strong narratives of circumstances implying that Lubie Griffith and Nathan Bell had engaged in intercourse. Instead, their narratives primarily focused on Griffith's own behavior and statements in which she demonstrated jealousy and defensiveness over her alleged connection with Bell. While one might note that the jury, trial judge, and appellate court in this case elected to believe the testimony of the state's black female witnesses over Griffith's and her white supporters', Griffith's refusal to conform to the restrictive behavioral expectations for white women likely influenced the white men determining her fate negatively.

In all three of these cases, gender interwove with race to shape how the appellate courts understood the narratives presented at trial. In the *Brewer* and *Jordan* cases, the crucial question was whether the appropriate gendered frame was one of an intimate relationship or of a master and servant, which could in this racial configuration incorporate some sexuality without crossing the boundary into miscegenation. In *Gilbert,* the black woman's narrative of rape was not recognized as such, though enough of the coercive nature of the encounter came through to invalidate one of the key elements of miscegenation. Finally, in *Griffith,* Griffith's transgressions of gendered norms likely contributed to the appellate court's willingness to accept circumstantial evidence to prove that she had transgressed racial norms as well.

Alabama's final comment on questions of racial definition came in the context of Hosea Agnew's appeal; Agnew was suspected of fathering a mixed-race child with Vena Mae Pendley and the trial centered around this child. Refusing to reopen the debate over racial classification, the appellate court dismissed Agnew's efforts to challenge the definition of whiteness and reaffirmed that the jury could appropriately consider testimony about appearance as a proxy for concrete information about heredity. The court also reinforced the principle of *Griffith* that circumstantial evidence, even when that evidence did not hint at all of any observation of an act of intercourse, could be sufficient to ground a conviction for miscegenation. Agnew avoided his prison term only because the trial court had violated a simple evidentiary principle known to most law students: it had improperly admitted legal documents for a collateral but noncriminal proceeding that had been subject to different standards of proof. While the substance of the improperly admitted document was a controversial racial definition, the court completely avoided the racial controversy by turning to a general rule of admissibility.

In all of these cases, the courts worked minor refinements in established principles, but these refinements underlined the developmental process that had been occurring over the last several decades. Common knowledge, circumstantial evidence, and appearances continued to be important. Even an overt act of intercourse did not have to be proven definitively if it could be inferred from other actions or statements of the defendants. Nonetheless, the relationship had to look like a familial bond or at least an adulterous one. Questions of racial categorization were simple matters for the jury, as long as the jury was reviewing permissible evidence. The courts were comfortable

with the principles they were applying, and the era featured no major the-
matic challenges to the application of the statute. What the era did feature
was conscious choices on the part of appellate judges to sidestep thorny questions about racial definition and the appropriate boundaries of racialized language and acts by the state's agents. The appellate courts thus signaled that
these nodes of conflict were closed.

Given the growing certainty of major unrest on racial issues, why would
this have been the case? Even in the early 1940s, white Southerners were
aware that federal attitudes toward race were beginning to shift toward a
more interventionist approach and some were promoting meaningful racial
reform. At the same time, isolated incidents of black protest and resistance
were taking place nationwide, and by the end of World War II, the tension
between the ideological commitment to democracy and racial tolerance
abroad and white supremacy at home had become overt. These factors were
likely prominent in reigniting the constitutional debate, albeit briefly, but
why did the courts not make more comprehensive rulings on the substance of
the crime of miscegenation?

The cases themselves do not reveal the answer; we must think about the
relationship between the prohibition against interracial intimacy and the
broader context of white supremacy. The narrowing scope for debate about
miscegenation portrayed the state's policies on race as stable, fully developed, and embedded as fundamental representations of and supports for the
state's racial interests. This was particularly evident in legal discourse, as the
courts as institutions were largely representatives of the conservative Democratic elites rather than emerging liberals or populist reformers. Race *had to*
appear as mostly stable, unquestionable, and simple to determine through
the exercise of reasonable white men's judgment. While a few questions were
permissible at the margins, the categories of race themselves had to be stable
overall. Knowledge of dangerous interracial connections *had to* be accessible
through the same men's evaluation of the circumstances in which the accusations were made. Judges had clarified in the 1930s that individual utterances
of racist invective were not permissible within the legal arena, and that white
supremacy was to be implemented in formal and facially neutral ways. These
cases built upon this development and portrayed a state that had answered
all of the major questions about race and supremacy, a state that was fully
developed and rationalized, where white male knowledge and white dominance intersected. Racial questions were simply not to be engaged in the context of miscegenation.

Unlike previous lines of cases, the two constitutional challenges did not emerge from earlier precedents and defense attorneys' ability to generate new questions from their conflicts and resolutions. However, like other lines of cases, the challenges arose within a concrete political and social context that strongly influenced their timing. A constitutional challenge to the prohibition on interracial intimacy was literally unthinkable by a member of Alabama's legal community in 1934. By 1954, it was not inevitable but was probably at least likely. Elbert Haltom's dogged efforts to force a substantive consideration of the constitutionality of the statute, while an elite tactic, resonated with the first stirrings of mass resistance and presented a new model for the white Alabaman as racial liberal.

Haltom and his associates were likely not surprised by the outcome in the cases, but the act of appealing implied that they believed that a radical departure from nearly a century of practice was possible. At least for them, it was thinkable within a legal framework. The timing of the cases as the *Brown* rulings wove through their appeals in the state and federal system made it politically far more difficult for the U.S. Supreme Court to use this issue to follow through on its own incremental dismantling of the legal support system for the supremacist state. Nonetheless, the stage was set for later appeals and the ultimate national invalidation of state-based criminal policies against interracial intimacy in *Loving v. Virginia* in 1967.

CHAPTER 8 *Race and the Legacy of the Supremacist State*

The developmental process that started in Alabama with the close of the Civil War saw profound disruptions with the initiation of the civil rights movement in the early 1950s. Nonetheless, the deep history of gradual rationalization of white supremacy and the white power structure's continual bargaining over the use of race as a political category suggest that the function of race in Alabama's politics and culture was too profound to be swept away easily. The civil rights movement, as chapter 7 suggests, did not arise spontaneously, but rather as a reaction to the confluence of social and political factors, not the least of which was the claustrophobic and insistently static way that the state portrayed itself to its citizens in the 1940s and 1950s. This state, however, would be the basis upon which a new state would have to be constructed. As in the transformation from an antebellum to a postbellum state, the transformation from a pre–civil rights to a post–civil rights state would build on the foundations laid by previous generations. The particular form of white supremacy that had organized politics and society would ultimately be purged from the legal code as it had been earlier from uncontrolled expression in the courtroom, and the formal barriers between white and black would be dismantled judicially and legislatively, often through the agency of the federal government. Nonetheless, the fundamental dichotomy of white and nonwhite, the political foundation of the version of white supremacy built in the early twentieth century, would persist. Race would continue to be a political and politicized concept, even as racial ascription was finally purged from the law. Even now, it remains politically salient, as the controversy in 2000 over amending Alabama's constitution to remove the prohibition against interracial marriage demonstrates.

The history of the legal regulation of interracial intimacy in Alabama is both a history of the politics of race and a history of development. The criminal ban on interracial intimacy was a crucial site where legal actors negotiated the meaning of race and racial division in the developing state. Reflecting on this history will show that race cannot be dismissed as a category with political significance, even though the state has largely purged overt references to it and has gradually erased it from its governing documents. The legacy of the supremacist state still has an impact on contemporary politics and policies. In addition, as the afterword notes, the connections among state development, subordinated identity, and marriage in the analysis of interracial marriage can provide an instructive, though not perfect, analogy for understanding the contemporary struggles over same-sex marriage.

Before reviewing the significance of the developmental narrative, a brief description of Alabama's dealings with interracial intimacy after 1954 is in order. This description will answer the basic question of what happened to the legal structure that supported so many prosecutions for generations, showing that its dismantling was not accomplished through the fiat of the U.S. Supreme Court.[1] It also underlines the fact that after 1954, the regulation of interracial intimacy ceased to be either the crucial developmental or reflective location that it was in earlier years, as racial controversies involving the state and the law recentered elsewhere.

The Demise of Criminal Sanctions against Interracial Intimacy

By the late 1950s, the main legal forum adjudicating Alabama's efforts to suppress interracial intimacy was the federal rather than the state courts, as noted in chapter 7. Nonetheless, both *Jackson* and *Naim* had failed to produce rulings from the U.S. Supreme Court, and the Court tacitly decided to defer consideration of the problem of criminal bans on interracial relationships while the heated battle over desegregation was taking place. Judicial reconsiderations in other states were sparse; only California's high court took this route to invalidation in the closely divided case of *Perez v. Sharp* in 1948. While unique in this era, the case was nonetheless highly significant.

Perez addressed a challenge to California's ban on interracial marriage, which extended to any relationship between a "white person" and "a Negro,

---

1. Eliminating the antimiscegenation regime was thus like the battle to eliminate formal legal school segregation, which required significant intervention after the Court's ruling in *Brown*.

mulatto, Mongolian or member of the Malay race" (*Perez v. Sharp*, 32 Cal.2d 711, 712 [Cal. 1948]). The case came in the posture of a proceeding in mandamus, as an interracial couple sought an order compelling the County Clerk of Los Angeles County to issue a marriage license to them. The clerk refused the license to Andrea Perez and Sylvester Davis because she was white and he was black. Perez grounded her suit in freedom of religion, arguing that they were entitled to receive the Roman Catholic sacrament of marriage (id.). Avoiding this line of constitutional argumentation by citing *Reynolds v. United States*, the court turned instead to an analysis of the underlying state interests. In the person of Chief Justice Roger Traynor, the court explained: "If the miscegenation law under attack . . . is directed at a social evil and employs a reasonable means to prevent that evil, it is valid regardless of its incidental effect upon the conduct of particular religious groups" (id. at 713–14). The right around which the case would pivot was the right to marry, a right "as fundamental as the right to send one's child to a particular school or the right to have offspring" (id. at 715). Traynor framed this right as individual rather than group-based in its nature.

The inquiry then turned to what might be a legitimate concern for the state, listed the expressed state interests, and demolished them one by one. The opinion considered in empirical terms objections based on the lack of healthiness of races other than the Caucasian and rejected these concerns. The court then looked to the origin of the statute, linking it to other laws passed at the same time rendering people of color ineligible as witnesses and citing the clearly racist language justifying this policy. After using this information to root the statute in racialized thinking, the court turned to an analysis of the meaning and definition of race, setting up the state's system of percentage-based definition against contemporary liberal anthropological data on race as a social construction. Additional arguments about black inferiority in general received short shrift from the court, which noted that blacks' social conditions were largely attributable to discrimination. The court also rejected the state's fears of inflaming racial prejudice by pointing out caustically that "it is no answer to say that race tension can be eradicated through the perpetuation by law of the prejudices that give rise to the tension" (id. at 725). Ultimately, the court had tied the policy thoroughly and effectively to an underlying justification of white supremacy, which it read as both empirically inaccurate and constitutionally unacceptable (id.).

In the wake of the *Perez* ruling, several states outside the South dealt with the issue legislatively by repealing their criminal prohibitions in the 1950s, beginning with Oregon in 1951 and followed by Montana, North and South Dakota, Colorado, Idaho, and Nevada (Wallenstein 2002: 254). By the mid-1960s, criminal prohibitions of interracial relationships were almost exclusively a Southern phenomenon, with seventeen states maintaining their laws until 1967: Alabama, Arkansas, Delaware, Florida, Georgia, Kentucky, Louisiana, Maryland, Mississippi, Missouri, North Carolina, Oklahoma, South Carolina, Tennessee, Texas, Virginia, and West Virginia (253–54).

For the South, these statutes were sufficiently important in a symbolic sense that their repeal was quite unlikely; further, even if prosecutions were uncommon, they could still be used to prevent the issuance of marriage licenses to mixed-race couples. Only national intervention seemed like a viable way of eliminating these laws. The first decisive step would take place in the 1960s, when the U.S. Supreme Court would again have the opportunity to reconsider its 1883 precedent of *Pace v. Alabama.*

In 1963, Florida's high court heard the appeal of Dewey McLaughlin and Connie Hoffman, a black Honduran hotel worker and white woman from Alabama who were convicted of "habitually liv[ing] in and occupy[ing] in the nighttime the same room" as an unmarried couple (Romano 2003: 188). While their punishment of a thirty-day sentence and a $150 fine was not nearly as severe as it would have been had they been convicted of miscegenation in Alabama, they nonetheless appealed (Wallenstein 2002: 208–9). Upon the Florida Supreme Court's affirmation of the constitutionality of the law on the basis of *Pace v. Alabama,* they appealed to the U.S. Supreme Court with representation from the Legal Defense Fund of the NAACP. The NAACP's decision that it was time to take up the issue was significant—it had not participated in earlier constitutional cases, having specifically declined to become involved in a challenge to Oklahoma's statute in federal court in the late 1940s (183–85).

Like the NAACP, the U.S. Supreme Court believed that the time was ripe to tackle bans on interracial relationships. In 1964, a unanimous Court invalidated Florida's racially based statute on equal protection grounds. With regard to *Pace,* Justice Byron White explained that the case "represents a limited view of the Equal Protection Clause which has not withstood analysis" (Wallenstein 2002: 209). The Court's opinion first dismantled *Pace*'s endorsement of the principle of superficial symmetry and then applied a straightforward analysis under strict scrutiny, finding that Florida had not provided any justification, much less a strong one, for punishing interracial cohabitation and promiscuity more severely than intraracial sexual misconduct (*McLaughlin v. Florida,* 379 U.S. 184, 192–93 [1964]). The majority noted that Florida's specific statute barring miscegenation (which Florida defined more strictly as intermarriage) could not provide the required justification but declined to address the constitutionality of Florida's law against miscegenation (id. at 194). Justices Stewart and Douglas concurred but argued for a broader principle that likely would have encompassed laws punishing interracial marriage as well as the law at issue in the case (id. at 198, Stewart, J., concurring).

McLaughlin v. Florida formally overruled the Supreme Court's specific ruling in *Pace,* but the broader principle that *Pace* established, favoring the constitutionality of laws against interracial relationships, remained alive though clearly under target. The direct confrontation was not long in coming. The American Civil Liberties Union (ACLU) was pursuing a promising Oklahoma case involving a denial of a marriage license to a Latino and a black woman, but their plans for appeal had to be dropped when the Latino eventually lost faith in the judicial process and married a white woman (Wallenstein 2002: 212–14).

In Alabama, the state's attorney general reassured the public that the high court's ruling would not affect the functioning of Alabama's legal regime. He pronounced that any effort to invalidate Alabama's law would have to go "all the way to the U.S. Supreme Court before we would let it be reversed" (*Montgomery Advertiser* 1964: 1). He reported that no cases from Alabama were currently working their way through the judicial system and that he knew of no attempts within the state to attack its laws (1).

The perfect case for the final national resolution of the issue arose instead in Virginia, resulting from a judicial action initiated in 1958 against Mildred Jeter and Richard Loving, who had married in Washington, DC, and were arrested for miscegenation a little more than a month after their wedding. Upon their conviction and Virginia state judge Bazile's issuance of a suspended sentence of a year in jail, the couple had returned to Washington. They nonetheless maintained close family connections across the state line, and Mildred Loving bore all three of their children in Caroline County, Virginia, with her extended family. Tired of their exile and need for extreme caution when visiting family, Mildred Loving lost patience in 1963 and wrote to Robert F. Kennedy for assistance. Her letter was forwarded to the American Civil Liberties Union, which assigned the case to Virginia lawyer and ACLU member Bernard Cohen. Cohen and another ACLU attorney, Philip Hirschkop, revived the case before Judge Bazile, secured an adverse ruling, and began the appellate process that ultimately led to *Loving v. Virginia* (id. at 217–20).

The Virginia Supreme Court obligingly upheld the state's criminal prohibition and set up the appeal in *Loving* to the U.S. Supreme Court, which granted certiorari in December 1966. While Virginia was able to rely on federal precedents from the 1880s to the 1940s upholding specific elements of the regime against miscegenation, Cohen and Hirschkop relied on more recent precedents expanding the scope of review under equal protection and touching on newer interpretations of liberty (id. at 221–23). On June 12, 1967, the U.S. Supreme Court announced its ruling in *Loving*, unanimously invalidating Virginia's statute. The high court characterized Virginia's expressed state interest in the earlier litigation over the case as unadulterated support for white supremacy, clearly not an acceptable state interest under any form of review, much less strict scrutiny (*Loving v. Virginia*, 388 U.S. 1, 6 [1967]). Nonetheless, reasoning in the case focused less on the genealogy of white supremacy than on the meaning of the Fourteenth Amendment. On the equal protection side, the Court explained, "We have consistently denied the constitutionality of measures which restrict the rights of citizens on account of race. There can be no doubt that restricting the freedom to marry solely because of racial classifications violates . . . the Equal Protection Clause" (id. at 11–12). Equality thus required the state to ignore the races of the parties seeking a marriage license.

The analysis of due process and liberty was equally succinct. The Court declared marriage to be a basic civil right, explaining that "to deny this fundamental freedom on so unsupportable a basis as the racial classifications embodied in these statutes . . . is surely to deprive all the State's citizens of liberty without due process of law. . . . the freedom to marry . . . a person of another race resides within the individual and cannot be infringed by the State" (id. at 12). While the analysis of liberty also rested upon a fundamental assumption that the underlying racial differentiation was illegitimate, here also the reasoning rested upon an analytical rather than a doctrinal or factual argument about the meaning and sources of racial discrimination. Except for a nondefinitive reading of the history of the Fourteenth Amendment's adoption, history was relatively unimportant in the Court's opinion. *Loving* provided a mirrored response to *Pace v. Alabama,* rereading the meaning of equality to encompass the freedom to choose marital partners without state intervention on the basis of race. The state was forbidden to see racial difference in sanctioning marital and other sexually intimate relationships.

Loving was thus quite different from *Perez* and perhaps reflected the high court's sentiment that, by 1967, the history of racial discrimination was known and the roots of the Jim Crow era had been laid bare by the struggles over desegregation. Regardless of the Court's motivation, it established an analytical structure for rejecting racialized limits on marriage that did not address in any substantial way the structural and institutional sources of state repression of socially subordinated racial minorities. *Perez* constituted a more thorough attempt to dismantle the embedded racism in law and culture through showing the way that the state had participated in the process of racial formation (to use a term that would not have occurred to Justice Traynor).

Loving, however, provided a necessary national mandate. Its expression of broad principles of equality and freedom to marry clearly directed the sixteen states with operational antimiscegenation provisions that their statutes could no longer be enforced either to prosecute mixed-race couples or to deny marriage licenses to them.[2] Nonetheless, several states, including Alabama, were not willing to acquiesce quietly to the Court's directive.

In November 1970, a white Army sergeant, Louis Voyer, went with his fiancée, Phyllis Bett, to the probate court of Calhoun County to obtain a marriage license. Voyer had been raised in Massachusetts and was a Vietnam veteran, while Bett was a seventeen-year-old native of Alabama. Voyer was serving at Fort McClellan, and Bett lived in the nearby town of Anniston. The probate judge, G. Clyde Brittain, refused to issue the license on the ground that Voyer was white and Bett was black; his clerk informed the couple that issuing the license to them was illegal (*Richmond Times-Dispatch,* Dec. 4, 1970). Alabama's statutes still dictated that the issuance of a license to or performance of a marriage ceremony for a mixed-race couple was a misdemeanor (Wallenstein 2002: 234).

Brittain, however, was likely not acting only out of fear of prosecution. Another mixed-race couple had applied for and received a marriage license in

2. Maryland had repealed its statute shortly before the Court announced its ruling in *Loving* (Wallenstein 2002: 252).

Tuskegee shortly before Voyer and Bett, and no appellate case in Alabama had involved a prosecution of a justice of the peace or probate judge since *Burns v. State* in 1872. While he testified later that his office had no set policy regarding interracial marriage, Brittain and his staff apparently disapproved of interracial relationships and did not view the ruling in *Loving* as having invalidated Alabama's criminal statutes (*Richmond Times-Dispatch*, Dec. 4, 1970).[3]

Voyer and Bett did not have to look far for support. The Nixon administration, concerned about the effect of such actions on U.S. military policy, took up the case and sued the state of Alabama and Brittain (Wallenstein 2002: 234). Attorney John Mitchell went to the federal district court for the northeast region of Alabama and sought an injunction against Alabama's antimiscegenation laws as violative of the U.S. Constitution (*United States v. Brittain*, 319 F. Supp. 1058 [N.D. Ala. 1970]).

Alabama defended its laws in court, first seeking to have the suit dismissed on the ground that it was moot, since Voyer and Bett had simply traveled to Clarksville, Tennessee, and gotten married after being thwarted in Anniston. The Justice Department responded that they were still subject to prosecution upon their return to Alabama for Sgt. Voyer to complete his term of service in the military. Federal district judge Sam Pointer, a recent Nixon nominee who had served in the army himself in the late 1950s, agreed and allowed the substantive challenge to proceed (Wallenstein 2002: 234). He explained that the case, being brought by the United States as plaintiff, involved more than just the substantive rights of the Voyers, though even if the Voyers had been the sole parties, the next question would have been the validity of their Tennessee marriage in Alabama (*United States v. Brittain* at 1060).

Alabama's next gambit, when confronted with the *Loving* decision, was to argue that the Supreme Court's ruling applied only to the Lovings. Deputy assistant attorney general John Bookout, assigned the task of defending Alabama's laws, argued, "The Alabama law is still law until it is stricken

---

3. Brittain had also been nominally involved in another case addressing Alabama's struggles with race in this era. In 1968, the city of Anniston had considered moving from having a commission-based government to a city council–manager form of government. The change was proposed by petition and adopted but was challenged first on state constitutional grounds and then under the Voting Rights Act. Brittain was the named defendant in the black challengers' failed suit to secure an injunction against the impending election of five city councillors. See *Brittain v. Weatherly*, 281 Ala. 683 (1968); *Oden v. Brittain*, 396 U.S. 1210 (1969).

down. They don't just wipe these laws off the book all over the United States because of one ruling" (Wallenstein 2002: 234). Pointer gave this argument short shrift as well, stating plainly that Alabama's laws violated the Fourteenth Amendment as the Supreme Court's opinion in *Loving* had established (*United States v. Brittain* at 1059). Judge Pointer took pains to make his ruling absolutely unambiguous, entering a judgment declaring the statute completely invalid and "enjoining the State of Alabama, its officers, agents, employees, and their successors, and all those acting in concert or participation with them from enforcing or giving any effect to such laws; and requiring the Attorney General of the State of Alabama to advise the Judges of Probate" across the state of the invalidity of Alabama's antimiscegenation laws (id. at 1060).

The governor, Albert Brewer, expressed distaste for the ruling. He told a reporter the next day, "I feel very strongly that our miscegenation laws ought to be upheld . . . . I don't find any sentiment of significance anywhere in this country for mixed marriages. I strongly believe miscegenation laws are in the best interests of all our people" (Bailey 1970: 23). He argued that the state legislatures had the right to represent the views of the people, and that Alabamans still had strong feelings against interracial intimacy. Nonetheless, he recognized the inevitability of the change, admitting that the state had no plans to appeal the ruling and faced certain defeat (23). A similar process involving legal actions took place in Louisiana, Florida, Arkansas, Mississippi, and Georgia in the late 1960s and early 1970s. Finally by the mid-1970s, interracial couples no longer had to worry that their applications for marriage licenses would be denied by hostile clerks or challenged by white supremacists (Wallenstein 2002: 235–38).[4]

The last formal legal barriers have gradually been eliminated. Since the

---

4. Even in the early 1970s, white Alabamans were not uniformly hostile to interracial marriage. A Tuskegee couple who had applied for a marriage license just a few months before the struggle in *Brittain* did not become social pariahs. Johnny Ford, a political organizer for Robert Kennedy and later the administrator of Tuskegee's Model Cities Program, married Frances "Tas" Rainer, daughter of a leading white family in Macon County. Although her family had a personal acquaintance with segregationist stalwart George Wallace and her father was a member of the local Citizens' Council, Rainer's work with the Welfare Department of Macon County caused her to rethink her presumptions about race. But two years after their marriage, Johnny Ford was elected the first black mayor in Tuskegee. After his election, accompanied by his wife and their infant daughter, Ford declared, "This is 1972 and people ought to have a right to do what they feel is constitutionally and morally right. We're just man and wife, that's all" (Romano 2003: 175–76). Between 1965 and 1970, the Gallup Poll reported that approval for laws barring interracial marriage had dropped from 72 percent to 56 percent among Southern whites (191).

ruling in *Loving*, discrimination against interracial couples has consistently been recognized legally as racial discrimination, rejecting utterly the framework of *Pace*. The Supreme Court ruled in *Palmore v. Sidoti* in 1984 that the custody of a child could not be denied to a parent because the parent was involved in an interracial relationship (*Palmore v. Sidoti*, 466 U.S. 429 [1984]). Judges have used federal fair housing laws to protect interracial couples from discrimination in housing, and Title VII's protections against employment discrimination have been used to alleviate harassment and discrimination in the workplace aimed at individuals involved in interracial relationships (Romano 2003: 248). Mississippi and South Carolina amended their constitutions in 1987 and 1998 respectively to remove their bans on interracial marriage (250). As described in the introduction, Alabama, the last state in the nation to have a constitutional provision forbidding the legitimation of interracial marriage, eliminated that provision from its constitution in 2000.

As Romano, Frankenberg, Root, and other scholars point out, the elimination of formal legal barriers to mixed-race relationships has not meant complete social acceptance for such relationships. Interracial couples have continued to struggle with the reactions of their families (particularly their white families) and their associates and friends (see Frankenberg 1993; Root 2001). Developing ways of negotiating the identities of their children has been of particular concern (see Romano 2003). Debate still rages over the conditions under which interracial adoption should be permitted or encouraged (see Kennedy 2003; Moran 2001; Woodhouse 1995; Bartholet 1999). While interracialism is increasingly a fact of life in the modern United States, marriages between blacks and whites remain less common than intermarriages among other racial groups and combinations, and interracial couples still must work to negotiate the fragmented terrain of race in the twenty-first century.[5]

Alabama's Final Repudiation of the Formal Ban on Interracial Marriage

These tensions surfaced in the campaign to remove Alabama's constitutional prohibition on the legitimation of interracial relationships. State representative Alvin Holmes, a black Democrat from Montgomery, had long been con-

---

5. While the rate of intermarriage has increased dramatically, by 2003 there were but 416,000 intermarriages between self-identified whites and blacks nationally. Overall, intermarriages between self-identified whites and blacks constituted 0.7 percent of all marriages in 2003 (Fields 2004: 19).

cerned with his state's troubled historical legacy. A member of the legislature since 1974, in 1992 he and other black legislators had boycotted the rededication of Alabama's capitol to protest Governor Guy Hunt's flying of the Confederate battle flag over it (Reeves 1992: B1). While the capitol was closed for renovations previously, Holmes and other black lawmakers were arrested and convicted of trespassing when they had attempted to remove the flag from the dome (Sznajderman 2000). In 1999 he spearheaded a successful campaign to remove the flag from Alabama's house chamber, characterizing it as an insult to blacks governed by the laws made there (Poovey 1999). After observing South Carolina's successful campaign in 1998 to remove its constitutional ban on interracial marriage, Holmes decided that the time was ripe to tackle the issue in Alabama.

The House Judiciary Committee passed Holmes's proposal quickly without dissent. In addition to supporters in the House, Holmes counted attorney general Bill Pryor as an early proponent of the change. Holmes characterized the easy passage of the proposed amendment in committee as a sign of Alabama's racial progress (Poovey 1999). The full House also approved the measure overwhelmingly in April 1999, with no negative votes and but two abstentions. Holmes was happy about the result but somewhat surprised about the margin, having expected more abstentions. He said that the vote demonstrated that Alabama was "moving in the right direction . . . I think it sends a good message across this country, that Alabama is getting in line with other states" (Sznajderman 1999a: 4B). The measure also passed in the Senate without dissent (Sznajderman 1999b: 3D).[6]

As noted earlier, the campaign for the amendment was low key. The language of the amendment itself was simple: it read, "Article IV, Section 102 of the Constitution of Alabama of 1901, is hereby annulled and set aside" (Alabama Const., Amendment No. 667 [2003]). Michael Chappell and his Confederate Heritage Political Action Committee provided the only visible opposition, claiming that the amendment was unnecessary and predicting the expenditure of $50,000 on a media campaign against it. As reported in the *Birmingham News* (2000), attorney general Pryor dismissed Chappell and his followers, claiming that the amendment was necessary and characterizing the

---

6. Holmes and other legislators expected the measure to be on the ballot for a special election already scheduled to be held that fall to address a proposed amendment authorizing a state lottery. The legislature, however, failed to pass a resolution placing the measure on the ballot for the special election, so the vote on it was deferred to the next general election, which was held in November 2000 (Rawls 1999: B2).

antimiscegenation provision in the constitution as "embarrassing and obsolete and . . . an example of the kind of deadwood in the constitution that ought to be removed." Chappell, realizing that he had little chance of success at the polls, attempted to fight the amendment in court. He sued in early October to have it removed from the ballot on the ground that it was vague and unnecessary because the Alabama constitution did not specifically ban any marriages (Johnson 2000).

The lawsuit failed, and the amendment passed in November, though more than 542,000 Alabamans, constituting 40 percent of those voting, opposed it in the silence and privacy of the voting booths (State and Local Proposed Amendments 2000). Support for the measure varied significantly across the state. Counties with larger urban centers like Montgomery and Birmingham supported the repeal of the prohibition strongly. In Montgomery County just over 70 percent of the voters favored it, and Jefferson County, containing Birmingham, approved it by a margin of almost 69 percent. In two low-population counties located in the former Black Belt, support topped 80 percent.

Nonetheless, in twenty-five counties the amendment failed outright, with the northwest region of the state providing the strongest opposition. In eight counties, each of which accounted for fewer than 10,000 votes, the amendment failed to garner even 40 percent approval. The county strongest in opposition was Lamar, in the northern half of the state next to Mississippi; there only 34 percent of the voters wanted the ban on interracial marriage removed from the state constitution. Close on its heels were Cleburne and Clay Counties, in the northeast part of the state, both of which voted against the amendment by a margin of 65 percent (State and Local Proposed Amendments 2000). These trends were all the more disturbing because turnout was high, representing 66 percent of registered voters and exceeding the turnout in all elections in the previous eight years (Statewide Voter Turnout 2003: 4).[7]

The removal of the ban had little practical effect, though its symbolic significance, particularly for intermarried couples, was great. Nonetheless,

---

7. In 2004, Alabama's voters rejected by a razor-thin margin an effort to amend the state constitution to remove language mandating racially segregated schools. The campaign was more than a referendum on segregation, however, as flamboyant former chief justice of the Alabama Supreme Court Roy Moore (well known for his staunch support for a public monument to the Ten Commandments) spearheaded the opposition. Many conservative voters feared that removing the provision might allow judges to mandate increases in school funding due to the removal of language declaring that Alabamans have no right to public support for their education (McGrew 2005).

while the constitutional amendment could erase the ban from Alabama's statute books, it could not eradicate the historical legacy of more than a century of vigorous enforcement in conjunction with the process of building a white state. The state constitution is no longer interpreted with white supremacy as its paramount goal, but the years of careful construction and accretion of white power remain a troubling backdrop to contemporary politics and society. And just as state constitutions were a significant site for articulating antiegalitarian visions of the state based on race in the early twentieth century, they are now becoming the primary site for the articulation of inegalitarian visions of citizenship based on differences in sexual orientation, just as the states are active partners and often leaders in restricting the rights of immigrants and naturalized citizens.

The Ban on Interracial Intimacy and the Construction of Race and Gender

We see the troubling legacy of this history most clearly in the ways that the regime against interracial relationships interacted with beliefs about race and gender and their meaning in the post–Civil War years. The South's loss in the Civil War did not sweep away the previously negotiated relations of race and gender, but set forth a new political context for their articulation, performance, and transformation. The law, in particular laws punishing interracial intimacy, constituted part of the process of racial and gender-based formation and served as a key site for conflicts over the boundary between whiteness and other races and the meaning of this boundary. At the same time, considerations of interracial intimacy highlighted an analytical separation between commodified sexuality and reproductive familial formation, which played out in racialized and gendered ways.

The ban on interracial relationships emerged immediately as the main location for racial and gender-based anxieties wrought by the war, emancipation, and the North's victory. Fairly stable racial readings of blacks not simply as subordinates but as utterly other slaves were thrown into disarray, and free contractual rights seemed to imply the right for blacks to engage in close transactions, including romantic ones, with whites. An immediate controversy broke out, sparked by the coinage of the term *miscegenation* to refer to intimacy between different racial groups, most notably black and white. Upon the constitution of new governing bodies, Southern states worked quickly to ban interracial intimacy, often punishing it more stringently under the law than it had been prior to the war.

These bans were politically uncontroversial but raised significant legal questions in light of congressional acts seeking to establish new standing and equality for black citizens. The late 1860s and early 1870s saw debate in Alabama, as the state supreme court first upheld and then invalidated Alabama's criminal prohibition of interracial relationships. In 1872, the *Burns* court endorsed a vision of race as a simple matter of identity and not as a status or barrier to citizenship. The appellate cases in the era of constitutional controversy all involved white women and black men, and many involved couples who had clearly understood emancipation as erasing strictures on the formation of meaningful romantic relationships with members of different races. As the immediate white anxieties about emancipation centered on precisely this dyad, the post-Reconstruction state's response to move against these couples systematically was unsurprising. After conservative Democrats had returned to power in Alabama, they worked to dismantle the adverse precedent of *Burns,* articulating a conception of race (explicitly blackness but by implication whiteness as well) as an irrevocable and unquestionable status. This conception of race enabled the reading of statutes as discriminating properly between adulterous relationships that merely undermined public mores and miscegenous relationships that threatened the fundamental framework of the state. The state itself was understood to stand upon the white family, not the white individual. The sanctity of the white family was both the ultimate target of state protection and the most powerful foundation for the state itself. By 1883, racial differentiation had become more than a biological or social fact for the courts; they understood it as the basic political divide on which the state would stand, and their reading of race as status made this understanding more plausible.

In the years between 1883 and 1917, major work on race and gender developed these initial efforts on the part of the state to justify impenetrable barriers between black and white. This process took place around substantive evidentiary questions about the crime of miscegenation, and the courts used these cases to clarify that sexual encounters had to be accompanied by a desire to continue the relationship to qualify as criminal miscegenation. While this principle was parasitic on race-neutral rules for intraracial adultery and fornication, it took on a significant cast in the context of miscegenation as the prohibition of any effort to establish a mixed-race family.

Black and white were left relatively undefined, but the courts clarified that these qualities or statuses were evident to any ordinary observer, ruling that the jury could determine both race and gender from their observations of defendants in the courtroom. These cases thus drew upon an increasing tendency to understand race in the South in binary terms. The courts saw the question of what constituted adultery and fornication as a problem of distinguishing between prostitutes and women in intimate ongoing relationships. Apparently, the question "what kind of woman would have sexual intercourse across the racial boundary?" had but these two answers; the third possibility of individual casual sexual encounters was not visible to the courts, so they had to classify the women in the cases as prostitutes or miscegenators. These classifications incorporated racialized beliefs about women involved in prostitution, but centered on questions about the nature of the relationship. Evidence that a man had paid a woman did not necessarily lead to a finding that she was a prostitute; rather, it could show that the man was "keeping" her and supporting her by procuring a residence for her in which they could continue a relationship.

This distinction had different implications depending on the race of the woman in question, as *Story v. State,* a case addressing interracial rape, indicated. Other scholars have demonstrated convincingly that black women were viewed as hypersexual and that they were presumed to have consented to sexual contact, while white women were increasingly viewed as asexual, sheltered beings. Confronted with unchaste white women, courts placed them beyond the boundaries of Southern white womanhood by classifying them either as prostitutes or as race mixers. Martha Linton and Lizzie White were convicted upon the presentation of evidence that they were being kept by black men, and Ophelia Smith only escaped conviction because the confession of her partner, Jackson Jones, was excluded on nonracialized grounds. While the woman whom Clarence Story was accused of raping was not charged with miscegenation, the high court used the case to clarify that specific proof would be necessary to demonstrate that a prostitute regularly accepted black clients. No appeals of miscegenation cases involved white women who protested that they had not consented to intercourse. In this era this was unsurprising, as such a claim would more likely have reached Alabama's criminal courts in the form of a rape prosecution or more ominously never would have reached the courts at all due to the lynching of one of the potential defendants.

Given the sexualization of black women in this era, one notes with interest how few defendants evaded their convictions for miscegenation on appeal because the black woman or her white male partner was able to convince the appellate courts that they were not engaged in an ongoing relationship. Alice Pinckard's partner John Love made this argument, as did Mattie Leonard's partner George Smith. Love's conviction stood, and while Smith's conviction was overturned on other grounds, the court made sure to point out that his statements about his feelings for Leonard were all admissible.

Taken together, these cases developed more nuanced conceptions of race and gender, particularly for the women involved in them. Both race and gender were still understood to be transparent and ascertainable through the observation of physical characteristics and interactions. Nonetheless, the reliance on evidentiary conceptions of confession and admission set up the conflict over the meaning of race that would dominate the next era.

An intense debate over the meaning and proper proof of race emerged in the years between 1918 and 1928, as defendants challenged their convictions on the ground that the state had not adequately proven that they had participated in a mixed-race relationship. While the main evidentiary problem was proving blackness within the statute's terms of requiring one black great-grandparent, claims also reached the appellate courts based on challenges to the state's proof of whiteness. The appellate courts had to devise rules to accommodate increasingly popular hereditary definitions of race with common understandings of racial transparency based on appearance and association. Their rules increasingly assumed a binary racial universe, reading out the old category of mulatto.

Their task was further complicated by the reality and myth of Native American ancestry in Alabama's history. Alabama's constitutional framers had intentionally excluded Native Americans from their 1901 prohibition on the legitimation of marriages between whites and blacks, but the folk understandings emerging in the trial records clearly marked Native Americans as people of color and subordinates, though just as clearly not as black. As in Virginia, some of Alabama's older families claiming pioneer roots also claimed descent from "noble" Native Americans, rendering the stigmatization of Native American ancestry problematic for the regime of white supremacy. The reality was that some Alabamans with both black and white ancestors indeed descended from Native Americans as well, but these ties were difficult to trace definitively by the 1920s, based largely in oral family histories. The language and application of the antimiscegenation statutes required the classification of individuals as white, black, and not-black as the prosecutions worked out in practice. The contradictory nature of Native American ancestry as a mark of color and of noble descent provided a loophole for defendants who could claim that their racial characteristics, family history, and associations were ambiguous.

Ultimately the courts and the legislature developed ways of circumventing this problem. Rather than relying on strictly hereditary definitions of race, the courts adopted the principle that appearances and associations could serve as admissions. While the *Williams* cases demonstrated that in practice this standard could still be problematic for some defendants, most defendants could be definitively categorized through this means. A year after the courts came to this solution, the legislature added another defense, the initiation of a one-drop definition of blackness. Now there would be no need to prove that a particular defendant had a black great-grandparent rather than a mulatto great-grandparent; any degree of black ancestry would suffice.

The cases of this era also demonstrated that the perceived dangers of interracial intimacy to the supremacist state transcended the gender-based and racial configuration of the couple involved. While scholars have often assumed that white Southerners perceived the primary threat to racialized and gender-based norms to be the connection between the white woman and the black man, the prosecutions of Ophelia Metcalf and Sarah Wilson demonstrated that prosecutors, juries, and courts also worried about black women and white men. One reason for this concern appeared in the prosecution of Percy Reed, a man of ambiguous race: the state alleged that he was the great-grandson of a slave, but he countered that his great-grandmother had been a Native American who became involved with her white employer. Women of color, when they had children with white men, would themselves compound the problem of maintaining racial boundaries by producing children who would be difficult to classify even in a regime that allowed multiple forms of evidence to place individuals in the disfavored category of blackness.

More directly, the prosecution and appeal of Sarah Wilson demonstrated the potentially disruptive and dangerous nature of black women to the supremacist state. Allegedly defying all conventions of subordination and oppression, in the state's narrative Wilson ran her own shady business and lured white men into her ambit, entrapping Charles Medicus among others.

A direct threat to the white family, Wilson not only linked Medicus to herself in a romantic attachment but went even further, taunting his wife with her ability to violate the bonds of marriage and the strictures of racial categories. While Wilson was convicted, she may indeed have had the last laugh by securing a pardon from the governor despite the protests of middle-class white women offended by her multiple transgressions of racial and gender-based norms of behavior and submission. The legislators and judges in 1927 and 1928 who changed the standards did not mention Wilson's name or her case, but one wonders if any were aware of her case.

The more common danger in the appellate cases of this era was, however, the racially ambiguous man like Jim Weaver and Percy Reed. Witnesses largely agreed that they were men of color but could not agree about their racial ancestry. The *Reed* court, faced with maintaining a strict racial boundary or delegitimating several marriages in a community, ultimately chose to invalidate his sentence. Weaver was not so fortunate, and he and Maggie Milstead, definitively ruled black and white respectively despite the defense's challenge on both of these points, went to the state penitentiary.

The new definitions of race were in place in the 1930s, and the security provided by their settlement of most questions of categorization enabled the courts to take on a different project. In these years, the courts rationalized the application and operation of white supremacy by refining race-neutral evidentiary rules as applied in the racialized context of these cases. The repeated prosecutions and convictions of Jesse Williams bedeviled the appellate courts, which continued to find problems in the trials of the son of a woman accepted as white but with questions about his father. Relying on the rulings and statutory changes of the 1920s, the appellate courts did not focus directly on the prosecutor's burden to demonstrate race through heritage, appearances, or associations. The problems were mainly the prosecutor's inflammatory remarks about Williams's mother's alleged dalliance with a black man. Such a claim had to be made soberly and proven soberly; its mere allegation was not only insufficient evidence of Williams's race but actually rendered Williams's entire trial legally problematic.

The courts also continued their discussion of the appropriate proof and meaning of intercourse. Sam Jackson, whose racial coding as black was unambiguous to the court, admitted having had intercourse with Alexander Markos. Her race was somewhat in question at the trial, as some of the witnesses had trouble definitively categorizing a Greek as white, but the larger problem was her unreliability as a witness. The rule announced by the appellate court—that proof of intercourse alone was not proof of miscegenation—was not new, but Markos's questionable racial background likely did not help her credibility or the state's desire to protect her from black contamination.

Mappings of white Southern womanhood likely influenced the appeal of Elijah Fields as well as his conviction for miscegenation with Ollie Roden. Roden was a young white woman who had been caught with Fields in the middle of the night, but uncontroverted testimony portrayed her as dependent and sexually nonfunctional due to illness. Here again the prosecutor's introduction of threatening sexual imagery based on white Southern fears of predatory black men constituted an illegitimate intrusion in the jury's deliberative process for the appellate court.

Finally, Alice Murphy's unruliness, truculence, and drunkenness placed her outside of the bounds of endangered white femininity, despite statements from her that appeared to support a finding of a relationship between her and Coleman Cole. The appellate court's distaste for her and Cole was palpable and rendered the court incapable even of narrating the facts. Cole and Murphy escaped their convictions through the high court's categorization of Cole as an impotent clown rather than a genuine threat to the racial boundary. Perhaps both defendants' perceived degradation placed them far enough from society not to require the kind of close governance and monitoring that more conventional couples did.

By the 1930s, a binary conception of race had been established as a political and normative dividing line in Alabama. Most laypersons likely would still have identified a biological component to race, but the trials of the 1930s demonstrated that race was also understood as a social relation defined by interactions and associations among people. Its strength as a legal category was tested by cases involving attempts by white men to leave their property to black women and children, as the principle of free control over property collided with the principle of separation between the races. While only three of these cases reached the appellate level between 1914 and 1944, the Alabama courts endorsed the principle that white male authority over property had to be maintained even in the face of a social policy against interracial intimacy. This principle appeared most directly in *Dees v. Metts* in 1944, when the high court flatly rejected the idea that the relationship of a black paramour to her white lover constituted undue influence per se. While the court emphasized that such relationships were shameful and reprehensible, following the path of many earlier appellate rulings on this question, it refused to diminish white men's putative agency in these situations. Indeed, in order for the black heirs to inherit, the courts portrayed them as simple subordinate objects of white men's desires and control, despite significant evidence in trials that the black heirs involved had acted carefully and thoughtfully to preserve their legacies. Nonetheless, even such cases did not threaten the well-established dividing line between the races. A black heir with property was still black, even if clearly identified as the child of a white man. In a sense, such cases could be reassuring to those seeking to maintain a hard division between black and white, as they demonstrated that even bequests of substantial property to mixed-race children could not whiten them.

The cases of the 1940s and early 1950s portrayed a facade of stability and rigidity on the questions of race as a status and political category. As the nation and Alabama endured recovery from the Depression, war, and the postwar boom, the courts framed race as timeless and unchanging, subject to careful state management. Blackness continued to appear as a status but maintained its performative aspects, as did whiteness. The cases centered around lingering questions about what constituted the crime of miscegenation and what kinds of circumstantial evidence were sufficient to prove it. Moving subtly toward greater stringency, the courts ruled that proof of intercourse was not absolutely necessary to ground a conviction for miscegenation, even if the basis for the accusation was a connection of adultery or fornication rather than an attempt to intermarry. The courts refused to engage further debates about the meanings or definitions of race, despite opportunities to do so in some of the cases. Even when faced with a provocative direct challenge to the regime of antimiscegenation laws, the appellate court hearing the case avoided the question and relied upon the principle of stare decisis, citing previous rulings and declaring itself bound by the Alabama Supreme Court's validation of the statutes. The cases of the 1940s and early 1950s taken together portray an insistence that race was not under negotiation, even as events outside the courtroom, both in Alabama and nationally, demonstrated that unrest over race and its meaning was increasing rapidly.

The cases reaching the appellate level in these years involved a white man (Tom Jordan), four black women (Mary Brewer, Myra Gilbert, Linnie Jackson, and Gold Lilly Rogers), a white woman (Lubie Griffith), and a black man (Hosea Agnew). Several of the cases revealed the persisting beliefs about appropriate roles for men and women of different races; in some cases these stereotypes helped the defendants. For instance, Jordan and Brewer were able to evade their convictions by tapping into the alternative frame of white male master and subordinated black domestic worker. Myra Gilbert, while unable to convince the courts that the crime of rape had been committed by a white man against a black woman, was at least able to use a narrative of forced intercourse to undermine the requirement of acquiescence to continued sexual relations for grounding a conviction for miscegenation. Jackson and Rogers could not pursue Brewer's path successfully, despite apparent attempts to do so at trial; perhaps such arguments were more effective when advanced by the dominant partner. And Lubie Griffith's defiance of the norms for white feminine behavior helped to persuade the appellate court that she had indeed crossed the racial boundary, despite the lack of evidence of intercourse.

Struggles over interracial intimacy, as other scholars (particularly Victoria Bynum and Ariela Gross) have suggested, played a significant role in defining race and gender, as the courts considered the actions of the defendants as measured against the state's image of appropriate relations between blacks and whites and between men and women. Because miscegenation was a crime of violating boundaries, considering it legally implicated the meaning of the boundary itself as well as the discrete categories of masculinity/femininity and whiteness/blackness that the courts sought to present as hermetically sealed and binary. The multiple and evolving meanings of race over time shifted from an understanding of race as an immutable biological category to race as a political and social category that was fixed through performance, appearance, and custom. Race also increasingly became, in Alabama, a formal division between a universe of black and white.

These understandings of race played out in the context of increasingly rigid conceptions of masculinity and femininity. The re-creation of the antebellum era as one of sheltered white femininity, potent and honorable white masculinity, clownish but potentially dangerous black masculinity, and hypersexualized black femininity provided a standard against which the actions and appearances of real defendants were measured. Unruly behavior was understood as such in gendered terms, and the permissible range of behavior varied according to one's race and gender. Wherever the lines were drawn, their crossing had to be addressed, whether the violation was by a white man keeping rather than having intercourse irregularly and casually with a black woman or by a black man whose social interactions with a white woman implied more than extreme deference and delicacy. The problem of proof of a felonious interracial relationship shifted over time, just as questions about race, its definitions, and its meanings shifted. Over the years, the courts moved from the rule that exclamations or statements from one of the accused to the other could be used as evidence of a more-than-casual relationship to a final ruling that sexual intercourse could be implied from circumstantial evidence. Through all of this, the crime of miscegenation was progressively defined as a violation of sexual norms that tacitly allowed certain types of interracial relationships but harshly punished others. Black women's sexual availability to white men was strictly conditioned upon the white men's not engaging in an exclusive relationship with individual black women; white women could engage in intercourse with black men, but only if identified as prostitutes so degraded as to serve a black clientele or if the race of the black man in question was sufficiently ambiguous.

The Ban on Interracial Intimacy and the Process of State Building

Alabama's regulation of interracial intimacy, in addition to clarifying and sometimes shaping understandings of race and gender, served a significant purpose in the creation, evolution, and reflection of the state. As negotiating race was at the heart of the postbellum state's agenda, the regulation of interracial intimacy was a premier location for working through the role of race in a binary sense in the politics and culture of Alabama. The centrality of criminalizing interracial relationships in this process is highlighted by the two eras of constitutional debate that opened and closed state-level litigation over the criminal prohibition of interracial intimate relations. As Alabama moved through the initial re-creation of the state to the conscious creation of white supremacy as a constitutional order to the gradual institutionalization and rationalization of the supremacist regime, the ban on interracial intimacy remained a key point for the expression and negotiation of the building of the white state.

In the years between 1868 and 1882, the agenda of state building was a major concern but was a tumultuous process. Alabama's political structure was in turmoil between the end of the Civil War and the consolidation of conservative Democratic control in the mid-1870s, and even after the Democrats had regained control, they faced robust challenges from different corners. The crime of miscegenation was a key site around which the conflict over the structure and meaning of the new state was waged. The fundamental question for the postbellum state was to what extent blacks were to be accorded full citizenship, and the most controversial extent of full citizenship was the formation of intimate relations between blacks and whites. The initial upholding of laws barring interracial intimacy in the face of a challenge based on congressional statutes and then their invalidation under the authority of the Fourteenth Amendment likewise highlighted the anxieties that white Southerners felt about federalism and its new incarnation. Conservatives agreed that the new state had to develop a means of closely cabining black citizenship while maintaining sovereignty and not provoking federal intervention. Ultimately aided by the U.S. Supreme Court, Alabama's courts settled on a careful strategy of dismantling the idea that blacks' freedom of contract would have more than the narrowest of applications. Endorsing blackness as a status and identifying the white family as the principal unit of the state provided a means of maintaining social separation between blacks and whites even while paying lip service to political equality.

The years between 1883 and 1917 saw the consolidation of these principles and their full flowering as the political ideology of white supremacy. The idea of white supremacy had been around for generations, but now it moved to the center of Southern political ideation as the basis for the new Southern states. From the cases of the late 1870s and early 1880s that declared the white family to be the cornerstone of the state, judges and political elites constructed a legally driven regime, expressed first in statutes and then in the constitution of 1901. The constitution of 1901, in replacing the version adopted in the waning years of Reconstruction, explicitly established white supremacy as the guiding principle for the state. Again, the regulation of interracial intimacy was a highlight of the state's policies and a site where the development of the supremacist state was reflected. The evidentiary debates built on the earlier identification of the white family as the center of the state by emphasizing that interracial relationships approximating familial bonds were the most dangerous to the state. They also drew from legal rules developed in nonracialized contexts and applied them in the appeals of convictions for miscegenation, creating new rules with racialized content. Supremacy depended upon the separation of whites from supposedly inferior races and the implementation of state-based policies designed to underline the political and social subordination that blacks in particular experienced in their day-to-day lives. As the legal discourse on the crime of miscegenation developed, it articulated a vision of the state and its history in line with the narrative popularized in *The Birth of a Nation*. Whiteness required protection and guarding, but courts took care to distinguish casual sexual relationships or prostitution from far more dangerous attempts to forge interracial bonds. Those who breached the boundary between the races and meant it were rightfully labeled criminals of a different class, as their actions were directly destructive of the white state as well as bearing evidence of extreme moral degradation.

The years of debate over racial definition contributed to the process of state-level political development by refining the boundary on which the project of supremacy depended. Now that supremacy had been constitutionalized, the categories on which it was based had to be articulated as carefully and precisely as possible, and justified legally. The struggle over racial definition was shaped by the collision between scientific beliefs about heredity and race on the one hand and deeply rooted folk understandings of what constituted whiteness and blackness on the other. The significance of the struggle, however, went to the heart of the supremacist state that by now had been articulated in the constitution and laws of Alabama. The Klan reached the height of its political power both in Alabama and nationally during these years, and it contributed to an atmosphere of fear of contamination of whiteness. These fears were heightened by the apparent willingness of ambiguously raced individuals like Percy Reed and Jim Weaver to consort with whites. They were also manifest in the *Wilson* case, featuring a black female defendant who, rather than being subservient, fearful, and cowed by her encounter, hired an aggressive lawyer to exploit every perceived loophole in Alabama's statutory regime. A further threat was expressed in anxieties over what precisely constituted whiteness, an even more difficult legal category than blackness due to the lack of any clear statutory definition. The state underlined the importance of settling these problems by addressing them through two different branches: the legislature adopted a one-drop definition of blackness a year before the Alabama Supreme Court ruled that appearance and association could serve as an admission of race, circumventing difficult problems of proving heredity according to the statutory language. As supremacy became more established as a way of life as well as a political doctrine, the state worked to define and protect its foundation in racial differentiation. The state's embrace of racial binarism contributed to this process.

The constitutional era had set the broad outlines for white supremacy. The turn of the century had seen its constitutionalization and further statutory expression through the legal rise of Jim Crow. During the 1920s, the definitions of white and black were renegotiated and refined to provide for more rigid separation. The 1930s saw the consolidation and rationalization of the developed regime through the legal process. Jesse Williams, a man of unclear racial origins, would likely have given the appellate courts fits over his appropriate classification had his three appeals been heard in the 1920s. The courts of the 1930s that heard his appeals instead focused on problems of proof and the prosecutor's misconduct. Even as the Klan continued to ride and the defendants in the notorious Scottsboro case were tried and condemned repeatedly, courts in the lower-profile miscegenation cases insisted that white supremacy was not a license for the overt exercise of racial hostility by whites against blacks in legal forums. State actors were prohibited in trials from using racially inflammatory arguments without grounding them properly and soberly according to standard race-neutral evidentiary rules. While some conservative elites undoubtedly saw such rules as sensible precautions against negative publicity for Alabama and the possibility of federal intervention into Alabama's racial regime, the deeper narrative appeared to be about the legitimation of the legal expression of white supremacy. As a political doctrine, it would work more effectively if all unauthorized, random, personalized expressions of racial threat or invective were barred from the courtroom, leaving only the formal legal rules that made white political power a reality. The sanitized and rationalized operation of the racist state would, however, leave room for the gaudy excesses in which some private white individuals indulged. It further allowed the functioning of explicitly racially discriminatory laws, so long as they were applied dispassionately.

In some sense, the wills cases were a perfect example of this principle. The state, faced with a possible collision between social policies against interracial intimacy and social policies supporting individual control over property, tipped the balance in favor of allowing white testators' property rights to prevail. Such instances demonstrated that the racist legal order of the South, even at the height of Jim Crow repression, could operate to benefit individual black litigants, even when their claims were not completely uncontroversial. The appellate courts, when openly encouraged by white heirs to modify the ordinary operation of the law of bequests to cut out interracial beneficiaries, declined the invitation. In the absence of a highly rationalized and deeply institutionalized system of supremacy, the Alabama courts might not have been as willing to grant property to the Allen children (who could not even produce their father's will), to Estella Mathews (a black paramour whom the courts favored over the dead white man's own legitimate daughter), or to Nazarine Parker (whom the white intestate heirs portrayed as a scheming Jezebel who had plotted for years to get her hands on Ben Watts's property). The appellate victories of these subordinated black women and children should not, however, be misunderstood. They underlined rather than undermined the developmental process in progress. By the time of the Alabama high court's pronouncement in 1944 that the existence of an interracial relationship between a white man and a black woman could not be taken as per se evidence of undue influence by the black woman, the state had firmly established and rationalized white supremacy. Nazarine Parker's ownership of substantial property, while upsetting to the white intestate heirs of Ben Watts, could not threaten the racial order, rooted as it was in law and culture. Rather, the affirmation of Watts's own white male authority over property reiterated the state's commitment to bolstering its gendered and racially based conceptions of autonomy and liberty.

Finally, the 1940s and early 1950s completed the rationalization of the supremacist state and set the stage for the confrontations of the civil rights era. At first glance, one might be perplexed by reading the court cases addressing the criminal ban on interracial intimacy alongside the obvious stirrings of racial unrest arising from the aftermath of World War II. The cases considering appeals of convictions for miscegenation studiously avoided any recognition of the rising tensions and actively sidestepped debates that had predominated in previous eras. Relying more on generalized legal principles than on rules designed to address race specifically, the courts worked within the boundaries of the sanitized supremacist regime that had evolved in the 1930s. While some of the defendants achieved reversals on appeal, these reversals signaled closure of earlier debates. The reversal of Tom Jordan's conviction, which also led to Mary Brewer's vindication, was based on the unreliability of a witness and the inadmissibility of her testimony on grounds of hearsay. Myra Gilbert's conviction probably failed because her narrative of forced sex did not meet the formal criterion of agreement to continue a relationship, but the court ignored the implications of a black woman's accusation of a white man for rape. While Hosea Agnew's confession was deeply problematic, having been obtained under threat of mob violence, the court instead focused on the trial court's error of admitting a legal document adjudicated under a different standard of proof. Even here, the adoption paperwork whose mistaken entry as evidence freed Agnew simultaneously protected the state by stamping the child at the center of Agnew's trial as black for life. The era also saw a subtle tightening of standards: Lubie Griffith's conviction was upheld despite the lack of direct evidence that she had engaged in intercourse with a black man. This case contrasted sharply with the case of Alice Murphy, decided in the 1930s, in which the appellate court invalidated her conviction because the state's evidence suggested that intercourse did not take place due to her alleged paramour's extreme drunkenness.

The reemergence of constitutional debate stripped away the facade of stability but did not provoke the courts to reexamine either the policy against interracial intimacy or white supremacy itself. The invocation of stare decisis and the appellate court's references both to the era of federal constitutional debate and to the era of the legal and constitutional establishment of Jim Crow portrayed a static regime unaffected either by recent legal developments or the stirrings of the civil rights movement. Neither the *Jackson* nor the *Rogers* court gave any hint that serious questions about the viability of entrenched legal subordination of blacks were on the national and local agenda. Looking backward intentionally, they framed the legal question as answered definitively by history and practice and found it unworthy of detailed primary inquiry. Their stance was supported both by the Alabama Supreme Court and the U.S. Supreme Court, which refused to consider further appeals.

As the retelling of this history demonstrates, the ban on interracial intimacy was at times a significant locus for working out the operation and institutionalization of white supremacy. At other times, challenges to convictions enabled the courts to reflect the process of development and to determine the parameters within which white supremacy would function as an ideology. Ideology alone cannot function to organize political and social behavior either by private individuals or by state actors. The day-to-day workings must be implemented, and white supremacy operated through a complex negotiation between private racial oppression through violence and exploitation and a state-centered regime of legal repression and control exercised over both black and white citizens. Through appeals of convictions for miscegenation, the state's judges articulated the boundary between black and white and expressed the meaning of this boundary, both of which evolved over time. As white supremacy developed, it became increasingly ingrained and rationalized within the state's very structure; the diminishing of lynching and extreme violence against blacks after the 1920s was in part replaced by the state's efforts to control and channel black subordination.

White supremacy was not static, either as an ideology or as an organizing principle for the state. As the state modernized and developed, so did white supremacy as its basis. Many scholars since C. Vann Woodward have noted that the end of the Civil War did not immediately usher in the complete panoply of state-sponsored racism typified by Jim Crow laws. More recent work by Grace Elizabeth Hale and other cultural historians has revealed the significant work conducted in the early twentieth century to create both a new conception of whiteness for the postbellum era and a nostalgic and unificatory narrative of the "War between the States" emphasizing reconciliation over the principle that white Southerners should be given a free hand in regulating racial issues. Significantly less attention, however, has focused on the supposedly quiet years between the 1920s and the 1950s. The patterns of appellate rulings in cases involving interracial intimacy suggest that the racial politics of these years were not simple reiterations of a static racial regime. Rather, in Alabama the courts went through a detailed process of developing the racial boundaries on which white supremacy depended, and refined and rationalized its operation. Courts were grappling with very real questions of how to legitimate a regime of intentional and structural inequality based on overtly political categories that had nonetheless been established in the state constitution. This regime had to be squared with abstract principles of fairness and justice that would simultaneously legitimate the system for its immediate participants and shield the state from unwelcome national and, by the 1940s, international scrutiny. By the 1940s and particularly in the constitutional challenges of the early 1950s, the courts were portraying supremacy as static, but their rulings revealed additional development and consolidation of the regime to fortify it against the coming storm.

In light of these insights, we must reconsider the turn to color blindness, as Peggy Pascoe and others have advocated. Initiated in U.S. Supreme Court doctrine over race and expressed most forcefully by the rhetoric of Dr. Martin Luther King Jr., this principle began as a call for radical equality through the elimination of the racially based distinctions rooted in Southern law at the dawn of the civil rights era.[8] As implemented, however, it was vulnerable to being read into the process that had been going on since the constitutional convention of 1901. Since the constitutionalization of white supremacy, Alabama had gradually moved toward purging outright and uncontrolled expressions of racism in the law, focusing instead upon creating a legal structure that kept blacks explicitly subordinated by cutting off their access to political and social power. The process can be read as one of the gradual privatization, but not elimination, of overtly racist behavior.

In this sense, the adoption of color blindness by stripping all racial references from the law was a logical next step. This move continued the gradual practice of scaling back overt racial discrimination from the apparatuses of the state while leaving it free to operate within areas traditionally defined as private. It also built on the practice of adopting nonracialized precedent and applying these rules in racialized cases in a self-congratulatory way. Alabama and the rest of the South fought hard to maintain the authority to preserve segregation as a formal legal policy as well as to keep its primary control over issues of race. The state, however, was ultimately pitted against all three branches of the federal government and had to acquiesce to national regulations mandating the end of the era of formalized and legalized white supremacy as well as considerable federal oversight in racially charged areas traditionally under state control, ranging from voting to housing, employment, and elementary and secondary education.

The retreat to color blindness was a logical step for those who had been committed to white supremacy. With the legal regime forcibly dismantled in state law and racial issues now under closer federal scrutiny, the same type of alchemy that had transformed the Civil War into *The Birth of a Nation* provided an escape. The wrongs of segregation and Jim Crow were defined not as the inherent unfairness and discriminatory nature of white supremacy as an ideology, but rather as the intervention of government in a sphere in which it had no place: that of race. Segregation's recognition of race was defined as its most dangerous feature; thus, any governmental policy that recognized race was a threat. The end of juridical segregation of schools had to be accepted while busing was to be fought as illegitimate. Policies forbidding the hiring of blacks were viewed as belonging to an unenlightened era,

---

8. The phrase *color blind* as applied to race appears to have entered the U.S. legal lexicon in Justice Harlan's dissent in *Plessy v. Ferguson*. It did not make its way into Alabama's reported case law until 1964 in the context of a sit-in at the Talledega City Pharmacy (*Banks v. State*, 170 So.2d 417 [Ala. App. 1964]).

but affirmative action was seen as unfair. Blacks were to be permitted to vote, but the drawing of majority-minority voting districts was fraught with controversy.

These stances and others like them should not be taken as mere sophistry or winking efforts to circumvent racial remediation. Rather, they were part of a new moment of racial formation as the system both in the South and nationally responded to the disruptions of the civil rights era. Omi and Winant explain the dynamics behind the emergence of modern conservatism on race effectively, but the historical process of state-level development adds another significant element to the explanation for why color blindness was an effective response to the changes of the late 1960s and early 1970s. It also explains in part the striking differences between Justice Traynor's approach to invalidating California's ban on interracial marriage in 1948 in *Perez v. Sharp* and the U.S. Supreme Court's nullification of Virginia's law in 1967. This process has implications for the future of racial politics in the United States and the strategies that political and legal actors adopt for continuing challenges to the embedding of subordination in law and culture.

The Law and Its Agents

The history of the regulation of interracial intimacy reveals much about the law and its agents, the attorneys and judges who struggled over and shaped the evolution of white supremacy between 1868 and 1954. Attorneys and judges were locked within an institutional structure that predated the re-creation of the state in the wake of the Civil War. Even though many elements of the state changed dramatically in the tumultuous years of Reconstruction and the conservative elite's retaking of the state, the functioning of the judiciary and the adversarial system remained fairly stable. The different personnel who staffed the courts during Republican and Democratic control in the 1860s and 1870s operated within the same institutional context, which changed only gradually over time as formalism lost its dominance and newer modes of thought prevailed in the twentieth century.

As agents of the state, these judges and attorneys were all implicated in the state's systematic denial of full citizenship to black Americans after the Civil War, but their institutional roles left them room for maneuvering. In the initial phase of open debate, Republican judges who nonetheless had deep connections to Alabama's law and culture ruled that Alabama's criminal prohibition of interracial intimacy was unconstitutional and unenforceable.

Later judges used their institutional authority not just to repudiate but to dismantle carefully this viewpoint. In the process, they never mentioned in their formal opinions the previous Court's Republican bent, keeping partisan politics at arm's length from their judicial role. As they were creating an entire alternative framework for the constitutionality of policies against interracial intimacy, they backhandedly legitimated the earlier ruling by advocating clemency for the defendants who had relied upon it. Throughout the period of litigation over the crime of miscegenation, judges repeatedly supported supremacy while allowing individual defendants, some of whom probably had conducted interracial romances, to escape the full weight of criminal sanctions. Simple filters like the racial and gender-based composition of the couple appealing their sentences do not work to explain the judges' rulings, nor does consideration of the judges' own political backgrounds, as almost all were conservative Democrats. Rather, we must consider the interplay between institutional factors constraining judicial decision making and the sometimes contradictory state interests at stake in the individual case as well as the judge's own capacity to exercise agency.

Most judges have little capacity to set their own agendas. Even appellate courts that can limit their dockets through certiorari or other selective processes can only adjudicate the cases that are brought to them. While Alabama's judges engaged in sustained debates over particular issues and produced coherent strands of doctrine that were in conversation with earlier cases, they were hearing the cases within their cultural and temporal contexts. The sustained debate over racial definition, for instance, is hard to imagine in the form that it took in an era when eugenics was not a popular theory. Nonetheless, the judiciary's willingness to grapple with different questions in different eras signaled to defense and state attorneys that they should focus their briefs and arguments on appeal on the issues that were in flux at those moments. While it is unlikely that any individual judge in an appeal of a conviction for miscegenation saw himself as an architect of the state or as a builder of racial meaning, the words that the judges wrote ultimately had these effects as they closed some issues, opened others, and highlighted the issues that the legal system itself found to be problematic and liminal.

The attorneys, too, were bound by their institutional roles but nonetheless worked creatively within these roles in ways that sometimes had effects they could not have anticipated. The states' attorneys were charged with the simple duty to uphold the law and to ensure that trial prosecutors' convictions were sustained upon appeal. Nonetheless, their defenses of the convictions varied from vigorous, careful, and high-profile preparation as in the constitutional cases to lower-stakes arguments to uphold convictions about which they themselves might not have been completely enthusiastic. Their arguments ultimately bolstered white supremacy, but their immediate goals of maintaining convictions obtained in trials were for the most part not so lofty. Some likely took into account the structural significance of the ban on interracial intimacy, while others appeared simply to be looking for practical guidance from the appellate courts so that the prosecutors at trial could immunize later prosecutions from challenges.

Some may wonder what kind of attorney would defend a client accused of engaging in interracial sex in Alabama during the Jim Crow era. The question is hard to answer, but the little data available on attorneys like Elbert Haltom, Jr., who pushed forward the constitutional appeals of the 1950s, suggests that they were not viewed as unusual or radical characters in their communities. While interracial sex was culturally understood by white elites in particular as odious, defense attorneys helping these defendants likely also defended accused bootleggers, prostitutes, con artists, and the occasional murderer. Still, the passion and commitment of some of the attorneys like Edward Grove, defender of Sarah Wilson in the 1920s, leaps from the pages of the trial transcripts and appellate documents. These white men were often deeply engaged with their clients, not simply fulfilling the state's ethical (if not yet legal) obligation to provide them with representation for a fair trial. By and large, the arguments that defense attorneys made on behalf of their appellate clients approached Grove's creative and committed standard far more often than the notoriously awful standard set by the Alabama attorneys appointed to defend the Scottsboro rape defendants.

Together, these individual attorneys and judges, focusing on the individual appeals of defendants in particular sets of circumstances, worked together to forge a shifting narrative that was open for consumption by state actors and others outside of the legal system. Often exercising creative agency within the bounds of the particular case, these actors nonetheless participated in an often undirected and unconscious process of development that was always in conversation with the society and culture around it. Appellate judges crafted their opinions to generate appropriate answers to the legal questions at hand, but they also sought to bolster the state's authority and legitimacy, sometimes leading them to weigh the interests of the state in maintaining control over racial policies more heavily than the outcomes for defendants in individual cases. Later judges and attorneys would also reweave these decisions into a coherent narrative of the role of the state with respect to race, and regardless of defense attorneys' motivations, interests, or stances, they mostly had only the option of trying to define their clients' actions as outside of the statute rather than being able to confront the statute itself in direct terms. The appeals and their framing, however, show the extent to which white supremacy itself was always under negotiation and malleable. The ultimate hard line that Alabama and other states took when confronted by the civil rights movement was not inevitable. It was rather the result of a gradual accretion of individual choices and decisions by thousands of state actors, important and not so important, over a span of decades leading up to the 1950s.

As the legal community worked through issues in stages, their actions resonated through other institutions and in society. The resonation was most obvious in the debate over racial definitions, which prompted direct legislative intervention, but struggles over other issues drew from and reflected back Alabamans' notions about race, family, and the white state. High-profile prosecutions put potential interracial couples on notice of the danger of their actions, just as some couples' ability to evade their convictions helped to signal what kinds of sexual relationships between blacks and whites would provoke the state's punitive intervention and what kinds might escape scrutiny and punishment. The distinction between the misdemeanors of prostitution, adultery, fornication, and other sexual crimes, on the one hand, and the felony of miscegenation, on the other, framed the kinds of sexual offenses that merely violated generally held mores versus those that threatened the state's structure and operation. In this regard, one may note with interest that sodomy, whether forcible or consensual, fell into the more dangerous category along with miscegenation. In fact, until a constitutional amendment in 1996, a conviction for either offense also worked permanent disenfranchisement upon the perpetrator, demonstrating vividly the link between the state's vision of citizenship and certain types of sexual misconduct (Ala. Const. Art. VIII, Sec. 182).[9]

---

9. The list of crimes for which permanent disenfranchisement was enforced included treason, murder, arson, embezzlement, malfeasance in office, larceny, receiving stolen property, obtaining property or money under false pretenses, perjury, subornation of perjury, robbery, assault with intent to rob, burglary, forgery, bribery, assault and battery on the wife, bigamy, living in adultery, sodomy, incest, rape, miscegenation, and crime against nature. "Idiots and insane persons" and "any person who shall be convicted as a vagrant or tramp," as well as those implicated in any kind of electoral fraud, all lost the franchise permanently (Ala. Const. Art. VIII, Sec. 182 [2003]).

Alabama's history of legally regulating interracial intimacy is ultimately the story of how an important manifestation of white supremacy functioned and evolved over time. As the courts and lawyers did their everyday work of interpreting the law, they did so against a formidable backdrop of white supremacy, but the political and legal structure of supremacy was never completely closed. At some moments and for some defendants, there was room for maneuvering and even cautious resistance. While barring interracial relationships was a crucial element in the development and articulation of white supremacy, the appellate cases addressing interracial intimacy demonstrate that supremacy itself was never so solid, monolithic, and uncontested as its staunchest supporters perceived and hoped for it to be. Still, the lengthy and often incremental development of supremacy led to the entrenching of socially and culturally embedded racial inequality that persists today.

Would that this history could close with some simple formula for achieving racial equality and healing the wounds of centuries of racism! The existing racial order, however, did not arise without hard work engaged through decades of struggle, and it will not be dismantled without the same work, struggle, and commitment on the part of private individuals and public policymakers. Forging the political will to create an achievable dream of an equal and just society will undoubtedly be difficult and may prove impossible. As inheritors of the white state and its burdened legacy, however, none of us are morally free from the obligation to try.

Afterword: The Analogy between Bans on Interracial Marriage and Same-Sex Marriage—A Usable Past?

Can the history of Alabama's efforts to prevent interracial couples from forming legitimate families inform the contemporary battle over same-sex marriage? Historically inclined left scholars have highlighted the similarities in state justifications for the bans on both types of marriage and have looked to the history of the United States' elimination of bans on mixed-race sexual relationships for guidance. Scholars on the right have argued that the racial focus of bans on interracial intimacy renders them fundamentally different from the gendered regulation of marriage, and have emphasized that racial regulations are constitutionally suspect in a way that regulations based on sexual orientation are not. Still other scholars and activists have argued about the similarities and differences between historic discrimination against African Americans in particular and contemporary discrimination against members of the lesbian-gay-bisexual-transgender (LGBT) community. What is missing in this three-cornered struggle is a close analysis of the meaning of these bans to the states and people who enact them.

While the analogy is helpful, it is not perfect because of the particular historical situation of the battle over removing the ban on interracial marriage. Because regulations against interracial marriage were at the heart of defining and perpetuating the political and institutional system of white supremacy, they served a different purpose than the bans on same-sex marriage. Nonetheless, in reviewing the history with an eye toward determining the value of the analogy, one can see how thinking about the bans potentially as state work and as reflections of state developmental processes can shift the questions we should ask.

The history of the struggle over regulating interracial intimate relationships demonstrates a few key developmental points that can help to frame questions about the analogy. First, bans on interracial marriage were implemented consciously in the postbellum era first as a strategy to cordon off the radical implications of black equality and later as an articulation of a political ideology of white supremacy. Second, the bans highlighted the significance of the family as a unit of the state and helped to place the white family as a normative center around which both the state as an abstract entity and concrete actual states were organized. (The centering of the white family also embedded heteronormativity, although not in such an overt fashion.) Third, the contentious process through which the bans were removed demonstrated alternative paths for challenging white supremacy. The path ultimately taken by the U.S. Supreme Court embraced an abstract conception of equality, privileging this reasoning over a substantive engagement with the political and ideological roots of white supremacy.

So to consider the nature of the analogy, let us ask the questions that arise from the history of regulating interracial intimacy. What is the impetus behind the contemporary struggle over same-sex marriage? What conceptions of marriage, its relationship to the state, and the centrality of heterosexuality in all of this arise from progressive court rulings? And what implications does the unfolding of this debate have for the state and for marriage?

A stark—and for those who would use the analogy aggressively, troubling—contrast appears immediately. The establishment of the antimiscegenation regime was part and parcel of the development of a white supremacist state. The contemporary state is thoroughly heterosexist when we look to the structure of its institutions. Nonetheless, the process through which the contemporary state bans have been established was not based upon an agenda of imposing heterosexual supremacy as a basis for legitimation. Nor was same-sex marriage specifically identified as a site for privileging the heterosexual family as the fundamental unit.

This observation is more significant than the standard objection rooted in comparative oppression (often framed as the claim that heterosexist oppression is less bad than racist oppression). It also sets aside the tautological objection that the constitutional standard of review for racially based state policies is higher than for those policies based on sexual orientation.[1] Note

---

1. This objection is tautological because part of what the contemporary legal struggle over same-sex marriage has put into play is the appropriate standard of review for differentiations based in sexual orientation.

that I am not arguing that the wave of bans on same-sex marriage is insignificant from a developmental standpoint. Clearly, those pushing such bans legislatively and constitutionally see themselves as engaging in a process of state construction. Perhaps, though, it is more accurate to characterize this process as a reconstruction of the place of marriage within the state, and an effort to reprioritize heterosexual marriage as a public near-obligation of full citizenship. This differs substantially from the criminal regime of policing the racial boundary through prosecutions of interracial couples as a means to mark "other" races as tainted, polluting, dangerous, and subordinate.

Another contrast is that bans on interracial marriage were often operationalized through the criminal law, while contemporary bans on same-sex marriage rest in the realm of civil law. One could argue that the struggle leading up to the U.S. Supreme Court's ruling in *Lawrence v. Texas* invalidating criminal antisodomy laws is a more appropriate comparator. This objection, however, minimizes the work that marriage does in both cases. Further, the goals of antisodomy laws seem at least upon cursory investigation to be fairly far removed from the goals of the ban on interracial sexuality. Antisodomy legislation was largely about preventing same-sex *sexual relationships,* whereas antimiscegenation laws targeted interracial *intimacy.* Intimacy—or at least some evidence of an ongoing relationship—was largely beside the point for state actors seeking to prosecute individuals under sodomy laws, whereas it was consciously defined as an element of miscegenation in states that criminalized interracial adultery and fornication.

What has the state-level debate over same-sex marriage revealed about its sources and role in defining the state? This process has had—thus far—two distinct stages. First was a wave of constitutional litigation over the legitimacy of denying marriage licenses or significant privileges to same-sex couples. Begun in Hawaii in 1993 and reaching its most visible moment in 2003 with Massachusetts' ruling in *Goodridge,* this phase demonstrated the scope of conflict over the state's preexisting interests in heterosexual marriage. The second stage has been the wave of constitutional changes seeking to bar state high courts from mandating the recognition of same-sex marriage. This struggle demonstrates in stark terms how the debate over same-sex marriage is shifting rapidly and has suddenly developed the potential to become a site for the articulation of an exclusionary conception of marriage, citizenship, and state functioning.

Recent case law on same-sex marriage established the initial boundaries of the conflict. In the last several years, several state courts (Alabama not among them)[2] have heard direct constitutional challenges to their limits on same-sex marriage. Their discussions provide significant insights into what the states understand themselves to be doing in limiting marriage to male-female dyads.

The debate over the meaning and status of interracial marriage was sparked by the legislative and constitutional changes of Reconstruction. For same-sex marriage, while some scattered litigation took place prior to 1993, the Hawaii supreme court's ruling in *Baehr v. Lewin* was the watershed moment. While the court rejected a fundamental right to marry a person of the same sex, it found that barring same-sex marriage constituted sex discrimination under Hawaii's state constitution. The court remanded the case for the state to attempt to articulate a compelling interest in differentiating between same-sex and opposite-sex couples. Upon remand, the circuit court found that the state had not met this burden with its claims that the traditional nature of marriage should ground the limit. In order to prevent the high court from upholding this ruling, voters in the state amended Hawaii's constitution to limit marriage to a man and a woman, the first such amendment. This struggle in the most geographically isolated of the fifty states sparked litigation over state actors' refusing to marry same-sex couples and a nearly simultaneous wave of state constitutional amendments presented as defenses of traditional marriage.

Vermont was next. *Baker v. State* represented a court's effort to split the difference, with the opinion announcing that "the State is constitutionally required to extend to same-sex couples the common benefits and protections that flow from marriage under Vermont law" (*Baker v. State*, 170 Vt. 194, 197 [1999]). The court explicitly declined to decide whether only marriage would suffice, leaving the door open for the legislature to embrace civil unions. In reaching this decision, the court identified the state's interest as legitimating and providing permanent support for marital children (id. at 881). Allowing same-sex marriage, in this view, would undermine the link

---

2. In Alabama, same-sex marriage was mentioned in *Ex parte H. H.*, a case in which a mother challenged a trial court's denial of her request to modify a custody order. While some evidence suggested abusive behavior on the part of the father, the appellate court agreed with the trial court that this evidence did not warrant modifying the original joint custody order, in part because the mother was living in California in a committed lesbian relationship. The case featured a lengthy concurrence by then-chief justice Roy Moore, who discussed extensively the immorality and dangers of homosexuality and the inherent unfitness of homosexuals as custodial parents (*Ex parte H. H.*, 830 So.2d 21 [Ala. 2002]).

between procreation and child-rearing and would devalue the roles of mothers and fathers in this process. The court relied on *Loving,* citing a principle of freedom to marry and the need to extend the benefits and protections of marriage on an equal basis (id. at 220).

Despite extensive reliance on this parallel, however, the court did not look to the role of maintaining exclusivity in marriage as a means of reinforcing the fundamental nature of the state. The justices relied instead on requiring the state to articulate a strong justification for refusing to allow some citizens to enjoy the protections freely provided to others. The majority, in refusing to endorse an outright command that the state extend marriage, explicitly noted that the analogy to criminal sanctions on miscegenation was problematic, because "the exclusion of same-sex couples from the definition of marriage was [not] intended to discriminate against women or lesbians and gay men, as racial segregation was designed to maintain the pernicious doctrine of white supremacy" (id. at 226). The conflation of segregation with the specific policy of barring interracial marriage was likely unconscious but demonstrates how the issues were linked retrospectively in the public mind.

Additional states considered the question directly, with Arizona ruling against same-sex marriage in October 2003 and Indiana following suit in early 2005. Arizona's consideration focused on *Lawrence v. Texas* and its potential application to legitimate same-sex marriage (*Standhardt and Keltner v. Superior Court,* 206 Ariz. 276 [2003]), and an Indiana appellate court articulated the novel argument that accidental procreation through heterosexual carelessness generated a rational basis for limiting marriage to heterosexual couples (*Morrison v. Sadler,* 821 N.E. 2d 15 [Ind. App. 2005]). The issue initially produced confusion in New York, with two trial courts issuing opposing opinions, although the court of appeals settled the question against same-sex marriage in the summer of 2006 in an opinion addressed later. An intermediate appellate court in New Jersey ruled against same-sex marriage in the summer of 2005 on the ground that New Jersey's Domestic Partnership Act sufficiently addresses the inequities created by limiting marriage to opposite-sex couples (*Lewis and Winslow v. Harris,* 2005 N.J. Super. LEXIS 186 [NJ App. 2005]).

The best-known case, however, is *Goodridge v. Department of Public Health,* decided by the Supreme Judicial Court of Massachusetts in late 2003. It seems likely to remain the definitive presentation of the case for same-sex marriage. The Massachusetts court relied upon several provisions of the Massachusetts constitution mandating equality and limiting the scope of government (*Goodridge v. Department of Public Health*, 440 Mass. 309, 316 [2003]). While pro–same-sex marriage advocates have frequently compared it to *Loving v. Virginia*, the much stronger parallel is to *Perez v. Sharp*. Like the *Perez* court, the *Goodridge* court carefully and empirically deconstructed the state's justifications for maintaining exclusionary marriage laws.

The court observed that civil marriage itself is a creature of the state and has been throughout the history of Massachusetts. More than mere private choice or contract, civil marriage was the transformation of a private relationship into a set of publicly defined and enforced rights, benefits, and obligations. In contrast to advocates for the state's conception of marriage, the court read the flow of benefits and obligations in two directions: between the married individuals and from the state to the marital unit (id. at 322–25). While the court acknowledged that marriage can be limited by "appropriate government restrictions in the interests of public health, safety, and welfare," the majority systematically rejected the state's numerous attempts to implicate one of these categories (id. at 328, 331–36). Empirical justifications based on children's best interests were swept aside along with pleas based in the traditions of marriage and views that homosexuality is immoral; where possible, the court rested its reasoning on other areas of Massachusetts law recognizing discrimination based on sexual orientation as problematic.

Civil marriage survived the court's analysis in *Goodridge* but emerged in a novel form. The court defined it as "the voluntary union of two persons as spouses, to the exclusion of all others," and identified its public basis in the state's interests in "providing a stable setting for child rearing and conserving state resources" (id. at 343). Marriage was both a private relationship governed by free individual choice and a public imprimatur of legitimacy, bringing the relationship within the boundaries of ordinary law.

The dissent, like the dissent in *Perez v. Sharp*, took issue with nearly every element. The Massachusetts dissenters, like their counterparts in Vermont, noted that Massachusetts did not establish an explicit ban on same-sex marriage in order to generate and preserve an exclusionary state (id. at 352). In language reminiscent of that used in *Pace v. Alabama*, the dissenters embraced a thin conception of equality, noting that all individuals are free to marry (id.). Much more central for the dissenters, however, was the claim of judicial usurpation of a legislative function.

Additional high profile rulings were issued by the New York Court of Appeals and the Washington Supreme Court in the summer of 2006, opposing rights to same-sex marriage, and New Jersey's ruling in the fall of 2006 in *Lewis and Winslow v. Harris* asserting a qualified right to equal state recognition of partnerships between same-sex couples. The New York high court refused to recognize a right to same-sex marriage under the New York constitution's due process or equal protection clauses, provoking a vigorous dissent from Chief Judge Judith Kaye. The majority firmly placed the case within the ambit of rational basis review and found that the primary purpose on the part of the state was to protect children. The opinion then identified two specific rational connections between the policy and the protection of children: first, that heterosexual relationships in general tend to lead naturally to childbirth and therefore require the additional inducements of marriage to stabilize them for the sake of accidentally produced children, and second that the legislature could rationally conclude "that it is better, other things being equal, for children to grow up with both a mother and a father" (*Hernandez v. Robles*, 855 N.E. 2d 1, 7 [N.Y. 2006]). In countering the argument that *Loving* extended logically to the issue of same-sex marriage, the majority claimed that the situations were not similar because "the traditional definition of marriage is not merely a by-product of historical injustice," unlike the relationship between antimiscegenation laws and the "long and shameful history" of racism (id.).

In New York, the interpretations the majority presented on due process and equal protection were significantly narrower than in *Goodridge;* the majority defined the due process right at stake as a narrow right to same-sex marriage rather than a right to marry generally (id. at 9–10). On equal protection, the court rejected the invitation to see the question as one of gender and ruled that rational basis scrutiny was sufficient for policies that differentiate on the basis of sexual orientation in instances where the courts are reviewing "legislation governing marriage and family relationships" (id. at 11). The majority then handed the issue over to the legislature with a commendation of the democratic process. The dissent took issue with both portions of the analysis and relied on a parallel to bans on interracial marriage. It also noted the constructed and shifting nature of marriage over time (*Hernandez v. Robles*, Kaye, J., dissenting 2006).

Washington's high court was more divided on the issue, with the consolidated cases producing a majority of six in favor of allowing the legislature to limit marriage to opposite-sex couples and three justices in dissent. However, Justice Barbara Madsen's lead opinion only attracted two cosigners, and the three other justices agreeing with the outcome wrote or endorsed concurrences. Madsen's opinion, like the New York Court of Appeals' approach, denies that lesbians and gay men are a suspect class and identifies the right at stake narrowly as "the right to marry a person of the same sex" (*Andersen v. King County*, 138 P.3d 963, 968 [Wash. 2006]). Refusing to analyze critically the legislature's reliance upon the state interests of furthering procreation and protecting children's well being, Madsen's opinion explicitly situated the court as highly deferential to the legislature's judgment (id.). Madsen distinguished *Loving*'s identification of marriage as a fundamental right on the ground that the ruling confirmed the direction of recent history and tradition in removing limits on interracial marriage, and then went on to link marriage with procreation (id. at 977–80). While Madsen ended her opinion with a suggestion that "the legislature may want to reexamine the impact of the marriage laws on all citizens of this state" and acknowledged the hardships that same-sex couples face in the absence of a means to secure formal state recognition of their relationships, she did not see these hardships rising to an unconstitutional level (id. at 990). Justice J. M. Johnson concurred, with another justice signing on, finding Madsen's opinion to be too narrowly drawn. He wrote separately to "analyz[e] and reject[] all constitutional claims to achieve finality" (*Andersen v. King County*, 138 P.3d 963, 990, Johnson, J., concurring [2006]).

The primary dissent by Justice Mary Fairhurst relies upon a structural, precedential, and analogy-driven analysis, resting primarily upon marriage as a fundamental right and chiding the majority for defining the right too narrowly. In considering the state interests, Fairhurst employs a rational basis test but fails to find a rational basis for the legislature's choice to limit marriage, identifying the interest as fundamentally based in animus. Another dissent takes issue with the plurality opinion's analysis of Washington's privileges or immunities clause, reading it more broadly than federal constitutional equal protection doctrine (*Andersen v. King County*, 138 P.3d 963, Chambers, J., dissenting [2006]). Justice Bridge also dissented separately to underline the proper role of the judiciary and the real discrimination and animus that lesbians and gay men face in everyday life (138 P.3d 963, Bridge, J., dissenting [2006]).

New Jersey's court is the most recent to acknowledge an egalitarian stake in marriage rights for same-sex couples. While the court declined to find a fundamental right to same-sex marriage (and construed the question in this fashion), the majority reasoned that "the unequal dispensation of rights and benefits to committed same-sex partners can no longer be tolerated under our State Constitution (*Lewis and Winslow v. Harris,* 908 A.2d 196, 217 [N.J. 2006]). While the court left the legislature to determine whether to extend marriage rights or create an alternative but equal regulatory structure for same-sex partnerships, it rested its reasoning simultaneously in an interpretation of same-sex relationships as structurally and morally equal to opposite-sex marriages and in a strong reading of the liberty guarantee outlined in New Jersey's constitution.

In addressing the liberty piece of the argument, the majority endorsed the standard mode of considering deeply rooted history and tradition while defining the proposed right narrowly. As a result, the justices were unable to find a fundamental right at stake, having defined the right as one to same-sex marriage (id. at 208–9). In doing so, the court explicitly rejected the parallel to *Loving,* both reading the case as resting primarily upon federal equal protection grounds and claiming that the primary problem in antimiscegenation laws was the "intolerable racial distinctions that patently violated the Fourteenth Amendment" (id. at 210). Nonetheless, the court was able to find a significant commitment to equality in New Jersey's laws regarding sexual orientation, which the justices read as endorsing a broad principle of "protect[ing] gays and lesbians from sexual orientation discrimination in all its virulent forms" (id. at 215). Because marriage itself as a particular institution had been read out of the analysis through the court's position on liberty, the court reduced the inquiry to one of the inequality of benefits and privileges for two similarly situated groups. This inquiry grounded the court's finding that same-sex couples' unequal access to the benefits and privileges associated with marriage had no rational basis, especially given the broad range of other protections written into New Jersey's laws to eliminate discrimination based on sexual orientation.

The court's simultaneous rejection of marriage as an equally accessible fundamental right and endorsement of a strong principle of nondiscrimination left it in the position of directing the legislature to make the final choice between allowing marriage and creating civil unions (id. at 224). Three members of the court objected to the decoupling of liberty and equality, however, and argued that only full access to marriage would be justifiable. Justice Poritz's opinion, concurring with the equal protection discussion but dissenting on the framing of the right at stake and the outcome allowing for civil unions, drew a direct and structural parallel to *Loving v. Virginia*. In his view, endorsed by two other justices, the court's discussion of a right to same-sex marriage as not rooted in history and tradition improperly contradicted *Loving*'s framing of the right at stake as more than a right to interracial marriage (*Lewis and Winslow v. Harris*, Poritz, J., concurring in part and dissenting in part, A-68: 227–28). He saw *Loving* as clear and binding precedent, arguing that "*Loving* teaches that the fundamental right to marry no more can be limited to same-race couples than it can be limited to those who choose a committed relationship with persons of the opposite sex" (id. at 228).

These cases, while they reach radically different outcomes, all share some themes. First is the state's explicit avoidance of animus as a justification for limiting marriage to opposite-sex couples. As the parallel to interracial marriage is so immediately salient, particularly in the wake of *Lawrence*, state legislatures have been careful not to heighten the parallel by situating their efforts as an attempt to embed state practices based in dislike, distaste, or hatred for homosexuals and homosexuality. Rather, the conflict has been framed over the normative organization of the family and the extent to which the state may privilege certain family structures as healthy and desirable.

Two central questions in these cases have been what the family is for and why it must be protected. In all of the cases, the courts identify the family as a significant and central institution worthy of state recognition and protection. Only those judges who rule for same-sex marriage, however, see the family as a state-created institution; the judges allowing exclusionary marriage to continue seem to see the family as a prepolitical, natural living arrangement that the state merely legitimates. All agree that marriage plays a crucial role in creating family but disagree about the point at which state intervention makes the family. For supporters of same-sex marriage, committed relationships are about liberty and individual choice, and the state merely encourages, acknowledges, or refuses to acknowledge these choices based upon its attitude toward the participants. For those opposed to same-sex marriage, the state's acknowledgment is more active, in that it renders particular kinds of relationships acceptable and desirable through the state's recognition. It is also ironically less active, in that limits on same-sex marriage simply reflect and reinforce the perceived universal traditional organization of the family under state rubrics.

The third question has been about the significance of procreation and its mechanics. Courts upholding limits on marriage have placed great weight upon the capacity of the married heterosexual couple (as an ideal type) to procreate without "outside" intervention into the biological sanctity of the married couple's presumed pact of sexual exclusivity. These stances range from Indiana's concerns about creating incentives for managing unplanned heterosexual procreation to one of the New York trial courts' reliance on the "unique and distinct social benefit" in "natural procreation and child-rearing." The place of procreative sex has been hotly debated in arguments over same-sex marriage, and these arguments need not be reviewed here.[3] The point is simply that the silent assumption of exclusive heterosexual procreative intercourse in marriage undergirds state support for preventing same-sex marriage. Rulings that invalidate exclusionary practices center child rearing and families in their justifications but do so in a different way. Rather than focus on the process through which the children have been conceived, these rulings note the importance of protecting intact families through the provision of state recognition and benefits. The children themselves are centered rather than the biological process through which they have been created.

These cases, however, also show dramatically how indebted the debate over same-sex marriage is to the looming shadow of *Loving v. Virginia,* which itself was indebted to its developmental context. As in the high court's analysis there, these courts all see marriage as a simple extension of public benefits and recognition to a private relationship. The cases turn on the dual pivots of equality and liberty, with the courts struggling over whether limits on marriage partners are unacceptable breaches of equality and how to define the liberty interest at stake. The family is still important as a unit of the state, but the need for protection of the family is circular rather than reciprocal. Marriage emerges as the state's way to acknowledge and shelter the family (as a contested concept), but the family does not have direct and independent responsibilities to the state.

---

3. The points raised most frequently in response to claims about the natural procreation of children are that many heterosexual couples cannot procreate "naturally" or choose not to procreate and that the children born and/or raised within many heterosexual marriages are not the biological children of both of the members of the opposite-sex couple.

Unlike the first round of constitutional debate over antimiscegenation laws, this burst of litigation did not involve an active and directed process of constitutional development on the part of the state. Instead, the struggle produced second-order questions about the relationship between marriage and the state. The raising of these questions, however, prompted a debate with significantly stronger parallels to the question of interracial marriage. Alerted to the possibility of marriage's extension to same-sex couples, the religious right swung into action, first through the mobilization of state-level defense of marriage acts (DOMAs) in the 1990s and more recently through amendments of state constitutions to prohibit same-sex marriage directly. By the summer of 2006, nineteen states had placed bans in their constitutions, and seven more followed suit in the fall election of 2006, though Arizona became the first state to reject a constitutional ban. Alabama's voters approved a state constitutional amendment banning same-sex marriage in June 2006.[4]

This has provoked a node of conflict not directly rooted in the courts or judicial decisions. Instead, the battle has been fought on the political ground of the state constitutional amendment process. The push to define marriage as a relationship solely between a man and a woman both through barring recognition of other states' definitions and by limiting marriage directly does implicate state development. At least for some members of the religious Right and their strongest opponents, the struggle has become a debate over the wisdom of embedding heterosexual supremacy in constitutional law and policy.

While a few more overtly political groups and individuals have assisted conservative Christian organizations, the religious orientation of the primary movers behind the wave of constitutional amendments is worth noting (Leaming 2004). This is in stark contrast to the political elite's initiation and backing for bans on interracial marriage in the late nineteenth and early twentieth centuries. One might respond that politics has changed, and that mass organizations and social movements are now much more direct players in the political process than when bans on interracial relationships were being debated. Such a distinction, however, would overlook the success that

---

4. The amendment had almost no difficulty going through Alabama's legislature. Representative Alvin Holmes, who also spearheaded the campaign to remove Alabama's ban on interracial marriage from the state constitution, mounted a filibuster against the amendment in Alabama's House, but the amendment passed there by a vote of 85 to 7 and unanimously in the Senate (McGrew and Davis 2005). Alabama's voters approved the amendment by more than 80 percent, and a majority of residents in every county voted in favor of it (Information for Election 2006).

private progressive organizations had in the early twentieth century in passing state-level legislation. Further, the example in the late 1800s and early
1900s of a largely religiously based temperance movement that brought pro-
fessional politicians on board as participants also undercuts the claim that
political mobilization itself has changed.

What work is the wave of constitutional initiatives and referenda doing?
This process involves conscious state development more directly than the
more ambiguous judicially considered challenges to exclusive rules. In seeking
to embed a particular vision of marriage in state constitutions, advocates for
bans on same-sex marriage are also promoting a vision of the state based in
families organized around heterosexually married couples as the foundation.

For their part, advocates for same-sex marriage within the LGBT community have relied principally upon arguments of simple equality, equal dig-
nity and citizenship, and protection for families. Seasoned by years of legal
struggle, these advocates have relied upon the legal, ethical, and constitutional themes that opened doors to beat back discrimination in other arenas
(Andersen 2004). These themes have recurred both in legal arguments in
favor of extending marriage to same-sex couples and in public campaigns
against exclusionary constitutional amendments and statutes. They have
been strikingly ineffective, as state after state, with the exception of Arizona,
passed constitutional bans on the recognition of same-sex marriage. These
bans have ranged from Oregon's simple declaration that marriage may only
be recognized between a man and a woman, leaving open the possibility of
civil unions or domestic partnerships (which the legislature indeed adopted in
2007), to the versions passed in Ohio and Michigan that bar any attempt to
create a status akin to marriage between unmarried couples of any gender.

The Oregon Supreme Court has provided an example of how the bans
can short-circuit judicial debates. Finding Oregon's Measure 36 to dispose
definitively of the issue of same-sex marriage, the court wiped out approximately 3,000 marriages that had taken place mostly in Multnomah County in
the spring of 2004. The plaintiffs had filed a suit similar to the previously discussed litigation prior to the passage of Measure 36 but argued in the wake
of its passage that it merely expressed an aspirational view of marriage. The
court disagreed, reading Measure 36 as a clear indication of the voters' will
to deny marriage to same-sex couples (*Li v. State*, 110 P.3d 91 [Ore. 2005]). In
the court's reading, the passage of Measure 36 foreclosed any close inquiry
into the possibly nefarious intentions of the voters. Because Measure 36 was
a constitutional amendment, the court was unwilling to question the inten-

tions and state interests behind the preexisting statutory language defining marriage as a relationship between men and women (id.). As other states confront their amendments, similar outcomes seem likely. The constitutional amendments foreclose further judicial debate over the meaning of marriage and family, allowing only room for procedural questions about the scope and nature of the amendments themselves. The amendments thus move the locus of conflict over the meaning of same-sex marriage directly into the political and cultural arena, where religious activists see stronger chances of victory.

As with interracial marriage, we can review the recent controversy over same-sex marriage to understand how this struggle links with state development. In doing so, two things become evident. First, the analogy between state recognition for interracial and same-sex intimate relationships is not perfect. The initial conflict over interracial marriage took place in the context of the bans implemented in the postbellum era to limit the scope of black (and other races') equality with whites. The bans were refined around the turn of the century to articulate and embed white supremacy. In contrast, the opening salvos in the battle over same-sex marriage implicated the meaning of family and the state's relationship to the family but were not in the immediate sense based in efforts to articulate a state based fundamentally in heterosexual supremacy. The controversy, however, raised the political salience of questions about the relationship between the heterosexual family and the state. A wave of right-wing political organization leading to constitutional amendments in many states implicated state development much more directly, in a fashion similar to the efforts of racial state-builders in the late 1800s and early 1900s, triggering major struggles that remain unresolved. Here, those promoting limits on same-sex marriage saw themselves more explicitly acting to embed the heterosexual family at the center of the state and to exclude same-sex relationships and ultimately those individuals who engage in them from recognition by the polity.

Even here, though, the cases diverge. The political actors who wrote bans on interracial intimacy into state laws and constitutions in the late 1800s and early 1900s were primarily concerned with establishing white supremacy. Other goals were significant—in Alabama, the state constitution of 1901 also consolidated power in a Montgomery-based conservative Democratic elite—but supremacy was a political end, not a means. In the contemporary struggle over same-sex marriage, the establishment of a heterosexually supremacist state would be embraced by those promoting the amendments, but their ultimate aim seems to be different. They seek the embedding of conservative

Christian values at the center of the contemporary state, an agenda that transcends its flashpoint cultural struggles over same-sex marriage and, prior to this battle, abortion.

What Work Can the Analogy Do?

The history of regulating interracial intimacy in the modern era is a history of the thoroughgoing connection between interracial marriage and white supremacy. In the years following the Civil War, limits on interracial marriage first centered the white family and circumscribed equality, and then became a key site for articulating the white state. This regime was formally dismantled through the law from 1948 through the late 1960s and early 1970s. However, the mode through which the U.S. Supreme Court and later federal courts lifted the ban on interracial intimacy failed to achieve a redefinition of race and the uprooting of racial subordination.

The initial calls for state recognition of same-sex marriage revealed the extent to which the marriage statutes themselves did not consciously embed a regime of heterosexual supremacy. Instead, these statutes merely assumed a heterosexist social context. While more work could specify the developmental path taken, the indifferently gendered marriage laws likely relied upon the background criminal regime suppressing same-sex sexual activity to define the state as implicitly heterosexual. Such a process would explain why the question has become more salient of late, as first several states and finally the federal legal system took steps to eliminate the remaining sodomy bans in recent years.

The differences in developmental histories of struggle over interracial and same-sex marriage demonstrate the need for a more nuanced comparison of how supremacist impulses based on race and sexual orientation have interacted with the state. How do the conscious animus and overt supremacy operating primarily in the context of race differ from the active exclusion, silencing, and rendering invisible operating primarily in the context of sexual orientation? The left scholars best poised to consider this question have avoided it in part because of the political power of analogies between racist and heterosexist oppression. A close examination could, however, lead to useful payoffs, especially in considering what removing the ban on same-sex marriage will mean.

The state work performed in the initial struggle over same-sex marriage has been thinking through the role of marriage and family in the state. The legal controversy centered questions about the public significance and meaning of gender roles and highlighted the way that the family's centering in the state has changed over time. While the raising of children is still an activity imbued with public interest, this public interest is largely protective, with children's roles as future citizens relegated to the background. The constitutional amendments have moved the process to a more overt effort to embed the heterosexual (and, sub rosa, patriarchal) family at the center of the state and to reorient the state around this normative family. Behind all of this is the effort to reinvigorate civic and political culture with religious values connected to particular normative gender roles. In this sense, the struggle over abortion as described by Kristin Luker—a struggle over worldviews and the meaning of gender—provides a striking parallel to the fight over same-sex marriage (Luker 1984).

It is worth reinforcing, though, that the meaning of this struggle is part of the struggle itself. The struggle cannot be completely defined by one side, and those fighting for recognition of same-sex relationships have the opportunity to articulate their vision of what this fight means both in the legal and political arenas. The history of removing bans against interracial marriage provides two possible models: the equality-based model of *Loving v. Virginia* and a more concretely critical model suggested by *Perez v. Sharp*.

Analogizing to *Loving v. Virginia* is tempting, as evidenced by the pro–same-sex marriage judges and legal activists who have tacked in this direction. Marriage can be seen through the lens of *Loving* as a simple matter of equality. The state's responsibility is to invest institutionally in the support through recognition of the loving family and to protect the individual liberties of those who choose to engage in state work by creating a family. Abstract equality and individual liberty resonate strongly, and claiming that the state should not be able to withhold its sanction from couples on the basis of their subordinated identities is a powerful argument.

The seductiveness of this simple claim should not overshadow its risks. We know from history that *Loving* did not engineer a fundamental rethinking of race or of marriage. Rather, it extended marriage to interracial couples on its own existing terms. The case, while rejecting formal white supremacy, did not challenge the historically embedded placement of the white family as the normative center of the state. Instead, it incorporated interracial couples into the existing model and promoted color blindness as a response to the state's conscious privileging of whiteness. The ruling thus imposed no responsibility on the state to dismantle the social and cultural apparatus of racism that was supported through the previous one hundred years of post-bellum state-level political development.

Asking harder questions inspired by *Perez v. Sharp* might ultimately prove more fruitful. Why have we had a wave of constitutional amendments banning same-sex marriage, and what state work are these amendments doing? What is accomplished by the emphasis on heterosexual marriage not only as protection for children but as the only legitimate tradition? Is the process we see evolving right now a developmental moment in which the Right is attempting to articulate and embed heterosexual supremacy? And is heterosexual supremacy itself an end or only a means to develop a new porousness of the state to religion?

A developmental deep critique can help us to sort out how state laws and policies have institutionalized heteronormativity on the ground over time. Much of this work has been done through the lenses of law and history (see Canaday 2003; Eskridge 1999; Colker 1996; Robson 1992; among many), but a comprehensive study of the ways that questions of constitutional and political development implicate sexual orientation remains on the horizon. Justice Traynor's account of the history and significance of racialized state development in the context of marriage laws can provide a useful model for a critical analysis of marriage regulations and their role in creating and embedding the heterosexual state.

This approach can also draw upon the emerging questions about the purpose and significance of marriage. The initial round of legal considerations of limits on same-sex marriage has begun this process of critical consideration and reevaluation. Not since debates over the meaning of marriage and family in the late nineteenth century in the context of race and plural marriage has there been such an opportunity for a close legal consideration of marriage's relationship to the state. In particular, we can and should think about the ways that marriage has changed, as expressed both in gradual shifts in the law through repeal and desuetude and through the sharp conflict over extending marriage's benefits to same-sex couples. In order to have this debate, we as a society are fully considering what these benefits are and what they mean to the couples who enjoy them or choose to eschew them and those from whom they are consciously withheld.

The *Perez* example, embedded as it is within a particular developmental history, teaches us to look critically at the messages of inclusion and exclusion that the state sends through its laws on marriage. By extending this inquiry, we can move toward a cautious deconstruction. Such an approach can help us to sort out the extent to which marriage is a relationship that can and should be imbued with normative content that the state supports and acknowledges. We can reveal the work that state recognition of marriage is doing both for marriage and for the state. In the process we can consider critically what the state interest is in recognizing intimate relationships and how the state can best articulate this interest. Ultimately, the debate could lead to an informed and pragmatic reconfiguration of marriage that recognizes its deep spiritual significance to those who choose it but decouples that significance from a silent privileging of state structures dedicated to exclusive heterosexuality. While this outcome may take years to achieve, having the historical example of the struggle over interracial marriage can serve to alert us to the meaning of the developmental process that is unfolding now. We can also use this history to weigh models for argument and change. In the end, using the history of regulating interracial marriage can spark discursive examinations that will restructure marriage rather than simply opening it on a thinly egalitarian basis that does not undercut the fundamental and developmental nature of exclusion that has supported it throughout modern legal history.

Bibliography

This bibliography is divided into three main sections: legal primary sources, documentary primary sources, and documentary secondary sources. The lists are organized chronologically or alphabetically.

Legal Primary Sources

Alabama State Cases Addressing Miscegenation (listed chronologically)

Ellis v. State, 42 Ala. 525 (1868)
Burns v. State, 48 Ala. 196 (1872)
Ford v. State, 53 Ala. 150 (1875)
Green v. State, 58 Ala. 190 (1878)
Hoover v. State, 59 Ala. 58 (1878)
Green et al. v. State, 59 Ala. 69 (1878)
Pace and Cox v. State, 69 Ala. 231 (1881)
Pace v. Alabama, 106 U.S. 583 (1883)
White v. State, 74 Ala. 31, 33–34 (1883)
Linton v. State, 7 So. 261, 88 Ala. 216 (1890)
McAlpine v. State, 117 Ala. 95 (1897)
Love v. State, 27 So. 217, 124 Ala. 82 (1899)
Pumphrey v. State, 156 Ala. 103 (1908)
Jones v. State, 47 So. 100, 156 Ala. 175 (1908)
Toles v. State, 54 So. 511 (Ala. 1911)
Story v. State, 59 So. 480 (Ala. 1912)
Allen v. Scruggs, 67 So. 301 (Ala. 1914)
Smith v. State, 75 So. 627, 16 Ala. App. 79 (1917)
Metcalf v. State, 78 So. 305, 16 Ala. App. 389 (1918)
Simmons v. State, 78 So. 306 (Ala. App. 1918)
Lewis v. State, 89 So. 904, 18 Ala. App. 263 (1921)
Rollins v. State, 92 So. 35 (Ala. App. 1922)
Reed v. State, 92 So. 511 (Ala. App. 1922)
Wilson v. State, 101 So. 417 (Ala. App. 1924)
Weaver v. State, 116 So. 893 (Ala. App. 1928)
Williams v. State, 125 So. 690 (Ala. App. 1930)
Jackson v. State, 129 So. 306 (Ala. App. 1930)
Fields v. State, 132 So. 605 (Ala. App. 1931)
Williams v. State, 146 So. 422 (Ala. App. 1933)

Williams v. State, 152 So. 264 (Ala. App. 1934)
Murphy v. State, 176 So. 473 (Ala. App. 1937)
Rogers v. State, 193 So. 872 (Ala. 1939)
Bailey v. State, 193 So. 873 (Ala. 1939)
Rogers v. State, 193 So. 871 (Ala. App. 1940)
Bailey v. State, 193 So. 871 (Ala. App. 1940)
Mathews v. Stroud, 196 So. 885 (Ala. 1940)
Jordan v. State, 5 So.2d 111 (Ala. 1941)
Brewer v. State, 5 So.2d 111 (Ala. 1941)
Dees v. Metts, 17 So.2d 137 (Ala. 1944)
Gilbert v. State, 23 So.2d 22 (Ala. App. 1945)
Griffith v. State, 50 So.2d 797 (Ala. App. 1951)
Pendley v. State, 53 So.2d 811 (Ala. App. 1951)
Agnew v. State, 54 So.2d 89 (Ala. App. 1951)
Jackson v. State, 72 So.2d 114 (Ala. App. 1954)
Jackson v. State, 72 So.2d 116 (Ala. 1954)
Rogers v. State, 73 So.2d 389 (Ala. App. 1954)

Other Alabama Cases (listed chronologically)

McQueen v. Wilson, 31 So. 94, 95 (Ala. 1901)
Locklayer v. Locklayer, 35 So. 1008 (Ala. 1904)
Mullen v. Johnson, 47 So. 584 (Ala. 1908)
Yarbrough v. Harris, 52 So. 916 (Ala. 1910)
Councill v. Mayhew, 55 So. 314 (Ala. 1911)
Smith v. Smith, 56 So. 949 (Ala. 1911)
Scarbrough v. Scarbrough, 64 So. 105 (Ala. 1913)
Posey v. Donaldson, 66 So. 662 (Ala. 1914)
Watkins v. Yeatman, 66 So. 707 (Ala. 1914)
Kirby v. Arnold, 68 So. 17 (Ala. 1915)
Barnett v. Freeman, 72 So. 395 (Ala. 1916)
Sharpe v. Hughes, 80 So. 797 (Ala. 1918)
Howell v. Howell, 98 So. 630 (Ala. 1923)
Ritchey v. Jones, 97 So. 736 (Ala. 1923)
Cox v. Parker, 101 So. 657 (Ala. 1924)
Hobson v. Morgan, 110 So. 406 (Ala. 1926)
Batson v. Batson, 117 So. 10 (Ala. 1928)
East v. Karter, 118 So. 547 (Ala. 1928)
McLendon v. Stough, 118 So. 647 (Ala. 1928)
Zeigler v. Coffin, 123 So. 22 (Ala. 1929)
Wainwright v. Wainwright, 137 So. 413 (Ala. 1931)
Abrams v. Abrams, 144 So. 828 (Ala. 1932)
Towles v. Pettus, 12 So.2d 357 (Ala. 1943)
Dees v. Metts, 17 So.2d 137 (Ala. 1944)

Malone v. State, 26 So.2d 916 (Ala. App. 1946)
Tipton v. Tipton, 32 So.2d 32 (Ala. 1947)
Hyde v. Norris, 35 So.2d 181 (Ala. 1948)
King v. Aird, 38 So.2d 883 (Ala. 1949)
Banks v. State, 170 So.2d 417 (Ala. App. 1964)
Brittain v. Weatherly, 281 Ala. 683 (1968)
Ex parte H. H., 830 So.2d 21 (Ala. 2002)

Federal/Other State Cases (listed chronologically)

State v. Gibson, 36 Ind. 389 (1871)
Pace v. Alabama, 106 U.S. 583 (1883)
Maynard v. Hill, 125 U.S. 190 (1888)
Plessy v. Ferguson, 163 U.S. 537 (1896)
Powell v. Alabama, 287 U.S. 45 (1932)
Smith v. Allwright, 321 U.S. 649 (1944)
Korematsu v. US, 323 U.S. 214 (1944)
State v. Eaton, 195 S.W.2d 457 (Mo. 1946)
Smith v. State, 165 P.2d 381 (Okla. 1946)
Perez v. Sharp, 32 Cal.2d 711 (1948)
Smith v. State, 211 P.2d 538 (Okla. 1949)
Davis v. Schnell, 81 F. Supp. 872 (S.D. Ala. 1949)
Schnell v. Davis, 336 U.S. 933 (1949)
State v. Wagstaff, 68 S.E.2d 858 (N.C. 1952)
Brown v. Board of Education I, 347 U.S. 483 (1954)
Jackson v. State, 348 U.S. 888 (1954)
Brown v. Board of Education, 348 U.S. 886 (1954)
Brown v. Board of Education II, 349 U.S. 294 (1955)
Naim v. Naim I, 350 U.S. 891 (1955)
Naim v. Naim II, 350 U.S. 985 (1956)
McLaughlin v. Florida, 379 U.S. 184 (1964)
Loving v. Virginia, 388 U.S. 1 (1967)
Oden v. Brittain, 396 U.S. 1210 (1969)
U.S. v. Brittain, 319 F. Supp. 1058 (N.D. Ala. 1970)
Palmore v. Sidoti, 466 U.S. 429 (1984)
Bowers v. Hardwick, 478 U.S. 186 (1986)
Baehr v. Lewin, 74 Haw. 530 (1993)
Baker v. State, 170 Vt. 194 (1999)
Standhardt and Keltner v. Superior Court, 206 Ariz. 276 (2003)
Gratz v. Bollinger, 539 U.S. 244 (2003)
Grutter v. Bollinger, 539 U.S. 306 (2003)
Lawrence v. Texas, 539 U.S. 558 (2003)
Goodridge v. Department of Public Health, 440 Mass. 309 (2003)
Morrison v. Sadler, 821 N.E.2d 15 (Ind. App. 2005)

Seymour v. Holcomb, 790 N.Y.S. 2d 858 (2005)
Hernandez et al. v. Robles, 805 N.Y.S. 2d 354 (2005)
Li v. State, 110 P.3d 91 (Ore. 2005)
Lewis et al. v. Harris, 875 A.2d 259 (N.J. Super. 2005)
Hernandez v. Robles, 855 N.E. 2d 1 (N.Y. 2006)
Andersen v. King County, 138 P.3d 963 (Wash. 2006)
Lewis and Winslow v. Harris, 908 A.2d 196 (N.J. 2006)

Statutes and Legislative Materials (listed chronologically)

Alabama Statutes (1852): Art. I, sec. 1956
Alabama Statutes (1852): Art. I, sec. 4
Alabama Statutes (1852): Art. X, sec. 3307
Alabama Statutes (1866): Art. I, sec. 61
Boswell Amendment
Journal of the Proceedings of the Constitutional Convention of the State of Alabama, (Montgomery, May 21, 1901)
Official Proceedings of the Constitutional Convention of the State of Alabama, May 21, 1901–September 3, 1901 (Wetumpka, AL: Wetumpka Printing Co. 1940), vol. 2: 2650
Journal of the Alabama House (Montgomery, June 15, 1927)
Alabama Statutes (1928): sec. 5001
Alabama Constitution, Amendment No. 55 (1946)
Alabama Constitution, Amendment No. 579 (1996)
Alabama Constitution, Amendment No. 667 (2003)
Alabama Constitution, Art. VIII, sec. 182 (2003)

Alabama Supreme Court and Appellate Court Records (records listed chronologically by date of appellate ruling, with witness testimony and other documents from record listed in order from record)

Ellis v. State, 42 Ala. 525 (1868), Trial Record. Alabama Department of Archives and History, Montgomery (hereinafter ADAH)
Green v. State, 58 Ala. 190 (1877), Trial Record. ADAH
Hoover v. State, 59 Ala. 58 (1878), Trial Record. ADAH
Pace and Cox v. State, 69 Ala. 231 (1881), Trial Record. ADAH
McAlpine v. State, Bill of Exceptions, Testimony of C. Bishop 1897, Alabama Supreme Court Records, ADAH
McAlpine v. State, Bill of Exceptions, Testimony of Alice Madison 1897, Alabama Supreme Court Records, ADAH
McAlpine v. State, Bill of Exceptions, Testimony of Annie Bishop 1897, Alabama Supreme Court Records, ADAH
McAlpine v. State, Bill of Exceptions, Testimony of Caroline Turner 1897, Alabama Supreme Court Records, ADAH

Love v. State, Bill of Exceptions, Testimony of Mills, Nov. Term 1899, Alabama Supreme Court Records, ADAH

Love v. State, Bill of Exceptions, Testimony of John Love, Nov. Term 1899, Alabama Supreme Court Records, ADAH

Jones v. State, Bill of Exceptions, Testimony of W. M. Burge 1908, Alabama Supreme Court Records, ADAH

Jones v. State, Bill of Exceptions, Testimony of Officer Nation 1908, Alabama Supreme Court Records, ADAH

Jones v. State, Bill of Exceptions, Testimony of Officer Parker 1908, Alabama Supreme Court Records, ADAH

Pumphrey v. State, Bill of Exceptions, Testimony of Anne Crimm 1907, Alabama Supreme Court Records, ADAH

Pumphrey v. State, Bill of Exceptions, Testimony of J. T. Powell 1907, Alabama Supreme Court Records, ADAH

Pumphrey v. State, Bill of Exceptions, Testimony of W. C. Kyle 1907, Alabama Supreme Court Records, ADAH

Toles v. State, Bill of Exceptions, Judgment Entry 1910, Alabama Supreme Court Records, ADAH

Toles v. State, Bill of Exceptions, Testimony of J. C. Fonville 1910, Alabama Supreme Court Records, ADAH

Toles v. State, Bill of Exceptions, Testimony of Claire Fonville 1910, Alabama Supreme Court Records, ADAH

Toles v. State, Bill of Exceptions, Testimony of Mrs. J. C. Fonville 1910, Alabama Supreme Court Records, ADAH

Toles v. State, Bill of Exceptions, Testimony of J. B. Sikes 1910, Alabama Supreme Court Records, ADAH

Toles v. State, Bill of Exceptions, Testimony of W. L. Tatum 1910, Alabama Supreme Court Records, ADAH

Toles v. State, Bill of Exceptions, Testimony of J. C. McLendon 1910, Alabama Supreme Court Records, ADAH

Story v. State, Bill of Exceptions, Testimony of Beatrice McClure 1911, Alabama Supreme Court Records, ADAH

Story v. State, Bill of Exceptions, Testimony of Clarence Story 1911, Alabama Supreme Court Records, ADAH

Story v. State, Bill of Exceptions, Testimony of J. H. Hyde 1911, Alabama Supreme Court Records, ADAH

Story v. State, Bill of Exceptions, Testimony of W. V. Burns 1911, Alabama Supreme Court Records, ADAH

Story v. State, Bill of Exceptions, Testimony of W. M. Wallace 1911, Alabama Supreme Court Records, ADAH

Story v. State, Bill of Exceptions, Testimony of J. D. Jones 1911, Alabama Supreme Court Records, ADAH

Story v. State, Bill of Exceptions, Assignments of Error 1911, Alabama Supreme Court Records, ADAH

Allen v. Scruggs, Bill of Exceptions, Testimony of Kit Allen, Alabama Supreme Court Records, No Number in Original (1913), ADAH

Allen v. Scruggs, Bill of Exceptions, Testimony of O. H. Watson, Alabama Supreme Court Records, No Number in Original (1913), ADAH

Allen v. Scruggs, Bill of Exceptions, Testimony of Lucy Randolph, Alabama Supreme Court Records, No Number in Original (1913), ADAH

Allen v. Scruggs, Bill of Exceptions, Testimony of J. A. Green, Alabama Supreme Court Records, No Number in Original (1913), ADAH

Allen v. Scruggs, Bill of Exceptions, Testimony of Thomas H. Callis, Alabama Supreme Court Records, No Number in Original (1913), ADAH

Allen v. Scruggs, Bill of Exceptions, Testimony of Joe Allen, Alabama Supreme Court Records, No Number in Original (1913), ADAH

Allen v. Scruggs, Bill of Exceptions, Testimony of Charley Williams, Alabama Supreme Court Records, No Number in Original (1913), ADAH

Allen v. Scruggs, Bill of Exceptions, Testimony of Robert Noble, Alabama Supreme Court Records, No Number in Original (1913), ADAH

Allen v. Scruggs, Bill of Exceptions, Testimony of Joseph N. Scruggs, Alabama Supreme Court Records, No Number in Original (1913), ADAH

Allen v. Scruggs, Bill of Exceptions, Testimony of O. H. Watson, Alabama Supreme Court Records, No Number in Original (1913), ADAH

Allen v. Scruggs, Bill of Exceptions, Testimony of W. S. Melton, Alabama Supreme Court Records, No Number in Original (1913), ADAH

Allen v. Scruggs, Bill of Exceptions, Testimony of Thomas H. Callis, Alabama Supreme Court Records, No Number in Original (1913), ADAH

Allen v. Scruggs, Bill of Exceptions, Judgment Entry, Alabama Supreme Court Records, No Number in Original (1913), ADAH

Allen v. Scruggs, Bill of Exceptions, Testimony of Frank Watson, Alabama Supreme Court Records, No Number in Original (1913), ADAH

Smith v. State, Bill of Exceptions, Charge, Alabama Court of Appeals Records, 4 Div. 481 (1917), ADAH

Smith v. State, Bill of Exceptions, Judgment Entry, Alabama Court of Appeals Records, 4 Div. 481 (1917), ADAH

Metcalf v. State, Indictment, Alabama Court of Appeals Records, 6 Div. 482 (1916), ADAH

Metcalf v. State, Judgment of Conviction, Alabama Court of Appeals Records, 6 Div. 482 (1917), ADAH

Metcalf v. State, Bill of Exceptions, Testimony of Henry Tice, Alabama Court of Appeals Records, 6 Div. 482 (1917), ADAH

Reed v. State, Bill of Exceptions, Testimony of Henry Rivers, Alabama Court of Appeals Records, 1 Div. 433 (1920), ADAH

Reed v. State, Oral Charge, Alabama Court of Appeals Records, 1 Div. 433 (1920), ADAH

Reed v. State, Jury Charges and Verdict, Alabama Court of Appeals Records, 1 Div. 433 (1920), ADAH

Wilson v. State, Bill of Exceptions, Brief of Edward Grove, Alabama Court of Appeals Records, 1 Div. 527 (1923), ADAH

Wilson v. State, Bill of Exceptions, Testimony of Ivy Medicus, Alabama Court of Appeals Records, 1 Div. 527 (1923), ADAH

Weaver v. State, Bill of Exceptions, Testimony of Dudley Weaver, Alabama Court of Appeals Records, 1 Div. 756 (1927), ADAH

Weaver v. State, Bill of Exceptions, Testimony of Wade Weaver, Alabama Court of Appeals Records, 1 Div. 756 (1927), ADAH

Weaver v. State, Bill of Exceptions, Testimony of J. W. Henson, Alabama Court of Appeals Records, 1 Div. 756 (1927), ADAH

Weaver v. State, Bill of Exceptions, Testimony of Jim Dudd Weaver, Alabama Court of Appeals Records, 1 Div. 756 (1927), ADAH

Williams v. State, Bill of Exceptions, Alabama Court of Appeals Records, 4 Div. 515 (1930), ADAH

Williams v. State, Bill of Exceptions, Testimony of Sarah Bryant, Alabama Court of Appeals Records, 4 Div. 515 (1930), ADAH

Williams v. State, Bill of Exceptions, Testimony of Dr. L. E. Broughton, Alabama Court of Appeals Records, 4 Div. 515 (1930), ADAH

Williams v. State, Bill of Exceptions, Testimony of H. C. Johnson, Alabama Court of Appeals Records, 4 Div. 515 (1930), ADAH

Williams v. State, Bill of Exceptions, Testimony of W. Jack Stanley, Alabama Court of Appeals Records, 4 Div. 515 (1930), ADAH

Williams v. State, Bill of Exceptions, Testimony of H. I. Mitchell, Alabama Court of Appeals Records, 4 Div. 515 (1930), ADAH

Williams v. State, Bill of Exceptions, Testimony of A. J. Williams, Alabama Court of Appeals Records, 4 Div. 515 (1930), ADAH

Williams v. State, Given Charges, Alabama Court of Appeals Records, 4 Div. 515 (1930), ADAH

Williams v. State, Oral Charge, Alabama Court of Appeals Records, 4 Div. 515 (1930), ADAH

Williams v. State, Bill of Exceptions, Alabama Court of Appeals Records, 4 Div. 515 (1930), ADAH

Jackson v. State, Bill of Exceptions, Appeal Bond, Alabama Court of Appeal Records, 6 Div. 769 (1930), ADAH

Jackson v. State, Bill of Exceptions, Oral Charge to Jury, Alabama Court of Appeal Records, 6 Div. 769 (1930), ADAH

Jackson v. State, Bill of Exceptions, Assignment of Error, Alabama Court of Appeal Records, 6 Div. 769 (1930), ADAH

Jackson v. State, Bill of Exceptions, Testimony of Alexander Markos, Alabama Court of Appeal Records, 6 Div. 769 (1930), ADAH

Jackson v. State, Bill of Exceptions, Testimony of Ivy Collins, Alabama Court of Appeal Records, 6 Div. 769 (1930), ADAH

Jackson v. State, Bill of Exceptions, Testimony of Jessie Collins, Alabama Court of Appeal Records, 6 Div. 769 (1930), ADAH

Fields v. State, Bill of Exceptions, Testimony of Brigs Wright, Alabama Court of Appeal Records, 8 Div. 84 (1929), ADAH

Fields v. State, Bill of Exceptions, Judgment Entry, Alabama Court of Appeal Records, 8 Div. 84 (1929), ADAH

Fields v. State, Bill of Exceptions, Testimony of Elijah Fields, Alabama Court of Appeal Records, 8 Div. 84 (1929), ADAH

Fields v. State, Bill of Exceptions, Affidavit of Ollie Roden, Alabama Court of Appeal Records, 8 Div. 84 (1929), ADAH

Fields v. State, Bill of Exceptions, Testimony of Rufus Roden, Alabama Court of Appeal Records, 8 Div. 84 (1929), ADAH

Fields v. State, Bill of Exceptions, Testimony of Elijah Fields, Alabama Court of Appeal Records, 8 Div. 84 (1929), ADAH

Fields v. State, Bill of Exceptions, Testimony of Mrs. Roden, Alabama Court of Appeal Records, 8 Div. 84 (1929), ADAH

Fields v. State, Bill of Exceptions, Alabama Court of Appeal Records, 8 Div. 84 (1929), ADAH

Williams v. State, Bill of Exceptions, Testimony of Sara Bryant, Alabama Court of Appeals Records, 4 Div. 43 (1933), ADAH

Williams v. State, Bill of Exceptions, Testimony of Jerry M. Woodall, Alabama Court of Appeals Records, 4 Div. 43 (1933), ADAH

Williams v. State, Bill of Exceptions, Testimony of Jesse Williams, Alabama Court of Appeals Records, 4 Div. 43 (1933), ADAH

Murphy v. State, Bill of Exceptions, Testimony of Felix Perry, Alabama Court of Appeal Records, 8 Div. 448 (1936), ADAH

Murphy v. State, Bill of Exceptions, Testimony of E. L. Bailey, Alabama Court of Appeal Records, 8 Div. 448 (1936), ADAH

Murphy v. State, Bill of Exceptions, Testimony of Clarence Ingram, Alabama Court of Appeal Records, 8 Div. 448 (1936), ADAH

Murphy v. State, Bill of Exceptions, Testimony of Ray Blakely, Alabama Court of Appeal Records, 8 Div. 448 (1936), ADAH

Murphy v. State, Bill of Exceptions, Testimony of Ernest McClure, Alabama Court of Appeal Records, 8 Div. 448 (1936), ADAH

Murphy v. State, Bill of Exceptions, Testimony of Coleman Cole, Alabama Court of Appeal Records, 8 Div. 448 (1936), ADAH

Murphy v. State, Bill of Exceptions, Testimony of Buster Murphy, Alabama Court of Appeal Records, 8 Div. 448 (1936), ADAH

Murphy v. State, Bill of Exceptions, Testimony of Elmer Murphy, Alabama Court of Appeal Records, 8 Div. 448 (1936), ADAH

Murphy v. State, Bill of Exceptions, Testimony of Alice Murphy, Alabama Court of Appeal Records, 8 Div. 448 (1936), ADAH

Murphy v. State, Bill of Exceptions, Judgment Entry for Cole, Alabama Court of Appeal Records, 8 Div. 448 (1936), ADAH

Murphy v. State, Bill of Exceptions, Judgment Entry for Murphy, Alabama Court of Appeal Records, 8 Div. 448 (1936), ADAH

Mathews v. Stroud, Bill of Exceptions, Bill of Complaint, Alabama Supreme
Court Records, 4 Div. 131 (1939), ADAH

Brewer v. State, Bill of Exceptions, Court's oral charge to the jury, Alabama
Court of Appeal Records, 8 Div. 59 (1940), ADAH

Brewer v. State, Bill of Exceptions, Testimony of Clara Sinbeck, Alabama Court
of Appeal Records, 8 Div. 59 (1940), ADAH

Brewer v. State, Bill of Exceptions, Testimony of Mrs. Grover Goodwin,
Alabama Court of Appeal Records, 8 Div. 59 (1940), ADAH

Brewer v. State, Bill of Exceptions, Testimony of Tom Jordan, Alabama Court
of Appeal Records, 8 Div. 59 (1940), ADAH

Brewer v. State, Bill of Exceptions, Testimony of Mrs. William Mefford,
Alabama Court of Appeal Records, 8 Div. 59 (1940), ADAH

Brewer v. State, Bill of Exceptions, Testimony of Onice Graham, Alabama
Court of Appeal Records, 8 Div. 59 (1940), ADAH

Brewer v. State, Bill of Exceptions, Testimony of James Horrace, Alabama
Court of Appeal Records, 8 Div. 59 (1940), ADAH

Brewer v. State, Bill of Exceptions, Testimony of Sam Smith, Alabama Court of
Appeal Records, 8 Div. 59 (1940), ADAH

Brewer v. State, Bill of Exceptions, Testimony of Granville Brackeen, Alabama
Court of Appeal Records, 8 Div. 59 (1940), ADAH

Brewer v. State, Bill of Exceptions, Testimony of Mary Brewer, Alabama Court
of Appeal Records, 8 Div. 59 (1940), ADAH

Jordan v. State, Bill of Exceptions, Testimony of Onice Graham, Alabama
Court of Appeal Records, 8 Div. 59 (1941), ADAH

Jordan v. State, Bill of Exceptions, Testimony of O. R. Fielder, Alabama Court
of Appeal Records, 8 Div. 59 (1941), ADAH

Jordan v. State, Bill of Exceptions, Testimony of R. M. Sims, Alabama Court of
Appeal Records, 8 Div. 59 (1941), ADAH

Jordan v. State, Bill of Exceptions, Testimony of M. J. Carter, Alabama Court
of Appeal Records, 8 Div. 59 (1941), ADAH

Jordan v. State, Bill of Exceptions, Testimony of Arthur South, Alabama Court
of Appeal Records, 8 Div. 59 (1941), ADAH

Jordan v. State, Bill of Exceptions, Testimony of J. D. Moseley, Alabama Court
of Appeal Records, 8 Div. 59 (1941), ADAH

Jordan v. State, Bill of Exceptions, Testimony of Ed Brewer, Alabama Court of
Appeal Records, 8 Div. 59 (1941), ADAH

Jordan v. State, Bill of Exceptions, Testimony of Carl Copeland, Alabama
Court of Appeal Records, 8 Div. 59 (1941), ADAH

Jordan v. State, Bill of Exceptions, Testimony of Tom Jordan, Alabama Court
of Appeal Records, 8 Div. 59 (1941), ADAH

Dees v. Metts, Bill of Exceptions, Testimony of Leonard Wiggins, Alabama
Supreme Court Records, 1 Div. 186 (1943), ADAH

Dees v. Metts, Bill of Exceptions, Testimony of Loxley Dees, Alabama Supreme
Court Records, 1 Div. 186 (1943), ADAH

Dees v. Metts, Bill of Exceptions, Testimony of A. C. Lee, Alabama Supreme
    Court Records, 1 Div. 186 (1943), ADAH
Dees v. Metts, Bill of Exceptions, Testimony of Nevada Nelson, Alabama
    Supreme Court Records, 1 Div. 186 (1943), ADAH
Dees v. Metts, Bill of Exceptions, Testimony of Dill Brooks, Alabama Supreme
    Court Records, 1 Div. 186 (1943), ADAH
Dees v. Metts, Bill of Exceptions, Testimony of J. L. Bowden, Alabama
    Supreme Court Records, 1 Div. 186 (1943), ADAH
Dees v. Metts, Bill of Exceptions, Testimony of E. M. Salter, Alabama Supreme
    Court Records, 1 Div. 186 (1943), ADAH
Dees v. Metts, Bill of Exceptions, Testimony of W. G. Daniels, Alabama
    Supreme Court Records, 1 Div. 186 (1943), ADAH
Griffith v. State, Bill of Exceptions, Testimony of Miley More, Alabama Court
    of Appeal Records, 2 Div. 798 (1950), ADAH
Griffith v. State, Bill of Exceptions, Testimony of Mattie Leonard, Alabama
    Court of Appeal Records, 2 Div. 798 (1950), ADAH
Griffith v. State, Bill of Exceptions, Testimony of Lubie Griffith, Alabama
    Court of Appeal Records, 2 Div. 798 (1950), ADAH
Griffith v. State, Bill of Exceptions, Testimony of Louise Stallworth, Alabama
    Court of Appeal Records, 2 Div. 798 (1950), ADAH
Griffith v. State, Bill of Exceptions, Testimony of R. B. Williams, Alabama
    Court of Appeal Records, 2 Div. 798 (1950), ADAH
Griffith v. State, Bill of Exceptions, Alabama Court of Appeal Records, 2 Div.
    798 (1950), ADAH
Agnew v. State, Bill of Exceptions, Testimony of Sherman Brasher, Alabama
    Court of Appeal Records, 6 Div. 235 (1950), ADAH
Agnew v. State, Bill of Exceptions, Testimony of Dr. J. H. Ashcraft, Alabama
    Court of Appeal Records, 6 Div. 235 (1950), ADAH
Agnew v. State, Bill of Exceptions, Testimony of Dr. B. W. McNease, Alabama
    Court of Appeal Records, 6 Div. 235 (1950), ADAH
Agnew v. State, Bill of Exceptions, Testimony of Hosea Agnew, Alabama
    Court of Appeal Records, 6 Div. 235 (1950), ADAH
Agnew v. State, Bill of Exceptions, Testimony of Oscar Watkins, Alabama
    Court of Appeal Records, 6 Div. 235 (1950), ADAH
Agnew v. State, Bill of Exceptions, Testimony of Clara Courington, Alabama
    Court of Appeal Records, 6 Div. 235 (1950), ADAH
Agnew v. State, Bill of Exceptions, Testimony of Edna Franklin, Alabama
    Court of Appeal Records, 6 Div. 235 (1950), ADAH
Agnew v. State, Bill of Exceptions, Testimony of Aline Williams, Alabama
    Court of Appeal Records, 6 Div. 235 (1950), ADAH
Agnew v. State, Bill of Exceptions, Exhibit B, Alabama Court of Appeal
    Records, 6 Div. 235 (1950), ADAH
Agnew v. State, Bill of Exceptions, Exhibit C, Alabama Court of Appeal
    Records, 6 Div. 235 (1950), ADAH

Jackson v. State, Bill of Exceptions, Demurrer to Indictment, Alabama Court of Appeal Records, 8 Div. 382 (1953), ADAH

Jackson v. State, Bill of Exceptions, Given Charges for Defendant, Alabama Court of Appeal Records, 8 Div. 382 (1953), ADAH

Jackson v. State, Bill of Exceptions, Given Charges for the State, Alabama Court of Appeal Records, 8 Div. 382 (1953), ADAH

Jackson v. State, Bill of Exceptions, Oral Charge, Alabama Court of Appeal Records, 8 Div. 382 (1953), ADAH

Rogers v. State, Bill of Exceptions, Oral Charge, Alabama Court of Appeal Records, 8 Div. 425 (1953), ADAH

Rogers v. State, Bill of Exceptions, Defendant's Refused Charges, Alabama Court of Appeal Records, 8 Div. 425 (1953), ADAH

Rogers v. State, Bill of Exceptions, Demurrer to Indictment, Alabama Court of Appeal Records, 8 Div. 425 (1953), ADAH

Materials from the Alabama Attorney General

Biennial Report of the Attorney General of Alabama. Montgomery: State of Alabama: 1892.

Biennial Report of the Attorney General of Alabama. Montgomery: State of Alabama: 1894.

Biennial Report of the Attorney General of Alabama. Montgomery: State of Alabama: 1896.

Biennial Report of the Attorney General of Alabama. Montgomery: State of Alabama: 1898.

Biennial Report of the Attorney General of Alabama. Montgomery: State of Alabama: 1900.

Biennial Report of the Attorney General of Alabama. Montgomery: State of Alabama: 1902.

Biennial Report of the Attorney General of Alabama. Montgomery: State of Alabama: 1906.

Biennial Report of the Attorney General of Alabama. Montgomery: State of Alabama: 1908.

Biennial Report of the Attorney General of Alabama. Montgomery: State of Alabama: 1910.

Biennial Report of the Attorney General of Alabama. Montgomery: State of Alabama: 1912.

Biennial Report of the Attorney General of Alabama. Montgomery: State of Alabama: 1914.

Biennial Report of the Attorney General of Alabama. Montgomery: State of Alabama: 1916.

Biennial Report of the Attorney General of Alabama. Montgomery: State of Alabama: 1918.

Biennial Report of the Attorney General of Alabama. Montgomery: State of Alabama: 1920.

Biennial Report of the Attorney General of Alabama. Montgomery: State of
    Alabama: 1922.
Biennial Report of the Attorney General of Alabama. Montgomery: State of
    Alabama: 1924.
Biennial Report of the Attorney General of Alabama. Montgomery: State of
    Alabama: 1926.
Biennial Report of the Attorney General of Alabama. Montgomery: State of
    Alabama: 1928.
Biennial Report of the Attorney General of Alabama. Montgomery: State of
    Alabama: 1930.
Biennial Report of the Attorney General of Alabama. Montgomery: State of
    Alabama: 1932.
Biennial Report of the Attorney General of Alabama. Montgomery: State of
    Alabama: 1934.
Biennial Report of the Attorney General of Alabama. Montgomery: State of
    Alabama: 1936.
Biennial Report of the Attorney General of Alabama. Montgomery: State of
    Alabama: 1938.
Quarterly Report of the Attorney General of Alabama. Vol. 28. Montgomery:
    State of Alabama: 1942.

Other Primary Legal Documents

Attorney General of Alabama. *Biennial Reports.* Montgomery: State of
    Alabama, 1884–1938.
Tompkins, John. *Brief for the Plaintiff in Error.* Filed in U.S. Supreme Court,
    1882.
Tompkins, Henry. *Brief and Argument for Appellee.* Filed in U.S. Supreme
    Court, 1882.

Documentary Primary Sources

Contemporary Newspaper Articles

Bailey, Stan. "Brewer Thinks Old Marriage Law Was Best." *Alabama Journal,*
    Dec. 9, 1970, 23, col. 5. Accessed through the Tuskegee Institute News
    Clippings File, Alabama Department of Archives and History (hereinafter
    ADAH).
Birmingham Herald. "Court Upholds Woman's Sentence." February 17, 1954,
    3. Accessed through the Tuskegee Institute News Clippings File, ADAH.
Black Dispatch. "Adultery in Alabama?" Oklahoma City, October 9, 1954, 4.
    Accessed through the Tuskegee Institute News Clippings File, ADAH.
Montgomery Advertiser. "Cohabitation Law in State Not Involved." December
    8, 1964, 1. Accessed through the Tuskegee Institute News Clippings File,
    ADAH.

Birmingham News. "Groups Are Against Interracial Marriage Amendment."
August 27, 2000.

Jackson, Emory O. "Blond Husband Fights to Free Wife From Jail: Lawyer
Mum as Both Sides Seek to Hide Details from Press." *Afro-American,*
Baltimore, October 16, 1954, 2. Accessed through the Tuskegee Institute
News Clippings File, ADAH.

Johnson, Bob. "Lawsuit Filed to Remove Interracial Marriage Amendment
from Ballot." Associated Press State and Local Wire, October 4, 2000.

McGrew, Jannell. "Lawmakers Debate Constitution Changes." *Montgomery
Advertiser,* January 31, 2005.

McGrew, Jannell, and John Davis. "Same-Sex Marriage Ban Clears Hurdle."
Montgomery Advertiser, February 9, 2005.

"Mississippi Repeals Ban on Interracial Marriages." *Jet* 73 (9): 18, November
23, 1987.

"Mobile Women Protest Against Parole of 'Shreveport Sarah': League of
Women Voters Expose Record of Notorious Mulatto and Threaten Expose
of Parties Concerned in Application to Governor Brandon and Appeal to
K.K.K. for Relief." *Pittsburgh American,* August 17, 1923. Accessed
through the Tuskegee Institute News Clippings File, ADAH.

Montgomery Advertiser. "Appellate Court Upholds Sentence of Negro
Woman." February 17, 1954, sec. B: 14. Accessed through the Tuskegee
Institute News Clippings File, ADAH.

Poovey, Bill. "Lawmakers Vote to End Ban on Interracial Marriages; Flag Not
Returning." *Associated Press State and Local Wire,* March 11, 1999.

Rawls, Phillip. "Alabama Goofs Special Election; Interracial Marriage
Amendment Off the Ballot." *Chattanooga Times Free Press,* June 19, 1999,
B2.

Reeves, Jay. "Rebel Flag at Capitol Stirs Alabama Boycott." *Commercial
Appeal,* November 29, 1992, Memphis Metro, B1.

Richmond Times-Dispatch. "Alabama Marriage Law Contested." December 4,
1970, A13.

Richmond Times-Dispatch. "Alabama Marriage Law Ruled Unconstitutional."
December 9, 1970, A8.

Roig-Franzia, Manuel, "Alabama Vote Opens Old Racial Wounds; School
Segregation Remains a State Law as Amendment Is Defeated." *Washington
Post,* November 28, 2004, A1.

Sengupta, Somini. "Marry at Will." *New York Times,* November 12, 2000, sec.
4, 2, col. 3.

Sheppard, Judy. "Alabama Voters May Bury Interracial Marriage Ban; It
Hasn't Had Legal Force for Decades." *Atlanta Journal and Constitution,*
September 26, 2000, sec. A: 11A.

Sznajderman, Michael. "Marriage Ban, Lottery May Be on Same Ballot."
Birmingham News, April 16, 1999a, sec. B: 4B.

Sznajderman, Michael. "Voters to Get Say on Interracial Marriage Ban."
    Birmingham News, June 2, 1999b. 3D.
Sznajderman, Michael. "Rebel Flag Raiser Not Charged; AG Says Evidence
    Not Enough to Stick." *Birmingham News,* April 29, 2000.

Web Sites

Information for Election 2006. Alabama Secretary of State, Elections Division.
    http://www.sos.state.al.us/election/2006/index.aspx
State and Local Proposed Amendments. Election Results, 2000 Election
    Information, Alabama Secretary of State, Elections Division.
    http://www.sos .state.al.us/election/2000/2000.htm
Statewide Voter Turnout. Alabama Secretary of State, Elections Division. 2003.
    http://www.sos.state.al.us/election/st-tout.htm

Other Documentary Sources

Allen, William G. *The American Prejudice Against Color: An Authentic
    Narrative, Showing How Easily the Nation Got into an Uproar.* London:
    W. and F. G. Cash, 1853.
American Institute of Public Opinion. "American Institute of Public Opinion—
    Surveys." *Public Opinion Quarterly* 2 (1938).
Bailey, Thomas Pearce. *Race Orthodoxy in the South and Other Aspects of the
    Negro Question.* New York: Neale Publishing, 1914.
Baker, Ray Stannard. *Following the Color Line: An Account of Negro
    Citizenship in the American Democracy.* Williamstown: Corner House,
    1973. Original publication, 1908.
Bancroft, Hubert Howe. "A Historian's View of the Negro." In *The
    Development of Segregationist Thought,* ed. I. A. Newby, 79–83.
    Homewood, IL: Dorsey Press, 1968.
Bardin, James. "Science and the 'Negro Problem.'" In *The Development of
    Segregationist Thought,* ed. I. A. Newby, 29–36. Homewood, IL: Dorsey
    Press, 1968.
Barringer, P. B. *The American Negro: His Past and Future.* 3d ed. Raleigh, NC:
    Edwards and Broughton, 1900.
Bean, Robert Bennett. "The Negro Brain." In *The Development of
    Segregationist Thought,* ed. I. A. Newby, 46–53. Homewood, IL: Dorsey
    Press, 1968.
Bilbo, Theodore. "World War II: Increasing Racial Tensions." In *The
    Development of Segregationist Thought,* ed. I. A. Newby, 134–45.
    Homewood, IL: Dorsey Press, 1968.
Bowers, Claude. "Negroes and the South in Reconstruction." In *The
    Development of Segregationist Thought,* ed. I. A. Newby, 84–90.
    Homewood, IL: Dorsey Press, 1968.

Bratton, Theodore DuBose. "Christian Principles and the Race Issue." In *The Development of Segregationist Thought,* ed. I. A. Newby, 106–11. Homewood, IL: Dorsey Press, 1968.

Bruce, Alexander. "In Defense of Southern Race Policies." In *The Development of Segregationist Thought,* ed. I. A. Newby, 70–78. Homewood, IL: Dorsey Press, 1968.

Bryce, James. *The Relations of the Advanced and the Backward Races of Mankind.* Oxford: Clarendon Press, 1902. Reprinted in *Racial Determinism and the Fear of Miscegenation Post-1900.* Vol. 8 of *Race and the Negro Problem,* ed. John David Smith. New York: Garland, 1993.

Chesnutt, Charles. *The House Behind the Cedars.* New York: Collier, 1971.

Clark, Frank. "A Politician's Defense of Segregation." In *The Development of Segregationist Thought,* ed. I. A. Newby, 91–97. Homewood, IL: Dorsey Press, 1968.

Clemens, Samuel. *The Tragedy of Pudd'nhead Wilson.* New York: New American Library, 1980.

Cox, Earnest Sevier. *The South's Part in Mongrelizing the Nation.* Richmond, VA: White America Society, 1926.

Davenport, Charles B. *Heredity of Skin Color in Negro-White Crosses.* Washington, DC: Carnegie Institute, 1913.

Dixon, Thomas. *The Leopard's Spots: A Romance of the White Man's Burden, 1865–1900.* New York: Doubleday, Page and Co., 1902.

Dixon, Thomas. *The Clansman: An Historical Romance of the Ku Klux Klan.* New York: Grosset and Dunlap, 1905.

Douglas, William O., and Walter Murphy. *Transcriptions of Conversations between Justice William O. Douglas and Professor Walter F. Murphy.* Recorded April 5, 1963. Cassette tape. Princeton University Library, Princeton, 2000.

Ellender, Allen. "Changing Attitudes in the 1930's." In *The Development of Segregationist Thought,* ed. I. A. Newby, 128–33. Homewood, IL: Dorsey Press, 1968.

Faulkner, William. *Light in August.* New York: Random House, 1968.

Faulkner, William. *Absalom! Absalom!* New York: Vintage Books, 1991.

Ferber, Edna. *Show Boat.* New York: Grosset and Dunlap, 1926.

George, Wesley Critz. *The Biology of the Race Problem.* Report prepared by commission of the Governor of Alabama, 1962.

Heflin, J. Thomas. "A Segregationist Discusses Interracial Marriage." In *The Development of Segregationist Thought,* ed. I. A. Newby, 123–27. Homewood, IL: Dorsey Press, 1968.

Hoffman, Frederick. *Race Traits and Tendencies of the American Negro.* New York: Macmillan (for the American Economic Association), 1896.

Miller, Kelly. "An Appeal to Reason on the Race Problem: An Open Letter to John Temple Graves." January 30, 1912.

Miscegenation Indorsed by the Republican Party. New York: E. P. Patten, 1864.

Miscegenation: The Theory of the Blending of the Races, Applied to the American White Man and Negro. New York: H. Dexter, Hamilton, 1864.

Mitchell, Margaret. *Gone With the Wind.* New York: Scribner Books, 1936.

Moore, David Presley. *The Place for the Negro or Heaven, Hell or Africa.* Prichard, AL: Lowrey Printing, 1933.

Morgan, John T. "The Race Question in the United States: An Overview in 1890." In *The Development of Segregationist Thought,* ed. I. A. Newby, 22–28. Homewood, IL: Dorsey Press, 1968.

Murphy, Edgar Gardner. *Child Labor in Alabama: Pamphlets by Edgar Gardner Murphy.* Montgomery: Alabama Child Labor Committee, 1901–2.

Norwood, Thomas M. *Address on the Negro.* Savannah: Braid and Hutton, 1907.

Odum, Howard. "The Education of Negroes." In *The Development of Segregationist Thought,* ed. I. A. Newby, 63–69. Homewood, IL: Dorsey Press, 1968.

Pickett, William. *The Negro Problem: Abraham Lincoln's Solution.* New York: G.P. Putnam's Sons, 1909.

Putnam, Carleton. *Race and Reality: A Search for Solutions.* Washington, DC: Public Affairs Press, 1967.

Reed, Rev. William B. *A Race between Two Straits.* Newport, RI: W. B. Reed, 1912.

Reuter, Edward Byron. *The Mulatto in the United States.* 1918. New York: Negro Universities Press, 1969.

Rogers, J. A. *Sex and Race.* St. Petersburg, FL: Helga M. Rogers, 1940–41.

Russell, Sylvester. *The Amalgamation of America: Normal Solution of the Color and Inter-Marriage Problem.* Chicago: Sylvester Russell Book Concern, 1920.

Schultz, Alfred Paul Karl Eduard. *Race or Mongrel.* Boston: L. C. Page, 1908.

Seaman, L. *What Miscegenation Is! And What We Are to Expect Now that Mr. Lincoln Is Re-elected.* New York: Waller and Willetts, 1865.

Shaler, Nathaniel Southgate. "The Permanence of Racial Characteristics." In *The Development of Segregationist Thought,* ed. I. A. Newby, 54–62. Homewood, IL: Dorsey Press, 1968.

Shannon, A. H. *Racial Integrity and Other Features of the Negro Problem.* Nashville: Smith and Lamar, ca. 1920.

Smith, William Benjamin. "The Color Line: A Brief in Behalf of the Unborn." In *Racial Determinism and the Fear of Miscegenation Post-1900, 1905,* ed. John David Smith, vol. 8. New York: Garland, 1993.

Stone, Alfred. *Studies in the American Race Problem.* New York: Doubleday, Page and Co., 1908.

Subgenation: The Theory of the Normal Relation of the Races; An Answer to "Miscegenation." New York: John Bradbury, 1864.

Sumner, William Graham. "Legislation Cannot Make Mores." In *The Development of Segregationist Thought,* ed. I. A. Newby, 44–45. Homewood, IL: Dorsey Press, 1968.

Thomas, William. "The Psychology of Race Prejudice." In *The Development of Segregationist Thought,* ed. I. A. Newby, 37–43. Homewood, IL: Dorsey Press, 1968.

White Intervenors in *Stell v. Savannah-Chatham Co. Bd. of Educ.* "In Defense of School Segregation." In *The Development of Segregationist Thought,* ed. I. A. Newby, 146–53. Homewood, IL: Dorsey Press, 1968.

Windham, Festus. *A Bible Treatise on Segregation: An Analysis of Biblical References to Determine the True Relationship of the Races.* New York: William-Frederick Press, 1957.

Secondary Sources

Allen, J. Michael, III, and Jamison Hinds. "Alabama Constitutional Reform." *Alabama Law Review* 53 (2001): 1–30.

Allen, Thomas C. *Integration Is Genocide.* Franklinton, NC: TC Allen, 1997.

Andersen, Ellen Ann. *Out of the Closets and Into the Courts: Legal Opportunity Structure and Gay Rights Litigation.* Ann Arbor: University of Michigan Press, 2004.

Appiah, Kwame Anthony. *In My Father's House: Africa in the Philosophy of Culture.* New York: Oxford University Press, 1992.

Arendt, Hannah. *Eichmann in Jerusalem: A Report on the Banality of Evil.* New York: Penguin Books, 1994.

Bair, Barbara. "Remapping the Black/White Body: Sexuality, Nationalism, and Biracial Antimiscegenation Activism in 1920s Virginia." In *Sex, Love, Race: Crossing Boundaries in North American History,* ed. Martha Hodes, 399–421. New York: New York University Press, 1999.

Baker, Lee D. *From Savage to Negro: Anthropology and the Construction of Race, 1896–1954.* 1998. Berkeley: University of California Press, 1998.

Bank, Steven. "Anti-Miscegenation Laws and the Dilemma of Symmetry: The Understanding of Equality in the Civil Rights Act of 1875." *University of Chicago Law School Roundtable* 2 (1995): 303–44.

Bardaglio, Peter. *Reconstructing the Household: Families, Sex, and the Law in the Nineteenth-Century South.* Chapel Hill: University of North Carolina Press, 1995.

Bartholet, Elizabeth. *Nobody's Children: Abuse and Neglect, Foster Drift, and the Adoption Alternative.* Boston: Beacon Press, 1999.

Bell, Derrick. *Faces at the Bottom of the Well: The Permanence of Racism.* New York: Basic Books, 1992.

Berger, Raoul. "Robert Bork's Contribution to Original Intention." *Northwestern University Law Review* 84 (1990): 1167–89.

Berry, Mary Frances. "Judging Morality: Sexual Behavior and Legal Consequences in the Late Nineteenth-Century South." *Journal of American History* 78 (1991): 835–56.

Blight, David. *Race and Reunion: The Civil War in American Memory.* Cambridge: Harvard University Press, 2001.

Boone, Dorothy. *A Historical Review and a Bibliography of Selected Negro Magazines, 1910–1969.* EdD diss., Language and Literature, University of Michigan, 1970.

Bowler, Peter. *Theories of Human Evolution: A Century of Debate, 1844–1944.* Baltimore: Johns Hopkins University Press, 1986.

Brandwein, Pamela. *Reconstructing Reconstruction: The Supreme Court and the Production of Historical Truth.* Durham: Duke University Press, 1999.

Brandwein, Pamela. "The *Civil Rights Cases* and the Lost Language of State Neglect." In *The Supreme Court and American Political Development,* ed. Ronald Kahn and Ken I. Kersch, 275–325. Lawrence: University Press of Kansas, 2006.

Bridges, Amy. "Path Dependence, Sequence, History, Theory." *Studies in American Political Development* 14 (2000): 93–112.

Brodkin, Karen. *How Jews Became White Folks and What That Says about Race in America.* New Brunswick: Rutgers University Press, 1998.

Bybee, Keith. *Mistaken Identity: The Supreme Court and the Politics of Minority Representation.* Princeton: Princeton University Press, 1998.

Bynum, Victoria. *Unruly Women: The Politics of Social and Sexual Control in the Old South.* Chapel Hill: University of North Carolina Press, 1992.

Bynum, Victoria. "'White Negroes' in Segregated Mississippi: Miscegenation, Racial Identity, and the Law." *Journal of Southern History* 44 (1998): 247–75.

Canaday, Margot. "Building a Straight State: Sexuality and Social Citizenship under the 1944 G.I. Bill." *Journal of American History* 90 (2003): 935–54.

Clemon, U. W., and Bryan Fair. "Making Bricks without Straw: The NAACP Legal Defense Fund and the Development of Civil Rights Law in Alabama, 1940–1980." *Alabama Law Review* 52 (2001): 1121–52.

Colker, Ruth. *Hybrids: Bisexuals, Multiracials, and Other Misfits under American Law.* New York: New York University Press, 1996.

Collins, Patricia Hill. "Gender, Black Feminism, and Black Political Economy." *Annals of the American Academy of Political and Social Science* 568 (2000): 41–52.

Cook, Raymond Allen. *Thomas Dixon.* New York: Twayne, 1974.

Cott, Nancy. *Public Vows: A History of Marriage and the Nation.* Cambridge: Harvard University Press, 2000.

Davis, Adrienne. "The Private Law of Race and Sex: An Antebellum Perspective." *Stanford Law Review* 51 (1999): 221–88.

Davis, F. James. *Who Is Black? One Nation's Definition.* University Park: Pennsylvania State University Press, 1991.

Davis, Peggy Cooper. *Neglected Stories: The Constitution and Family Values.* New York: Hill and Wang, 1998.

Doss, Harriet Amos. "White and Black Female Missionaries to Former Slaves During Reconstruction." In *Stepping Out of the Shadows: Alabama Women, 1819–1990,* ed. Mary Martha Thomas, 43–56. Tuscaloosa: University of Alabama Press, 1995.

Dudziak, Mary. "Desegregation as a Cold War Imperative." *Stanford Law Review* 41 (1988): 61–120.

Dudziak, Mary. *Cold War Civil Rights: Race and the Image of American Democracy.* Princeton: Princeton University Press, 2000.

Dunlap, Leslie. "The Reform of Rape Law and the Problem of White Men: Age-of-Consent Campaigns in the South, 1885–1910." In *Sex, Love, Race: Crossing Boundaries in North American History,* ed. Martha Hodes, 352–72. New York: New York University Press, 1999.

Elliott, Michael. "Telling the Difference: Nineteenth-Century Legal Narratives of Racial Taxonomy." *Law and Social Inquiry* 24 (1999): 611–34.

Eskridge, William. *Gaylaw: Challenging the Apartheid of the Closet.* Cambridge: Harvard University Press, 1999.

Federal Judicial Center. *Judges of the United States Courts: Elbert Bertram Haltom, Jr.* 2003. Web site. Available: http://www.fjc.gov/servlet/tGetInfo?jid+954. May 5, 2003.

Feldman, Glenn. *Politics, Society, and the Klan in Alabama, 1915–1949.* Tuscaloosa: University of Alabama Press, 1999.

Ferber, Abby. *White Man Falling: Race, Gender, and White Supremacy.* Landham: Rowman & Littlefield, 1998.

Fields, Barbara J. "Ideology and Race in American History." In *Region, Race, and Reconstruction: Essays in Honor of C. Vann Woodward,* ed. J. Morgan Kousser and James M. McPherson, 143–77. New York: Oxford University Press, 1982.

Fields, Jason. *America's Families and Living Arrangements, 2003.* Washington, DC: Census Bureau, November 2004.

Filene, Peter. "The Secrets of Men's History." In *The Making of Masculinities: The New Men's Studies,* ed. Harry Brod, 103–20. Boston: Allen & Unwin, 1987.

Finkelman, Paul. "The Crime of Color." *Tulane Law Review* 67 (1993): 2063–2112.

Finkelman, Paul. *Slavery and the Founders: Race and Liberty in the Age of Jefferson.* Armonk, NY, and London: M. E. Sharpe, 1996.

Fitzgerald, Michael. "Republican Factionalism and Black Empowerment: The Spencer-Warner Controversy and Alabama Reconstruction, 1868–1880." *Journal of Southern History* 64 (1998): 473–95.

Flynt, Wayne. "Alabama's Shame: The Historical Origins of the 1901 Constitution." *Alabama Law Review* 53 (2001): 67–76.

Foner, Eric. "Hiring Quotas for White Males Only." In *Critical White Studies:*

Looking Behind the Mirror, ed. Richard Delgado and Jean Stefancic, 24–26. Philadelphia: Temple University Press, 1997.

Fox-Genovese, Elizabeth. "Stewards of their Culture: Southern Women Novelists as Social Critics." In *Stepping Out of the Shadows: Alabama Women, 1819–1990,* ed. Mary Martha Thomas, 11–27. Tuscaloosa: University of Alabama Press, 1995.

Franke, Katherine. "Becoming a Citizen: Reconstruction Era Regulation of African American Marriages." *Yale Journal of Law and the Humanities* 11 (1999): 251–309.

Frankenberg, Ruth. *White Women, Race Matters: The Social Construction of Whiteness.* Minneapolis: University of Minnesota Press, 1993.

Franklin, Clyde. "Surviving the Institutional Decimation of Black Males: Causes, Consequences, and Intervention. In *The Making of Masculinities: The New Men's Studies,* ed. Harry Brod, 155–70. Boston: Allen & Unwin, 1987.

Gallagher, Charles A. "White Racial Formation: Into the Twenty-First Century." In *Critical White Studies: Looking Behind the Mirror,* ed. Richard Delgado and Jean Stefancic, 6–11. Philadelphia: Temple University Press, 1997.

Garvey, John, and Noel Ignatiev. "Toward a New Abolitionism: A *Race Traitor* Manifesto." In *Whiteness: A Critical Reader,* ed. Mike Hill, 346–49. New York: New York University Press, 1997.

Gilmore, Glenda. *Gender and Jim Crow: Women and the Politics of White Supremacy in North Carolina, 1896–1920.* Chapel Hill: University of North Carolina Press, 1996.

Giroux, Henry. "Racial Politics and the Pedagogy of Whiteness." In *Whiteness: A Critical Reader,* ed. Mike Hill, 294–315. New York: New York University Press, 1997.

Gordon-Reed, Annette. *Thomas Jefferson and Sally Hemings: An American Controversy.* Charlottesville: University of Virginia Press, 1997.

Gould, Stephen J. *The Mismeasure of Man.* New York: W. W. Norton, 1981.

Graber, Mark. *Dred Scott and the Problem of Constitutional Evil.* Cambridge: Cambridge University Press, 2006.

Green, Venus. "The 'Lady' Telephone Operator: Gendering Whiteness in the Bell System, 1900–70." In *Racializing Class, Classifying Race: Labour and Difference in Britain, the USA, and Africa,* ed. Peter Alexander and Rick Halpern, 57–86. Oxford: Macmillan, 2000.

Griffith, Lucille. *Alabama: A Documentary History to 1900.* Rev. ed. University: University of Alabama Press, 1968.

Gross, Ariela J. "Litigating Whiteness: Trials of Racial Determination in the Nineteenth-Century South." *Yale Law Journal* 108 (1998): 109–85.

Grossberg, Michael. *Governing the Hearth: Law and Family in Nineteenth Century America.* Chapel Hill: University of North Carolina Press, 1985.

Guterl, Matthew Pratt. *The Color of Race in America, 1900–1940.* Cambridge: Harvard University Press, 2001.

Hale, Grace Elizabeth. *Making Whiteness: The Culture of Segregation in the South, 1890–1940.* New York: Pantheon Books, 1998.

Haney López, Ian. *White by Law: The Legal Construction of Race.* New York: New York University Press, 1996.

Harris, Cheryl. "Whiteness as Property." *Harvard Law Review* 106 (1993): 1707–91.

Harris, Cheryl. "Finding Sojourner's Truth: Race, Gender, and the Institution of Property." *Cardozo Law Review* 18 (1996): 309–409.

Hickman, Christine. "The Devil and the 'One Drop' Rule: Racial Categories, African Americans, and the U.S. Census." *University of Michigan Law Review* 95 (1997): 1161–1265.

Higginbotham, F. Michael. "Soldiers for Justice: The Role of the Tuskegee Airmen in the Desegregation of the American Armed Forces." *William and Mary Bill of Rights Journal* 8 (2000): 273–321.

Hill, Mike. "Introduction: Vipers in Shangri-La: Whiteness, Writing, and Other Ordinary Terrors." In *Whiteness: A Critical Reader,* ed. Mike Hill, 1–18. New York: New York University Press, 1997.

Hodes, Martha. *White Women, Black Men: Illicit Sex in the Nineteenth-Century South.* New Haven: Yale University Press, 1997.

Hodes, Martha. "Introduction: Interconnecting and Diverging Narratives." In *Sex, Love, Race: Crossing Boundaries in North American History,* ed. Martha Hodes, 1–9. New York: New York University Press, 1999.

Igatiev, Noel. *How the Irish Became White.* New York: Routledge, 1995.

Jackson, Harvey. "The Middle-Class Democracy Victorious: The Mitcham War of Clarke County, Alabama, 1893." *Journal of Southern History* 57 (1991): 453–78.

Jacobson, Matthew Frye. *Whiteness of a Different Color: European Immigrants and the Alchemy of Race.* Cambridge: Harvard University Press, 1998.

Jones, D. Marvin. "Darkness Made Visible: Law, Metaphor, and the Racial Self." *Georgetown Law Journal* 82 (1993): 437–511.

Kaplan, Sidney. "The Miscegenation Issue in the Election of 1864." *Journal of Negro History* 34, no. 3 (1949): 274–343.

Kennedy, Randall. *Interracial Intimacies: Sex, Marriage, Identity, and Adoption.* New York: Pantheon Books, 2003.

Key, V. O. *Southern Politics in State and Nation.* New York: Vintage Books, 1949.

King, Desmond. *Making Americans: Immigration, Race, and the Origins of Diverse Democracy.* Cambridge: Harvard University Press, 2000.

King, Desmond, and Rogers Smith. "Racial Orders in American Political Development." *American Political Science Review* 99 (2005): 75–92.

Kinney, James. *Amalgamation! Race, Sex, and Rhetoric in the Nineteenth-Century American Novel.* Westport, CT: Greenwood, 1985.

Klarman, Michael. *From Jim Crow to Civil Rights: The Supreme Court and the Struggle for Racial Equality.* Oxford: Oxford University Press, 2004.

Klinkner, Philip, and Rogers Smith. *The Unsteady March: The Rise and Decline of Racial Equality in America.* Chicago: University of Chicago Press, 1999.

Kluger, Richard. *Simple Justice: The History of* Brown v. Board of Education *and Black America's Struggle for Equality.* New York: Vintage Books, 1977.

Kolchin, Peter. *First Freedom: The Responses of Alabama's Blacks to Emancipation and Reconstruction.* Westport, CT: Greenwood, 1972.

Kolchin, Peter. "Whiteness Studies: The New History of Race in America." *Journal of American History* 89 (2002): 1–41.

Kryder, Daniel. *Divided Arsenal: Race and the American State during World War II.* Cambridge: Cambridge University Press, 2000.

Kull, Andrew. *The Color-Blind Constitution.* Cambridge: Harvard University Press, 1992.

Leaming, Jeremy. "Unholy Matrimony: President Bush, Religious Right Join Hands to Push for Marriage Amendment." *Church and State* (April 2004): 80–82.

Lee, Taeku. *Mobilizing Public Opinion: Black Insurgency and Racial Attitudes in the Civil Rights Era.* Chicago: University of Chicago Press, 2002.

Linder, Doug. *The 'Scottsboro Boys' Trials: 1931–1937.* Web page. Available: http://www.law.umkc.edu/faculty/projects/FTrials/scottsboro/scottsb.htm. April 9, 2003.

Lowndes, Joseph. *The Southern Origins of Modern Conservatism.* New Haven: Yale University Press, forthcoming, 2008.

Luker, Kristin. *Abortion and the Politics of Motherhood.* Berkeley and Los Angeles: University of California Press, 1984.

MacLean, Nancy. *Behind the Mask of Chivalry: The Making of the Second Ku Klux Klan.* New York: Oxford University Press, 1994.

Marcosson, Samuel. "Colorizing the Constitution of Originalism: Clarence Thomas at the Rubicon." *Law and Inequality* 16 (1998): 429–91.

Marx, Anthony. *Making Race and Nation: A Comparison of the United States, South Africa, and Brazil.* New York: Cambridge University Press, 1999.

McConnell, Michael. "Originalism and the Desegregation Decisions." *Virginia Law Review* 81 (1995): 947–1140.

Michaels, Walter Benn. "Against Formalism: Chickens and Rocks." In *The State of the Language,* ed. Leonard Michaels and Christopher Ricks, 410–20. Berkeley: University of California Press, 1980.

Miles, Robert. *Racism after "Race Relations."* London: Routledge, 1993.

Mills, Gary. "Miscegenation and the Free Negro in Antebellum 'Anglo'

Alabama: A Reexamination of Southern Race Relations." *Journal of American History* 68 (1981): 16–35.

Moore, Albert Burton. *History of Alabama*. Vol. 2. University: Alabama Book Store, 1954.

Moran, Rachel. *Interracial Intimacy: The Regulation of Race and Romance.* Chicago: University of Chicago Press, 2001.

Morris, Aldon. *The Origins of the Civil Rights Movement: Black Communities Organizing for Change*. New York: Free Press, 1984.

Morris, Aldon. *The Origins of the Civil Rights Movement: Black Communities Organizing for Change*. New York: Free Press, 1986.

Mumford, Kevin. *Interzones: Black/White Sex Districts in Chicago and New York in the Early Twentieth Century*. New York: Columbia University Press, 1997.

Murphy, Karen Lin. *Reconstructing the Nation: Race, Gender and Restoration, the Progressive Era*. PhD diss., American Studies, University of Minnesota, 1996.

Nelson, Scott. "Livestock, Boundaries, and Public Space in Spartanburg: African American Men, Elite White Women, and the Spectacle of Conjugal Relations." In *Sex, Love, Race: Crossing Boundaries in North American History*, ed. Martha Hodes, 313–29. New York: New York University Press, 1999.

Newitz, Annalee, and Matthew Wray. "What Is 'White Trash'? Stereotypes and Economic Conditions of Poor Whites in the United States." In *Whiteness: A Critical Reader*, ed. Mike Hill, 168–84. New York: New York University Press, 1997.

Norrell, Robert. "Law in a White Man's Democracy: A History of the Alabama State Judiciary." *Cumberland Law Review* 32 (2001): 135–63.

Novkov, Julie. *Constituting Workers, Protecting Women: Gender, Law, and Labor in the Progressive Era and New Deal Years*. Ann Arbor: University of Michigan Press, 2001.

Novkov, Julie. "Racial Constructions: The Legal Regulation of Miscegenation in Alabama, 1890–1934." *Law and History Review* 20 (2002): 225–77.

Omi, Michael, and Howard Winant. *Racial Formation in the United States: From the 1960s to the 1990s*. 2d ed. New York: Routledge, 1994.

Oshinsky, David. *"Worse than Slavery": Parchman Farm and the Ordeal of Jim Crow Justice*. New York: Free Press, 1996.

Owen, Thomas. *History of Alabama and Dictionary of Alabama Biography*. Vol. 3. Spartanburg, SC: Reprint Company, 1978.

Painter, Nell. " 'Social Equality,' Miscegenation, Labor, and Power." In *The Evolution of Southern Culture*, ed. Numan Bartley. Athens: University of Georgia Press, 1988.

Palmer, Phyllis. *Domesticity and Dirt: Housewives and Domestic Servants in the United States, 1920–1945*. Philadelphia: Temple University Press, 1989.

Pascoe, Peggy. "Miscegenation Law, Court Cases, and Ideologies of 'Race' in

Twentieth-Century America." *Journal of American History* 83 (1996): 44–69.

Pascoe, Peggy. "Sex, Gender, and Same-Sex Marriage." In *Is Academic Feminism Dead? Theory in Practice,* ed. Social Justice Group at the Center for Advanced Feminist Studies, University of Minnesota, 86–129. New York: New York University Press, 2000.

Payne, Charles. *I've Got the Light of Freedom: The Organizing Tradition and the Mississippi Freedom Struggle.* Berkeley: University of California Press, 1995.

Pierson, Paul. "Not Just What, but *When:* Timing and Sequence in Political Processes." *Studies in American Political Development* 14 (2000): 72–92.

Pleck, Joseph. "The Theory of Male Sex-Role Identity: Its Rise and Fall, 1936 to the Present." In *The Making of Masculinities: The New Men's Studies,* ed. Harry Brod, 21–38. Boston: Allen & Unwin, 1987.

Regosin, Elizabeth. *Freedom's Promise: Ex-Slave Families and Citizenship in the Age of Emancipation.* Charlottesville: University of Virginia Press, 2002.

Robinson, Charles F. T. "The Antimiscegenation Conversation: Love's Legislated Limits (1868–1967)." PhD diss., University of Houston, 1998.

Robinson, Charles F. *Dangerous Liaisons: Sex and Love in the Segregated South.* Fayetteville: University of Arkansas Press, 2003.

Robson, Ruthann. *Lesbian (Out)Law: Survival under the Rule of Law.* Ann Arbor, MI: Firebrand Books, 1992.

Roediger, David. *The Wages of Whiteness: Race and the Making of the American Working Class.* London: Verso, 1991.

Rogers, William Warren. *The One-Gallused Rebellion: Agrarianism in Alabama, 1865–1896.* Baton Rouge: Louisiana State University Press, 1970.

Rogers, William Warren, Robert David Ward, Leah Rawls Atkins, and Wayne Flint. *Alabama: The History of a Deep-South State.* Tuscaloosa: University of Alabama Press, 1994.

Rogin, Michael. *Blackface, White Noise: Jewish Immigrants in the Hollywood Melting Pot.* Berkeley: University of California Press, 1996.

Romano, Renee. *Race Mixing: Black-White Marriage in Postwar America.* Cambridge: Harvard University Press, 2003.

Root, Maria P. P. *Love's Revolution: Interracial Marriage.* Philadelphia: Temple University Press, 2001.

Russell, Sylvester. *The Amalgamation of America: Normal Solution of the Color and Inter-Marriage Problem.* Chicago: Sylvester Russell Book Concern, 1920.

Saks, Eva. "Representing Miscegenation Law." *Raritan* 8 (1988): 39–69.

Saxton, Alexander. *The Rise and Fall of the White Republic: Class Politics and Mass Culture in Nineteenth-Century America.* London: Verso, 1990.

Sharfstein, Daniel. "The Secret History of Race in the United States." *Yale Law Journal* 112 (2003): 1473–1509.

Siegel, Reva. "Why Equal Protection No Longer Protects: The Evolving Forms of Status-Enforcing State Action." *Stanford Law Review* 49 (1997): 1111–1148.

Simon, Bryant. "The Appeal of Cole Blease of South Carolina: Race, Class, and Sex in the New South." In *Sex, Love, Race: Crossing Boundaries in North American History*, ed. Martha Hodes, 373–98. New York: New York University Press, 1999.

Smith, Rogers. *Civic Ideals: Conflicting Visions of Citizenship in U.S. History*. New Haven: Yale University Press, 1997.

Smith, Rogers. "Black and White after *Brown*: Constructions of Race in Modern Supreme Court Decisions." *University of Pennsylvania Journal of Constitutional Law* 5 (2003): 709–33.

Sommerville, Diana Miller. *Rape and Race in the Nineteenth-Century South*. Chapel Hill: University of North Carolina Press, 2004.

Stanton, William. *The Leopard's Spots: Scientific Attitudes toward Race in America, 1815–59*. Chicago: University of Chicago Press, 1960.

Swain, Martha. "Loula Dunn: Alabama Pioneer in Public Welfare Administration." In *Stepping Out of the Shadows: Alabama Women, 1819–1990*, ed. Mary Martha Thomas, 132–53. Tuscaloosa: University of Alabama Press, 1995.

Talty, Stephan. *Mulatto America: At the Crossroads of Black and White Culture; A Social History*. New York: HarperCollins, 2003.

Tarpley, Joan. "Blackwomen, Sexual Myth, and Jurisprudence." *Temple Law Review* 69 (1996): 1343–86.

Thomas, Mary Martha. "White and Black Alabama Women during the Progressive Era, 1890–1920." In *Stepping Out of the Shadows: Alabama Women, 1819–1990*, ed. Mary Martha Thomas, 75–95. Tuscaloosa: University of Alabama Press, 1995.

Tolnay, Stewart, and E. M. Beck. *A Festival of Violence: An Analysis of Southern Lynchings, 1882–1930*. Urbana: University of Illinois Press, 1995.

Van Tassel, Emily Field. " 'Only the Law Would Rule between Us': Antimiscegenation, the Moral Economy of Dependency, and the Debate over Rights after the Civil War." *Chicago-Kent Law Review* 70 (1995): 873–926.

Wallenstein, Peter. "Race, Marriage, and the Law of Freedom: Alabama and Virginia, 1860s–1960s." *Chicago-Kent Law Review* 70 (1994): 371–437.

Wallenstein, Peter. *Tell the Court I Love My Wife: Race, Marriage, and Law; An American History*. New York: Palgrave, 2002.

Welke, Barbara Y. "When All the Women Were White, and All the Blacks Were Men: Gender, Class, Race, and the Road to *Plessy*, 1855–1914." *Law and History Review* 13 (1995): 261–316.

Welke, Barbara Y. *Recasting American Liberty: Gender, Race, Law, and the Railroad Revolution, 1865–1920*. New York: Cambridge University Press, 2001.

Wells-Barnett, Ida B. "Mob Rule in New Orleans: Robert Charles and His

Fight to the Death." In *On Lynching.* 1900. The American Negro: His History and Literature. New York: Arno Press, 1969a.

Wells-Barnett, Ida B. "A Red Record: Tabulated Statistics and Alleged Causes of Lynchings in the United States, 1892–1894." In *On Lynching.* n.d. The American Negro: His History and Literature. New York: Arno Press, 1969b.

Wells-Barnett, Ida B. "Southern Horrors: Lynch Law in All Its Phases." *On Lynching.* 1892. The American Negro: His History and Literature. New York: Arno Press, 1969c.

White, G. Edward. "The American Law Institute and the Triumph of Modernist Jurisprudence." *Law and History Review* 15 (1997): 1–47.

Wiggins, Sarah Woolfolk. *The Scalawag in Alabama Politics, 1865–1881.* Tuscaloosa: University of Alabama Press, 1977. Reprint, 1991.

Williamson, Joel. *New People: Miscegenation and Mulattoes in the United States.* New York: Free Press, 1980.

Willrich, Michael. "The Two Percent Solution: Eugenic Jurisprudence and the Socialization of American Law, 1900–1930." *Law and History Review* 16 (1998): 63–111.

Wood, Betty. *The Origins of American Slavery: Freedom and Bondage in the English Colonies.* New York: Hill & Wang, 1997.

Woodhouse, Barbara Bennett. "'Are You My Mother?' Conceptualizing Children's Identity Rights in Transracial Adoptions." *Duke Journal of Gender Law and Policy* 2 (1995): 107–29.

Woodward, C. Vann. *The Strange Career of Jim Crow.* 3d ed. New York: Oxford University Press, 1974.

Wyatt-Brown, Bertram. *Honor and Violence in the Old South.* New York: Oxford University Press, 1986.

Yamin, Priscilla. "Nuptial Nation: Marriage and the Politics of Civic Membership in the United States." PhD diss., Political Science, New School University, New York, 2005.

Yamin, Priscilla. "The Search for Marital Order: Immigration, Marriage, and the Politics of the Progressive Era." Article under review, 2006.

Zack, Naomi. *Race and Mixed Race.* Philadelphia: Temple University Press, 1993.

Zangrando, Robert L. *The NAACP Crusade against Lynching, 1909–1950.* Philadelphia: Temple University Press, 1980.

Index